Qualitative Research in Sport Management

Qualitative Research in Sport Management

Allan Edwards
James Skinner

AMSTERDAM · BOSTON · HEIDELBERG · LONDON · NEW YORK · OXFORD · PARIS · SAN DIEGO
SAN FRANCISCO · SINGAPORE · SYDNEY · TOKYO
Butterworth-Heinemann is an imprint of Elsevier

Butterworth-Heinemann is an imprint of Elsevier
Linacre House, Jordan Hill, Oxford OX2 8DP, UK
30 Corporate Drive, Suite 400, Burlington, MA 01803, USA

First edition 2009

British Library Cataloguing in Publication Data
A catalogue record for this book is available from the British Library

Library of Congress Cataloging-in-Publication Data
A catalog record for this book is available from the Library of Congress

ISBN: 978-0-7506-8598-6

For information on all Butterworth-Heinemann
publications visit our website at www.elsevierdirect.com

Printed and bound in Hungary

09 10 11 12 10 9 8 7 6 5 4 3 2 1

Working together to grow
libraries in developing countries

www.elsevier.com | www.bookaid.org | www.sabre.org

ELSEVIER   BOOK AID International   Sabre Foundation

Contents

Part 6 Writing the Sport Management Research Report

Author Biographies

Dr Allan Edwards was formerly the Head of Sport and Business Management at Hartpury College, University of the West of England. Now a faculty member at the University of Ulster Dr Edwards has published extensively on the use of qualitative research methods and theoretical frameworks for sport management research. His research brings sociological theory to the study of sport management. Dr Edwards has extensive sport industry experience and has conducted a number of consultancies for national and international sports organisations. His academic and practical experiences allow him to blend theory and practice when undertaking sport management research.

Associate Professor James Skinner is a faculty member at Griffith University, Gold Coast Campus. His research has appeared in leading sport management journals such as the Journal of Sport Management, European Sport Management Quarterly, Sport Management Review and the International Journal of Sport Management. Dr Skinner has published extensively in the use of qualitative research methods and theoretical frameworks for sport management research. His research focuses on culture as it relates to organisational change and sporting studies, drugs in sport, sport as a vehicle for social change and sport globalisation studies.

Special Acknowledgement

The authors would like to thank Ms Ruth Watkins for her dedication in bringing this book to publication. As a research assistant there is no better. Her commitment, enthusiasm and valuable suggestions about the book have been greatly appreciated.

PART 1

The Context of Sport Management Research

CHAPTER 1

Introduction to Sport Management Research

INTRODUCTION

Costa (2005) suggests that sport management defined itself as a discipline in the mid-1980s "as signaled by the founding of the North American Society for Sport Management (NASSM) in 1985" (p. 117), and the subsequent formation of the European Association of Sport Management (EASM) in 1993 and the Sport Management Association of Australia and New Zealand (SMAANZ) in 1995.

A key element in a discipline's growth and development is the publication of scholarly works (Chelladurai, 2005). As Pitts (2001) suggests, "a field of study cannot exist without a body of knowledge and literature" (p. 2) that has been formed through the process of research. Historically, positivistic, quantitative methodologies have served as the dominant approaches for research exploration in the field of sport management (Amis & Silk, 2005). Recently, however, an increasing number of scholars have acknowledged the need to consider and embrace alternative worldviews and eclectic methodological approaches to examine questions about the social world (Quatman, 2006). Quatman (2006) identified how these issues have been raised by a number of sport management researchers (e.g., Chalip, 2006; Pitts, 2001; Slack, 1996, 1998). Concerns have also been expressed about the lack of domain diversity and limited range of topics being explored (Pitts, 2001; Slack, 1998).

Wendy Frisby in her acceptance speech of the 2004 Earle F. Zeigler award challenged the sport management research community to embrace multiple research paradigms. Frisby (2005) writes:

> *The paradigm we operate from as researchers, whether it be positivism, pragmatism, interpretivism, critical social science, postmodernism or a combination of these paradigms, shape the questions we ask, the methods we use, and the degree to which our findings will have an impact on society. (p. 2)*

Frisby (2005) while not making judgments concerning certain paradigms, speaks of the importance in writing with paradigmatic lenses in mind. Although this can be a complex undertaking, it is the foundation of qualitative research.

Others have supported Frisby's contentions (Amis & Silk, 2005; Skinner & Edwards, 2005) that the field of sport management tends to be overly focused on the same theories and paradigms (Quatman, 2006). Drawing on the work of Amis and Silk (2005), Quatman (2006) suggests there is a trend "toward "expanding the horizons" and extending the idea space of a scientific discipline through the promotion of alternative approaches to inquiry has made its way into the sport management literature" (p. 14). Quatman, however, suggests that the rate at which these approaches have been embraced implies "a culture of guarded optimism at best toward these new approaches" (p. 14). As Amis and Silk (2005) articulated:

> There is little doubt that some related disciplines – such as education,
> cultural studies, leisure studies, and the sociology of sport – have
> progressed more rapidly than sport management in their
> acknowledgment of the value of different ideological, epistemological,
> and methodological approaches. (cited in Quatman, 2006, p. 14)

Quatman (2006) indicates that the 2005 special issue in the *Journal of Sport Management* reflected on the "constrained idea space (i.e., content and diversity of knowledge circulating) in the field and focused on "expanding the horizons" of sport management research through critical and innovative approaches" (p. 2). The special edition raised hopes that future sport management research would lead to a range of counter-hegemonic approaches. By recognizing, and in essence advocating for the alternative methods presented, Amis and Silk (2005) sought to "aid the power of those in the academy to apply research so that it impacts, and is meaningful to, the various communities that sport management has the potential to touch" (cited in Quatman, 2006, p. 2). Quatman goes on to suggest that the core theme of the special edition clearly suggests there is a need to move beyond current research practices and embrace socially inclusive approaches to understanding the lived experiences of sport managers in order to promote a more inclusive culture for the generation of knowledge in the field. This book takes up this challenge by presenting research paradigms that can provide new and innovative ways to conceptualize and investigate issues of interest to both the sport management academic and sport management practitioner. In this light, this book aims to offer potential solutions to emerging problems in the world of sport management research.

Research Brief

Title: An Exploratory Qualitative Study of the Projection of Images by Organisations Operating within the Context of a Professional Sport League
Who: Bastien, F., Concordia University

This study used an exploratory qualitative analysis of the projection of images by organizations operating within the context of a professional sport league. The research focused on a professional sport league as the organizational setting (i.e., cultural industry) for investigating and analyzing the particularities of English football (soccer) clubs' images,

operationalized as they are presented on club websites. This research established theoretical relationships between the identity of organizations, the images that these organizations project, and the environment in which they operate. In doing so, the analysis contributed to our understanding of what types of images professional sport organizations must manage in order to be perceived as attractive to different stakeholders that control the resources on which professional sport organizations are dependent on for funding.

WHY QUALITATIVE SPORT MANAGEMENT RESEARCH?

Despite our strong endorsement of qualitative research, we suggest that there is a strong position for quantitative research within sport management; indeed some suggest (Amis & Silk, 2005; Cunningham & Mahoney, 2004; Cuskelly & Boag, 2001; Fink et al., 2003; Murray & Howat, 2002; Quatman, 2006; Shilbury, 2001; Skinner & Edwards, 2005) that quantitative approaches to sport management research continue to dominate the discipline. Despite calls to embrace new paradigms, there remains considerable institutional pressure on sport management researchers to remain within a quantitative framework approach so as to maintain an aura of academic respectability. As a consequence, much sport management research seems to have adopted a somewhat naive and unreflecting empiricism.

We strongly support both quantitative and qualitative approaches, and the notion of mixed research approaches combining both quantitative and qualitative approaches. Meuller's (2004) study of 'Customer Relationship Management (CRM) for Selected Stakeholder Groups in the Professional German Soccer Industry' is an example of qualitative analysis of quantitative data. One of the major themes of this book is that there is no one best research approach, but rather that the approach most effective for the resolution of a given problem depends on a large number of variables, not least the nature of the problem itself. Research methodology is always a compromise between options in the light of tacit philosophical assumptions, and choices are frequently influenced by the availability of resources. In this book, we will advance criteria for choice of methodology by reviewing emergent approaches to sport management research and, through examples, their appropriateness to finding answers to particular research questions. The book aims to open up the unlimited possibilities for the production of new sport management knowledge through the application of qualitative approaches.

Research Brief

Title: Customer Relationship Management (CRM) for Selected Stakeholder Groups in the Professional German Soccer Industry

Who: Meuller, W.

Meullers' analysis of several German Bundesliga soccer companies showed that sports managers acted instinctively. Inadequate use of modern management instruments, or in some cases even a complete lack thereof, led to deficient strategies (or no pursuance of a strategy) resulting in stagnating revenues.

Meullers' qualitative analysis drew on quantitative data to analyze the opportunities and potentials of customer relationship management for professional soccer companies in the B2C segment. He argued that management identified the need of a long-term and future oriented strategy and recognized the key role that customers and their relation with the soccer company play was crucial to the long-term success of a soccer company. In conclusion, he argues that when formulating a CRM strategy, management needs to take both economic and non-economic side-conditions into account.

THE MIXED METHOD APPROACH TO SPORT MANAGEMENT RESEARCH

In a true mixed method approach, qualitative and quantitative methods have to be combined in order to produce sound sociological explanations. If qualitative and quantitative methods are combined in this way to answer a specific research question, in principle, one of the following three outcomes may arise:

1. Qualitative and quantitative results may 'converge'.

2. Qualitative and quantitative results may relate to different objects or phenomena, but may be 'complementary' to each other and thus can be used to 'supplement' each other.

3. Qualitative and quantitative results may be 'divergent' or 'contradictory'.

The construction of a multi-method design requires that methodological tools are selected in regard to theoretical assumptions about the nature of the social reality under investigation. Quantitative and qualitative methods usually provide information on different levels of sociological description: quantitative analyses show phenomena on an aggregate level and can thereby allow the description of macro-social structures. Although qualitative data may also relate to phenomena on a macro-societal level, their specific strength lies in their ability to lift the veil on social micro-processes and to make visible unknown cultural phenomena. In order to formulate adequate sociological explanations of certain social phenomena, it will often be necessary to combine both types of information.

It is not sufficient to discuss the integration of qualitative and quantitative methods exclusively on the basis of epistemological considerations and methodological models but that methodological reflections on the integration of methods have to be based on theoretical considerations about the social processes under investigation. Thereby one must pay attention to the nature of social structures and social actions in the empirical field, and to the ways that structures and actions are related to each other.

In sport management research using more than one method to study the same phenomenon has the potential to strengthen the validity of the results. A typical design might start out with a qualitative segment such as an interview, which will alert the researcher to issues that should be explored in a survey of participants, which in turn is followed by semi-structured interviews to clarify some of the survey findings. A mixed method approach may also lead sport management researchers to modify or expand the research design and/or the data collection methods.

Research Brief

Title: The Commitment of Volunteers in Junior Sport Organisations: A Mixed Methods Study

Who: Estella (Terry) Engelberg, Griffith University

The purpose of this research was to examine the dimensionality and targets of the commitment of volunteers (including committee members, coaches, officials, and volunteers in various other roles) in junior sport organizations, and the links between commitment and behavioral outcomes, specifically, intention to stand down from a volunteer role, intention to cease volunteering for the club or center, and self-assessed performance. A sequential explanatory mixed methods design consisting of a quantitative (two studies) and a qualitative phase (one study) was employed. Drawing on Meyer and Herscovitch's (2001) general commitment model, the quantitative studies assessed commitment to three organizational targets: the organization (defined as the center or the club), the team of volunteers, and the volunteer role. The qualitative study explored and explained the findings of the quantitative phase in more depth and to allow volunteers to "use their own voice" in discussing their commitment. This study consisted of focus group discussions. Taken together, the results of the three studies indicate that commitment is a multidimensional construct that can be applied to various organizational targets. Volunteers held distinctive affective, normative, and, to a lesser extent, continuance commitments to their organizations, their team of volunteers, and their volunteer roles. There are also differences in commitment amongst volunteer subgroups, such as committee members and volunteers in other roles, and volunteers with children and volunteers without children.

IN PROFILE - Associate Professor Brad Humphreys

Brad Humphreys is currently an Associate Professor in the Department of Economics at the University of Alberta, where he is the Chair in the Economics of Gaming. His previous academic positions include Associate Professor in the sport management program at the University of Illinois and Assistant and Associate Professor of Economics at the University of Maryland, Baltimore County. Brad has also been a visiting scholar at the Congressional Budget Office in Washington DC and a Fulbright Scholar at CERGE-EI in Prague, Czech Republic. He received a PhD in economics from the Johns Hopkins University in 1995.

His research interests include the economic impact of professional sports, the financing of sports facilities, the economics of intercollegiate athletics, competitive balance in sports leagues, the economic determinants of participation in physical activity, and economic aspects of sports betting markets. His research has been published widely in economics journals, public policy journals and sport management journals, including the *Journal of Urban Economics, Contemporary Economic Policy*, the *Journal of Policy Analysis and Management*, and the *Journal of Sport Management*. As an economist, Brad's research is primarily quantitative in nature. He is primarily interested in the statistical and econometric analysis of secondary data. However, as a quantitative researcher, he also recognizes and appreciates the important role of qualitative research in sport management, and other fields. Brad believes that while quantitative research provides the researcher with important evidence and can uncover interesting and informative patterns in data, it cannot provide the rich and detailed evidence that emerges from qualitative research. Qualitative research also allows the researcher to gain a better understanding of detailed aspects of human behavior, including powerful insights into causality that quantitative research cannot adequately address. In sport management, scientific inquiry needs both qualitative and quantitative research to advance. Brad sees the relationship between qualitative and quantitative research as synergistic. When used together, they generate much more powerful insights than either approach could provide separately.

STRUCTURE OF THE BOOK

In Chapter 2 – Research Paradigms in Qualitative Sport Management Research – of **Section 1**, we explain the assumptions of research paradigms. In particular, we (1) explain the assumptions about the nature of knowledge and reality that underlie research paradigms; (2) describe the research paradigms the sport management researcher can draw on to frame their research; and (3) comment on how the sport management research process can be shaped by applying different theoretical perspectives. We outline how sport management research involves a systematic exploration, guided by well-constructed questions, producing new information or reassessing old information. In doing this though we recognize that sport management researchers' own value systems inevitably come into play. We also argue that sport management researchers therefore need to look carefully at the claims of others, judging for themselves whether they are convincing. To do that, they need to understand the process by which other researchers have come to their conclusions, and this means understanding both their methodologies and the intellectual frameworks within which they have operated.

In **Section 2**, Chapter 3 – *The Sport Management Research Process* – we highlight that undertaking a research study requires careful and methodical planning on the part of the sport management researcher. It identifies that from the initial idea that sparks the sport management researcher's interest, the conduct of the literature review, refining the research problem, formulating the questions to be answered in the research topic through to the design of the research plan, the sport management researcher must carefully review and plan each step of the research journey. Chapter 4 – *Research Ethics for Sport Management* – provides an understanding of the basic concepts of research ethics and identifies the major ethical considerations involved in sport management research. This chapter therefore discusses what research ethics are, why they are important and the concerns around valuing the knowledge that can be obtained through research against the value of non-interference in the lives of potential research participants.

In **Section 3**, we turn our attention to understanding the different data collection methods employed in sport management research and identifying data collection methods suitable for use in sport management research. Chapter 5 – *Methods of Data Collection for Sport Management Research* – discusses the need for sport management researchers to use a range of data collection techniques including fieldwork, observation, interviews and document analysis.

Section 4 focuses on analyzing the sport management data. Chapter 6 – *Modes of Analysis in Sport Management Qualitative Research* – outlines that the purpose of modes of analysis is to make sense of the data so that evidence can be obtained to answer the research question. However, there is a lack of a commonly accepted method of qualitative analysis. It is suggested that the key is to ensure that your analysis is appropriate to achieve your research objectives.

In **Section 5**, we discuss some fundamental philosophical issues concerning the choice and justification of research methods. Chapter 7 – *Reflection in Sport Management Research* commences this section of the book. We do this because each research method discussed has embedded within it the need for critical reflection. The remaining chapters in this section – Chapters 8 – 21 – discuss a range of research methods and "unpack" them while directly linking them to the study of sport management. In each chapter, research briefs and case study examples are used to demonstrate how each method has been applied to a sport context. Chapter 8 explores the various methodologies of *Action Research*, particularly

Emancipatory and Participatory Action Research, both of which have features that make them applicable to the field of sport management research. Chapter 9 identifies and discusses the principles that underpin *autoethnographic approaches* to research in sport settings. It discusses the strengths and limitations associated with this approach and advocates that autoethnography is a viable methodology for sport management research. Chapter 10 focuses on *case study* as a research method and provides an understanding of the basic tenets that underpin case study research designs. It also identifies what is involved in designing a case study approach to sport management research. Chapter 11 explores the controversial methodology of *deconstruction* – which many critics claim is not a legitimate methodology. It provides an introduction and overview to the concept of deconstruction and some suggestions as to possible frameworks from which to start the process of deconstruction in the reading of sport management literature. Chapter 12 explores the methodology of *discourse, discourse analysis* and *critical discourse analysis* and their possible applications to the field of sport management research. It argues that in the context of sport management research, the analysis of discourses can provide new and exciting insights into the reasons behind the adoption of certain sport policies, and the acceptance of certain research outcomes as "truth". Chapter 13 explores the qualitative research approach of *Ethnography*. Although traditional ethnography has been applied to the field of sport for many years, from the late 1990s, sport researchers started to embrace ethnographic frameworks underpinned by critical and postmodern theories. We suggest that the benefit for sport management researchers in applying critical and postmodern thought to ethnographic approaches is that it sharpens their own critical consciousness. Chapter 14 builds on Chapter 13 by discussing *emerging ethnographies* and demonstrates how they can be situated in the sport management research field. Chapter 15 explores a qualitative research methodology that aims to study, understand and articulate how people make sense of themselves and each other in everyday life – *ethnomethodology*. The basic tenets of ethnomethodology and how these can be applied to the field of sport management research in useful and practical ways that can facilitate the development of practices that enhance sport management education are discussed. Chapter 16 turns its attention to *Gender Theories*. In particular, it argues that while gender methodologies are still in an evolving and emerging state, the developing recognition of the importance of difference and the need to empower and give voice to research participants offers the sport management researcher scope to investigate issues specifically related to gender, and the impact these issues may have on the sport management environment. Chapter 17 examines the debates surrounding the application of *grounded theory* to research and identifies and discusses the principles that underpin grounded theory approaches to research in sport management settings. It is suggested that the grounded theory approach is compatible with the aims of sport management researchers because it enables the research to capture and explicate on a theoretical level the complexity of organizational situations and processes. Chapter 18 focuses on *narrative inquiry* as a research method. Interest in narrative inquiry is attributed to the postmodern perspective of truth and knowledge. This chapter presents the qualitative research methods of "story", "narrative" and "voice" and highlights how they can provide rich descriptions of the sport management environment and at the same time provide an alternative research approach. Chapter 19 explores the methodology of *phenomenology,* and looks at some possible applications in the field of sport management research. It suggests that in sport management literature, phenomenology offers researchers a different perspective and opportunity to explore previously unchartered waters. Chapter 20 presents two emerging approaches that have significance for sport management research – *globalization and postcolonial studies.* In doing this, it provides an understanding of the concepts of globalization and postcolonialism while identifying the implications of the application of these approaches to research in sport management. The final chapter of this section – Chapter 21 – discusses some emerging issues for the *future direction of sport management research* and demonstrates how they can be situated in the sport management research field.

The final section of the book – **Section 6** – *Writing the Research Report* – dedicates a chapter to the preparation of the sport management research report. It identifies strategies with which to begin writing the research report and the key chapters in the research report. It notes that there is no definitive format for a qualitative research report; however, this chapter seeks to guide the new researcher in writing up a report in a systematic way.

In closing, we turn to the comments of Stewart (cited in Edwards et al., 2002) who notes that sport management is a respectable academic discipline. It has its own peer-reviewed journals, higher degree programs, international conferences, and research agendas. There are also more higher degree students than ever before undertaking research programs, and an increasing number of government grants are being allocated to sport management issues. However, the one area where sport management studies are under-developed is research design. Researchers, for the most part, have been forced to go to the generic management literature for their theories and conceptual frameworks. In many respects, this has not been a bad thing, but it often means that some of the "nuances" and special features of sport are not given sufficient focus. We believe this book fills a significant gap by customizing its discussion of qualitative research to the sport management researcher.

REFERENCES

Amis, J. & Silk, M. 2005. Rupture: promoting critical and innovative approaches to the study of sport management. *Journal of Sport Management*, **19**, 355–366.

Costa, C. A. 2005. The status and future of sport management: a Delphi study. *Journal of Sport Management*, **19**, 117–142.

Chelladurai, P. 2005. Managing Organizations for Sport and Physical Activity: A Systems Perspective, 2nd ed. Scottsdale, AZ: Holcomb Hathaway.

Chalip, L. 2006. Toward a distinctive sport management discipline. *Journal of Sport Management*, **20**, 1–21.

Cunningham, G. B. & Mahoney, K. 2004. Self-efficacy of part-time employees in university athletics: the influence of organizational commitment, valence of training, and training motivation. *Journal of Sport Management*, **18**, 59–73.

Cuskelly, B. & Boag, A. 2001. Organisational commitment as a predictor of committee member turnover among volunteer sport administrators: results of a time-lagged study. *Journal of Sport Management*, **4**, 65–88.

Edwards, A., Gilbert, K. & Skinner, J. 2002. Extending the Boundaries: Theoretical Frameworks for Research in Sports Management. Melbourne, Victoria: Common Ground.

Fink, J. S., Pastore, D. L. & Riemer, H. 2003. Managing employee diversity: perceived practices and organizational outcomes in NCAA division III athletic departments. *Sport Management Review*, **6**, 147–168.

Frisby, W. 2005. The good, the bad, and the ugly: critical sport management research. *Journal of Sport Management*, **19**, 1–12.

Meuller, W. 2004. *Customer Relationship Management (CRM) for Selected Stakeholder Groups in the Professional German Soccer Industry*. Unpublished master's thesis, Bond University, Queensland, Australia.

Meyer, J. P. & Herscovitch, L. 2001. Commitment in the workplace. Toward a general model. *Human Resource Management Review*, **11**, 299–326.

Murray, D. & Howat, G. 2002. The relationships among service quality, value, satisfaction, and future intentions of customers at an Australian sports and leisure centre. *Sport Management Review*, **5**, 25–43.

Pitts, B. G. 2001. Sport management at the millennium: a defining moment. *Journal of Sport Management*, **15**, 1–9.

Quatman, C. 2006. *The Social Construction of Knowledge in the Field of Sport Management: A Social Network Perspective*. Unpublished doctoral dissertation, The Ohio State University, Columbus.

Shilbury, D. 2001. Examining board member roles, functions and influence. A study of Victorian sporting organisations. *International Journal of Sport Management*, **2**, 253–281.

Skinner, J. & Edwards, A. 2005. Inventive pathways: fresh visions of sport management research. *Journal of Sport Management*, **19**, 404–421.

Slack, T. 1996. From the locker room to the board room: changing the domain of sport management. *Journal of Sport Management*, **10**, 97–105.

Slack, T. S. 1998. Is there anything unique about sport management? *European Journal for Sport Management*, **5**, 21–29.

CHAPTER 2

Research Paradigms in Qualitative Sport Management Research

OBJECTIVES

The main objective of this chapter is to explain the assumptions of research paradigms. In particular, it will

1. explain the assumptions about the nature of knowledge and reality that underlie research paradigms.

2. describe the research paradigms the sport management researcher can draw on to frame their research.

3. comment on how the sport management research process can be shaped by applying different theoretical perspectives.

KEY TERMS

Positivism: a theoretical perspective based on notions of impartiality and objectivity and assumptions that the researcher can remain separate from, and not influence, the research field.

Constructivism: a construction of the human mind shaped by experiences of the world.

Crisis of representation: how to locate the sport management researcher and their subjects in reflective texts.

Structuralism: decisive shaping factors in structural forms discoverable within society or the unconscious, or both.

Post-structuralism: challenges the very idea of structure, including the idea of a center, a fixed principle, a hierarchy of meaning and a solid foundation.

Ontology: refers to how one sees the world and the nature of one's reality.

Epistemology: what is the relationship between the enquirer and knowledge?

Paradigm: is a set of prepositions that explain how the world is perceived, and it contains a worldview, a way of breaking down the complexity of the real world, telling researchers and social scientists in general what is important, what is legitimate, and what is reasonable.

KEY QUESTIONS

The key questions raised in this chapter are as follows:

1. How has qualitative research been shaped by differing theoretical perspectives?

2. How are Ontology, Epistemology and Methodology related to the sport management research process?

3. How does who we are influence the research process?

CHAPTER OVERVIEW

This chapter explains that sport management research involves systematic exploration, guided by well constructed questions, producing new information or reassessing old information. Sport management researchers spend a great deal of time evaluating other people's research, deciding what the strengths and weaknesses are in each case, and hoping to apply their conclusions to their own reading and to the procedures they follow in their research. In this chapter, we recognize that sport management researchers' own value systems inevitably come into play. We also argue that sport management researchers therefore need to look carefully at the claims of others, judging for themselves whether they are convincing. To do that, they need to understand the process by which other researchers have come to their conclusions, and this means understanding both their methodologies and the intellectual frameworks within which they have operated.

RESEARCH PARADIGMS

We believe that it is important that sport management researchers understand research *paradigms* and that they have an understanding of the major frameworks that they will come across in their reading. This is because it is not a matter of having a theory and putting it into practice, nor of doing something and deriving a theory from it, but of both theory and practice happening simultaneously, interactively and continuously. Understanding the range of possible frameworks, and how others have used them is key to understanding your own processes of thought.

Even if they are unable to articulate it, most sport management researchers have an intellectual framework that governs the way they perceive the world and their own place within it. This framework shapes research from the beginning to the end, because it provides the structure within which choices (including the initial choice of a research subject) are made. This framework comes partly from the institutional setting within which research takes place – the position taken by employers or those who commissioned the research, or by supervisors, by the department within which researchers work, and by the university/college which employs them. Part of it will come from the personal position of the sport management researcher which has been shaped by their biography of experiences as well as their previous education, political and religious beliefs, gender, sexual preference, race and class affiliations.

What we have called a *paradigm* is sometimes called a *framework*: a paradigm/framework allows some questions to be asked and some research methods to be applied to these questions, while at the same time denying the validity of other questions and other methods.

COMPETING PARADIGMS – THE DIFFERENT WAYS OF "SEEING"

The word paradigm comes from the Greek language *"paradeigma"* meaning model, pattern or example (Barker 1992). In the philosophical meaning, "…it is a way of viewing the world that underlies the theories and methodology of science in a particular period of history…" (The New Shorter Oxford English Dictionary, 1993). Adam Smith in his book *"Powers of the Mind"* describes paradigms as "A shared set of assumptions. The paradigm explains the world to us and helps us to predict its behaviour" (cited in Barker, 1992, p. 31). Covey (1989) explains paradigms as the way we see the world in terms of perceiving, understanding and interpreting, a theory, explanation, model or map. Covey (1989) says that humans interpret everything they experience through their individual, personal mental maps. Mental maps are rarely questioned. Humans assume that what they see is "reality". Our basic attitudes and behaviors are derived from our paradigms which affect the way people interact with each other. People see the world as they are conditioned to see it through their perceptions, paradigms or mental maps.

Covey (1989) writes that when a person sees the world from a different viewpoint, they experience a paradigm shift, nearly every breakthrough in research has been derived from a paradigm shift. Zohar (1990) describes a worldview as a living truth, which is taken for granted. It is only when there is change do people try to understand and articulate their worldview.

Senge (1990) calls paradigms mental models and describes them as: "…deeply ingrained assumptions and generalisations that influence how people see the world and behave" (p. 8). People are not always aware of their mental model. Senge et al. (1994) say that people cannot steer through the environment of life without a mental model and that all mental models are, in some way, flawed. Pascale (1990) prefers the term paradigm to mind set because it encompasses the sharing of a belief system by a community, whereas a mind set or worldview refers to an individual. Guba and Lincoln (1994) describe a paradigm as a set of basic beliefs dealing with first principles. It is a worldview describing the nature of the world, a person's place in it and their relationship to the world.

Paradigm definition

Within the discipline of inquiry, the concept of existing paradigms has been strongly associated with Thomas Kuhn who through his own enquiring activity began to question how "the practice of astronomy, physics, chemistry, or biology normally failed to evoke the controversies over fundamentals that today often seem endemic among, say, psychologists or sociologists" (Kuhn, 1962, p. 9). Kuhn coined the word *paradigm* as a framework to assist in the true understanding of past research enquiry, emerging practices and as a means of identifying "models from which spring particular coherent traditions of scientific research" (Kuhn, 1962, p. 10). As stated by Kuhn, "the road to a firm research consensus is extraordinarily arduous" (Kuhn, 1962, p. 15).

Kuhn (1970) defines a paradigm as, "a set of values and techniques which is shared by members of a scientific community, which acts as a guide or map, dictating the kinds of problems scientists should address and the types of explanations that are acceptable to them" (p. 175). In simple terms, a paradigm is a set of prepositions that explain how the world is perceived, and it contains a worldview, a way of breaking down the complexity of the real world, telling researchers and social scientists in general what is important, what is legitimate, and what is reasonable (Patton, 1990; Sarantakos, 2002). Paradigms allow researchers to identify the relationship between variables and to specify appropriate methods for conducting particular research (Guba & Lincoln, 1994; Lincoln & Guba, 2000).

A paradigm may be viewed as a set of basic beliefs that deals with ultimates or first principles. It is the basic belief system or *worldview* that guides enquiry, or the individual, regarding their place in that world, the range of possible relationships to it and its parts (Guba & Lincoln, 1994, 1998). "There are many paradigms that we use in guiding our actions: the adversarial paradigm that guides the legal system, the judgmental paradigm that guides the selection of Olympic winners, the religious paradigms that guide spiritual and moral life … [and] those that guide disciplined inquiry" (Guba, 1990, p. 18).

The outcome of "good research" is the satisfactory achievement of a desired result or outcome. The determination of what upholds good research has been the issue that drives the paradigm debate. As history would suggest, the debate is evolutionary and one that has prevailed in all schools of enquiry. The school of natural or physical sciences has been no exception. While the evolutionary debate has continued, and as original schools of thought gradually disappeared (Kuhn, 1962), the realities are that scientific methods such as physics, chemistry, economics and psychology, for example, are often seen as the crowning achievements of Western civilization.

Denzin and Lincoln (1994) present a doctrine based on the premise that good inquiry or research should be able to contribute quantifiable facts and truth, free from personal bias. Social science, while originally seduced by an equal desire to contribute and "achieve rapid maturation" (Guba & Lincoln, 1994, p. 106) as a field of inquiry, as early as the late nineteenth century began to broaden the research paradigm debate. It did this by posing questions such as "whether or not social scientists could and/or should "borrow" the methodology of the physical sciences, especially physics, to investigate the social and human world" (Smith, 1983, p. 6). The debate continues today and shows little sign of abating (Denzin & Lincoln, 2000).

> Inquiry paradigms define for inquirers what it is they are about, and what falls within and outside the limits of legitimate inquiry. The basic beliefs that define inquiry paradigms can be summarized by the responses given by proponents of any given paradigm to three fundamental questions, which are interconnected in such a way that the answer given to any one question, taken in any order, constrains how the others may be answered. (Guba & Lincoln, 1989, p. 108)

Such development is further preceded by the nature of the inquiry itself, the question being asked, "what is available in the context, and what the researcher can do in that setting" (Denzin & Lincoln, 1994, p. 2), and the worldview of the researcher.

Research Brief

Title: Sport and New Media: A Profile of Internet Sport Journalists in Australia
Who: Lange, K.M., Victoria University, Australia
Lange utilized qualitative research methods to construct a profile of Australian Internet sport journalists within the context of recent developments in the field of sport and new media. Her data sources included a range of material such as books, newspapers, magazines, journals, WWW-sites and interviews. Lange utilized semi-structured interviews with Internet sport journalists. Key research questions that guided the study were: How did the subjects become Internet sport journalists? What are their work routines? What

Continued

are their experiences of online sport journalism and what is their perception of the future of sport journalism? Lange discovered that, with certain limitations, traditional journalism skills still apply to the Internet sport environment. In comparison to print media, Internet sport journalists tend to write shorter articles, have to respond to a continuous deadline and do not work within a traditional beat system. In addition, it can be noted that the interactivity of the Internet forces Internet sport journalists to continually re-evaluate their skills and the manner in which they respond to their audience. Lange suggested that her study provided important insights into the changing working practices of Australian Internet sport journalists and the online environment.

THE THREE PERSPECTIVES: ONTOLOGICAL, EPISTEMOLOGICAL AND METHODOLOGICAL

Denzin and Lincoln (2000) offer the following useful explanation of how a paradigm shapes our thinking processes:

> *A paradigm encompasses four concepts: ethics, epistemology, ontology and methodology. Ethics asks, How will I be as a moral person in the world? Epistemology asks, How do I know the world? What is the relationship between the inquirer and the known? Ontology raises basic questions about the nature of reality and the nature of the human being in the world. Methodology focuses on the best means for gaining knowledge about the world. (p. 157)*

1. The ontological perspective

Ontology refers to how one sees the world and the nature of one's reality. Under a positivist guise, reality is singular, static, objective and apart from the inquirer. For a positivist, reality is something which exists "Out There", waiting to be discovered by the objective observer and revealed as scientific "truth" (Denzin & Lincoln, 1998). In this way, it is surmised that truth can be measured and quantified. Interpretivists, by contrast, do not assume that social realities can be reduced to a numerical state (Denzin, 2002). Viewing the social world through a more postmodern lens, interpretivists acknowledge realities, which can be observed and explained in a multiplicity of ways (Bryman & Burgess, 1994). In other words, there is no one correct way of interpreting social phenomena. Thus, ontology is concerned with the nature of reality and poses questions such as:

■ What is the nature *of* reality?

■ What is already known about *this* reality?

■ What is already known about the *real* world?

■ Is this how things *really* work?

This leads to the second perspective, the epistemological perspective.

2. The epistemological perspective:

The second question is the *epistemological* question. This asks what is the relationship between the inquirer and knowledge? Guba and Lincoln (1994) postulate that no one answer can be given to this question; the answer is dependent on the answer to the ontological question. For example, if the world is considered "real" then the researcher's position is one of objective separation from the object of research.

Under Lincoln and Guba's (2000) positivist paradigm of "reality" the researcher can research the object of inquiry without impact. However, there are implications for validity if either the researcher or object of the research is influenced. Set research procedures are followed to eliminate bias; repetition produces the same results.

Under post-positivism, according to Guba and Lincoln (1994), the dualism of positivism is discarded; however, there is still objectivity guarded by questions such as 'do the results fit existing knowledge'. The research is also usually reviewed by peers. Guba and Lincoln (1994) write that under the critical theory epistemological position the researcher and the subject of the research interact to the point where the values of the researcher influence the research. This is taken further under constructivism where the researcher and the subject of the research are actually linked to the extent that research findings are created during the research (Lincoln & Guba, 2000). The epistemology of the participatory worldview, write Heron and Reason (1997), involves the researcher participating in the known and expressing this through experience, presentation, proposing and practice.

Epistemology refers to the relationship researchers have with the reality they have created, their justified belief and the truth of their final research findings (Guba & Lincoln, 1994). Therefore, epistemology poses the social questions such as:

■ What is the relationship between the sport management researcher and the reality, as they perceive it?

■ Is the reality shared by others or only by the sport management researcher?

■ Has the perceptions of the sport management researcher, shaped the desired reality, or is it a "true" representation of the reality? (Guba & Lincoln, 1994)

This leads to the third perspective, the methodological perspective.

3. The methodological perspective:

The third question is the *methodological* question. Guba and Lincoln (1994) write that this asks how the researcher will go about the research. This leads to the following question: "What technique can be used to measure the perceived reality"?

The answer to this question is also constrained by the answers to the previous meta-physical questions. If, for example reality is "real" the objectivist or positivist researcher controls the factors being researched. The research methodology for Guba and Lincoln's (1994) *positivist* paradigm involves empirical analysis to test stated hypotheses. The conditions of the experiment are controlled to prevent bias. *Post-positivism*, say Guba and Lincoln (1994), emphasizes falsifying hypotheses. Data that are collected about a situation allows for the discovery of knowledge, viewpoints are solicited, without interaction, to interpret people's actions.

Critical theory requires a dialectical methodology so that misconceptions are transformed into an informed understanding of the research subject. *Constructivism* requires interaction between the researcher and the subject of the research to form an agreed, informed construction through dialectical exchange (Guba & Lincoln, 1994). Heron and Reason (1997) write that a *participative* paradigm requires a collaborative form of inquiry through democratic dialog as co-researchers and co-subjects. People determine the questions to be answered and the methodology to explore them. This is applied in their world of practice, which leads to new experiences and new ways of representing their understanding.

HISTORICAL MOMENTS IN RESEARCH AND PARADIGM DEVELOPMENT

Denzin and Lincoln (2005) argue that any investigation of qualitative research must take into account the historical moments, as qualitative research takes a different meaning in each of these moments. They posit at least eight historical moments "that overlap and simultaneously operate in the present" (p. 3). These moments are defined as "the *traditional* (1900–1950); the *modernist,* or golden age (1950–1970); *blurred genres* (1970–1986); the *crisis of representation* (1986–1990); the *postmodern,* a period of experimental and new ethnographies (1990–1995); *post-experimental inquiry* (1995–2000); the *methodologically contested present* (2000–2004); and the *fractured future,* which is now (2005 to the present)" (Denzin and Lincoln, 2005, p. 3).

Whilst these moments are "somewhat artificial" (Denzin and Lincoln, 2005, p. 2) they provide a way of locating and understanding the different research paradigms.

THE TRADITIONAL PERIOD AND POSITIVISM

The traditional period (1900–1950) encompasses a focus on providing "objective" accounts of experiences. "*Positivism* asserts that objective accounts of the real world can be given" (Denzin & Lincoln, 2005, p. 27). Positivism as a theoretical perspective is based on notions of impartiality and objectivity and assumptions that the researcher can remain separate from, and not influence, the research field. A positivist perspective presents the social world as existing independent of human consciousness and therefore data are not affected by the participants' or the researcher's interpretation. Internal and external validity are sought with the results being presented in the form of scientific report (Denzin & Lincoln, 2000).

Positivism was probably the most powerful intellectual framework of the nineteenth and twentieth centuries, across all disciplines. It is built upon a realist assumption that the world is out there waiting to be known. It has faith in the scientific method, which it sees as leading to the growth of objective and verifiable knowledge (rather than mere superstition and guesswork). The grip of positivism on the scientific world has been weakening over recent decades, as scientific research methodology begins to shift away from the goal of absolute truth, based on claims to objectivity, generalization and prediction, and find ways to deal with concepts such as "uncertainty" and "chaos". (As indicated in Chapter 1, this change is evident in a recent issue of *Journal of Sport Management* (October, 2005) which was devoted to emergent research paradigms).

The French writer Auguste Comte (1798–1857) was largely responsible for the extension of the term "positivism" to cover more than the physical sciences: he proposed that all forms of knowledge (both physical and social) had passed through three stages over the course of human history – theological, meta-physical, and scientific. The logical positivists of the Vienna Circle in the 1920s and 1930s required the scientist (including the social scientist) to seek invariable natural laws, which were to be discovered by subjecting empirical data to logical analysis, ideally by a combination of operationalizing (turning into quantitative statements) and verification (testing on all possible samples), though they acknowledged that perfect verification is not possible on data from human subjects (Potter, 1996). Since then, the definition of positivism has been further expanded. It may now include any approach which operates on the general assumption that the methods of the physical sciences (such as measurement, or the search for general laws) can be carried over into the social sciences (Jary & Jary, 1991).

Sport management research to a large extent grew out of this view that researchers should use research methods that were similar to those which had seemed to lead to the discovery of objective laws and regularities in the natural sciences. Therefore, in this tradition, there is a concern with measurement, reliability, prediction and replicability. The appropriate way of going about knowledge production is thought to be by means of the hypothetico-deductive method in which the sport management researcher begins with a clearly articulated theory, deduces hypotheses which are logically consistent with the theory, and then tests the hypotheses under experimental conditions. But since social science hypotheses do not often lend themselves to laboratory experimentation, statistical analysis of large samples usually counts as objective testing. Such methodology assumes that through observation and precise measurement, social reality, which is external to and independent of the mind of the observer, may be rendered comprehensible to the social scientist.

It is in approaches to theorization, as much as in the methodology itself, according to Sharp and Green (1975), that the "inherent weakness" of such deductive research is revealed. Qualitative sport management theorists could attack the positivist, logical empiricist tradition and argue that while "fact finding" and "head counting" produces voluminous statistical data, it does not address the social circumstances out of which such data arise. Quantitative, positivist sport management studies assume the existence of a natural social order with an underlying value consensus. According to Sharp and Green, this limits both the formulation of problems to be studied and the conceptualization of possible solutions:

> *Methodologically, this tradition tends to engage in positivistic "fact finding" procedures with arbitrarily imposed categories for differentiating the data. It fails to do justice to the complexity of social reality, which cannot be "grasped" by merely reducing sociologically significant characteristics of men to their external and objective indicators. (pp. 2–3)*

In the positivist tradition (Kuhn, 1962), emphasis is placed upon the search for generalizations or laws, which will enable not only explanation but also the prediction of social behavior, and therefore social intervention and control (Berstein, 1978; Fay, 1975). Fay further indicated that by treating conventional activities and social circumstances as if they are naturally occurring entities, the positivist approach reifies the social institutions and customs of the society it is studying. By reification, Lukacs (1971) explained that social arrangements are treated as if they were immutable things that must necessarily be the way they are. Social structures and the structural relationships are regarded as inevitably functioning the way they currently do regardless of the wishes of the social actors.

In sum, the main contemporary criticisms of positivism are well summarized by Burrell and Morgan (1979) as follows:

> *Science is based on 'taken for granted' assumptions, and thus, like any other social practice, must be understood within a specific context. Traced to their source all activities which pose as science can be traced to fundamental assumptions relating to everyday life and can in no way be regarded as generating knowledge with an 'objective', value-free status, as is sometimes claimed. What passes for scientific knowledge can be shown to be founded upon a set of unstated conventions, beliefs and assumptions, just as every day, common-sense knowledge is. The difference between them lies largely in the nature of rules and the community which recognises and subscribes to them. The knowledge in both cases is not so much 'objective' as shared. (p. 255)*

Positivism in this light could be viewed as excessively narrow and inflexible and therefore unlikely to successfully capture either the hidden complexities or the commercial and cultural contexts of sport or the sport management environment. What is required is the means to provide sport management researchers with a more sophisticated understanding of the epistemological and sociological sciences.

THE MODERNIST PERIOD AND POST-POSITIVISM

The *post-positivist* position (1950–1970) began in the middle of the twentieth century, with Karl Popper (1902–1994), who demonstrated that falsification (finding the case that does not fit, and so requires a change in the theory) is a more logically achievable goal than verification.

The term "post-positivism" is harder to define than positivism. There are, broadly speaking, two families of definition. The more limited definition is represented by Lincoln and Guba (2000). They attribute to post-positivism an ontology of critical realism, an epistemology that still seeks knowledge (but admits that verification is not achievable and judges success on Popper's principles and the search for relative objectivity through the critical community of scholars), and a methodology more open to qualitative methods.

A more inclusive definition proposes post-positivism as the covering term for all the intellectual frameworks which have positioned themselves against positivism. Researchers from this perspective (see Lather, 1991), see the research process to some degree as circular or spiral or cumulative (rather than linear and sequential), prefer qualitative over quantitative methods of research, and apply hermeneutic and contextual explanatory systems within a constructivist epistemology.

The aim of research within a post-positivist framework is to gain as thorough an understanding of reality as possible by subjecting it to comprehensive and critical examination (Guba & Lincoln, 1994). Grounded Theory, with its emphasis on rigorous qualitative analysis, developed during this period.

Because positivism was more openly acknowledged within the social sciences than within the humanities, it is primarily in these fields (particularly sociology, education and psychology) that the debate between positivism and post-positivism has developed: within the humanities (literary studies, history), opposition to positivism tends to use a slightly different vocabulary. Such debates about terminology clearly demonstrate how important definitions are in the research process. In this book, we often use *"non-positivist"* when we wish to refer to all those categories positioned against positivism.

THE BLURRED GENRES AND CONSTRUCTIVIST-INTERPRETIVIST AND CRITICAL PARADIGMS

The next period was labeled the "blurred genres" (1970–1986) where qualitative researchers had a variety of paradigms, methods and strategies at their disposal (Denzin & Lincoln, 2000). Denzin and Lincoln (2005) connect the modernist and blurred genre periods with post-positivist arguments as well as the emergence of new interpretive perspectives "including hermeneutics, structuralism, semiotics, phenomenology, cultural studies and feminism" (p. 3). Developments in the Blurred Genres moment, included *constructivist* and *interpretivist* paradigms, *symbolic interactionism* and *critical theory*.

Constructivism

Constructivism moves away from the traditional positivist criteria of internal and external validity and seeks instead trustworthiness and authenticity (Denzin & Lincoln, 2005). "The constructivist paradigm assumes a relativist ontology (there are multiple realities), a subjectivist epistemology (knower and respondent co-create understandings), and a naturalistic (in the natural world) set of methodological procedures" (Denzin & Lincoln, 2005, p. 24). Constructivism sees knowledge as pertaining to the world we experience (von Glasersfeld, 1997) and all theory as lacking in certainty.

Crotty (1998) argues that we cannot be both objectivist, that is, take the "view that things exist as *meaningful* entities independently of consciousness and experience, that they have truth and meaning residing in them as objects" (p. 5), and constructionist or subjectivist. Constructivism posits that: "Truth, or meaning, comes into existence in and out of our engagement with the realities of our world … Meaning is not discovered, but constructed … different people may construct meaning in different ways, even in relation to the same phenomenon … subject and object emerge as partners in the generation of meaning" (p. 8). Therefore meaning or "truth" cannot be described as "objective".

Constructivists "desire participants to take an increasingly active role in nominating questions of interest for any inquiry and in designing outlets for findings to be shared more and widely within and outside the community." (Lincoln & Guba, 2000, p. 175). Constructivism accepts the idea of multiple voices and multiple representations. Constructions of events will be influenced by the socio-cultural and historical environment; hence the researcher cannot speak with authority nor assume objective impartiality.

Interpretivism

Interpretivism also arose as a reaction to positivism. Denzin and Lincoln (2000) summarize this as a difference in the view of science as a means of providing causal explanations (positivism) or of developing understanding of human action (interpretivism). The authors state that from an interpretivist perspective "what distinguishes human (social) action from the movement of physical objects is that the former is inherently meaningful" (p. 191).

Interpretivists take the view that objectivity can be achieved believing that "it is possible to understand the subjective meaning of action … the interpreter reproduces or reconstructs … the original meaning of the action" (Denzin & Lincoln, 2003, p. 193). To achieve this level of objectivity, interpreters must employ methods that enable them to step outside their own frames of reference and take a theoretical attitude as a neutral observer. This paradigm sees reality as created by people assigning meaning; however patterns of behavior "emerge" due to social conventions. Interpretive research aims to explain and understand social life, using an inductive approach, and presenting reality symbolically. Understanding subjective meaning is important and "value neutrality is neither necessary or possible" (Sarantakos, 1998, p. 38).

The interpretivist stance requires the use of qualitative research methodologies as these enable researchers to explore how people make sense of their lives (Miles & Huberman, 1994), their experiences and reactions to those experiences. These research methods allow for in-depth exploration of the issues as perceived by the participants, to ascertain their view of events and hear their story. An interpretivist approach involves:

> … the systematic analysis of socially meaningful action through the direct detailed observation of people in natural settings in order to arrive at understandings and interpretations of how people create and maintain their social worlds. (Neuman, 2000, p. 71)

A person's definition of a situation therefore tells him or her how to assign meaning in constantly shifting conditions. For example, the social reality of a "fan" includes ways they interact with their team and other fans. They attend games, buy merchandise and have a collective social identity with other fans. These behaviors are developed and shaped by cultural, social and masculinist factors; however, the social reality of the relationship is not fixed. The definition of the situation can change dramatically. The social reality may be influenced for example if the team were to relocate to a new area, merge with an existing team for the purpose of rationalization, or at worst cease to exist (Skinner & Edwards, 2005). Interpretive approaches to sport management research posit that research cannot be value-free. It is not possible to "suspend values in order to understand" (Maykut & Morehouse, 1994, p. 12) as values are embedded in all aspects of the research, from what is chosen as the topic, how it is examined, and in the relationship between researcher and researched (Maykut & Morehouse, 1994). Moreover, the relationship between the researcher and the informant affects the gathering, interpretation, and writing up of data (see Denzin, 1989; Fraenkel & Wallen, 1993).

The constructivist–interpretivist paradigm is embodied in many theoretical perspectives including symbolic interactionism (Crotty, 1998), which was particularly influential in the development of Grounded Theory.

Research Brief

Title: An Interpretive Analysis of Hartford Whalers Fans' stories
Who: Hyatt, C., University of Massachusetts
This study examined the experience of being a fan of the National Hockey League's Hartford Whalers from the perspective of the insider. Twenty-four fans were interviewed in-depth to gain an understanding of the process of becoming a Whalers fan, being a Whalers fan, living through the franchise re-location, and living life without the Whalers. By examining the stories, existing concepts and definitions in the sport marketing and fan loyalty literature were questioned by Hyatt.

Symbolic interactionism

Symbolic interactionism did not accept the prevailing thinking that human behavior is the consequence of external forces that impact upon people. Symbolic interactionism focused on the meaning that things and events have for people. Blumer (1969) writes that to "bypass the meaning in favour of factors alleged to produce the behaviour is seen as a grievous neglect of the role of meaning in the formation of behaviour" (p. 3).

Symbolic interactionism "sees meanings as social products, as creations that are formed in and through the defining activities of people as they interact" (Blumer, 1969, p. 4). It differs from behaviorist models, based in objectivist epistemologies, in its belief that people act reflectively, consciously construct what they do and are able to modify or alter the meanings and symbols they use in their interactions. It is therefore the patterns of action and interaction that make up groups and societies (Ritzer, 1996), and interactionists "study how people produce their situated versions of society" (Denzin, 1992, p. 23). The focus is on the generation of meaning and its interpretation.

Symbolic interactionism rests on three main premises: "that human beings act toward things on the basis of the meanings that the things have for them ... that the meaning for such things is derived from, or arises out of, the social interaction that one has with one's fellows ... that these meanings are handled in, and modified through, an interpretative process used by the person in dealing with the things he encounters." (Blumer, 1969, p. 2).

Thus, individuals learn the meanings of objects through socialization, both as children and in all other interactions where meanings are developed and refined. Physical objects (a chair), social objects (a student), and abstract objects (including ideas and moral principles), all have learned meanings (Ritzer, 1996). Some of these will be learned differently by different groups of people at varying places and times.

The basic principles of symbolic interactionism are set out by Ritzer (1996):

1. Human beings ... are endowed with the capacity for thought.

2. The capacity for thought is shaped by social interaction.

3. In social interaction, people learn the meanings and the symbols that allow them to exercise their distinctly human capacity for thought.

4. Meanings and symbols allow people to carry on distinctly human action and interaction.

5. People are able to modify or alter the meanings and symbols that they use in action and interaction on the basis of their interpretation of the situation.

6. People are able to make these modifications and alterations because, in part, of their ability to interact with themselves, which allows them to examine possible causes of action, assess their relative advantages and disadvantages, and then choose one.

7. The intertwined patterns of action and interaction make up groups and societies.

Human behavior then is a response to events and situations and the researcher must either "enter into the defining process or develop a sufficient appreciation for the process so that understanding can become clear" (Berg, 2001, p. 9). Symbolic interactionism's "most important methodological premise is that all social inquiry must be grounded in the particular empirical world studied" (Locke, 2001, p. 24), and from the detailed description gained by observing behavior researchers can formulate interpretations.

Critical theory

Critical inquiry, unlike positivism and constructivism–interpretivism, seeks to challenge the status quo. Critical theorists do not share the confidence of interpretivists in people's accounts of experience: "Where most interpretivists today embrace such accounts as descriptions of authentic "lived experience", critical researchers hear in them the voice of an inherited tradition and prevailing culture" (Crotty, 1998, p. 159). Critical research views "claims to truth as always discursively situated and implicated in relations of power" (Kincheloe & McLaren, 2005, p. 327) with each set of meanings supporting particular power structures and resisting change toward greater equity (Crotty, 1998).

Freire (1972) writes that people can only begin to move and change when the oppressed find the power within themselves to free both themselves and their oppressors from the existing order. To do this, they "must perceive their state not as fated and unalterable, but merely as limiting – and therefore challenging" (p. 57). Critical theorists believe that people are capable of change and the role of research is to actively uncover the conditions that affect people's lives. People will then understand the conditions of their oppression and be able to act upon them. The role of the researcher is to study reality to provide data that people can use to understand their condition and to be an activist for change.

Critical theory was developed in Germany by the Frankfurt school over 70 years ago. It follows the tradition of Marx, Kant and Hegel (Kincheloe & McLaren, 1994, 2000). Kincheloe and McLaren define a criticalist as a researcher who uses research as a social or cultural criticism. A critical researcher aims to produce a social or cultural criticism within certain assumptions. The assumptions of critical theory, according to Kincheloe and McLaren, are that:

- thought is modified by power relations;

- facts are value mediated;

- the relationship between concept and object is mobile;

- language is central to developing subjectivity;

- society has a social status hierarchy;

- there are many faces of oppression; and

- research often, unwittingly, reproduces the class system.

Kincheloe and McLaren (1994, 2000) further say that modern critical analysis is a hybrid and not confined to a specific school of analysis. Critical researchers try to understand the ideologies that inform their research so that assumptions can be transparent. Information for critical theorists is an act of human judgment or interpretation, knowledge that must be interpreted by people. This interpretation and development of theory requires an understanding of the relationship between the parts of the whole (Wack, 1985a,b). Creswell (1998) notes that there are a number of themes for the critical researcher; one of the core themes is to critique and imagine a different society. Critical research aims to confront issues in a society or part of it and to change the wrongs that emerge from the research as perceived by the researcher. To just increase knowledge is not enough for the critical researcher (Kincheloe & McLaren, 1994, 2000). In contrast to empirical research, critical research depends on meaning being derived from interpretation of data (Kincheloe & McLaren, 1994) "...what we see is not what we see but what we perceive" (p. 144). According to Kincheloe and McLaren, knowledge comes from interpreting data by people who are part of the world and understanding the relationships between parts of the world. Critical research is a process of offering hope where there is contempt.

THE CRISIS OF REPRESENTATION AND FEMINIST/ POST-STRUCTURALIST PARADIGMS

The crisis of representation period (1986–1990) appeared with writings that "called into question the issues of gender, class and race" (Denzin & Lincoln, 2000, p. 16). Researchers struggled with "how to locate themselves and their subjects in reflective texts" (Denzin & Lincoln, 2005, p. 3). Writers challenged older models of meaning and truth and moved away from gathering data as something separate from the researcher to including the researcher in the experience and questioning issues such as validity, reliability and objectivity.

This period represents changes in thinking about how knowledge is created, understood and used, leading to the more recent historical periods of postmodern, post-experimental, methodologically contested present and fractured future and the paradigm of post-structuralism. Post-structuralism, the fourth paradigm presented by Denzin and Lincoln (2003), emerges as clearly different from positivist paradigms and structuralism.

Structuralism "looks for decisive shaping factors in structural forms discoverable within society or the unconscious, or both" (Crotty, 1998, p. 204), whereas post-structuralism "challenges the very idea of structure, including the idea of a center, a fixed principle, a hierarchy of meaning and a solid foundation (Alvesson, 2002, p. 30). Post-structuralism places a strong focus on the origins of language linking "language, subjectivity, social organization and power … Language … produces meaning and creates social reality … Language is how social organization and power are defined and contested and the place where one's sense of self – one's subjectivity – is constructed" (Richardson & St Pierre, 2005, p. 961). Richardson and St Pierre view post-structuralism as a particular kind of postmodernist thinking, a view also taken by authors who see post-structuralism as "a more specific form of thought" (Crotty, 1998, p. 195) and therefore subsumed under postmodernism. An alternate view holds that post-structuralism, which developed in France, provides the "orientations and ideas that postmodernism, a much broader movement geographically and conceptually, has made its own, enlarged and applied to an extended range of subject areas" (Crotty, 1998, p. 195). In this view, post-structuralism provided the foundations for postmodernism. Alvesson (2002) suggests that it is almost impossible to establish a clear relationship between post-structuralism and postmodernism as authors use the terms in different ways, but that postmodernism tends to be used more frequently due to the familiarity emanating from "the term's use in the most varied of contexts" (p. 31).

Research Brief

Title: The Role of the Digital Sports Games in the Sports Media Complex
Who: Baerg, A., The University of Iowa
Baerg investigated how the culture of sport is changed as it is mediated. He examined the mediation of sport through four digital sports games produced by Electronic Arts – *Fight Night Round 2*, *Tiger Woods PGA Tour 2004*, *MVP Baseball 2005*, and *John Madden Football 2005*.

Baerg employed a multi-level method of textual analysis in engaging the representation and gameplay of these respective titles. He used three case studies to tease out the ideological implications of these games as they position their users. A fourth case study examined how the digital sports game audience responds to the ideologies and positioning identified in the textual analysis section.

THE POSTMODERN, POST-EXPERIMENTAL, THE METHODOLOGICALLY CONTESTED PRESENT AND THE FRACTURED FUTURE

The postmodern (1990–1995) and post-experimental (1995–2000) demonstrate a concern for narrative and the "refusal to privilege any method of theory" (Denzin & Lincoln, 2005, p. 3). The postmodern period (1990–1995) struggled to make sense of the crises of the preceding periods and develop ways to represent the "other", with the concept of "aloof observer" abandoned (Denzin & Lincoln, 2000, p. 17). Postmodernism has at its core "the doubt that any method or theory, any discourse or genre, or any tradition or novelty has a universal and general claim as the "right" or privileged form of authoritative knowledge" (Richardson & St Pierre, 2005, p. 961).

Postmodernist research, in a similar vein to critical theory, seeks to expose the hidden structure of the social world and aims to deconstruct or dissolve all distinctions by breaking down boundaries. Knowledge takes numerous forms and therefore cannot be generalized (Crotty, 1998; Neuman, 2000). "Reality" is constructed by the discourse of each social and historical context so what is "real" is "what is represented as such" (Locke, 2001, p. 11). Postmodernists break down boundaries within research seeing research as a form of art in which the presence of the researcher must be evident. The value of research is to stimulate thought in others. It is certainly not to make predictions or reinforce existing power relations (Neuman, 2000).

With the incorporation of critical and postmodern views into the field of sport management, sport management scholars have emphasized "the need to understand sport management in its wider, political, economic, and ideological context and be concerned with exposing patterns of inequality and intervening in local communities" (Amis & Silk, 2005, p. 357). While this is of course important in a grander sociological sense, it is also important to recognize the significance that these needs hold within the sport management research. That is, researchers in the field of sport management need to be concerned with the political, economic, and ideological patterns of inequality that may exist in terms of scholarly interactions with one another. Certainly, the dream of an open-minded and diverse culture of scholarship is not an uncommon goal for researchers in the field. As Amis and Silk (2005) expressed: "In keeping with a field that is inherently multidisciplinary in nature, we envision an academic landscape that is not dominated by any single overarching meta-narrative that marginalizes and obfuscates alternative approaches" (Amis & Silk, 2005, p. 358). Despite this commentary, critical and postmodern approaches, at this time, still remain at the fringes of sport management research (Edwards et al., 2002).

Denzin and Lincoln (2005) suggest that at the start of the twenty first century qualitative research "confronts the methodological backlash associated with the evidence-based social movement … [and] asks that the humanities become sites for critical conversations about democracy, race, gender, class, nation-states, globalisation, freedom, and community" (p. 3). They argue that what is needed is an interpretive social science that "blurs both boundaries and genres" (p. 1083) and is committed to social change. Denzin and Lincoln (2005) suggest this requires researchers who are able to navigate between the oppositional forces of the methodological conservatives, neo-traditionalist methodologists and the ethical right whom they perceive as threatening the advances in qualitative research. This historical moment is evolving now as the *Fractured Future* with the outcome yet unknown.

Sport management researchers embracing these new research paradigms signal a growing awareness in the sport management research community that there is no single or right way to understand social reality. Qualitative methods, and more recently the support for emergent theoretical approaches to sport management research, have provided an alternative to the positivistic testing of formal theories developed by empirical researchers. Furthermore, our understanding of how social reality is depicted is being continually challenged and subsequently, as Richardson (2000) suggested, the research process is becoming harder to master. It is therefore important that as sport management academics and students we grapple with questions regarding the nature of the knowledge that informs our discipline and we assess particular research practices before they adopt them. A failure to do so may lead us to unwittingly generate knowledge that is inimical to their particular quest.

In endeavoring to emulate rigorous standards of research, sport management researchers should be encouraged to take more methodological "risks" and embrace more eclectic research approaches. Through embracing such concerns, the sport management researcher will increasingly identify dimensions of the reflexive nature of researcher and participant intersubjectivity and the reflexive moments of research interaction. Because of their vantage point in interacting intensively at multiple levels and in an enduring way with people from all walks of life sport management researchers are well positioned to take up many of the challenges that qualitative research paradigms can offer.

PARADIGMS MODEL

Following on from the development of research approaches, a number of researchers have attempted to develop models based on paradigms.

The paradigm categories proposed by Lincoln and Guba (1994; 2000) provide a useful model across all forms of sport management research. These categories are *positivism, post-positivism, critical theory, constructivism,* and *participatory* and mirror somewhat the historical development of research discussed previously.

1. *Positivism:* according to Guba and Lincoln is where a simple reality is assumed governed by natural laws; knowledge is context free and controlled by cause and effect laws. The goal of research is to discover the "truth".

2. *Post-positivism:* say Guba and Lincoln is where imperfect reality is assumed because of imperfect human intelligence and the complex nature of phenomena.

3. *Critical theory:* write Guba and Lincoln is where "reality" is shaped by social, political, cultural, economic, ethnic and gender values. Over time, this "reality" is assumed to be "real".

4. *Constructivism:* "reality" is intangible, a construction of the human mind shaped by experiences of the world, it is dependent on the individual and can be changed with new information (Guba & Lincoln, 1994; 2000).

5. *Participatory:* Lincoln and Guba (2000) have drawn on the work of Heron and Reason (1997) and included a fifth paradigm, participatory, to their list of alternative inquiry paradigms. As this paradigm has not been discussed in as great a detail as the above paradigms, a brief discussion of this paradigm will now be given.

The *participatory paradigm* is mostly associated with *co-operative inquiry:* a person centered inquiry that does research *with* people, not *on* them or *about* them. This means people become co-researchers involved in all levels of the research design (Heron, 1996). The participatory paradigm allows researchers and participants to "be co-participants in defining and altering" situations (Joyappa & Martin, 1996, p. 2). It is an approach that seeks to empower both individuals and communities in a way that allows and perhaps even facilitates eventual social change (Joyappa & Martin, 1996). As argued by Heron and Reason (1997), the participatory worldview allows us, as researchers, to unite with other persons in a collaborative approach to inquiry.

An important aspect of participatory research is its attempt to share control of the actual research process with those involved in it. What becomes important in this research approach is who produces, validates, and is empowered by knowledge. Participatory research is ultimately a bottom-up approach that is participant driven and favors individual meaningful outcomes over a broader generalizability of findings (Joyappa & Martin, 1996).

Ontology: In terms of how we view the world, the participatory paradigm asserts that in no way can we ever have absolute experiential knowledge, and as such, what must be remembered about experiential knowing is that "the very process of perceiving is also a meeting, a transaction" (Heron & Reason, 1997, p. 278). Heron and Reason state: "To experience anything is to participate in it, and to participate is both to mould and to encounter; hence experiential reality is always subjective-objective" (p. 278). This relationship means that we come to know a world at an interactive interface, which exists between one and what is encountered.

Epistemology: Heron and Reason (1997) describe that a knower comes to know in four different ways; that is an experiential, presentational, propositional, and practical way. The first kind of knowing, experiential, stems from an "empathic resonance with a being … it is also the creative shaping of a world" (p. 280). There inherently is an acceptance of our perspective of knowledge, and while authentically valuing that, we recognize its biases and articulate this consciousness and awareness.

Methodology: Heron and Reason (1997) suggest that from a participatory worldview, methodologies need to reflect this democratic dialog creation between both the participants and the researchers through co-operative methods of inquiry. They also posit that a co-operative method means that:

People collaborate to define the questions they wish to explore and the methodology for that exploration (propositional knowing); together or separately they apply this methodology in the world of their practice (practical knowing); which leads to new forms of encounter with their world (experiential knowing); and they find ways to represent this experience in significant patterns (presentational knowing) which feeds into a revised propositional understanding of the original question. (p. 282)

Table 2.1 summarizes these basic beliefs that underpin the alternative inquiry paradigms. We agree with Denzin and Lincoln's (2000) proposition that "the borders and boundary lines separating these paradigms and perspectives have begun to blur" (p. 157). A model like that of Lincoln and Guba (2000) acknowledges the necessary connection between our processes of thought and our actions. It also allows us to see not only that methods can cross discipline boundaries, but also that both the social sciences and the humanities share common frameworks. Although some variants of each framework may be incompatible with some variants of another, it is not uncommon to find that individual researchers subscribe to more than one framework at a time, and move about among them (and among variants within them) over the course of their research career.

We suggest that there is no single paradigm, and/or methodology, that meets the needs of all sport management researchers and all research questions, when investigating our diverse, complex and changing contemporary field. Therefore, it is crucial that the most appropriate paradigm(s) and thereby the most appropriate methodology to conduct the research is adopted by the sport management researcher.

Research Brief

Title: Playing with Traditions: Fenway Park and Urban Culture
Who: Borer, M., Boston University

Borer analyzed the situation concerning the removal or renovation of Fenway Park in Boston. He utilized qualitative research methods including participant observation, archival research, and intensive interviewing with fans, non-fans, workers in the park, current and former Red Sox players and personnel as well as those who ultimately make the decision about the future of the park (e.g., Red Sox owners and Executives, city officials, and the Boston Redevelopment Agency). In this way, Borer uncovered the way people in and outside of Boston utilized the ballpark and responded to the debate about its future.

Table 2.1   Basic Beliefs of Alternative Inquiry Paradigms

Issue	Positivism	Post-Positivism	Critical Theory	Constructivism	Participatory
Ontology	Naïve realism – "real" reality but apprehensible	Critical realism! – "real" reality but only imperfectly and probabilistically apprehensible	Historical realism – virtual reality shaped by social, political, cultural, economic, ethnic, and gender values; crystallized over time	Relativism – local and specific co-constructed realities	Participative reality – subjective–objective reality, co-created by mind and given cosmos
Epistemology	Dualist/object; findings true	Modified dualist/objectivist; critical tradition/community; findings probably true	Transactional/subjectivist; value-mediated findings	Transactional/subjectivist; co-created findings	Critical subjectivity in participatory transaction with cosmos; extended epistemology of experiential, propositional, and practical knowing; co-created findings
Methodology	Experimental/manipulative; verification of hypotheses; chiefly quantitative methods	Modified experimental/manipulative; critical multiplism; falsification of hypotheses; may include qualitative methods	Dialogic/dialectical	Hermeneutical/dialectical	Political participation in collaborative action inquiry/primacy of the practical; use of language grounded in shared experiential context

Source: Lincoln, Y.S., & Guba, E.G. (2000). Paradigmatic controversies, contradictions, and emerging confluences. In N.K. Denzin & Y.S. Lincoln (Eds), *The Handbook of Qualitative Research*, 2nd edn, (p. 168). Thousand Oaks: Sage.

CONCLUSION

It was once possible to define each academic "discipline" in terms of its research paradigm, built upon a specific ontology and epistemology. The fields of "mathematics" or "physics" or "biology" or "history" or "literature" or "classics" recognized boundaries not only of what knowledge was appropriate for the discipline but also of how the appropriate knowledge could be obtained. But now, not only are many frameworks operating simultaneously, but they are also operating across disciplines. This is where this book is positioned – on the boundary between the humanities and the social sciences. We believe that good sport management research can come out of both these academic traditions, and from all intellectual positions past rigid positivism.

A model like that of Lincoln and Guba (2000) acknowledges the necessary connection between our processes of thought and our actions. It also allows us to see not only that methods can cross discipline boundaries, but also that both the social sciences and the humanities share common frameworks. Although some variants of each framework may be incompatible with some variants of another, it is not uncommon to find that individual sport management researchers subscribe to more than one framework at a time, and move about among them (and among variants within them) over the course of their research career.

Until quite recently, it was considered both unwise and unprofessional to articulate a particular framework in a research report. However, as the positivist paradigm, with its claim to objectivity and its assumption that research must be value-free, has been increasingly challenged, more sport management researchers feel free, or even obliged, to express their position openly. Frisby (2005) identifies her research as aligning with neo-Marxism, feminism and post-structuralism. Her research is also a good example of empirical research from a non-positivist perspective.

We do not propose that all these frameworks are equal, or even equally valid, only that all are currently in use, so you are likely to find them represented in the reading you do, and you are likely to have absorbed some at least of this into your own ways of thinking. We hope here to provide you with a map of the terrain – a way of understanding how all these various philosophical frameworks, the fundamental methodological approaches, and the practical methods within each relate to each other. With this knowledge, we hope you will be empowered to understand your own framework(s) and so to select your methodology wisely – choosing those methods that are appropriate for your project, and understanding the implications of your choices.

IN PROFILE - Dr Laura L Cousens

Dr Cousens' graduate education in sport management was completed at the University of Alberta (Ph.D.) and the University of Ottawa (MA), after completing an undergraduate degree in Recreation Administration at the University of Waterloo. Dr Cousens is currently an Associate Professor in the Department of Sport Management at Brock University. Prior to accepting a tenure-tracked position at Brock University in 2002, Dr Cousens lectured at the University of British Columbia and at Central Queensland University in Australia. The courses she has taught are in the areas of organization theory, marketing, sponsorship, strategic alliances, and professional sport. Over the last 15 years, Dr Cousens' program of research has evolved from a focus on marketing and sponsorship to studies designed to investigate change at the organizational and industry levels of analysis. Her doctoral research used a historical-comparative approach to explore changes in North America's professional sport industry between 1970 and 1997. Institutional theory was used to inform this investigation of the logics of action (ideas and beliefs), inter-organizational linkages, governance structures, and communities of actors that shaped and constrained decision-making by the leaders of the four major professional sport leagues on this continent. More recently, Dr Cousens has investigated networks of community sport providers with a focus on local basketball and swimming clubs in the Niagara Region of Ontario. This research explores the density, centrality, and multiplexity of ties characteristic of community sport networks. Furthermore, this research also seeks to investigate the institutional context that shapes the logics, governance, and values of the leaders of community sport organizations. Qualitative approaches to exploring sport organizations, their institutional context, and their changes are central to Dr Cousens' research efforts. It was through a textual analysis of secondary sources of data, and through the analysis of in-depth interviews conducted with individuals in the sport industry, that she was able to learn about values, ideas, and beliefs that have shaped both professional and community sport delivery. These interpretative approaches have facilitated a heightened level of scrutiny of social phenomena that help us to understand why, for example, particular decisions are made. Institutional theorists seek to explore the ideas and beliefs, and values that shape and constrain organizations. Uncovering the scripts or rules characteristic of a sport organization's institutional environment necessitates adopting research approaches that pay attention to the meanings of social events and the subjective nature of human life.

REVIEW AND RESEARCH QUESTIONS

1. Summarize the historical moments in qualitative research and the related theoretical paradigms.

2. Distinguish between Ontological, Epistemological and Methodological perspectives in the context of sport management research.

3. Explain what is meant by the term "paradigm" and the different types of paradigms that are associated with sport management research.

REFERENCES

Alvesson, M. 2002. Understanding Organizational Culture. London: Sage.

Amis, J. & Silk, M. 2005. Rupture: promoting critical and innovative approaches to the study of sport management. *Journal of Sport Management*, **19**, 355–366.

Barker, J. 1992. Future Edge: Discovering the New Paradigms of Success. New York: William Morrow.

Berg, B. L. 2001. Qualitative Research Methods for the Social Sciences, 4th ed. Boston: Allyn & Bacon.

Berstein, F. 1978. The Restructuring of Social and Political Theory. Philadelphia: University of Pennsylvania Press.

Blumer, H. 1969. Symbolic Interactionism: Perspective and Method. Englewood Cliffs, NJ: Prentice-Hall.

Bryman, A., & Burgess, R.G. (Eds.), 1994. Analyzing Qualitative Data. London: Routledge.

Burrell, G. & Morgan, G. 1979. Sociology of Paradigms and Organizational Life: Elements of the Sociology of Corporate Life. London: Heinemann.

Covey, S. R. 1989. The Seven Habits of Highly Effective People. New York: Fireside.

Creswell, J. W. 1998. Qualitative Inquiry and Research Design: Choosing among Five Traditions. Newbury Park, CA: Sage.

Crotty, M. 1998. The Foundations of Social Research: Meaning and Perspective in the Research Process. Sydney, NSW:: Allen and Unwin.

Denzin, N. K. 1989. Interpretive Interactionism. Newbury Park, CA: Sage.

Denzin, N. K. 1992. Symbolic Interactionism and Cultural Studies: The Politics of Interpretation. Cambridge, MA: Blackwell.

Denzin, N. K. 2002. Interpretive Interactionism, 2nd ed. Newbury Park, CA: Sage.

Denzin, N. K., & Lincoln, Y. S. (Eds.), 1994. Handbook of Qualitative Research. Thousand Oaks, CA: Sage.

Denzin, N. K., & Lincoln, Y. S. (Eds.), 1998. The Landscape of Qualitative Research. London: Sage.

Denzin, N. K., & Lincoln, Y. S. (Eds.), 2000. Handbook of Qualitative Research (2nd ed.). Thousand Oaks, CA: Sage.

Denzin, N. K., & Lincoln, Y. S. (Eds.), 2003. The Landscape of Qualitative Research (2nd ed.). London: Sage.

Denzin, N. K., & Lincoln, Y. S. (Eds.), 2005. Handbook of Qualitative Research (3rd ed.). Thousand Oaks, CA: Sage.

Edwards, A., Gilbert, K. & Skinner, J. 2002. Extending the Boundaries: Theoretical Frameworks for Research in Sports Management. Melbourne, Victoria: Common Ground.

Fay, B. 1975. Social Theory and Political Practice. London: Allen and Unwin.

Fraenkel, J. R. & Wallen, N. E. 1993. How to Design and Evaluate Research. New York, NY: McGraw-Hill.

Freire, P. 1972. Pedagogy of the Oppressed. Harmondsworth, UK: Penguin.

Frisby, W. 2005. The good, the bad, and the ugly: critical sport management research. *Journal of Sport Management*, **19**, 1–12.

Guba, E. G. (Ed.), 1990. The Paradigm Dialog. Newbury Park, CA: Sage.

Guba, E. G. & Lincoln, Y. S. 1989. Fourth Generation Evaluation. Newbury Park, CA: Sage.

Guba, E. G. & Lincoln, Y. S. 1994. Competing paradigms in qualitative research. In: *Handbook of Qualitative Research* (Ed. by N. K. Denzin, Y. S. Lincoln), pp. 105–117. Thousand Oaks, CA: Sage.

Guba, E. G. & Lincoln, Y. S. 1998. Competing paradigms in qualitative research. In: *The Landscape of Qualitative Research* (Ed. by N. K. Denzin, Y. S. Lincoln), pp. 195–222. Thousand Oaks, CA: Sage.

Heron, J. 1996. Co-operative Inquiry: Research into the Human Condition. Newbury, CA: Sage.

Heron, J. & Reason, P. 1997. Qualitative Inquiry. London: Sage.

Jary, D. & Jary, J. 1991. Sociology of Education: The Harper Collins Dictionary of Sociology. USA: Harper Perennial.

Joyappa, V. & Martin, D. 1996. Exploring alternative research epistemologies for adult education: participatory research, feminist research, and feminist participatory research. *Adult Education Quarterly*, **47** (1), 1–14.

Kincheloe, J. L. & McLaren, P. L. 1994. Rethinking critical theory and qualitative research. In: *Handbook of Qualitative Research* (Ed. by N. K. Denzin, Y. S. Lincoln), pp. 138–157. Thousand Oaks, CA: Sage.

Kincheloe, J. L. & McLaren, P. L. 2000. Rethinking critical theory and qualitative research. In: *Handbook of Qualitative Research* (Ed. by N. K. Denzin, Y. S. Lincoln), pp. 279–313, 2nd ed. Thousand Oaks, CA: Sage.

Kincheloe, J. L. & McLaren, P. L. 2005. Rethinking critical theory and qualitative research. In: *Handbook of Qualitative Research* (Ed. by N. K. Denzin, Y. S. Lincoln), pp. 303–342, 3rd ed. Thousand Oaks, CA: Sage.

Kuhn, T. S. 1962. The Structure of Scientific Revolutions. Chicago: University of Chicago Press.

Kuhn, T. S. 1970. The Structure of Scientific Revolutions, 2nd ed. Chicago: University of Chicago Press.

Lather, P. 1991. Getting Smart: Feminist Research and Pedagogy with/in the Postmodern. New York: Routledge.

Lincoln, Y. S. & Guba, E. G. 2000. The only generalization there is: there is no generalization. In: *Case Study Method: Key Issues, Key Texts* (Ed. by R. Gomm, M. Hammersley, P. Foster), pp. 27–44. London: Sage.

Locke, K. 2001. Grounded Theory in Management Research. London: Sage.

Lukacs, G. 1971. History and Class Consciousness. Cambridge: MIT Press.

Maykut, P. & Morehouse, R. 1994. Beginning Qualitative Research: A Philosophic and Practical Guide. London: Routledge.

Miles, M. B. & Huberman, M. A. 1994. Qualitative Data Analysis. Thousand Oaks, CA: Sage.

Neuman, W. L. 2000. Social Research Methods: Qualitative and Quantitative Approaches, 4th ed. Boston: Allyn & Bacon.

Pascale, P. 1990. Managing on the Edge. New York: Touchstone.

Patton, M. Q. 1990. Qualitative Evaluation and Research Methods, 2nd ed. Newbury Park, CA: Sage.

Potter, J. 1996. Representing Reality: Discourse, Rhetoric and Social Construction. Newbury, CA: Sage.

Richardson, L. 2000. Writing: A method of inquiry. In NK Denzin & YS Lincoln (Eds.), Handbook of Qualitative Research (2nd ed., pp. 923–948).

Richardson, L. & St Pierre, E. A. 2005. Writing: a method of inquiry. In: *Handbook of Qualitative Research* (Ed. by N. K. Denzin, Y. S. Lincoln), pp. 959–978, 3rd ed. Thousand Oaks, CA: Sage.

Ritzer, G. 1996. The McDonaldization of Society: An Investigation into the Changing Character of Contemporary Social Life, Rev. ed. Newbury Park, CA: Pine Forge Press.

Sarantakos, S. 1998. Social Research. Melbourne: Macmillan Education Australia.

Sarantakos, S. 2002. Beyond domestic patriarchy: marital power in Australia. *Nuance*, **4**, 12–34.

Senge, P. 1990. The Fifth Discipline: The Art and Practice of the Learning Organization. New York: Doubleday.

Senge, P., Kleiner, A. & Roberts, C. 1994. The Fifth Discipline Fieldbook. London: Nicholas Brealey.

Sharp, R. & Green, A. 1975. Education and Social Control. London: Routledge & Kegan Paul.

Skinner, J. & Edwards, A. 2005. Inventive pathways: fresh visions of sport management research. *Journal of Sport Management*, **19**, 404–421.

Smith, J. K. 1983. Quantitative versus qualitative research: an attempt to clarify the issue. *Educational Researcher*, **March**, 6–13.

The New Shorter Oxford English Dictionary, 1993, 4th ed. New York, NY: Oxford University Press.

von Glasersfeld, E. 1997. Amplification of a constructivist perspective. *Issues in Education*, **3** (2), 203–209.

Wack, P. 1985a. The gentle art of reperceiving scenarios: uncharted waters ahead (part 1 of a two-part article). *Harvard Business Review*, **Sept–Oct**, 73–89.

Wack, P. 1985b. The gentle art of reperceiving scenarios: shooting the rapids (part 2 of a two part article). *Harvard Business Review*, **Nov–Dec**, 2–14.

Zohar, D. 1990. The Quantum Self. New York, NY: William Morrow.

PART 2

Planning the Sport Management Research Study

CHAPTER 3

The Sport Management Research Process

OBJECTIVES

By the end of this chapter, you should be able to

- understand the basic steps involved in formulating a Research Plan.

- identify primary and secondary sources used for a literature review.

- identify some strategies for sourcing research ideas for a sport management research study.

KEY TERMS

Literature review: A critical study of existing literature that is relevant to the study being conducted by the researcher.

Research problem: The statement that provides the context for the research study, and which generates questions that aim to be answered within the scope of the research study.

Reliability: consistency, dependability. The results can be replicated.

Validity: truthfulness of the research outcomes.

Authenticity: how "real" are the results.

Credibility: how believable or credible something is.

Population: all members of a specified group.

Target population: the population to which the researcher ideally wants to generalize.

Accessible population: the population to which the researcher has access.

Sample: a subset of a population.

Subject: a specific individual participating in a study.

Sampling technique: the specific method used to select a sample from a population.

Probability sampling: A random sample of a population, which ensures that each member of the population has a chance of being selected for the sample. This type of sampling technique is used in quantitative research.

Non-probability sampling: The sample is not random, as in probability sampling, as the researcher aims to select participants that have a greater chance of having relevance to the research topic.

KEY QUESTIONS

The key questions raised in this chapter are as follows:

- What is a research plan?
- What is a literature review?
- Where does the sport management researcher get research ideas from?

- Why are the concepts of rigor and trustworthiness so important to the sport management researcher?
- What is Sampling and why is selecting an appropriate sampling technique important?

CHAPTER OVERVIEW

This chapter highlights that undertaking a research study or investigation requires careful and methodical planning on the part of the sport management researcher. It identifies that from the initial idea that sparks the sport management researcher's interest, the conduct of the literature review, refining the research problem, formulating the questions to be answered in the research topic through to the design of the research plan, the sport management researcher must carefully review and plan each step of the research journey.

INTRODUCTION

Research involves systematic exploration, guided by well-constructed questions, producing new information or reassessing old information. Sport management researchers spend a great deal of time evaluating other people's research, deciding what the strengths and weaknesses are in each case, and hoping to apply their conclusions to their own reading and to the procedures they follow in their research. Sport management researchers' own value systems inevitably come into play in such an exercise, but they still try to be fair to other researchers, no matter how different those approaches and methods are from their own. Sport management researchers therefore need to look carefully at the claims of others, judging for themselves whether they are convincing. To do that they need to understand the process by which other researchers have come to their conclusions, and this means understanding both their methodologies and the intellectual frameworks within which they have operated.

Part of what we want you to take away from this book is enough knowledge of qualitative research to judge what you read for yourselves.

In this book, the main purpose is to assist the qualitative sport management researcher first and foremost to think about research, to reflect and to plan, or to design (and to redesign) a study, to acquire competence in methods and techniques associated with qualitative inquiry and to use writing as a way of researching and also as a means of presenting the study upon completion. We view the role of writing in the whole research process as a tool for *reflection* and as a tool of *composition*. In other words, throughout the research journey, the sport management researcher will write as a way of:

- *clarifying* their thoughts
- *documenting* theoretical information
- *developing and refining* the topic
- *documenting* data
- *refining* their understanding of theory
- *developing* their problem statement
- *planning* the inquiry and setting out the design
- *arguing* the strength of the design, and ultimately
- *composing* the report/dissertation

Therefore, if you have decided upon a research project with a qualitative approach, you will find this book useful. In qualitative research, we want to find out not only *what* happens, but also *how* it happens, and, importantly, also *why* it happens.

FEATURES OF QUALITATIVE RESEARCH

Several writers have identified what they consider to be the prominent characteristics of qualitative, or naturalistic, research. The list that follows represents a synthesis of these authors' descriptions of qualitative research:

1. Qualitative research uses the natural setting as the source of data. The researcher attempts to observe, describe and interpret settings as they are, maintaining what Patton (1990) calls an "empathic neutrality" (p. 55).

2. The researcher acts as the "human instrument" of data collection.

3. Qualitative researchers predominantly use inductive data analysis.

4. Qualitative research reports are descriptive, incorporating expressive language and the "presence of voice in the text" (Eisner, 1991, p. 36).

5. Qualitative research has an interpretive character, aimed at discovering the meaning events have for the individuals who experience them, and the interpretations of those meanings by the researcher.

6. Qualitative researchers pay attention to the idiosyncratic as well as the pervasive, seeking the uniqueness of each case.

7. Qualitative research has an emergent (as opposed to predetermined) design, and researchers focus on this emerging process as well as the outcomes or product of the research.

8. Qualitative research is judged using special criteria for trustworthiness (these will be discussed in some detail in a later section).

Patton (1990) points out that these are not "absolute characteristics of qualitative inquiry, but rather strategic ideals that provide a direction and a framework for developing specific designs and concrete data collection tactics" (p. 59). These characteristics are considered to be "interconnected" (p. 40) and "mutually reinforcing" (Lincoln & Guba, 1985, p. 39).

It is important to emphasize the emergent nature of qualitative research design. Because the researcher seeks to observe and interpret meanings in context, it is neither possible nor appropriate to finalize research strategies before data collection has begun (Patton, 1990). Qualitative research proposals should, however, specify primary questions to be explored and plans for data collection strategies.

The particular design of a qualitative study depends on the purpose of the inquiry, what information will be most useful, and what information will have the most credibility. There are no strict criteria for sample size (Patton, 1990). "Qualitative studies typically employ multiple forms of evidence … [and] there is no statistical test of significance to determine if results "count"" (Eisner, 1991, p. 39). Judgments about usefulness and credibility are left to the researcher and the reader.

THE ROLE OF THE RESEARCHER IN QUALITATIVE INQUIRY

Before conducting a qualitative study, a researcher must do three things: *First*, he/she must adopt the stance suggested by the characteristics of the naturalist paradigm. *Second*, the researcher must develop the level of skill appropriate for a human instrument, or the vehicle through which data will be collected and interpreted. *Finally*, the researcher must prepare a research design that uses accepted strategies for naturalistic inquiry (Lincoln & Guba, 1985).

Glaser and Strauss (1967) and Strauss and Corbin (1990) refer to what they call the *"theoretical sensitivity"* of the researcher. Theoretical sensitivity refers to a personal quality of the researcher. It indicates an awareness of the subtleties of meaning of data. … [It] refers to the attribute of having insight, the ability to give meaning to data, the capacity to understand, and capability to separate the pertinent from that which isn't (Strauss and Corbin, 1990, p. 42).

Strauss and Corbin (1990) believe that theoretical sensitivity comes from a number of sources, including professional literature, professional experiences, and personal experiences. The credibility of a qualitative research report relies heavily on the confidence readers have in the researcher's ability to be sensitive to the data and to make appropriate decisions in the field (Eisner, 1991; Patton, 1990).

Lincoln and Guba (1985) identify the characteristics that make humans the "instrument of choice" for naturalistic inquiry. Humans are responsive to environmental cues, and are able to interact with the situation; they have the ability to collect information at multiple levels simultaneously; they are able to perceive situations holistically; they are able to process data as soon as they become available; they can provide immediate feedback and request verification of data; and they can explore atypical or unexpected responses.

THE RESEARCH PROCESS

Qualitative research traditions

The ability of qualitative data to more fully describe a phenomenon is an important consideration not only from the researcher's perspective, but also from the reader's perspective. "If you want people to understand better than they otherwise might, provide them information in the form in which they usually experience it" (Lincoln & Guba, 1985, p. 120). Qualitative research reports, typically rich with detail and insights into participants' experiences of the world: "may be epistemologically in harmony with the reader's experience" (Stake, 1978, p. 5) and thus more meaningful.

Table 3.1 provides a summary of *Qualitative Research Traditions* which are most often used in sport management research.

Table 3.1	Qualitative Research Traditions				
Tradition	Basic Position	Methods Used	Research Outcomes	Key Concepts	Relevance to SM
Ethnography	Used to describe and understand the behavior of a particular social or cultural group	Extended field immersion to understand the perspective of that group	Appreciation of how understandings and behavior are generated in cultural groups	An insider's perspective – "emic", and outsider's perspective "etic" – derived from anthropology	Understanding professional world and the worlds of Sport managers
		Fieldwork observation, field notes, interviews		Triangulation	
				Thick description	
Grounded theory	Theory building from the ground up	Observation, interviews, photos, documents etc.	A theory may emerge of a dominant view	Coding procedure (open, axial, selective)	Provides a systematic way of analyzing data
	Groundwork is data collection	Further data collection guided by what emerges from initial data		Categories are "in vivo" (from actors themselves) or "in vitro" (constructed by researcher	
	Theory is derived from analysis of data.				
Phenomenology	To understand the essential meaning of human experiences	Interviews	In-depth interviews	Avoid contamination presuppositions – bracketing (removing)	We inevitably have preconceived notions, so something that tries to take these away is useful

Method					
	Understanding from within	No preconceived expectations – focus on what data reveals		Results in epoche	
	Interpretive orientation	Researcher moves from general to specific questions	General questions – open ended leading to more specific questions, e.g., "the experience of …"	Ideation – particular to general	
	People involved are active participants	is open/passive – no influence on interviewee			
Case Study	Focus of research on a unit or set of units	Interviewing most popular supported by observation and recording	Notes features of particular interest, relates to broader issues, developing explanations where appropriate	Sampling is likely to be purposeful	Power of a case study can resonate across cultures
	Can be quantitative and/or qualitative				
Narrative	Tells a life story	Prolonged interview (series of interviews)	To deepen understanding of a chosen topic	Progressive focusing	Important to understand the lives and beliefs of people in this field
	The context plays an important part	Triangulation important for reliability		Epiphanies emerge with particular significance	
				Respondent validation	

(continued)

Table 3.1 Qualitative Research Traditions *continued*

Tradition	Basic Position	Methods Used	Research Outcomes	Key Concepts	Relevance to SM
Action Research	Involves investigation, producing recommendations/ implementation	Cyclical – planning/ acting/observing/ reflecting and planning	Designing appropriate interventions	Cycle of activities	Rich source of professional understanding
	Aims to improve practice, and understanding situation	Journal keeping interviews, observations, and documents	Development of appropriate classroom strategies	Empowerment	Improvement of practice
				Emancipatory potential	
Conversation analysis	Ordinary conversation provides insight into ways people understand and build their social worlds	Focus is on sequential development of conversations	Close attention to organizational interaction can provide useful information on the nature of interaction and possibility of changing interactional patterns	Participant design and procedural relevance	Interaction is at heart of management. Particular area of interest is cross cultural encounters
	Interest in how people jointly construct conversation	Uses naturally occurring data		Attention to features – turn taking, repair of talk, preference organization and pre-sequences	
		Moves from observation to hypothesis Rule out nothing			

THE QUALITATIVE RESEARCH PROCESS

Eisner (1991) claims there is a "paucity of methodological prescriptions" for qualitative research, because such inquiry places a premium on the strengths of the researcher rather than on standardization (p. 169). Lincoln and Guba (1985) provide a fairly detailed outline for the design of naturalistic inquiry, which includes these general steps:

1. Determine a focus for the inquiry. This should establish a boundary for the study, and provide inclusion/exclusion criteria for new information. Boundaries, however, can be altered, and typically are.

2. Determine the fit of the research paradigm to the research focus. The researcher must compare the characteristics of the qualitative paradigm with the goals of the research.

3. Determine where and from whom data will be collected.

4. Determine what the successive phases of the inquiry will be. Phase one, for example, might feature open-ended data collection, while successive phases will be more focused.

5. Determine what additional instrumentation may be used, beyond the researcher as the human instrument.

6. Plan data collection and recording modes. This must include how detailed and specific research questions will be, and how faithfully data will be reproduced.

7. Plan which data analysis procedures will be used.

8. Plan the logistics of data collection, including scheduling and budgeting.

9. Plan the techniques that will be used to determine trustworthiness.

Denzin and Lincoln (1994) however suggest the selection of a Qualitative Research Process involves five sequential steps. These are as follows:

1. locate the field of inquiry in terms of either the use of a qualitative, interpretive approach or a quantitative, verificational approach.

2. select a theoretical paradigm that is capable of informing and guiding the research process.

3. link the chosen theoretical paradigm to the empirical world through a methodology.

4. select a method of data collection.

5. select a method of data analysis.

The procedure of Sarantakos (1998) for selecting a research design involves three steps. These are as follows:

1. select an appropriate paradigm.

2. select a methodology.

3. select a set of methods for collecting and analyzing the data.

Within this ongoing debate Crotty (1998) notes that the terminology with regard to the construction of the social research process is far from consistent in research literature and social science texts. One frequently finds the same term used in a number of different, sometimes contradictory ways. Different process elements are often thrown together in grab-bag style as if they were all comparable terms. To overcome this confusion, Crotty (1998) suggests an approach to the research process that involves the posing and answering of four associated questions. These are as follows:

1. What *methods* do we propose to use?

2. What *methodology* governs our choice and use of methods?

3. What *theoretical perspective* lies behind the methodology in question?

4. What *epistemology* informs this theoretical perspective?

Within these four questions are embedded the basic elements of the research process:

- *Methods:* the techniques or procedures used to gather and analyze data related to some research question or hypothesis.

- *Methodology:* the strategy, plan of action, process or design lying behind the choice and use of particular methods and linking the choice and use of methods to the desired outcomes.

- *Theoretical perspective:* the philosophical stance informing the methodology and thus providing a context for the process and grounding its logic and criteria.

- *Epistemology:* the theory of knowledge embedded in the theoretical perspective and thereby in the methodology.

Depending on whether you decide to employ the approach suggested by Lincoln and Guba, that of Denzin and Lincoln, Sarantakos' process, or that of Crotty, you begin to formulate your research plan.

Research Brief

What: Exploring the Coaching Process in Football Practice
Who: Matsakis, M., Kansas State University
Matsakis utilized qualitative research to answer the question: What is involved in the Coaching Process of experienced college assistant football coaches in practice?

Qualitative research interviews were conducted and their transcripts were analyzed through the methods of description, analyzation and interpretation. Matsakis indicated that this research provides some key understanding for personnel involved in the coaching process.

SOURCES OF RESEARCH IDEAS

Before beginning the planning and design process, the sport management researcher needs to source ideas for the research study. Several sources of research ideas include concepts and ideas already mentioned in the research literature, topics of public interest in the media, ideas gleaned from personal experience and those topics of interest to authorities that may be attached to funding opportunities. A brief discussion of these sources of ideas is outlined below.

Theory and research literature

Whilst reviewing the current available literature on a particular topic, the sport management researcher may identify other topics or areas that warrant further investigation, or which pose unanswered questions and opportunities for further study. For example, an article documenting the experiences of disabled athletes at a major sporting event may pose questions for the sport management researcher around the event or organizational management that are not covered in the original study.

Public issues

The media is quick to report or sensationalize news about sporting stars – either in a positive or negative way. Publicity around favorable sporting outcomes, for example successful medal wins in an Olympic Games is certainly of major appeal to the sporting public. But is there something in the reporting of a successful or favorable outcome for the sport management researcher to investigate further?

The reporting of conflict, bad behavior, illegal activities, and sporting events gone wrong do have the opportunity to provide ideas for the sport management researcher. It is important, however, for the researcher to consider why these reported events are problems at all. Is there an issue that needs to be investigated with the possibility of resolution or providing solutions to public concerns, or are these issues only important because of the publicity or coverage surrounding them.

Issues surrounding the bad behavior of athletes or illicit drug taking could imply a deficit in the management structure of a sporting organization which could benefit from some investigation by a sport management researcher.

Personal experiences and opportunities

The sport management researcher may, in roles other than that of researcher, have personal experience that may translate into the beginnings of a research idea. Whether as a club director, employee, coach (either professional or amateur), an athlete or parent of an athlete, the researcher can draw on personal experience to recognize issues that would benefit from further investigation.

Funding opportunities

Government authorities or sporting organizations may at times identify topics of specific interest that it is determined warrant investigation. These topics may be deemed to be of public interest or concern – such as illicit drug taking, behavior of sporting stars, or of particular interest to a sporting organization, such as in the organization of a major sporting event. Such research opportunities will often have funding attached, which is of significant advantage to the sport management researcher.

REVIEW OF THE LITERATURE

When designing or planning any research study, it is important for the researcher to review what has been written or researched on the topic the researcher intends to investigate. A literature review is important in the development of the research questions, methodology and identifying areas or issues for investigation relevant to the topic. This is often conducted as part of a secondary data review where other information sources are explored on the topic. A literature review may involve published and unpublished material, which can be sourced through hard copy such as reports, books or journals, or electronically, such as CDRoms and the Web. The searches can lead to various sites such as university libraries, statutory or voluntary organizations and national or international agencies.

A literature review is essentially a critical look at existing research that is relevant to the work you are carrying out. It is not just a summary of other people's work, but requires information gathering, and evaluation and appraisal skills. A good literature review identifies relevant research and explains why it is important, and justifies why further research is needed.

The main purpose of a literature review is to give a comprehensive review of previous works on the general and specific topics to be considered in your research. The literature review needs to report on the state of the literature in the field, its limitations and research directions as well as identifying any competing conceptualizations or any errors. Typically the review shows how the study fits into the broader scheme of research in the field and includes reference to classic and recent studies. When compiling your literature review it is important to utilize appropriate software packages such as Endnote, that allow you to manage your sources effectively.

Conducting a literature review

There are a number of strategies that can be employed by the researcher when conducting a literature review. These are as follows:

- read all studies that are closely related to the research problem.

- a review of the literature can help in limiting the research problem and in defining it better. It can also reveal gaps in the organized knowledge in the area.

- look at research critically before accepting the conclusions of the previous studies in the area.

- new research areas usually lack an organized body of source information to provide a general background, and thus it is necessary to do a fairly broad review.

- in more thoroughly researched areas greater depth is available so a more narrow range may be covered.

Reviewing the literature for research projects

When reviewing the literature for research projects, it is important for the researcher to keep in mind the following:

- learn the history of the problem; its disciplinary base, theoretical conception, the changing ways it has been addressed over time.

- identify the broad context from the specific problem.

- become familiar with theoretical backgrounds, develop a conceptual framework, and assess the strengths and weaknesses of previous studies.

- become aware of which research methods are most promising in studying this problem.

- identify key terms.

Making and keeping notes

Keeping notes is essential and should be done on all the literature the researcher reads on the topic. They should summarize succinctly and make notes on the following:

- What is the problem addressed in the study, the context, the purpose?

- What general and specific procedures were used in the study?

- What did the researcher find, the results?

- What conclusions were made?

- What implications were discussed or recommendations made that are relevant to the problem under consideration?

- Develop a matrix with the main information relevant to your focus for all the literature you read.

Writing the review

When writing the literature review, the researcher should describe the work that has been done, and be critical where necessary. This can be done by using the following as a guide:

- Summarize the main facts and conclusions, which emerge, synthesizing the material to explicate the main themes, directions, contradictions, challenges, etc.

- Point out the areas of the field that are still inadequately covered.

- Organize your information carefully, summarize the salient details of the research, the conclusions and any weaknesses in them.

- Combine the information in ways that allow adequate description of the literature and insightful conclusions about its meaning for the context in which you are going to be researching.

- Critically analyze and synthesize the material.

- This synthesis becomes the foundation of the conceptual framework for your study.

Literature search and the internet

There is no question that the Internet and its associated software have changed the methodologies of qualitative research. Searching the Internet for resources, using software to manage citations and some aspects of data analysis, interviewing by means of e-mail or in dedicated chat rooms, and using dialogs and interactions online as sites for study are all now part and parcel of much scholarship in the social sciences and applied fields. The *Handbook of Qualitative Research* (Denzin & Lincoln, 1994, 2000, 2005) is dedicated to some discussion of the use of computers in qualitative research.

Some questions to consider regarding website information

Most government agencies have websites that offer copies of recent reports, etc., whether for free or at a cost. These websites can be a useful source of information. Also some electronic journals are useful if they are peer reviewed ones, but beware of websites that offer inaccurate, erroneous or fabricated information. Evaluate documents carefully. In general though when using the web as a source for information you may want to ask yourself the following questions:

- Whose website is it? Is it a well known and reputable organization?

- Is it a reputable individual's website? Be cautious and consider the credibility of the individual who is operating and maintaining the website.

- Is the material dated?

- Can the information be corroborated?

THE RESEARCH PLAN

A research plan is a detailed description of the procedures that will be used to investigate a topic or problem. The purposes of the plan are threefold: Firstly, the plan forces the researcher to think through every aspect of the study.

Secondly, it facilitates the evaluation of the proposed study. Finally, it provides detailed procedures to guide the conduct of the study.

Typically a qualitative research plan will

- identify the general research issue,

- detail the steps to be followed in conducting the study,

- explain how the researcher intends to gain entry to the research site,

- identify the participants,

- estimate the time that will be spent in the field,

- determine the best ways to collect data, and

- identify appropriate ways to analyze the data.

Issues to consider

Three general issues need to be considered in developing a research plan: (1) Ethics of research, (2) Legal restrictions, (3) Cooperation from participants. These issues are summarized below.

1. Ethics of research

- *Adhering to ethical principles of:*

  - Competence

  - Integrity

  - Professional and scientific responsibility

  - Respect for people's rights and dignity

  - Concern for other's welfare

  - Social responsibility

- *Additional ethical issues in qualitative research*

  - Unique emerging nature of qualitative designs increase the likelihood of unanticipated and unreviewed ethical issues

  - Unique personal involvement and engagement of the researcher with the research context and participants raise issues related to the objective collection and interpretation of data as well as the possibility of observing potentially illegal or unprofessional behavior

2. Legal restrictions

- *National Research Legislation*

  Protecting participants

  - Protection from harm

  - Informed consent

  Stipulating that proposed research activities involving human subjects must be reviewed and approved by an authorized group

  Requirements of Internal Review Boards and Committees on Human Subjects

- *Privacy Act*

  Protection of participants' privacy

  Deception

- Situations in which complete information related to the study is not given to participants

  - Focus is on the likelihood that such information would influence or change the participant's responses

  - Some research studies can be negatively affected by informing participants of certain details

  - Use of deceptive practices must be undertaken very, very carefully

3. Cooperation of participants

- *Gaining entry to the research site*

  - Approval needed at several levels

  - Site

  - Gatekeepers

- *Strategies to enhance cooperation*

  - Clearly explain the benefits of the study

  - Afford stakeholders the opportunity to review drafts of the report for their approval

- Brief stakeholders on the findings

- Provide professional development sessions for stakeholders

FIVE MAJOR RESEARCH PLAN COMPONENTS

The five major areas of the research plan are listed below.

- Introduction

- Method

- Data analysis

- Time schedule

- Budget

Each area requires discussion of specific issues. These are outlined below and discussed in greater detail and unpacked further in the final chapter.

1. Introduction

The introduction normally has three sections. These are as follows:

- Statement of the topic

- Review of the literature

- Statement of problem

Within each of these sections discussion should focus on a number of points. These are as follows:

- *Statement of the topic*

  – The topic is identified with a discussion of the background and rationale

  – Whilst quantitative topics are stated at the beginning of the research plan the qualitative statements emerge as the research is conducted

- *Review of the literature*

  – Provides an overview of the topic and positions the study in the context of what is known, and more importantly what is not known, about the topic

  – Whilst quantitative reviews are done in the beginning of the study the qualitative reviews are ongoing as issues are identified

■ *Statement of problem/hypotheses*

    – A formal statement specifying the hypothesis, support for specific expected relationships between variables, and operational definitions of all variables

    – Quantitative statements reflect deductively reasoned hypotheses while qualitative studies do not usually discuss hypotheses

The research problem provides the context for the research study and typically generates questions which the research hopes to answer. In considering whether or not to move forward with a research project, the researcher will generally spend some time considering the problem.

The statement of the problem is the first part of the paper to be read [we are ignoring the title and the abstract]. The problem statement should "hook" the reader and establish a persuasive context for what follows.

It is important for the researcher to be able to clearly answer the question: "what is the problem"? and "why is this problem worth my attention"? At the same time, the problem statement limits scope by focusing on some variables and not others. It also provides an opportunity for you to demonstrate why these variables are important.

Problem importance

The importance of the problem should receive considerable and persuasive attention and answer questions such as these:

■ Is the problem of current interest? Is it topical?

■ Is the problem likely to continue into the future?

■ Will more information about the problem have practical application?

■ Will more information about the problem have theoretical importance?

■ How large is the population affected by the problem?

■ How important, influential, or popular is this population?

■ Would this study substantially revise or extend existing knowledge?

■ Would this study create or improve an instrument of some utility?

■ Would research findings lead to some useful change in best practice?

■ Is there evidence or authoritative opinion from others to support the need for this research?

The problem statement should persuasively indicate that major variables can be measured in some meaningful way. If you can identify likely objections to the study, identify and respond to them here. The problem statement should also be well focused, manageable and not too general. Good quality research questions are: Clear, concise, focused, informed by the literature and manageable and do-able.

2. Method

The research plan should have a "broad strategic approach" and a coherent way of addressing the problem/question being explored. Different kinds of questions will require different research methods to get good quality information and knowledge on the topic of investigation.

Within the method five sections can be identified. These are as follows:

- Participants

- Instruments

- Materials/apparatus

- Design

- Procedures

Within each of these sections discussion should focus on a number of points. These are as follows:

- *Participants*

  - Identifies the number, source, characteristics of the population and sample, and sampling procedures;

  - Quantitative studies identify large samples and probability sampling techniques whereas qualitative studies identify small samples and non-probability sampling techniques;

  - Sampling is the process of selecting and accessing individuals or groups for inclusion in the research process. We will now have a more detailed discussion of sampling before returning to the *Instruments* section of the Methods.

Sampling

For the qualitative researcher, sampling is based upon their relevance to the research topic as opposed to their representativeness which determines the way in which the participants to be studied are selected. Sport management researchers will in general utilize techniques that are defined as "non-probability" sampling techniques, as they aim to select participants with a connection to, involvement in, or interest in the research topic under investigation.

In a *non-probability* sample, some subjects have a greater, but unknown, chance (probability) than others of selection. Non-probability sampling is frequently used in qualitative research where in-depth understanding of particular groups or individuals' experiences are more important than representativeness. Qualitative researchers aim to find cases that enhance what the researcher will learn within a specific context – for the sport management researcher a sample drawn from a specific group who are involved in, or have an interest in an area related to the research study – i.e., individual athletes, spectators at specific sporting events, employees of sport management companies, families of athletes – will be more likely to provide relevant data and a deepened understanding of the research topic, rather than a random sample drawn from the general public which may provide no relevant information to the topic at hand. When choosing the sample population, the sport management researcher aims to obtain a range of responses or ideas, and seeks to explore issues to generate research questions; the sample therefore aims to include a wide variety of people likely to be able to share experiences relating to a given topic.

There are many different types of non-probability sampling, some of which are more applicable to the sport management researcher than others. *Purposive sampling* for example, has definite applicability to the sport management research context, whereas convenience or quota sampling have flaws that make them less suited for sport management research.

Purposive samples are often referred to as "judgment samples", because researchers select participants subjectively. The sport management researcher would use purposive sampling in studies where unique cases are required to provide especially informative data – for example athletes in a specific sport, parents of athletes competing in a specific sport. Also the researcher may use purposive sampling when aiming to identify particular types of cases for further in-depth investigation.

With purposive sampling the sport management researcher is thinking and planning ahead to the analysis process and the social explanations or interpretations they intend to construct. *Snowballing* is a technique to identify further respondents who fit the characteristics of the research focus or situation. In snowball sampling, the researcher obtains additional samples by their connection to or referral from the original sample source. Snowball sampling is particularly useful when researchers are investigating aspects of organizations or people that are interconnected in some way – and for the sport management researcher this could relate to branches of a worldwide sporting agency, or athletes competing in a local, national or international competition. The cases may not know or even interact with other cases in the sample, but they have a link – either direct or indirect. Snowball sampling is a multistage technique – it starts with either one, or a few cases, and then "snowballs" to include other cases, based on their links to the original cases.

Convenience sampling is frequently used in qualitative research concerned with exploring views and experiences. In this type of sample, anyone from the study population who is available can be interviewed. Although this method can save time, money and effort, it does so at the expense of information and credibility (See Miles & Huberman, 1994; Pope & Mays, 2000). An example of a sport management researcher using this type of sampling would be to conduct interviews on the street or in a shopping center – the people interviewed are convenient, but they do not represent everyone, and will not necessarily have any knowledge of, or interest in, the research topic. Another example would be the sport management researcher distributing a survey via a letter box drop or via publication in a newspaper, and asking people to complete the survey and mail it in. Not everybody reads the newspaper or unsolicited mail, and those that do may or may not have an interest in the topic. Some people will respond, but a sample obtained this way could not be used to generalize accurately. It therefore tends to produce ineffective, unrepresentative samples and is not recommended for the sport management researcher.

Quota sampling is where the researcher firstly identifies the categories of subjects relevant to the study, then decides how many cases to obtain in each of those categories. There are concerns with accessibility, representation, and generalizability, although it is an improvement over convenience/haphazard sampling. The researcher can ensure that there are some differences in the sampling because there are differentiated categories; however the cases within each category are generally chosen in a haphazard manner, so misrepresentation is still a distinct possibility.

We shall now return to our discussion of *Instruments* within the Methods section.

- *Instruments*
  - Descriptions of the specific measures of each variable, the technical characteristics of the instruments, and the administration and scoring of the instruments

- Quantitative studies describe non-interactive instruments (e.g., tests, questionnaires, surveys, etc.,) while qualitative studies describe interactive techniques (e.g., interviews and unstructured observations)

- *Materials/apparatus*

  - Descriptions of specific material such as manuals, computer programs, etc.)

- *Design*

  - Descriptions of the basic structure of the study and the specific research design chosen

  - Quantitative studies describe structured, static designs while qualitative studies describe flexible, emergent designs

- *Procedures*

  - Detailed descriptions of all the major steps that will be followed in conducting the study, assumptions of the study, and limitations of the study

  - Quantitative and qualitative studies differ in terms of the emphasis placed on different steps, but they do not differ in terms of the steps discussed

3. Data analysis

In the data analysis, there are two main issues that need to be considered. These are as follows:

- Descriptions of the techniques used to analyze the data

- Quantitative studies focus on the selection and application of appropriate statistical procedures to analyze numerical data while qualitative studies use appropriate procedures to interpret narrative data

The researcher needs to analyze and explore the patterns, similarities, differences and unusual aspects of the data. They need to explore ways to translate or interpret the data analysis into findings. Through interpretation of findings the researcher examines concepts, ideas, theories, arguments, models of explanations, so as to move analysis of the data to judgments which can be defended. In qualitative research trustworthiness and rigour are accepted terms used to discuss the reliability and validity of the data.

Trustworthiness

The literature regarding validity and reliability in qualitative research contains a variety of terms. These various terms reflect different authors' views on ways of ensuring validity and minimizing threats to validity in qualitative research. Some authors use terms that have their roots in the quantitative paradigm, for example, validity (both external and internal), reliability and objectivity. Lincoln and Guba (1985), and subsequently other researchers, have argued that the umbrella term trustworthiness criteria is more appropriate than the traditional quantitative criteria of validity and reliability. Others use the terms credibility, transferability, dependability and confirmability to address similar concepts (Lincoln & Guba 1985; Patton, 1990). Lincoln and Guba (1985) use the term "trustworthiness" to refer to a set of criteria that have been offered for judging the quality or goodness of qualitative enquiry.

Rigor

Similarly, the concept of rigor in qualitative studies has received much commentary and criticism and one would hope after years of significant qualitative research that the debate could be put to rest. Nonetheless, it has been the view of some authors that the transfer of validity and reliability of criteria from a quantitative to a qualitative paradigm is inadequate. As such, a number of criteria to evaluate rigor in qualitative studies have been proposed although there is no one agreed upon framework, Koch (1996) argues that the qualitative researcher should choose a method that suits the nuances of the study at hand.

Methodological rigor is demonstrated through the documentation of the actual research processes (Rice & Ezzy, 1999), including: (1) how the participants were chosen; (2) engagement of access to the sample and individual participants; (3) the development of trust and rapport with participants; (4) data collection and recording processes; and (5) data analysis methods. Guba and Lincoln (1981) use the term "auditability" to explain the premise of methodological rigor. The research processes must be adequately documented to allow another researcher to follow the procedural and decision trail. The text provides a detailed account of the methodological procedures used. These include tape recording the interviews; accurately transcribing the dialog; providing an in-depth description of the data collection and analysis strategies including contexts; describing the informants; providing definitions of the categories, including their theoretical antecedents; reviewing the emergent theory to ensure interpretive truth; and maintaining an audit trail detailing decision making (Rice & Ezzy, 1999).

Theoretical rigor can be demonstrated if both the theory and concepts have been appropriately chosen to ensure that the strategies are consistent with the objectives of the research study. As well, arguments and analysis should be soundly constructed and written to demonstrate relatedness and a contextual fit with the literature available on the phenomenon (Rice & Ezzy, 1999).

The resultant theory which accurately reflects the understanding of events and processes within the framework and the world view of those engaged in the phenomenon demonstrate the achievement of *interpretative rigor* (Rice & Ezzy, 1999). Although some researchers do not believe in an end point of accuracy within such qualitative research it is possible to demonstrate how the interpretation was obtained. This area of rigor is linked to methodological rigor but goes a step further by providing if necessary the primary text to other researchers so that they can make their own determination of the adequacy of interpretation of the data.

In qualitative research, the terms reliability and validity are often used instead of trustworthiness and rigour. In this book we use these terms interchangeably.

Reliability

Reliability is sometimes referred to as *Auditability* which refers to the replicability of a study, which is usually understood in terms of the stability and consistency of measurement instruments or procedures. In qualitative research the concept of stability is largely rejected in favor of consistency (Lincoln & Guba, 1985). In this regard, consistency is a function of the explicability and replicability of a researcher's data gathering, coding, and analytic methods. Given this, a study is considered to be auditable if naive researchers can replicate a study under roughly similar circumstances as the original. This replicability, however, does not necessarily apply to a study's findings. This is particularly the case with hermeneutic research, where the interpretation of data is largely dependent on the unique perspective of the researcher. In this regard, replicability would apply only to the data gathering and coding process. This is usually achieved by providing explicit instructions on the coding process, while at the same time providing detailed definitions of the categories that emerged from the data. In this way, other researchers could examine the raw data, itemize it, categorize it, and arrive at roughly similar conclusions as the primary researcher.

Validity

Credibility is concerned with the believability or persuasiveness of a study. It is roughly analogous to the concept of internal validity. It consists of two related concepts: structural corroboration and confirmability. Based on the ontological assumption of multiple constructed realities (see Lincoln & Guba, 1985), structural corroboration consists of producing a knowledge structure roughly isomorphic with the lived experience of the research participants. This is accomplished through prolonged engagement (i.e., by spending sufficient time with participants to assess for distortions, impression management, or misunderstandings), persistent observation (i.e., exploring a participant's experience in great detail), member checks (i.e., presenting results to research participants to verify the depiction of their lived experiences), and by triangulation (i.e., obtaining data from a variety of sources or methods).

Confirmability refers to the "qualitative objectivity" of a naturalistic report. In this regard researchers must demonstrate that their findings were factually based, that the data were systematically collected, sorted, and categorized, and that the categorization processes were theoretically informed and explicable. Confirmability also concerns itself with the explicability of decisions affecting the course of the research, the researcher's own experience of the study, the researcher's life experiences, biases, and insights, or anything else that could shape the course and outcome of the study. Confirmability is accomplished by standardizing procedures as much as possible (e.g., audio-taping interviews, verbatim transcripts, interview schedules) and recording all insights, design decisions, logistical decisions, and peer debriefing sessions. Lincoln and Guba (1985) recommend that this material be recorded in a "reflexive journal". This would enable research consumers to evaluate influences on the research process that are typically not reported in orthodox science. Also included in the reflexive log is a chronicle of all peer debriefing sessions. Lincoln and Guba advocate this process, whereby researchers present their categorizations to neutral peers. This is intended to keep researchers "honest", to keep their interpretations "close to the data", and to ensure that the abstraction and categorizing processes are clear and explicit.

4. Time schedule

Although not as complex as the other sections the time schedule needs to be addressed. This should provide a

- Description of the major activities and corresponding anticipated completion dates

5. Budget

The budget is an important part of the research plan as it provides an indication of the resources required. The budget should therefore provide:

- Descriptions of anticipated costs that are likely to be incurred

THE RESEARCH REPORT/THESIS

Based upon the research plan a research report and/or thesis may be written. Usually various institutions and/or funding bodies have their own criteria for assessing the quality of the final product. Researchers are strongly advised to map their research plan against the requirements of their particular institution/funding body.

CONCLUSION

This chapter discussed the processes that underpin a research study or investigation. It has identified that ideas for research can be obtained from numerous sources. Once the research topic has been identified the sport management researcher needs an understanding of research planning, what constitutes a literature review and strategies to complete one. The

IN PROFILE - Professor Simon Chadwick

Dr Simon Chadwick is Professor of Sport Business Strategy and Marketing at Coventry University Business School (UK), where he is also Director of CIBS (Centre for the International Business of Sport). Chadwick is currently Editor of the International Journal of Sports Marketing and Sponsorship and is therefore regularly involved in reviewing paper submissions that utilize qualitative methodologies. His personal research interests lie in the areas of sport sponsorship, ambush marketing, fan behavior, and relationship marketing. Throughout his academic career, Chadwick has regularly used qualitative methodologies to gather and analyze data. Almost a decade ago, his exploratory work (with Beech and Tapp) on Internet use by professional sports clubs employed standardized templates for analyzing and assessing the content of websites, as well as for identifying where clubs could further develop their product offerings on the web. Later, Chadwick conducted a series of dyadic interviews with sponsors and sponsees in order both to build a research agenda by understanding specific sponsorship phenomena, and to confirm subsequent findings. Qualitative data analysis therefore played a key role in the overall triangulation of various research methods. More recently, the growth in ambushing activity around major sporting events has led Chadwick and his team to use a qualitative approach to examining how corporations attempt to undermine their rivals' official sponsorship activities at events like the Olympics. This involved constructing a database of ambushing cases, as well as analyzing the content of marketing communications campaigns, and has been successful in helping to generate a new definition of ambushing and in classifying different forms of ambushing. Chadwick believes that a qualitative approach to research has helped him in a number of ways, particularly how it has helped him to understand new or misunderstood phenomena. For example, it has been incredibly useful in helping him to understand contemporary developments, such as the Internet and ambushing, about which little had been known or written. This has enabled Chadwick to develop a greater understanding of the commercial activity that has evolved around custom and practice, something that has been especially important to Chadwick as he has built relations with front-line managers in sport.

formulation of the research plan requires careful and methodical planning on the part of the sport management researcher. A systematic approach to research that is guided by well-constructed questions will allow the sport management researcher to not only identify what happens, but how it happens, and, importantly, also why it happens.

REVIEW AND RESEARCH QUESTIONS

The design of the research study, including the formulation of ideas, questions, reviewing the literature and the research plan itself are the essential first steps for the sport management researcher intending to undertake research. Now having an overview of this process, attempt to answer the following questions:

- Is the Internet a primary and reliable source of literature and/or information for the sport management researcher?

- Identify those key features of the research plan that the sport management researcher must decide on before proceeding onto the next phase of the researcher process.

REFERENCES

Crotty, M. 1998. The Foundations of Social Research: Meaning and Perspective in the Research Process. Sydney, NSW: Allen and Unwin.

Denzin, N. K., & Lincoln, Y. S. (Eds.). 1994. Handbook of Qualitative Research. Thousand Oaks, CA: Sage.

Denzin, N. K. & Lincoln, Y. S. (Eds.). 2000. Handbook of Qualitative Research, 2nd ed. Thousand Oaks, CA: Sage.

Denzin, N. K. & Lincoln, Y. S. (Eds.). 2005. Handbook of Qualitative Research, 3rd ed. Thousand Oaks, CA: Sage.

Eisner, E. W. 1991. The Enlightened Eye: Qualitative Inquiry and the Enhancement of Educational Practice. New York, NY: Macmillan.

Glaser, B. & Strauss, A. 1967. The Discovery of Grounded Theory: Strategies for Qualitative Research. New York: Aldine.

Guba, E. G. & Lincoln, Y. S. 1981. Effective Evaluation: Improving the Usefulness of Evaluation Results Through Responsive and Naturalistic Approaches. San Francisco, CA: Jossey-Bass.

Koch, T. 1996. Implementation of a hermeneutic inquiry in nursing: philosophy, rigour and representation. *Journal of Advanced Nursing*, **24** (1), 174–184.

Lincoln, Y. S. & Guba, E. G. 1985. Naturalistic Inquiry. Beverly Hills: Sage.

Miles, M. B. & Huberman, M. A. 1994. Qualitative Data Analysis. Thousand Oaks, CA: Sage.

Patton, M. Q. 1990. Qualitative Evaluation and Research Methods, 2nd ed. Newbury Park, CA: Sage.

Pope, C. & Mays, N. 2000. Qualitative Research in Health Care. London: Blackwell.

Rice, P. L. & Ezzy, D. 1999. Qualitative Research Methods: A Health Focus. South Melbourne, Victoria: Oxford University Press.

Sarantakos, S. 1998. Social Research. Melbourne: Macmillan Education Australia.

Stake, R. 1978. The case study method in social inquiry. *Educational Researcher*, **7**, 5–8.

Strauss, A. & Corbin, J. 1990. Basics of Qualitative Research: Grounded Theory, Procedures and Techniques. Newbury Park, California: Sage.

Research Ethics for Sport Management

CHAPTER OVERVIEW

Historically, the issues around ethics and the politics of research have not been as influential or as high on the research agenda as they are currently. There have been many critiques within disciplines and across fields of research about the morality of conducting research in specific contexts and the approaches or way methodologies have been applied in specific topical areas. There are also critiques about the purpose for many research projects, why it is being done, to what end and who will benefit? In critical social science, there is an emphasis and critique on only doing research that will benefit the most disadvantaged groups in society and others critique the imbalance of power and control between the researched and the researcher in conventional research. To counter this, there is a need for ethics policy and standard procedures to protect all parties. This chapter therefore discusses what research ethics are, why they are important and the concerns around valuing the knowledge that can be obtained through research against the value of non-interference in the lives of potential research participants.

WHAT ARE RESEARCH ETHICS

Ethics define what is or is not legitimate or moral to do. Codes of behavior, and legal considerations in most countries will provide some fixed rules and principles for researchers, but the sport management researcher needs to look further than their legal responsibility to take into account their moral and professional obligations to be ethical. The sport management researcher will often face conflicts in their principles – and have to weight up the benefits of the knowledge to be obtained from the research versus the rights of those taking part in the research study.

Research ethics has a positive role to play in the design and conduct of human research, but it needs to be seen as an integral component of the research process. Commonly held beliefs about research ethics include the importance of the protection of vulnerable populations, maintaining professional standards, safeguarding the rights and well-being of participants, risk management, and ensuring public support for research, and these are no less relevant for the sport management researcher.

Ethical considerations need to be considered in every phase of the research study, not just in the research design or when the researcher receives any required ethical clearance and authorization to commence the research. The researcher needs to consider and act upon ethical responsibilities and considerations continue right through a project, even beyond the data collection phase into analysis, write up and publication.

Basic ethical considerations for the sport management researcher to consider when designing and implementing the research project include the following:

Integrity – A research project must constitute a "genuine search for knowledge".

Respect for persons – A research project must embody respect for persons, including a regard for the welfare, rights, perceptions, customs and cultural heritage of participants. Respect for the dignity and well-being of participants must take precedence over any expected benefits to knowledge.

Beneficence – A research project must minimize risks, discomfort and burdens to participants.

Justice – A research project must provide for the fair distribution of the benefits and burdens associated with participation in the research. Furthermore, the inclusion or exclusion of participants should not be based on the gender, race, age, etc. of these persons unless for valid research reasons.

Consent – In all but the most extraordinary circumstances, the informed and voluntary consent of potential participants must be obtained.

Research merit and safety – To be considered ethical, a research project must be justifiable on the basis of its potential contribution to knowledge and on the basis of a sound assessment of the safety of participation. Even though it is appropriate to conduct a project involving risk, this risk must be quantified and presented in a meaningful way to potential participants, along with any strategies to address that risk.

WHY IS RESEARCH ETHICS IMPORTANT?

The importance of research ethics extends beyond the moral imperative of the researcher to operate legally and ethically and can have some quite practical ramifications. Compliance with ethical standards is increasingly becoming a condition of eligibility of research funding from many public and private organizations as well as a condition of publication eligibility in many refereed journals. Access to certain research populations – such as schools, hospitals – can also often be governed by restrictions that require compliance with ethical standards. The community – and specifically the sport management community – is also increasingly interested in how research is conducted, and has expectations about the ethical compliance of any research. Finally, and of major importance to the sport management researcher, is the confidence of potential research participants in the ethical integrity of research being conducted. This confidence in the ethical integrity of the researcher will in part ensure that potential research participants/ subjects will be more likely to take part in research studies.

ETHICAL CONCERNS

Lincoln and Guba (2000) suggest that the positivist sees ethical problems as extrinsic to (outside) the research process. This leaves the researcher to decide what is ethical, for example, whether or not to deceive participants. According to this approach, if the goal is important (the improvement of human knowledge and/or quality of existence), then the end justifies the means (deception is acceptable). Some post-positivist researchers will probably agree with the positivist in principle; however, in practice they tend to accept greater responsibility for the effects of the research on research subjects.

Other non-positivists take a different position, seeing the moral dimension of the research as intrinsic – a necessary part of the decisions they must make. Lincoln and Guba (2000) suggest that critical theorists will try to act morally (so protecting the participants from harm), while the constructivist and the participatory researcher will have involved participants all along, so moral decisions will have become a necessary aspect of the process itself.

According to Cohen et al. (2000), ethical issues can arise at any stage of a research project and include such factors:

- The nature of the project itself;

- The context of the research;

- Procedures adopted;

- Methods of data collection;

- Nature of the participants;

- The type of data collected;

- What is done with the data and how it is disseminated. (p. 49)

Ethical approaches to research do not reduce the validity and reliability of it but highlight the contextual complexities within which it is carried out (Kelly,

1989). To be ethical, a research project needs to be designed to create trustworthy (valid) outcomes if it is to be believed to be pursuing truth. The generalizability of findings from one situation to another is dependent on research being carried out ethically. Trying to answer questions from an inappropriate sample or data set, or choosing an inappropriate unit of analysis, may lead to misleading findings, undermining their transferability (Bassey, 1998).

There are a number of ethical responsibilities associated with research in sport management.

Responsibility to the sport management profession

As a researcher (or aspiring researcher), a sport management researcher has firstly a responsibility to the good name of the sport management profession. This requires researchers to

- meet high standards, both in their behavior during the research and in the quality of the work produced;

- behave in such a fashion that others will have no difficulty in entering the field at a later date.

Professional organizations now have voluntary codes of conduct which help to protect ethical standards within the profession, but such organizations are distant and impersonal. You would be wise to have someone (a lecturer; your thesis supervisor; a departmental head) to whom you can turn, if ethical problems arise.

Definitions of professional ethical practice are often enshrined in codes to guide the decisions of researchers. Codes have been developed by professional organization to protect the integrity of research. Jones (2000) points out the importance of the code devised by the American Statistical Association in 1998. University ethics committees police such codes to ensure that research carried out under their auspices does not breach them.

Conflict of interest and ethics

A conflict of interest is an ethical consideration that applies to a wide spectrum of activity, including conducting sport management research. A conflict of personal interest can arise when the impartiality of the researcher can be questioned because of potential (either perceived or actual) influences of personal considerations, which could be financial or personal. A conflict of role could also occur when the researcher occupies multiple roles – for example, as manager of a team or event which is the focus of the research study.

The sport management researcher needs to be aware of the potential ramifications of conflicts of interest in relation to the research study, some of which can be an impact on the perceived validity or integrity of the research, increased risk to the research participants and a negative impact on the reputation of the researcher.

For the sport management researcher, conflicts of interest or role could arise in some of the following ways:

- the research is being sponsored by a body (such as the alcohol industry) that might have a significant interest in the research generating particular results, and/or are likely to be unsupportive of the communication of contrary results

- the researcher has some form of direct pecuniary interest in the results of the research (such as the researcher being paid a "per participant" fee by a sponsor, or the researcher being paid a bonus on the basis of a particular set of results)

- the research involves issues of interest to another body (such as non-compliance, negative attitudes) and the researcher is also an officer of that other body

- the research involves the assessment of a service or program that the researcher is responsible for (either in the design or conduct of that sport service or program)

The sport management researcher should ensure that actual conflicts as well as perceived conflicts of interest are dealt with prior to the start of the research study, either by disclosing the conflict to all parties with a vested interest in the research, including the research participants, or as much as possible nullifying the conflict. This sends an important message regarding the ethical nature of the research being conducted and is an important gesture of goodwill to research participants. Additionally, it enhances the degree to which others will view the research as being of the highest integrity.

Most research receives *funding* from one source or another, be it from a public or private organization, some of which will have a vested interest in achieving a particular outcome from the research study. The sport management researcher needs to consider whether this financial arrangement will represent a real or potentially perceived conflict of interest, and will it alter the design, conduct and publication of results from the research in a way contrary to externally valid and justifiable scientific reasons. Even if the sport management researcher is confident that the support for the research would not have such an impact, would a third party consider that the support could have such an impact?

Another conflict of interest can arise where the sport management researcher will receive some form of financial benefit from the research, which is distinct from competitive research funding, or where the research is a component of the researcher's employment. Non-financial interests can be harder to identify, but are equally of importance when considering real or potential conflicts. The researcher needs to consider whether this interest is likely to impact on the conduct of the research or the publication of the results. For the sport management researcher such an interest could be a club director conducting research into the efficiency of the organization – the outcome of which could determine their future tenure in the position.

POLITICS OF RESEARCH

Historically, the issues around ethics and the politics of research have not been as influential or as high on the research agenda as they are currently. There have been many critiques within disciplines and across fields of research about the morality of conducting research in specific contexts and the approaches or way methodologies have been applied in specific topical areas. There are also critiques about the purpose for many research projects, why it is being done, to what end and who will benefit? In some fields of study such as critical social science there is an emphasis and critique on only doing research that will benefit disadvantaged groups in society and critique the imbalance of power and control between the researched and the researcher in research. Within sport management research new areas of research are being opened up to investigation and this inevitably leads to questions of ethical research behavior.

Ethical sport management research involves balancing the value of the knowledge obtained through the research study against the value of non-interference in the lives of the potential research participants. Potential risks to research subjects, including physical or mental injury, humiliation, fear, or loss of privacy must be evaluated by the sport management researcher before the research project can begin.

INFORMED CONSENT

The modern approach to the governance of ethical conduct of human research places a strong focus on obtaining voluntary and informed consent from potential participants. Except in defined circumstances human research is generally only considered to be ethically justifiable and sound where informed consent is obtained from participants.

Whilst informed consent remains a standard expectation for most human research, there is now an explicit recognition that this consent process should be subject specific, relevant to the context in which the research will be conducted, and be respectful and appropriate for the potential participant pool.

Informed consent refers to the decision made by a potential participant as to whether they wish to participate in a research project. It should be a voluntary choice, and should be based on sufficient information and adequate understanding of both the proposed research and the implications of participation in it.

Informed consent process

A consent process should be appropriate for the potential participant pool (so the language, delivery and information will need to be accessible, relevant and respectful for the pool); the amount of detail required could be considered as positively related to the complexity, risks and other ethical issues associated with the research (e.g., you would expect that a project that involves significant risk will involve providing potential participants with a much greater level of information than projects that involve no greater than negligible risk); consent could be expressed in any number of ways (e.g., orally, by signing a form, by returning a completed questionnaire); rather than merely a discharge of a regulatory process, the informed consent process should provide an opportunity for dialog between the potential participant and the researcher(s), where questions can be asked and clarification sought; and it may be appropriate to provide time and space so that a potential participant can discuss the project with other parties before they decide whether to participate.

Often considered to be the "classic" or default approach to informed consent in human research, a written consent process involves the provision of an information sheet to a potential participant, who signs and returns a consent form. Despite the fact that this is the most familiar approach to informed consent for research ethics reviewers, regulatory or gatekeeper bodies, and even researchers, there can often be situations where the use of a written informed consent mechanism is impractical or potentially unethical. Generally, a written informed consent process is most appropriate where:

- the research involves a greater than low risk of harm to participants

- where the risk will not be significantly compounded by seeking a written confirmation of consent

- where it is possible to conduct the written informed consent process in a way that will be meaningful and appropriate for the participant pool

- where there is some reason why it might be necessary to clearly substantiate what potential participants were told and their consent

The design, phrasing and detail used in an informed consent package needs to be appropriate for the specifics of the research; the potential participant pool; the risks/burdens; and the context. Signing an "informed consent" document (most institutions have standard forms) protects research subjects:

- There should be provision to withdraw (up to an agreed final date) at any time, even if that inconveniences the researcher.

- There should be information on the format in which data will be collected (for instance, by written questionnaire or by telephone or by personal interview) and recorded (for instance on audiotape or videotape).

- There should be information about how and where the research data will be stored, for how long this will be kept, and who will have access to it.

- There should be information about the use to which the research will be put, to whom and when the research report will be made and where and when it is likely to be published.

- There should be a guarantee of confidentiality and option for the subject to remain anonymous at all times.

- There should be information about the procedure to follow if the subject wishes to make a complaint.

Verbal consent

A compelling ethical reason not to seek a written expression of consent can be because the researcher having a record of an individual's consent could expose them to at least a potential serious risk (e.g., a document that could be subpoenaed). Even when, in practical terms, such a risk is unlikely to occur, it may be sufficient to case a potential participants to rethink their involvement in the project. Consequently, the decision not to seek a written expression of consent might be intended to address both a genuine risk, or to provide confidence to potential participants (and in so doing improve the chances they will elect to participate). This kind of approach to informed consent will be the approach for some telephone-based research, where a potential participant will receive information they have time to digest before being phoned and asked to verbally consent to being interviewed.

Such a mechanism can be the most appropriate approach to some research designs (e.g., when conducting a "doorstop interview" about a relatively innocuous subject, it might seem strange to a potential participant if they were first asked to sign a consent form).

Nevertheless, when this kind of mechanism is used, the potential participant is still provided a written information sheet, which they are given time and space to consider, before being asked to verbally express their consent.

A variation of the consent process discussed is where potential participants are given a verbal briefing about the project, verbally express whether they wish to participate in the research, and are later (typically after the interview or other participation at an end) offered a written information sheet. Obviously, such a mechanism is not appropriate for highly vulnerable potential participants; and/or research where there is significant risk to participants. This mechanism may be the most respectful approach where the literacy level of potential participants are a concern, or where the potential participants are likely to be concerned about signing documents.

A further iteration of valid informed consent processes can be a completely verbal process. Such a mechanism involves only a verbal briefing and then a verbal expression of consent. Generally, rather than a completely verbal process, it is considered preferable to use either of the approaches outlined above. This is because the informed consent process must address both ethical objectives (e.g., that a potential participant is able to exercise a voluntary and informed decision) and regulatory objectives (e.g., that individuals are given a statement about how their personal information will be handled). Whilst it is frequently possible (and indeed preferable) to meet ethical objectives with a verbal process, the verbal delivery of the required regulatory information can be laborious (both the length and sometimes the stipulated language); and a completely verbal process denies the participant having documentation for their later reference about the research, their participation, and their rights. Consequently, a sport management researcher who plans to use a completely verbal process would need to justify how it addresses the ethical requirements, how the regulatory requirements will be addressed, and why it is considered a preferable consent mechanism for the particular project.

UNEQUAL RELATIONSHIPS

Human research, by definition, involves some degree of interaction between humans. In some cases, potential participants in a research project can be in an unequal relationship with the researcher(s) and/or perceived sponsors of research. This unequal relationship can raise serious ethical issues and can result in formal complaints about the ethical conduct of a project.

Such problems can arise across the range of human research activity, being just as serious in contexts such as education and business management, as in clinical contexts. It is also important to recognize that, whilst nearly all researchers and sponsors would have no intention of exploiting an unequal relationship, the perception that an unequal relationship has not been appropriately addressed can be almost as damaging.

An unequal relationship can result in potential participants feeling coercive pressure to participate in a project, and additional risk issues. If not appropriately managed, these issues can raise serious questions about the ethical appropriateness of a proposed project.

Examples of unequal relationships include (but are by no means limited to) the following:

1. Lecturers or teachers conducting research on their own students.

2. Employers or supervisors conducting research on their staff.

3. Medical practitioners conducting research on their patients.

4. Service providers sponsoring research on their clients.

COERCION

A significant ethical concern for research involving unequal relationships is the degree to which there may be coercive pressure (whether real or perceived) on potential participants to participate (e.g., because not participating might damage their relationship with the researcher(s) or sponsor, or a belief that participating might enhance their standing or access to services). Some typical strategies to address this issue are:

1. Participation is anonymous, so the researcher(s)/sponsor will not know who participates, or is coded in such a way that participants will be anonymous until after the period of unequal relationship has passed.

2. Recruitment is to be conducted by a third party.

3. The recruitment material includes a clear statement that participation will not impact upon standing/access to services/the relationship.

4. Potential participants are afforded time and space to consider their participation.

5. A clear distinction is made between the existing relationship and the research activity.

The above are by no means the only appropriate strategies to address potential coercive pressure on participants. The necessity for, and thoroughness of, strategies to address these issues will largely depend upon a combination of the:

- risks and burdens associated with the research;

- extent of the unequal relationship;

- vulnerability of potential participants; and

- sensitivity of the data to be collected.

In some cases, such as research on a relatively innocuous topic where the participants are students of a university lecturer, it may be sufficient to simply include in the informed consent materials a clear statement that participation is voluntary and their decision will in no way impact upon their grades or otherwise on their relationship with the lecturer. In other cases, a comprehensive and independently managed system might be required, because of the serious risks and/or vulnerability of potential participants.

RISK OF POTENTIAL HARM

Unequal relationships can raise the risk of potential harm to participants. For example, employees identifying their own inappropriate work activities could expose them to loss of employability or standing if the researcher is their supervisor. It can also raise other risks (e.g., to the organization where the research is based, or to the researchers themselves).

Sometimes the only way in which such a risk can be managed is if the researchers are unaware of the identity of individual participants, so data cannot be attributed to an individual respondent, and so the risk does not apply. However, in many cases, it may not be possible to conduct the research in such a manner, or the number and nature of participants might mean that identification by inference is a real possibility.

In some cases, there may be more than minimal risk of harm (harm not only being defined in the physical sense but also psychological, emotional, etc.) to participants involved in the research. For example, this may include research involving:

- vulnerable groups – for example, children and young people, those with a learning disability or cognitive impairment, or individuals in a dependent relationship

- sensitive topics – for example, participants' illegal or political behavior, their experience of violence, their abuse or exploitation, their mental health, their gender or ethnic status

- where permission of a gatekeeper is normally required for initial access to members – for example, ethnic or cultural groups, members of the armed forces or inmates and other members of custodial or health and welfare institutions

- deception or research conducted without participants' full and informed consent at the time the study is started

- access to records of personal or confidential information, including genetic or other biological information

- inducing psychological stress, anxiety or humiliation or causing more than minimal pain

- intrusive interventions – for example, the administration of drugs or other substances, vigorous physical exercise, that participants would not normally encounter in their everyday life

In these cases, specific strategies need to be developed to suit the research participants and the context of the research. For example, a debriefing session may need to occur to ensure that no adverse effects to the participants have occurred. This discussion about the ethical concerns that need to be considered for vulnerable groups is further addressed later in this chapter.

PRIVACY, CONFIDENTIALITY AND THE LAW

Privacy as an ethical issue relates to the ethical principles of respect for persons and beneficence. These ethical principles require that a researcher:

- have regard for the welfare, rights, beliefs, perceptions, customs and cultural heritage, both individual and collective, of persons involved in research

- minimize risks of harm or discomfort to participants in research projects

- ensure that the research protocol *is* designed to ensure that respect for the dignity and well-being of the participants takes precedence over the expected benefits to knowledge

In practice, any proposed access to identified personal information, the use of identified personal information, and the disclosure of personal information, needed to be considered in terms of whether it compromised the ethical principle of respect for persons, whether it exposed participants to risk, and whether it placed the imperative of the expected benefits to knowledge ahead of the rights of the participants.

Experience shows that concerns about privacy are quite often at the root of complaints about the ethical conduct of research. For example,

- Information about a person being accessed without their knowledge and consent.

- Disclosure of results and the potential harm to participants.

- Third parties being aware of who participates, or who has been excluded, and this being a source of potential harm.

Sometimes, the most appropriate and effective way to address the ethical issues relating to privacy is by protecting the confidentiality of participants. Strategies to protect confidentiality will need to address all stages of a research project (e.g., identification of participants, recruitment, during data collection, during analysis, in reporting and publication, and in storage and any subsequent use). The issues to be considered relate to those governed by privacy regimes but can be quite different.

Generally, confidentiality strategies will relate to the degree to which individual comments or data can be attributed to individual participants. Confidentiality is not an absolute ethical requirement, indeed some research participants will very much want their comments attributed to them. However, key ethical considerations are the degree to which potential participants understand whether they will be identifiable, whether they have consented to this identification, the degree to which they should be considered a vulnerable group, and whether their identification exposes them to any risks.

Anonymity refers to a situation that exceeds confidentiality where the identity of participants is not known. Unlike confidentiality measures, where the measures to protect confidentiality might only be limited to some parts of the research process (e.g., reporting/publication and storage), arrangements to protect the anonymity of participants generally apply to all parts of the research process. An important distinction is between:

Completely anonymous – which is research where not even the researchers will know the identity of participants (such as a questionnaire that does not seek identifying information that is distributed to a large research population).

Anonymous responses – which is research where the researcher will know the identity of participants, but cannot link specific data with specific respondents (such as a questionnaire that does not seek identifying information distributed to a small or specific research population).

Protected anonymity – which is research where the researcher will know the identity of participants, may be able to link specific data with specific respondents, but will take steps to ensure that third parties cannot determine the identity of participants (such as an interview where the data will be recorded, reported and stored in an aggregated form).

The decision to conduct a research project using a form of anonymity will generally reflect the presence of special ethical issues or risks that warrant additional protection for participants (or indeed non-participants) – for example, if a researcher intended to collect data from drug users about their attitudes to the effectiveness of rehabilitation programs, anonymity might be necessary to protect them from a range of potential harms.

Even though a researcher might believe that a confidentiality strategy, or even a protected anonymity strategy, might afford participants sufficient protection from harm, the researcher is encouraged to reflect upon their ability to protect their participants in the event of receiving a subpoena or other lawful directive to disclose research data. In some cases, the only true protection for participants (and sometimes researchers) is for their research data to be truly anonymous. These matters should be identified and addressed in any application for ethical clearance for a proposed human research protocol, and appropriately set out in the informed consent materials that are provided to potential participants in the research.

Even when a researcher believes that their planned protocol includes sufficient provisions to protect the confidentiality or anonymity of respondents, they should reflect upon whether or not participants are identifiable by inference. Identification by inference can occur where sufficient information is presented that, even though the respondent's name or identity number, etc. is not available, it is possible to determine their identity (e.g., if collecting data from a work team of five, it is highly likely that a combination of age, gender, marital status, and length of service, might enable for their identification by inference).

In some cases, limited identification by inference is unavoidable. In the above example, members of the work team are likely to be able to recognize themselves or other members of the team, even if much less demographic information is published.

Identification by inference can also occur in case study research, where the published "stories" might enable respondents to be identified in a way that may be a source of harm. The preferred strategy in such cases would be for respondents to be offered to review their own stories to enable them to check the de-identification and potential risks not to editorialize their commentary.

The more ethically vexed issue is where the law recognizes that a duty of disclosure may override a contract (including a contract of confidentiality) – such situations include the concealment of a crime, an imminent and real threat to life, a significant public health concern, etc. Such situations are more difficult because this effectively places the moral responsibility upon the researcher, and requires a reflection upon what action is more ethically justified (e.g., the protection of an assurance of confidentiality, or preventing the spread of an infectious disease).

RESPONSIBLE USE OF DOCUMENTS AND IMAGES

One of the key questions the researcher needs to address is: Who "owns" the information? This is of particular sensitivity when studying different groups, with different standards concerning the "ownership" and use of information. For example, some cultures are particularly sensitive about the use of images. Library and archival research may turn up incriminating or embarrassing private documents, or institutional records. If these have caveats in place on their use, the researcher must obey these (no matter how disappointing this is), and if they do not you still have the responsibility of dealing fairly and honestly (i.e., ethically) with them. Fair dealing provides considerable leeway, but does not absolve the researcher from considering the feelings of the person(s) implicated, or (if the person is already dead), their family.

The researcher may feel that they have a larger responsibility to the community, particularly when disclosure might result in re-shaping public opinion or future action. The decision to use certain information may also have legal implications that the researcher should investigate before publication.

ETHICAL GUIDELINES FOR RESEARCH WITH VULNERABLE GROUPS

The following discussion builds upon the previous discussion concerning ethical issues to be considered for vulnerable groups.

Respect for persons

Consideration of the impact of a proposed protocol on the vulnerable, disadvantaged or powerless is an important ethical consideration for all human research. Indeed, academic commentary suggests that, in the case of non-clinical research, this can be the most common source of ethical concern and harm to research participants.

When designing a human research protocol, a researcher must consider whether the potential participants in the research are likely to include persons who should be considered vulnerable, disadvantaged or powerless. Such persons can include, but are no means limited to persons who are subject to prejudice and discrimination; persons who are highly dependent upon the care or assistance of others; and persons who are destitute or homeless. When submitting an application for ethical clearance for a protocol, a researcher who fails to correctly identify that the potential participant pool for the research involves such persons, is likely to be considered to either be ignorant or indifferent to the special ethical issues that their presence raises. Such an assessment may result in avoidable delays in the approval for a protocol.

When conducting research involving humans, the guiding ethical principle for researchers is respect for persons which is expressed as regard for the welfare, rights, beliefs, perceptions, customs and cultural heritage, both individual and collective, of persons involved in research. Each research protocol must be designed to ensure that respect for the dignity and well-being of the participants takes precedence over the expected benefits to knowledge.

As such, the design of a human research protocol that involves the participation of persons who should be considered vulnerable, disadvantaged or powerless, must include provisions to safeguard their welfare and rights. Any potential impact upon these welfare or rights should be identified in the application for ethical clearance for the protocol, and an explanation provided of the measures to address this issue.

Beneficence

Beneficence is described in the following terms: In research involving humans, the ethical principle of beneficence is expressed in researchers' responsibility to minimize risks of harm or discomfort to participants in research projects. Each research protocol must be designed to ensure that respect for the dignity and well-being of the participants takes precedence over the expected benefits to knowledge.

As such, the design of a human research protocol that involves the participation of persons who should be considered vulnerable, disadvantaged or powerless, must adequately negate, minimize or manage any risks to the participants. Risks to such participants can be especially acute, and their ability to themselves address such risks or take actions against those who cause them harm can be severely limited.

When considering an application for ethical clearance for a protocol that involves the participation of persons who should be considered vulnerable, disadvantaged or powerless. An Ethics Committee will expect that the applicant(s) will take special care to identify and address any risks.

Justice

The ethical value of justice requires that, within a population, there is a fair distribution of the benefits and burdens of participation in research and, for any research participant, a balance of burdens and benefits. Accordingly, a researcher must:

- avoid imposing on particular groups, who are likely to be subject to over researching, an unfair burden of participation in research

- design research so that the selection, recruitment, exclusion and inclusion of research participants is fair

- not discriminate in the selection and recruitment of actual and future participants by including or excluding them on the grounds of race, age, sex, disability or religious or spiritual beliefs except where the exclusion or inclusion of particular groups is essential to the purpose of the research.

As such, the design of a human research protocol must not include, or exclude persons who should be considered vulnerable, disadvantaged or powerless, unless for a valid scientific reason. Furthermore, the researcher must consider the degree to which participation in the research might place special burdens upon participants (e.g., participation in research that involves one hour spent completing a questionnaire at 8 am, might represent an extra burden for single parents – so some flexibility might be required to accommodate their child care and daily arrangements, as well as sensitivity of how little personal time they otherwise have in their day).

A human research protocol, which involves the participation of persons who should be considered vulnerable, disadvantaged or powerless, is likely to require extra or special recruitment and consent measures. These measures will probably be necessary to ensure that the design of the protocol is consistent with the ethical principles of respect for persons, beneficence and justice.

In practice, for such research, the extra considerations and precautions are likely to be as follows:

- Potential participants who are vulnerable, disadvantaged or powerless are likely to suffer harm (or perceive that they will suffer harm) as a result of a recruitment process – the degree to which the recruitment process is anonymous is likely to be a significant factor.

- The degree to which the initial contact with potential participants may cause them anxiety or distress, and the degree to which the persons conducting this process are experienced and sensitive to this issue.

- The impact of inducements on potential participants may be different or more significant if they are vulnerable, disadvantaged or powerless – this may necessitate a rethink of the nature and value of an incentive, or the use of measures to ensure that the incentive is not coercive.

- The fact that the potential participants are vulnerable, disadvantaged or powerless, increases both the likelihood and the impact of any coercive impacts upon their decision about participation – consequently, the design of the protocol will need to ensure that the potential participants are given time and space to enable them to make a decision that is voluntary, informed and can be established.

- A single informed consent mechanism is unlikely to be sufficient, and it may be necessary for this to be "scaffolded" with additional information and processes to ensure that potential participants can exercise a voluntary and informed decision.

ETHICAL PRINCIPLES FOR THE SPORT MANAGEMENT RESEARCHER

The following are some key principles that can guide the sport management researcher in applying appropriate ethical guidelines to their research:

- Research should be designed, reviewed, and undertaken to ensure integrity and quality.

- Research staff and subjects must be informed fully about the purpose, methods and intended possible uses of the research, what their participation in the research entails and what risks, if any, are involved, including any risks or threats to anonymity that might arise during and beyond the project itself and how these might be minimized or avoided. Gaining participants' informed consent to participation means researchers giving prospective participants as much information as possible about the project so that they can make an informed decision on their possible involvement.

- The confidentiality of information supplied by research subjects and the anonymity of respondents must be respected.

- Research participants must participate in a voluntary way, free from any coercion. They should be informed of their right to refuse to participate or withdraw from an investigation. In cases where research involves vulnerable groups such as children or adults with learning difficulties, the issue of informed consent may need to be managed through proxies who should be either those with a duty of care or who can provide disinterested independent approval. In the case of children, researchers cannot expect parents alone to provide disinterested approval on their children's behalf.

- Harm to research participants must be avoided, including their wider family, kin and community. Research designs should consider potential harm to respondent's organizations or businesses.

- There is no simple rule for getting right the balance between potential risks to participants and benefits of the research to a wider community.

- There may be exceptional circumstances in some fields of research when, with the consent of the participants, some short-term and minimal degree of harm which causes no lasting effects or prolonged personal discomfort might be acceptable.

- The independence and impartiality of researchers must be clear and any conflicts of interest must be explicit.

- Research should be conducted so as to ensure the professional integrity of its design, the generation and analysis of data, and the publication of results, while the direct and indirect contributions of colleagues, collaborators and others should also be acknowledged.

CONCLUSION

This chapter has offered an overview of the ethics process and its implications for sport management research. It is not intended to provide a fully comprehensive understanding of the place of ethics in research but to provide a guideline to the sport management researcher of the issues to consider. There will be many times when the sport management researcher faces difficult choices in relation to the conduct of their research, and will need to weigh up the benefits of the research against any possible harm or detriment caused to participants in the research study. A system of research ethics will serve to guide the sport management researcher in making the moral choices that will ultimately benefit both the research study and the research participants.

IN PROFILE - Dr Dwight Zakus

Dr Dwight Zakus is currently a senior lecturer in sport management at Griffith University. He graduated from UBC for the second time with a Master of Physical Education in Sport Management, as one of the first students to complete this specialty at that university. He followed this with a doctorate from the University of Alberta where he theoretically analyzed the Canadian government's establishment of a national sport structure. This followed several years of high school teaching and coaching and was concurrent with roles as a rugby CEO and coach. In both of these programs he used historical methods (Marxist based), interviews, and document analyses to complete his scholarly output. In subsequent research he has continued to use these qualitative methods, including his work with honors, masters, and doctoral students (including ethnographic methods), and with consultancy projects (most of which used interviews, focus groups, and document analysis). In most of these cases, only qualitative approaches are employed, although mixed methods have evolved in recent projects. This work involves research on social capital and community sport development, volunteers, the Olympic movement, ethics, high performance sport systems, and any other topic he finds challenging. While most of this research continues the historical materialism of his postgraduate work, other qualitative methods have been part of triangulation approaches to seek outcomes that explore at a deeper level data obtained through quantitative tools or simply to produce "thick" descriptions of the data. Quantitative data and ahistorical approaches are incomplete and limited. It is only through mixed methods and various forms of triangulation that true social scientific work can be completed. By implication, this means that qualitative methods are central to the overall scientific approach.

REVIEW AND RESEARCH QUESTIONS

Research ethics should be central to the design of the research study. They are necessary to protect the right of the sport management researcher to conduct the research, to ensure the research subjects are not placed at any risk of physical, emotional or financial harm, and to reduce the likelihood of legal action by research subjects against researchers and their institution. With this understanding attempt to answer the following questions:

- Investigate the process of gaining ethical clearance within your own institution.
- Discuss the ethical concerns associated with investigating the impact of a new sport development program on elite junior athletes.

REFERENCES

Bassey, M. 1998. Fuzzy generalization and professional discourse. *Research Intelligence*, **63**, 20–24.

Cohen, L., Manion, L. & Morrison, K. 2000. Research Methods in Education, 5th ed. London: Routledge Falmer.

Jones, K. 2000. A regrettable oversight or a significant omission? Ethical considerations in quantitative research in education. In: *Situated Ethics in Educational Research* (Ed. by H. Simons, R. Usher), pp. 147–161. London, UK: Routledge.

Kelly, A. 1989. Education or Indoctrination? The ethics of school based action research. In: *The Ethics of Educational Research* (Ed. by R. G. Burgess), pp. 100–113. London: Routledge.

Lincoln, Y. S. & Guba, E. G. 2000. The only generalization there is: there is no generalization. In: *Case Study Method: Key Issues, Key Texts* (Ed. by R. Gomm, M. Hammersley, P. Foster), pp. 27–44. London: Sage.

PART 3

Foundations of Sport Management Research

CHAPTER 5

Methods of Data Collection for Sport Management Research

By the end of this chapter, you should be able to

- understand the different data collection methods employed in sport management research

- identify data collection methods suitable for use in sport management research

KEY TERMS

Participant observation: the researcher observes the research study site by direct participation in the study.

Focus groups: small groups of participants that share characteristics or interests relevant to the topic of research.

Direct observation: The noting and recording of actions and behaviors, events and activities at the research site.

Fieldwork: Where the researcher engages in the research study in the natural setting pertaining to the topic of study, as opposed to a controlled environment.

KEY QUESTIONS

The key questions raised in this chapter are as follows:

- How does the sport management researcher determine the most applicable data collections to utilize?

- Which interview techniques are more suitable for the sport management research study?

- When are focus groups a preferable approach for data collection?

CHAPTER OVERVIEW

Data collection is the process of collecting or gathering information pertaining to a specific research topic that will be used by the sport management researcher in the latter process of analysis to formulate theories, produce recommendations or contextualize events and activities in the sport management setting. This chapter discusses the need for sport management researchers to use a range of data collection techniques including fieldwork, observation, interviews and document analysis.

DATA COLLECTION AND SPORT MANAGEMENT RESEARCH

In general, qualitative researchers utilize four main methods for gathering information – or "data collection". These are (1) fieldwork, (2) observation, (3) interviewing, and (4) analyzing documents and other materials. The sport management researcher may use some or all of these methods, and additionally utilize secondary and specialized methods of data collection, which are all dependent on the specific nature of the research being conducted.

The sport management researcher needs to take into account the following when deciding on the methods of data collection to be used in the research:

- What is the nature of the research? Is this traditional research or controversial and critical?

- How is the researcher positioned in relation to the participants? Do they view themselves as distant and objective or intimately involved in their lives?

- Is the research problem outward looking – is it externalized, or does it require inner contemplation?

- What is the primary purpose of the research? Is the end result of the research intended to be of benefit to the participants or the sport management site? Or is the research purely academic in nature intended to be of benefit to the researcher only?

- Who will be viewing the results of the study? Will it be the academic community or members of the sport management community?

- Is the research neutral or is there a political agenda?

- Are the researcher and the participants essentially passive or "engaged in local praxis"?

The answers the sport management researcher makes to these different questions can help shape how the specific data collection techniques are conceived for the study.

FIELDWORK

Fieldwork involves the researcher working for long periods of time in a natural setting. This natural approach steers clear from the controlled or laboratory situations used typically in experimental-type research. Observation, asking, "examining materials and recording information" are essential elements in fieldwork.

Fieldwork commences when one begins to ask questions. For example, "What are people doing here"? "What is the physical setting of this social setting" In fieldwork, researchers also make use of various data collection strategies to ensure the integrity of the data.

Field relations

Field relations are the complex relationships the researcher develops with others (e.g., gatekeepers, research participants) whilst in the field. These relationships have logistical, procedural, ethical and political dimensions (Schwandt, 2001).

OBSERVATION

Observation entails the systematic noting and recording of actions and behaviors (both verbal and non-verbal), events, and objects in the social or work setting that is the research site. There are two generally recognized observation techniques – *direct observation* or *participant observation*. *Direct observation*, where the researcher observes without engaging or interacting with the situation, is believed to be more objective and therefore protects the neutrality of the researcher. *Participant observation*, where researchers immerses themselves in the research setting, is more aligned with the naturalistic paradigm that argues that total objectivity and neutrality are not possible or, for many critics, desirable. Both techniques are time consuming and require clear reasons for using them (see Pope & Mays, 2000).

Direct observation

The researcher engaging in direct observation believes that they are not disturbing the environment and hence are able to maintain a greater level of neutrality and objectivity. This type of observation entails the researcher observing without engaging or interacting with the research situation. Some critics of the perceived neutrality of direct observation maintain that once a researcher appears on the scene, the actions and behaviors of those being observed will be affected, just by the presence of the researcher. Attempts at lack of involvement in whatever is going on in the setting will have some effects and cannot be judged to be the same as if the researcher were simply absent from the setting altogether. Engaging in covert observation – where the participants are unaware of the researcher's presence, raises ethical concerns, as participants may not have given informed consent for the observation to occur.

Participant observation

In this approach, the researcher attempts to immerse themselves in the setting they are observing. In this way, the researcher aims to experience and participate in the real-life activities alongside the research participants. This enables the researcher to collect data and understand the meanings of events as they occur. Some critics of this technique believe that it is impossible for researchers to really become totally immersed in the setting to the point where they are equal participants in terms of the knowledge gleaned and the experiences shared.

Spradley (1980) asserts that participant observation has two objectives when entering a social situation: (i) to be involved in activities appropriate to the setting, and (ii) to observe the activities, people and physical elements of the setting. Jorgensen (1989) makes the point that the methodology of participant observation is inappropriate where questions relate to fairly large populations – this is better addressed via surveys or experiments. In other words, participant observation is most suitable when minimal conditions exist such as:

- the observation pertains to human meanings and interactions as seen from the standpoint of insiders;

- the phenomenon of investigation can be surveyed in the here and now of an everyday life setting;

- the researcher is able to obtain access into the setting;

- the research problem can be addressed by qualitative information collected by participant observation pertinent to the field setting;

- the process of inquiry is open-ended and flexible providing direct experiential and observational access based on facts about human life grounded in the realities of daily existence; and

■ the researcher is able to use direct observation together with other
   techniques for collecting information.

Role of the researcher in observation

The role of the researcher in participant observation involves variations in
overt or *covert* dimensions. In terms of the *overt*, participants in the field are
fully aware who the observer is and that observations are being conducted
together with a complete explanation of the study. By contrast, in a *covert*
position, participants are not informed or aware of anything occurring. As
mentioned previously, researchers need to be aware of ethical considerations
around covert observation and the absence of informed consent on the part of
the unaware (and perhaps even unwilling) research participants.

The duration of observations could range from a limited one hour to long-
term (months or years; De Laine, 1997). Participant observation, if handled
correctly by the researcher can provide an opportune and creative process to
gain access to otherwise inaccessible dimension of human life and experiences (Jorgensen, 1989).

Fieldwork observation: sport organization example

Intrusion into the world of employees of the sport organization is a vital
means of obtaining contextual information about the organization, the
employees, and the supporting network committed to the sport. This aspect
of "being in the situation" (Kirk, 1986) can act as a means to becoming
sensitized to the research setting. This may involve time spent at the
research site in informed conversation with the members of the sport
organization and the broader sport community generally (e.g., volunteers,
supporters, players, etc.).

Furthermore, as a result of the time spent in the research site, this form of
observation can provide insight into the daily operational issues that confront
the sport organization. Such issues include preparation for high profile
matches; administrative issues that are related to all sections of the sport
organization's community; the monitoring and evaluation of coaching
programs and courses; liaising with the media to ensure pre and post match
publicity; servicing and communicating with sponsors to keep them informed
of leveraging opportunities; dealing with the concerns of other stakeholders;
and the general social interaction that occurred between all organizational
members and stakeholders. By observing these operational issues and being
present in the organizational setting, the sport management researcher is able
to develop a good rapport with a broad cross section of the sport organization's
community. This allows the researcher to engage in informal conversation

about the issues confronting the sport organization and can provide a greater understanding of the research issue under investigation.

The second dimension of observation could involve what is referred to as *systematic observation* and field note taking during meetings that occur within and outside the sport organization. Throughout the research a structured and defined method of systematic observation could be utilized to itemize and categorize responses. Meetings could be observed that address a variety of concerns with differing organizational stakeholders. In this way, systematic observation can provide a foothold in the world of the management of the sport organization (or other stakeholder groups), and provide the basis for interviews that could discuss issues that are relevant to the research.

INTERVIEWS

Face-to-face interviews are one of the most effective procedures used by the sport management researcher. There are three types of interviews: *structured*, *semi-structured*, and *unstructured*.

In addition to these generic interviewing approaches, there are several more specialized forms, including ethnographic interviewing, phenomenological interviewing, elite interviewing, focus-group interviewing, and interviewing children which require particular levels of expertise and guidance.

Structured interviews

Frey and Oishi (1995) defined structured interviews as a purposeful conversation in which one person asks prepared questions (interviewer) and another answers them (respondent). Structured interviews are very inflexible, because the number of possible responses is often limited and participants may be forced into giving responses, which may not reflect their true feelings about an issue (Kvale, 1996).

Burns (1997) suggests there are several *disadvantages* to this method of interviewing. First, the researcher has no flexibility to determine beliefs, feelings, attitudes, and perceptions of the respondent beyond that answered according to the pre-determined response categories. Second, in using a structured interview, the interviewer must become a neutral standardized medium wherein questions are presented without bias or subjectivity. As a result, the method fails to acknowledge the inherent humanness of the interviewer. Finally, the detachment and impersonal approach required can prevent trust and rapport from developing between the interviewer and the respondent.

Semi-structured interviews

Semi-structured interviews often have an initial question followed by probes. These types of interviews are favored widely by sport management researchers. These types of interviews are often based on the knowledge of, and/or the assumption that the respondents have had a particular experience they can elaborate upon. In these types of interviews, the situation has often been analyzed before the interview. Therefore, the researcher is seeking additional information. In a semi-structured interview, an interview schedule is formulated to address the topic and to guide the interview, yet "without fixed wording or fixed ordering of questions" (Minichiello et al., 1995, p. 65). The content of the interview is directed on matters that are foremost to the topic of the research. The manner in which questioning takes place allows room for flexibility, social interaction, exploration of ideas and "provides opportunities to observe participants in the face-to-face ongoing interaction of the focus group" (De Laine, 1997, p. 294).

The interviewer guides and specifies the topics for which information is sought. The interview focuses on the respondent's subjective experiences. This allows the respondents to describe in detail the situation, as it is meaningful to them. Moreover, it allows the interviewer to freely probe and ask follow-up questions (Doyle, 1994).

Judd et al. (1991) suggest the major disadvantage of semi-structured interviews is that the researcher is vulnerable to the interpretations and subjective insights of the informant. As a result, the researcher may be drawn into the informant's world view. According to Burns (1997), this problem of validity is acknowledged as inconsequential if the informant's behavior is congruent with their perception of reality.

Unstructured interviews

Unstructured interviews, by contrast, lean on social interaction between members and the interviewer to acquire information. Members are permitted to allow their thoughts to wander and, although structuring and ordering of questions are not utilized, there is an element of controlled communication relating to the interests of the interviewer. Field-workers are free to deal with the topics of interest in any order, and to phrase their questions as it is best suited (Nichols, 1991). An unstructured interview is particularly useful for a preliminary study to test what the responses might be to a particular issue (Doyle, 1994). The major disadvantage of unstructured interviews is that the researcher is vulnerable to the interpretations and subjective insights of the informant.

Quality of the interview data

There are usually seven steps involved in conducting interviews which ultimately affect the Quality of the Data:

- **Step one:** contacting the respondent.

- **Step two:** set time and setting.

- **Step three:** establishing rapport and neutrality.

- **Step four:** opening question.

- **Step five:** probe questions.

- **Step six:** inviting a summary.

- **Step seven:** concluding the interview.

Interviewers should have highly advanced listening skills and be skillful at personal interaction, question framing, and gentle probing for elaboration. Volumes of data can be obtained through interviewing, but these are time consuming to analyze. This raises the issue of the quality of the data. When the researcher is using in-depth interviews as the sole method of gathering data, they should demonstrate through the conceptual framework that the purpose of the study is to uncover and describe the participants' perspectives on events – that is, that the subjective view is what matters. Studies making more objectivist assumptions would triangulate interview data with data gathered through other methods. Of particular concern is that because interviews, at first glance, seem so much like natural conversations, researchers sometimes use them thoughtlessly, in an under-theorized manner, as if the respondent is surely providing "an unproblematic window on psychological or social realities" (Wengraf, 2001, p. 1).

Marcus and Fischer (1986) express concerns about the ways in which a generic researcher can influence the research, in both the methods of data collection and the techniques of reporting findings. This influence cannot be eliminated, but it can be neutralized if its assumptions and premises are made as clear as possible (Fontana & Frey, 1994). Fontana and Frey indicate that one way to reduce researcher influence is through polyphonic interviewing. Here the voices of participants are audiotaped with minimal influence from a generic researcher, and are not collapsed together and reported as one through the interpretation of the researcher. Instead the multiple perspectives of the various participants are reported and the differences discussed rather than glossed over (Krieger, 1983).

Issues in interviewing

Interviews have particular *strengths*. An interview yields data in quantity quickly. When more than one person participates (e.g., focus group interviews), the process takes in a wider variety of information than if there were fewer participants – the familiar trade-off between breadth and depth. Immediate follow-up and clarification are possible. Combined with observation, interviews allow the researcher to understand the meanings that everyday activities hold for people.

Interviewing also has *limitations and weaknesses*. Interviews involve personal interaction and cooperation is essential. Interviewees may be unwilling or may be uncomfortable sharing all that the interviewer hopes to explore, or they may be unaware of recurring patterns in their lives. The interviewer may not ask questions that evoke long narratives from participants because of a lack of expertise or familiarity with the local language or because of a lack of skill. Furthermore, they may not properly comprehend responses to the questions or various elements of the conversation. A major concern is that at times during the interview, interviewees may have good reason not to be truthful (see Douglas, 1976, for a discussion).

VALIDITY AND RELIABILITY OF THE RESEARCH INTERVIEW

Interviews can be conducted individually (one to one) or as a group. The reliability and validity of the data collected from the interview vary with the type of interview employed, as well the experience of the interviewer. Any potential participants to be interviewed should be carefully selected, because random selection is not usually recommended (Doyle, 1994; Seidman, 1998).

Validity in interviewing refers to the formation of suitable operational measures for the concepts being investigated (Emory & Cooper, 1991). Interviewing attempts to achieve construct validity through three tactics. *Firstly*, triangulation of interview questions is usually established in the research design stage by two or more carefully worded questions that look at the subject matter under investigation from different angles. *Secondly*, the interview method usually contains an inbuilt negative case analysis where, in each interview and before the next, the technique explicitly requires that the interviewer attempt to disprove emerging explanations interpreted in the data (Dick, 1990). *Finally*, the flexibility of the approach allows the interviewer to re-evaluate and re-design both the content and process of the interview program, thus establishing content validity.

Reliability in interviewing refers to how consistently a technique measures the concepts it is supposed to measure, enabling other researchers to repeat the study and attain similar findings (Sekaran, 2000; Emory & Cooper, 1991). Reliability is usually achieved through four tactics: Firstly, reliability is attained through the structured process of interviews. Secondly, reliability is achieved through organizing a structured process for recording, writing and interpreting data. Thirdly, research reliability is often achieved through comparison of the research findings between the interviewer and interviewee. Finally, the use of a planning committee to assist in the design and administration of the interview program is another way that reliability can be achieved (Guba & Lincoln, 1994). If a number of the members of the committee agree about a phenomenon, then their collective judgment is relatively objective.

Sport management interview example

In most instances, sport management researchers use semi-structured interviews. This is because in structured interviews, every informant receives the same questions in the same sequence. This forces the informants to respond only to the fixed question, and subsequently the information elicited reflects the depth and insight of the questions previously established by the designer of the interview protocol.

To overcome some of the disadvantages of semi-structured interviews, it is recommended that sport management researchers follow a combination of the Stewart and Cash (1994) topical sequence method and the Judd et al. (1991) funnel principle. Stewart and Cash defined a topical sequence as a technique that uses the natural discussion of interviews to develop *themes*. This sequence gives the interviewer the freedom to probe answers and adapt to any response the participant may give. The *funnel principle*, according to Judd et al. (1991), advocates that the interview should start with general questions and issues. For instance: "What are the major problems confronting the sport organization?" The initial questions should be easy and unchallenging for the participant. As the interview progresses the questions focus on more specific issues. To assist the interviewer, each question could contain a series of probes to aid the researcher in focusing on specific themes within the question; as such the funnel principle is also applied when probing for a deeper understanding of the research issue.

The benefits from this "funnel" approach can be highlighted in the following example of an interview with an organizational member about the change occurring within the sport and the sport organization. The interview should begin with the interviewer initiating conversation about the participant's background and interest in the sport he or she is associated with in order to address a particular theme. This leads to the interviewer asking a general question such as: "How long have you been employed by the sport organization?" From here, the interviewer would ask a more specific question such as: "During that time what changes have you seen occur within your sport organization?" This would then lead to a question requiring more specific information that would elicit more detail on a particular theme: for example, "What factors contributed to that change occurring?" By utilizing this approach, the participant is made to feel at ease and will more likely provide the interviewer with a detailed individual perspective of the type of change that has confronted the sport organization.

Recording the interview

Interviews should be, where possible, audio-taped. Research participants will in most cases agree to this process if it is established that confidentiality can be maintained, and tapes will be erased after transcription. Thomas and Nelson (1990) refer to the obvious advantages associated with the audio-taping of interviews for future analysis. They suggest it allows the researcher to concentrate more fully on the interview procedure and communication process. Attention can then be directed solely to the content of the interview providing increased time to dedicate toward developing and maintaining genuine rapport with the respondents. Hammersley and Atkinson (1983) also suggest audiotaping of interviews as advantageous to both the interviewer and interviewee. Reasons for this include the potential for the gathering of a more complete and detailed record of the content of the conversation, and the interviewer being more able to devote concerted attention to the interviewee without hasty note taking which may detract from the atmosphere and leave the respondent feeling distanced. Additionally, Hammersley and Atkinson indicate that note taking leads to the loss of much detailed verbal information that contributes to the content of the conversation and total content of responses.

Once the interviews are completed, they should be immediately transcribed verbatim. Ellen (1984) highlights the immense importance of immediate documentation and transcription of interviews to warrant them a serious analytical tool. Judd et al. (1991) outline the use of detailed verbatim responses of individuals as useful in the final evaluation of results. The sport management researcher consequently needs to ensure exact replication of the interview content.

Research Brief

Title: The Gender Structure of National Sport Organisations in Post-Reform China
Who: Ying Chui, University of Alberta
Ying Chui examined female sport administrators' organizational experience in the Chinese national sport hierarchy from 1978 to 2003. Through in-depth interviews with sport administrators, both male and female, most in senior leadership positions, she explored the underling reasons for women's under-representation in the decision making of Chinese national sport organizations. Ying Chui argued that women's absence from senior leadership positions and their powerlessness in the national sport management hierarchy is partly attributed to the national cultural thinking on social gender roles, but to a larger degree, is reinforced by a male-defined organizational culture. Processes such as recruitment, evaluation and promotion were examined. Ying Chui also discussed women's dual responsibilities of work and family and the different implications of the transformation from elite athletes to sport managers for both sexes. Based on the research findings, tentative recommendations were put forward with regard to enhancing women's equal career opportunities in sport management.

FOCUS GROUPS

Focus groups are semi-structured interviews with a number of participants that aim to explore a specific set of issues. They are useful in situations where participants have low levels of literacy and/or a strong oral tradition (Grbich, 1999). However, it takes a great deal of skill and preparation to run focus groups successfully so that useful information is generated. In addition, the facilitator must be aware that "public" rather than "private" accounts will be offered and therefore focus groups are unlikely to be the most appropriate method in sensitive situations.

Focus group discussions (or group interviews) capitalize on group interaction and communication to generate data. Focus group discussions can help researchers explore and clarify views in ways that are not possible/accessible in one-to-one interviews. The interviewer usually uses a series of open-ended questions to encourage discussion around issues important to participants, in their own vocabulary and explore their priorities.

Morgan (1997) elaborates on the significance of focus group interviews in terms of the importance of social context to the construction of meaning (and on which the analyst must focus) and the need to treat the group as the unit of analysis and not the individual. Morgan suggests that it is imperative to pay particular attention to the amount of consensus and interest that topics generate within and across groups, and how the dynamics of the group influences what is said, thus creating a greater diversity of communication than the more conventional methods of data collection (De Laine, 1997). A diversity of authors advocate that focus group interviews promote critical thinking abilities because group interaction triggers other ideas and argumentation, which involves the essential component of critical thinking (Burrows & Kendall, 1997; Glendon & Ulrich, 1997).

The method of interviewing participants in focus groups comes largely from marketing research but has been widely adapted to include social science and applied research. The groups are generally composed of seven to ten people (although groups range from as small as four to as large as 12) who are unfamiliar with one another and have been selected because they share certain characteristics relevant to the study's questions. The interviewer creates a supportive environment, asking focused questions to encourage discussion and the expression of differing opinions and points of view. These interviews may be conducted several times with different individuals so that the researcher can identify trends in the perceptions and opinions expressed, which are revealed through careful systematic analysis (Krueger, 1988).

This method assumes that an individual's attitudes and beliefs do not form in a vacuum: People often need to listen to others' opinions and understandings to form their own. Often, the questions in a focus-group setting are deceptively simple; the aim is to promote the participants' expression of their views through the creation of a supportive environment.

The *advantages* of focus-group interviews are that this method is socially oriented, studying participants in an atmosphere more natural than artificial experimental circumstances and more relaxed than a one-to-one interview. When combined with participant observation, focus groups are especially useful for gaining access, focusing site selection and sampling, and even for checking tentative conclusions (Morgan, 1997). The format allows the facilitator the flexibility to explore unanticipated issues as they arise in the discussion. The results have high "face validity": Because the method is readily understood, the findings appear believable. Furthermore, the cost of focus groups is relatively low, they provide quick results, and they can increase the sample size of qualitative studies by permitting more people to be interviewed at one time (Krueger, 1988).

There are, however, certain *disadvantages* to this method as well: First and foremost is the issue of power dynamics in the focus-group setting. Should the sport management researcher choose to use this method they should be aware of power dynamics and ensure that they are able to facilitate an open forum – these are crucial skills. In addition, the interviewer in focus groups may often have less control over a group interview than an individual one. Time can be lost while 'dead-end' or irrelevant issues are discussed. The groups can vary a great deal and can be hard to assemble and logistical problems may arise from the need to manage a conversation while getting good quality data. Data may also be difficult to analyze because the context is essential to understanding the participants' comments.

DOCUMENT ANALYSIS

Sport management researchers often supplement interviewing and observation with the analysis of documents produced in the course of everyday events. The history and context surrounding a specific organizational setting comes, in part, from reviewing documents. Marshall and Rossman (1995) suggested that "the review of documents is an unobtrusive method, rich in portraying values and beliefs of participants in a setting" (p. 116). As such, documents are essentially culturally standardized discourses associated with the value system an organization wants to promote (Miller, 1997).

The examination of documents, historical or archival records, and physical evidence can be considered an unobtrusive measure, in that the collection and review of this data do not require the cooperation of the research participants and, in fact, the subjects of the research may be completely unaware that this data collection and analysis is occurring. Webb et al. (1966) describe these measures as "nonreactive research" because the researcher is expected to observe or gather data without interfering in the ongoing flow of everyday events. Documents and archival records are the most frequently used in qualitative studies.

Knowledge of the history and context surrounding a specific setting comes, in part, from reviewing documents. Researchers supplement participant observation, interviewing, and observation with gathering and analyzing documents produced in the course of everyday events or constructed specifically for the research at hand. Minutes of meetings, logs, announcements, formal policy statements, letters, and so on are all useful in developing an understanding of the setting or group studied. Research journals and samples of free writing about the topic can also be quite informative. Archival data are the routinely gathered records of a society, community, or organization and may further supplement other qualitative methods. As with other methodological decisions, the decision to gather and analyze documents or archival records should be linked to the research questions developed in the conceptual framework for the study. Furthermore, documents must be viewed with the skepticism that historians apply as they search for truth in old texts. The use of documents often entails a specialized analytic approach called content analysis.

Content analysis

The raw material for content analysis may be any form of communication, usually written materials (textbooks, novels, newspapers, e-mail messages); other forms of communication – music, pictures, or political speeches – may also be included. Historically, content analysis was viewed as an objective and neutral way of obtaining a quantitative description of the content of various forms of communication; thus, counting the mention of specific items was important (Berelson, 1952). As it has evolved, however, it is viewed more generously as a method for describing and interpreting the artifacts of a society or social group. Probably the greatest strength of content analysis is that it is unobtrusive and non-reactive: It can be conducted without disturbing the setting in any way. The researcher determines where the emphasis lies after the data have been gathered. Also, the procedure is relatively clear to the reader. Information can therefore be checked, as can the care with which the analysis has been applied. A potential weakness, however, is the span of inferential reasoning. That is, the analysis of the content of written materials or film, for example, entails interpretation by the researcher, just as in the analysis of interactively gathered data.

Research Brief

What: An Examination of Online Relationship building of Professional Sport Leagues through their Website.

Who: Cuhn-Ju, R., Florida State University

Cuhn-Ju utilized content analysis to examine the online relationship of 13 selected sport organizations through their websites. Results indicated the most frequently used information to build relationships was Web based Sport Media Information followed by Value Added Service, Interactive Communication and Convenience. Cuhn-Ju also found that the results varied between team/individual and male/female websites.

Examining documents – historical analysis

A history is an account of some event or combination of events. Historical analysis is a method of discovering what has happened using records and accounts. It is particularly useful in qualitative studies for establishing a baseline or background prior to participant observation or interviewing. Sources of historical data are classified as either primary or secondary. Oral testimony of eyewitnesses, documents, records, and relics are primary.

Reports of persons who relate the accounts of eyewitnesses and summaries, as in history books and encyclopedias, are secondary.

The researcher should consider the following sources of historical data: (a) contemporary records, including instructions, stenographic records, business and legal papers, and personal notes and memos; (b) confidential reports, including military records, journals and diaries, and personal letters; (c) public reports, including newspaper reports and memoirs or autobiographies; (d) questionnaires; (e) government documents, including archives and regulations; (f) opinions, including editorials, speeches, pamphlets, letters to the editor, and public opinion polls; (g) fiction, songs, and poetry; and (h) folklore.

Historical analysis is particularly useful in obtaining knowledge of unexamined areas and in re-examining questions for which answers are not as definite as desired. It allows for systematic and direct classification of data. Historical research traditions demand procedures to verify the accuracy of statements about the past, to establish relationships, and to determine the direction of cause-and effect relationships. Many research studies have a historical base or context, so systematic historical analysis enhances the trustworthiness and credibility of a study.

The researcher needs to remember that documents may be falsified deliberately or may have been interpreted incorrectly by the recorder. Words and phrases used in old records may now have different meanings. The meanings of artifacts are perceived and interpreted by the investigator. Errors in recording, as well as frauds and forgeries, pose problems in dealing with the past. The researcher should retain a modest skepticism about such data.

Research Brief

Title: Establishing a World Anti-Doping Code: WADA'S Impact on the Development of an International Strategy for Anti-Doping in Sport
Who: Jenkins, C.A., University of Windsor
Jenkins' study evaluated how the formation of WADA impacted the development of an international strategy for anti-doping in sport. Conclusions were reached through the analysis of three primary sources of data: personal and organizational archives; media articles; and exploratory interviews. As revealed by the data, the formation of WADA brought together the necessary players to reach a solution for doping in sport. Jenkins suggested that this process provided a forum for sport and government to work co-operatively in generating ideas and focusing thinking. According to Jenkins, this led to an awakening within government and sport to the complexities of doping. Moreover, it embodied an independent/credible organization while raising/maintaining global awareness and interest in doping.

FILMS, VIDEOS AND PHOTOGRAPHY

Films, photographs, videos, DVDs, etc. are records of events and have the benefit of being used as permanent resources. For the sport management researcher, the concept and method of the research film is compatible with a variety of research methods to describe how people navigate in public places (Ryave & Schenkein, 1974) and how they use space (Whyte, 1980), particularly relevant to the event manager, to present findings and to empower participants (Ziller & Lewis, 1981). This represents, for the sport management researcher, a useful tool in examining issues relating to specific athletes and athletic events.

Films, photographs, videos, DVDs and any other digital forms of photography can be used for data collection and for organizing, interpreting, and validating qualitative inquiry (Szto et al., 2005). The visual record can enhance the data previously collected by a researcher, or be used as a historical background to a research topic. These visual records document a snapshot of real life – including death and disasters, celebrations and ceremonies. Major events are made available on a visual level to successive generations, and the platform also documents what may be considered minor social conflicts at the time – such as court proceedings, public speakers, etc., but which with the passage of time assume a different level of importance.

Film/video is especially valuable for discovery and validation. It documents nonverbal behavior and communication such as facial expressions, gestures, and emotions. Film/video preserves activity and change in its original form. It can be used in the future to take advantage of new methods of seeing, analyzing, and understanding the process of change. Film/video is an aid to the researcher when the nature of what is sought is known but the elements of it cannot be discovered because of the limitations of the human eye. It allows for the preservation and study of data from nonrecurring, disappearing, or rare events. Interpretation of information can be validated by another researcher or by participants.

The use of film/video does have weaknesses and limitations. The prevalence of "reality TV" has perhaps to some extent negated the positive effect of recording events, with the recognition that production schedule and rating targets ensure that to a large extent film/video footage is manipulated so that only salacious or biased footage is aired. For the sport management researcher without the pressures of television ratings or production schedules, however, there are still limitations in the use of film/video. Film/video can be expensive, and most research budgets have limitations. The researcher may not have the technical expertise to effectively document on film/video a particular situation without the filming process itself becoming so intrusive so as to detract from the research project itself. And again, the sport management researcher needs to take into account any ethical considerations around the use of film, particularly if intended to be used in a covert manner.

DATA COLLECTION AND QUALITATIVE RESEARCHER METHODS

The data collection techniques outlined in this chapter are those that to date have been most suited to the field of sport management research. The extent to which different techniques are relied upon will largely depend on the research paradigm from which the sport management researcher approaches the study. Table 5.1 lists some suggestions as to the preferred techniques for different research methodologies utilized by sport management researchers.

When collecting data, the mechanics of the process need to be considered; these have been discussed. There are, however, a number of other areas which the sport management researcher needs to consider prior to data collection. Without consideration of these issues, the ability of the sport management researcher to collect data may be restricted or at worst not provided. This is particularly the case in participant observation approaches to research. It is these areas that are now discussed.

ACCESS AND PROCEDURAL ISSUES IN SPORT MANAGEMENT RESEARCH

Gaining entry

Hammersley and Atkinson (1983) suggest appropriate tactics for gaining entry to a setting which include knowing whom to approach and how. Such knowledge is based upon some prior information about the temporal work rhythms that exist and the power alignments within the sport organization. The sport management researcher needs to garner information in order to present themselves to the right person at the right time to gain authorization to carry out an inquiry in a setting. When multiple entries are required to meet the purpose of the research, the sport management researcher should establish credibility and enter into positive relationships.

In many cases, entry into a sport organization or setting is gained through a contact located within that organization or setting, and with whom the sport management researcher may have established credibility through a previous encounters. According to Loftland (1984), the use of a contact or acquaintance to gain entry is not unusual amongst field workers: "It seems

Table 5.1 Design Types or Genres of Qualitative Research and Main Methods of Data Collection/Gathering

Methods	Observation	Interviewing	Documents and Artifacts
Case studies	Participatory observation Standardized observation with schedule	Individual and group interviews – semi-structured, structured and unstructured	Any relevant document or artifact
Ethnographic studies	Participatory observation	Individual and group interviews – semi-structured, structured and unstructured	Any relevant document or artifact
Ethnomethodological studies	Ethnomethodological observation		Any relevant document or artifact
Discourse analysis studies	Participatory observation non-participatory direct observation		Any relevant document or artifact
Grounded theory studies	Participatory observation	Individual and group interviews – semi-structured, structured and unstructured	Any relevant document or artifact
Action research	Participatory observation	Individual and group interviews – semi-structured, structured and unstructured	Any relevant document or artifact

quite typical for outside researchers to gain access to settings or persons through contacts they have already established. They cast about among their friends, acquaintances, colleagues, and the like for someone who is already favorably regarded by the person with access control" (p. 25). In this way the sport management researcher's contact can become and act as a "sponsor" in the organization, providing the sport management researcher with the opportunity to develop relationships which otherwise might have been more difficult and time consuming to achieve.

Gatekeepers

To secure entry to a sport organization, the researcher may be required to perform a presentation about the purpose of the research. This empowers organizational members as they can openly discuss the research and make comment. The sport management researcher's "sponsor" can also introduce the researcher to the appropriate individuals within the organization. Attention can then shift to the official gatekeeper of the sport organization and their support may be secured.

Hammersley and Atkinson (1983) indicate that gatekeepers will generally be concerned as to the "light" in which the organization will be portrayed, and will have a desire to see themselves and their colleagues presented in a favorable manner. As a consequence of this, the sport management researcher may be required to establish a research agreement with the organization.

Research agreement

In research that involves participant observation over a long period of time, the research agreement is primarily developed as a mechanism to provide guidelines in relation to the dissemination of information. In the researcher's initial discussion, it may be decided that a confidentiality agreement be established between the researcher, the researcher's supervisors, and the organization itself.

A sport organization may be concerned that any information that is provided to the researcher is only viewed by those directly associated with the research and is to be used for academic purposes only. For example, if the information provided is sensitive and has been developed in order to provide the sport organization with a competitive advantage over its rivals the organization would not want this information in the public domain. Additionally, an agreement, through the discretion of the Chief Executive Officer/President, could provide provision to terminate the study if any information was published or distributed in the broader private or public domain without prior agreement.

Finally, a verbal research agreement (in some cases a formal written contract is required) in relation to confidentiality is established. This occurs because information given by individuals may vary and as such may have potential to cause conflict between management members. In an interviewing context, one way to overcome this is prior to each interview the researcher should remind the participants that the interview is being conducted in complete confidentiality. Each individual can be arbitrarily assigned a label so that participants can be listed as "Respondent One", "Respondent Two", and so on. Thus, the rationale for confidentiality and negotiation of accounts is based on an ethical consideration of respect for persons who have guaranteed an intrusion into their world, and access to their opinions in regards to the research issues.

Preserving anonymity of participants

As discussed in Chapter 4, maintaining anonymity needs to be a consideration throughout the entire research project rather than only in the write-up. This requires the sport management researcher to use various procedures to help preserve anonymity. *First*, as previously mentioned, each interviewee should be identified by a number and labeled as a respondent/participant. *Second*, the researcher should be the only person who has access to the bulk of the data during the fieldwork stage. Fieldwork notes should not be presented to anyone, but treated as highly confidential. *Finally*, time itself helps to protect anonymity or at least to make identification more difficult. Over time, people tend to forget what others have said. They may even forget what they themselves said.

In spite of these procedures individuals who are familiar with the sport organization will speculate about statements made by individuals where positive identification is not possible. However, to present the information in such a way that even the people central to it are fooled by it is to risk removing the very aspects that make it relevant, insightful, and believable. The participants should be informed of this. Having been assured of confidentiality, individuals generally feel freer to talk about the organization This leads us to the notion of trust.

Trust

Wax (1971) emphasizes the importance of reciprocal relationships while gaining entry. Mutual trust, respect and co-operation are dependent on the emergence of an exchange relationship in which the researcher obtains information, and participants in a setting can identify something in that setting which will make their co-operation worthwhile.

Nelson (1969), however, suggests that restrictions can exist in achieving the desired amount of trust from participants. These potential barriers were highlighted through Nelson's direct participation in ethnographic fieldwork. His work focused on the notion of foreign and domestic participation. He believed participation in one's own formal organization is accompanied by a set of research constraints apparently not encountered if one participates in the activities of a foreign social group. The difference lies in the participants' perceptions of the researcher. While a researcher in a foreign culture might perceive him or herself as a participant, those in the group, are likely to perceive the researcher more as a guest participant rather than a full member.

Rosen (1991) related the problems raised by Nelson (1969) to the issue of *secrecy*. Rosen indicates that when a researcher occupies an official place in an organization, an office located in physical and temporal space, he or she becomes part of the first-order politics of the organization, and therefore not someone to be fully trusted by others located in the same political arena. This is opposed to how one might trust an outsider, the researcher as an observer. In this situation, the researcher is an outsider knowledgeable of the organization, yet at the same time probably marginal to its political processes.

This issue of secrecy, according to Rosen (1991), is related to the notion of trust. Rosen believed that when the researcher occupies a place in the first-order politics of an organization they are tied to the instrumental relations of organization, the means-ends processes of social intercourse. However, the researcher who occupies a role solely as an observer is tied to the moral relations among individuals, friendship-like relationships are developed and pursued. Rosen suggests that the instrumental and moral dimensions of a relationship are clearly embedded within the same discourse between actors. From a means–ends perspective, the researcher as an occupier of a role in instrumental relations will be informed according to other organizational members' perceived utility or disutility of doing so. On the other hand, the researcher as part of a friendship relationship (as an observer) will be informed of the discourse of the organization insofar as it is germane to the discourse of friendship.

Throughout a study that requires the researcher to spend a significant amount of time in a sport organization or setting the researcher can be perceived in a dual capacity depending on the role being fulfilled. Due to this, the sport management researcher needs to be aware of developing an impression of a person who would be discrete in handling information within the research setting, and who would honor promises of anonymity when collecting and discussing data. Therefore, it would be advisable that the sport management researcher not request at the outset full access to relevant and sensitive data. The researcher should decide to leave these requests, of what seem more delicate forms of access, until field relationships had been established. For example, although the researcher may be privy to a discussion of the detail of player contracts and their implications for management, the researcher should not request to see a copy of these contacts until a relationship of trust had been established between those concerned – if it is not, and the researcher's instincts suggest it is not appropriate, then this request should not be made. This approach to obtaining data at an appropriate time can be instrumental in allowing relationships to develop. As a consequence, this process can assist in participants being more open and candid in discussions. The outcome can be the development of relationships based on mutual trust, respect and co-operation.

Research Brief: Why Women don't watch Men's Sport

Title: Why Women don't watch Women's Sport: A Qualitative Analysis

Who: Farrell, A-M., Ohio State University

Farrell utilized qualitative methodology to investigate female consumption of women's sport through the voices and perspectives of female fans of men's basketball who do not attend women's events. The focus of this investigation included an understanding of how their attitudes and disinterest may be related to gendered media portrayals, socialization and distinct spectator motives. Aspects of social constructivism and critical theory framed Farrell's interpretation. Farrell indicated that while several fields in the social sciences have been dominated by qualitative studies for decades, their emergence in the sport management realm is a more recent development. She adds that lately, more scholars have utilized alternative paradigms to examine human behavior. To gather rich, detailed accounts of human behavior, semi-structured interviews were utilized, in conjunction with document analysis. Female season-ticket holders of university men's basketball, with no recent attendance at a women's basketball game, were interviewed using a semi-structured format. Semi-structured interviews allowed for the communication of study participants' thoughts, feelings, experiences and reactions in a way that would not be feasible using other research methods. The results of this study suggest the process of socialization favoring men's sports begins by watching sport with fathers and grandfathers, continuing with the glorification of their male siblings, and is later reaffirmed by boyfriends, husbands and sons. The study underscored the importance of socialization in the lives of women as sport consumers.

CONCLUSION

This chapter has explained the data collection methods that can be utilized to acquire data, and to address research aims. Observation can be utilized to provide the sport management researcher with a foothold in the world of the sport organization and provide the basis for further conversation in interviews. How documents can be utilized to collect data and compliment observations and interviews was also discussed. Finally, access and procedural issues were discussed. This includes issues such as gaining entry; gatekeepers; research agreement; preserving anonymity; and trust. Each of these issues is a vital part of the data collection process and need to be carefully considered.

IN PROFILE - Dr Sally Shaw

Dr Sally Shaw, Senior Lecturer in Sport Management, University of Otago. Dr Shaw relies on a consistent critical, post structural epistemology in her research. She has studied a number of aspects of sport management, starting with her Master's thesis on volunteering in 1996, and developing other interests, including gender relations in sport organisations, relationships between volunteer managers and volunteers, sponsorship, and inter-organisational relationships. She believes, and related research suggests, that qualitative research methods are useful in examining these areas because they encourage participants to talk openly and freely about their experiences. Qualitative methods thus lend themselves to depth within the data gathering process. This depth, and the subsequent data analysis, is particularly important when people are talking about potentially emotive topics, or when the researcher is interested in getting "below the surface" of a particular question. In particular, semi structured interviews have been the most useful to Dr Shaw. When she collected her PhD data in 1998–99, she refers to herself as a typically over-anxious PhD student, concerned about getting through a long list of questions, worried about taking up too much of her participants' time, and trying to make sure she got "good" data and quotes. Over time she evolved to become a more confident and competent researcher. Generally now, she uses fewer structured questions and tries to think more of a small number of themes to cover in an interview. The questions may change somewhat depending on the participant but the themes remain the same. Dr Shaw tries to engage in a somewhat directed conversation with participants, at times questioning their answers, offering more opportunity for the participants to expand on their ideas. This skill development has been invaluable over the years. After all, research is about the participants and providing an avenue for their views, not about the researcher!

REVIEW AND RESEARCH QUESTIONS

1. Distinguish between the different forms of observation and interviews and how these might be used by the sport management research.

2. Discuss how documents can be used by the sport management researcher to collect specific data.

Provide examples of the documents a sport management research may use in their research.

3. Explain the relationship between the issue of "gaining entry" the "research agreement" and developing "trust".

REFERENCES

Berelson, B. 1952. Content Analysis in Communication Research. Glencoe, IL: Free Press.

Burns, R. B. 1997. Introduction to Research Methods. Melbourne: Longman.

Burrows, D. & Kendall, S. 1997. Focus groups: what are they and how can they be used in nursing and health care research? *Social Sciences in Health*, **3**, 244–253.

De Laine, M. 1997. Ethnography: Theory and Applications in Health Research. Sydney: Maclennan and Petty.

Dick, B. 1990. Convergent Interviewing (Version 3). Brisbane: Interchange.

Douglas, J. D. 1976. Investigative Social Research. Beverly Hills, CA: Sage.

Doyle, P. 1994. Marketing Management and Strategy. London: Prentice Hall.

Ellen, R.F. (Ed.), 1984. Ethnographic Research: A Guide to General Conduct. London: Academic Press.

Emory, C. & Cooper, D. 1991. Business Research Methods. Homewood, IL: Irwin.

Fontana, A. & Frey, J. H. 1994. Interviewing: the art of science. In: *Handbook of Qualitative Research* (Ed. by N. K. Denzin, Y. S. Lincoln), pp. 361–376. London: Sage.

Frey, J. H. & Oishi, S. M. 1995. How to Conduct Interviews by Telephone and in Person. In: The Survey Kit, Vol. 4. Thousand Oaks, CA, Sage.

Glendon, K. & Ulrich, D. 1997. Unfolding cases: an experiential learning model. *Nurse Educator*, **22**, 15–18.

Grbich, C. 1999. Qualitative Research in Health: An Introduction. Thousand Oaks, CA: Sage.

Guba, G., & Lincoln, Y. S. 1994. Competing paradigms in qualitative research. In N. K. Denzin, & Y. S. Lincoln (Eds.), Handbook of qualitative research (pp. 105–117). Thousand Oaks, CA: Sage.

Hammersley, M. & Atkinson, P. 1983. Ethnography: Principles in Practice. London: Tavistock.

Jorgensen, D. L. 1989. Participant Observation: A Methodology for Human Studies. Thousand Oaks, CA: Sage.

Judd, C. M., Smith, E. R. & Kidder, L. H. 1991. Research Methods in Social Relations. Fort Worth: Harcourt Brace Jovanovich.

Kirk, D. 1986. Health related fitness as an innovation in the physical education curriculum. In: *Physical Education, Sport and Schooling: Studies in the Sociology of Schooling* (Ed. by F. Evans), pp. 167–181. London: The Falmer Press.

Krieger, S. 1983. The Mirror Dance: Identity in a Women's Community. Philadelphia: Temple University Press.

Krueger, R. A. 1988. Focus Groups: A Practical Guide for Applied Research. Thousand Oaks, CA: Sage.

Loftland, J. 1984. Analysing Social Settings: A Guide to Qualitative Observation and Analysis. Belmont, CA: Wadsworth.

Marcus, G. E. & Fischer, M. 1986. Anthropology as Cultural Critique: An Experimental Moment in Human Sciences. Chicago: University of Chicago Press.

Marshall, C. & Rossman, G. 1995. *Designing Qualitative Research*, 2nd ed. Thousand Oaks, London, New Delhi: Sage Publications.

Miller, G. 1997. Building bridges: the possibility of analytic dialogue between ethnography, conversation analysis and Foucault. In: *Qualitative Research: Theory, Method and Practice* (Ed. by D. Silverman), pp. 45–62. London: Sage.

Minichiello, V., Aroni, R., Timewell, E. & Alexander, L. 1995. In-Depth Interviewing: Principles, Techniques, Analysis, 2nd ed. Melbourne: Longman.

Morgan, D. L. 1997. Focus Groups as Qualitative Research, 2nd ed. Thousand Oaks, CA: Sage.

Nelson, R. K. 1969. Hunters on the Northern Ice. Chicago: University of Chicago Press.

Nichols, P. 1991. Social Survey Methods. Oxford: Oxfam.

Pope, C. & Mays, N. 2000. Qualitative Research in Health Care. London: Blackwell.

Rosen, M. 1991. Coming to terms with the field: understanding and doing organizational ethnography. *Journal of Management Studies*, **28** (1), 1–24.

Ryave, A. L. & Schenkein, J. N. 1974. Notes on the art of walking. In: *Ethno-methodology* (Ed. by R. Turner), pp. 265–278. Harmondsworth: Penguin.

Schwandt, T. 2001. Dictionary of Qualitative Inquiry, 2nd ed. Thousand Oaks, CA: Sage.

Seidman, I. 1998. Interviewing as Qualitative Research: A guide for Researchers in Education and the Social Sciences. New York: Teachers College Press.

Sekaran, U. 2000. Research Methods for Business, 3rd ed. New York: Hermitage.

Spradley, J. P. 1980. Participant Observation. New York: Holt, Rinehart & Winston.

Kvale, S. 1996. InterViews: An Introduction to Qualitative Research Interviewing. Thousand Oaks, CA: Sage.

Stewart, C. J. & Cash, W. B. 1994. Interviewing: Principles and Practices. London: McGraw-Hill.

Szto, P., Furman, R. & Langer, C. 2005. Poetry and photography: an exploration into expressive/creative qualitative research. *Qualitative Social Work*, **4**, 135–156.

Thomas, J. & Nelson, J. 1990. Research Methods in Physical Activity. Champaign, IL: Human Kinetics.

Wax, R. H. 1971. Doing Fieldwork: Warnings and Advice. Chicago: University of Chicago Press.

Webb, E. J., Campbell, D. T., Schwartz, R. D. & Sechrest, L. 1966. Unobtrusive Measures: Nonreactive Research in the Social Sciences. Newbury, CA: Sage.

Wengraf, T. 2001. Qualitative Research Interviewing: Biographic Narrative and Semi-Structured Methods. London: Sage.

Whyte, W. 1980. The Social Life of Small Urban Spaces. Washington, D.C: The Conservation Foundation.

Ziller, R. C. & Lewis, D. 1981. Orientations: self, social and environmental percepts through auto-photography. *Personality and Social Psychology Bulletin*, **7**, 338–343.

PART 4

Analyzing the Sport Management Data

CHAPTER 6

Modes of Analysis in Sport Management Qualitative Research

OBJECTIVES

By the end of this chapter, you should be able to

- identify modes of analysis process strategies.

- identify key methods in the coding process.

KEY TERMS

Modes of analysis: the process by which the researcher reviews the data collected with the aim of making sense of it so that evidence can be obtained to answer the research question.

Triangulation: examining the consistency of information generated by different data collection techniques, or by examining different data gathered by the same collection technique.

Crystallization: the process of suspending the modes of analysis process to reflect on the analysis experience itself thereby enabling the researcher to identify and articulate patterns or themes that may emerge.

Coding: the organization of raw data into conceptual categories.

KEY QUESTIONS

- Why is Data Entry and Storage important to the Sport Management Researcher?

- What is Coding?

CHAPTER OVERVIEW

This chapter discusses modes of analysis in sport management qualitative research. It notes that the purpose of modes of analysis is to make sense of the data so that evidence can be obtained to answer the research question. However, there is a lack of a commonly accepted method of qualitative analysis. It is suggested that the key is to ensure that your analysis is appropriate to achieve your research objectives.

ANALYSIS IN QUALITATIVE RESEARCH

Although there are many different modes of analysis in qualitative research, just two approaches or modes of analysis with particular relevance to sport management research will be discussed here: *hermeneutics* and *semiotics*.

Hermeneutics

Hermeneutics can be treated as both an underlying philosophy and a specific mode of analysis (Bleicher, 1980). As a philosophical approach to human understanding, it provides the philosophical grounding for interpretivism (see the discussion on Philosophical Perspectives in Chapters 1 and 2). As a mode of analysis, it suggests a way of understanding textual data. The following discussion is concerned with using hermeneutics as a specific mode of analysis.

Hermeneutics is primarily concerned with the *meaning* of a text or text-analog (an example of a text-analog is an organization, which the researcher comes to understand through oral or written text). The basic question in hermeneutics is: "what is the meaning of this text" (Radnitzky, 1970)? Taylor (1990) says that:

> *Interpretation, in the sense relevant to hermeneutics, is an attempt to make clear, to make sense of an object of study. This object must, therefore, be a text, or a text-analogue, which in some way is confused, incomplete, cloudy, seemingly contradictory – in one way or another, unclear. The interpretation aims to bring to light an underlying coherence or sense. (p. 153)*

The idea of a hermeneutic circle refers to the dialectic between the understanding of the text as a whole and the interpretation of its parts, in which descriptions are guided by anticipated explanations (Gadamer, 1976). It follows from this that we have an expectation of meaning from the context of what has gone before. The movement of understanding: "is constantly from the whole to the part and back to the whole" (p. 117). As Gadamer explains, "It is a circular relationship… The anticipation of meaning in which the whole is envisaged becomes explicit understanding in that the parts, that are determined by the whole, themselves also determine this whole" (p. 117). Ricoeur (1974) suggests that: "Interpretation…is the work of thought which consists in deciphering the hidden meaning in the apparent meaning, in unfolding the levels of meaning implied in the literal meaning" (p. xiv).

There are different forms of hermeneutic analysis, from "pure" hermeneutics through to "critical" hermeneutics; however a discussion of these different forms is beyond the scope of this section. For a more in-depth discussion, see Bleicher (1980) and Thompson (1981).

If hermeneutic analysis is used in an information systems study, the object of the interpretive effort becomes one of attempting to make sense of the organization as a text-analog. In an organization, people (e.g., different stakeholders) can have confused, incomplete, cloudy and contradictory views on many issues. The aim of the hermeneutic analysis becomes one of trying to make sense of the whole, and the relationship between people, the organization, and information.

Semiotics

Like hermeneutics, semiotics can be treated as both an underlying philosophy and a specific mode of analysis. The following discussion concerns using semiotics as a mode of analysis. Semiotics is primarily concerned with the meaning of signs and symbols in language. The essential idea is that words/signs can be assigned to primary conceptual categories, and these categories represent important aspects of the theory to be tested. The importance of an idea is revealed in the frequency with which it appears in the text. One form of semiotics is "content analysis".

Krippendorf (1980) defines content analysis as a research technique for making replicable and valid references from data to their contexts. The researcher searches for structures and patterned regularities in the text and makes inferences on the basis of these regularities. Another form of semiotics is "conversation analysis". In conversation analysis, it is assumed that the meanings are shaped in the context of the exchange (Wynn, 1979). The researchers immerse themselves in the situation to reveal the background of practices. A third form of semiotics is "discourse analysis." Discourse analysis builds on both content analysis and conversation analysis but focuses on "language games". A language game refers to a well-defined unit of interaction consisting of a sequence of verbal moves in which turns of phrases, the use of metaphor and allegory all play an important part. Both discourse analysis and conversation analysis are discussed in greater detail in the next section of the book.

MODES OF ANALYSIS

Although a clear distinction between data gathering and modes of analysis is commonly made in quantitative research, such a distinction is problematic for many qualitative researchers. For example, from a hermeneutic perspective it is assumed that the researcher's presuppositions affect the gathering of the data – the questions posed to informants largely determine what you are going to find out. The analysis affects the data and the data affect the analysis in significant ways. Therefore, it is perhaps more accurate to speak of "modes of analysis" rather than "data analysis" in qualitative research. These modes of analysis are different approaches to gathering, analyzing and interpreting qualitative data. The common thread is that all qualitative modes of analysis are concerned primarily with textual analysis (whether verbal or written).

MODES OF ANALYSIS PHASES AND FRAMEWORK

Miles and Huberman (1994) suggest that qualitative modes of analysis consist of three procedures: These are as follows:

1. *Data reduction*. This refers to the process whereby the mass of qualitative data you may obtain – interview transcripts, field notes, etc. – is reduced and organized, for example, coding, writing summaries, discarding irrelevant data and so on. This process should begin almost as soon as you begin the data collection, and is often an ongoing process throughout much of the research.

2. *Data display*. To draw conclusions from the mass of data, Miles and Huberman suggest that a good display of data, in the form of tables, charts, networks and other graphical formats is essential. Again, this is a continual process, rather than just one to be carried out at the end of the data collection.

3. *Conclusion drawing/verification*. Your analysis should allow you to begin to develop conclusions regarding your study. These initial conclusions can then be certified. That is, their validity can be examined through reference to your existing field notes, further data collection, or even critical discussion with your colleagues.

Modes of analysis framework

A useful *framework* to undertake the third procedure suggested by Miles and Huberman (1994) has been developed specifically for qualitative research. The Qualitative Research Unit at the National Centre for Social Research, London, has refined the approach, but the general principles remain applicable to a range of applied research studies (Ritchie & Spencer, 1993) including sport management research. The five stages of the framework are as follows:

1. **Familiarization** – Immersion in the raw data; listening to tapes, reading through transcripts, studying notes, to get a feel for the data and emerging themes.

2. **Identifying a thematic framework** – The process of identifying all key themes and concepts by which the data can be coded and referenced. The end product is a comprehensive coding index.

3. **Indexing** – Applying the thematic framework to all transcripts systematically; annotating the textual data with codes from the index.

4. **Charting** – The process of developing individual matrices for each key theme, and entering coded sections of text (plus identifiers) into appropriate charts.

5. **Interpretation** – Using the charts to map the range and nature of responses, create typologies, identify associations between themes, and attempt explanations.

The framework approach is a comprehensive, systematic and replicable modes of analysis process. It is designed so that it can be viewed and assessed by people other than the primary sport management researcher. This outcome enhances the trustworthiness of the findings and is particularly useful for sport management research.

Research Brief

Title: A Qualitative Study of Analysing Huntington Beach Surfers' Environmental Attitudes.
Who: Allen, A. California State University
Allen utilised grounded theory to explore the relationship between surfing and environmental attitudes amongst a group of surfers at Huntington Beach. Semi-structured interviews indicated that surfers had an awareness of environmental degradation but had their personal ways of dealing with these issues.

DATA REDUCTION STAGE

Bogdan and Biklen (1982) define qualitative modes of analysis as "working with data, organizing it, breaking it into manageable units, synthesizing it, searching for patterns, discovering what is important and what is to be learned, and deciding what you will tell others" (p. 145). Qualitative researchers tend to use inductive analysis of data, meaning that the critical themes emerge out of the data (Patton, 1990). Qualitative analysis requires some creativity, for the challenge is to place the raw data into logical, meaningful categories; to examine them in a holistic fashion; and to find a way to communicate this interpretation to others.

Sitting down to organize a pile of raw data can be a daunting task. It can involve literally hundreds of pages of interview transcripts, field notes and documents. The mechanics of handling large quantities of qualitative data can range from physically sorting and storing slips of paper to using one of the several computer software programs that have been designed to aid in this task.

At an early stage in qualitative analysis, the researcher should organize data into paper files or folders, or computer files, or onto index cards. The organization of these data is important because of the large amount of information generally gathered during a study. The researcher needs to develop a matrix or a table of sources that can help organize the material. Materials can be organized by type – for example, all interviews together, all observations, all documents, all photographs, etc. Alternatively materials could be organized by site, participant, location, or some other identifier or combination of identifiers. It is important that the organizational method is clear to the researcher and that all materials are easily retrievable. For safety/backup purposes, the researcher should also aim to keep a duplicate of all data. Whichever way the data are organized, they need to be stored in a secure manner so that records and information can be retrieved at some future time to verify the results presented in the final research report.

Coding data

The key process in the data reduction stage is that of *coding data*. Coding is the organization of raw data into conceptual categories. Each code is effectively a category or "bin" into which a piece of data is placed. Coding is the first stage to providing some form of logical structure to the data. Codes should be valid, that is, they should accurately reflect what is being researched, they should be mutually exclusive, in that codes should be distinct, with no overlap, and they should be exhaustive, that is, all relevant data should fit into a code.

A suggested framework for undertaking coding includes the following:

1. All data is carefully read, all statements relating to the research question are identified, and each is assigned a code, or category. These codes are then noted, and each relevant statement is organized under its appropriate code, either manually or on computer, along with any notes, or memos that the researcher wishes to add of their own. This is referred to as *open coding*. During *open coding*, the researcher must identify and tentatively name the conceptual categories into which the phenomena observed will be grouped. The goal is to create descriptive, multidimensional categories which form a preliminary framework for analysis. Words, phrases or events that appear to be similar can be grouped into the same category. These categories may be gradually modified or replaced during the subsequent stages of analysis that follow.

As the raw data are broken down into manageable chunks, the researcher must also devise an "audit trail"—that is, a scheme for identifying these data chunks according to their speaker and the context. The particular identifiers developed may or may not be used in the research report, but speakers are typically referred to in a manner that provides a sense of context. Qualitative research is characterized by the use of "voice" in the text; that is, participant quotes that illustrate the themes being described.

2. The next stage of analysis involves re-examination of the categories identified in stage 1 to determine how they are linked, a complex process sometimes called *"axial coding"* (Strauss & Corbin, 1990). The discrete categories identified in open coding are compared and combined in new ways as the researcher begins to assemble the "big picture." The purpose of coding is to not only describe but also, more importantly, to acquire new understanding of a phenomenon of interest. Therefore, causal events contributing to the phenomenon; descriptive details of the phenomenon itself; and the ramifications of the phenomenon under study must all be identified and explored. During *axial coding* the researcher is responsible for building a conceptual model and for determining whether sufficient data exists to support that interpretation.

3. Once the first two stages of coding have been completed, the researcher should become more analytical, and look for patterns and explanation in the codes. Questions should be asked such as:

   ■ Can I relate certain codes together under a more general code?

   ■ Can I organize codes sequentially?

   ■ Can I identify any causal relations?

4. The fourth stage is that of *selective coding*. This involves reading through the raw data for cases that illustrate the analysis, or explain the concepts. The researcher should also look for data that are contradictory, as well as confirmatory.

Another method of analysis is outlined by Biddle et al. (2001) whereby the data units (statements, sentences etc) are clustered into common themes (essentially the same as codes), so that similar units are grouped together into first order themes, and separated away from units with different meaning. The same process is then repeated with the first order themes, which are grouped together into second order themes. This is repeated as far as possible. A further discussion of Coding is presented in the next section of the book, in the chapter on Grounded Theory.

Research Brief

Title: Memory, Modernity, and the City: An Interpretive Analysis of Montreal and Toronto's Respective Moves From Their Historic Professional Hockey Arenas
Who: Gunderson, L.A. University of Waterloo, Ontario.
This study utilized a "radical interpretive" approach, involving a critical blend of interpretive theories and methodologies – including semiology, phenomenology, hermeneutics, and dialectical analysis to reflexively question the themes that the cases of the moves of the Toronto Maple Leafs and the Montreal Canadiens from Maple Leaf Gardens and the Montreal Forum themselves bring to light. The study thus concerns itself with issues of cosmopolitanism, globalization, and modernity as well as the concomitant questions of identity, commitment to place, and practical social action in the modern city.

SHOWING RELATIONSHIPS AMONG CATEGORIES

Once the data are coded the researcher looks for patterns or regularities that occur. Within each code the researcher should try to identify key words or phrases, such as "because", "despite", "in order to", "otherwise" and so on and try to make sense of the data through interpretation of the meaning and values that respondents assign to the phenomenon that they are interested in. Frankfort-Nachimas and Nachimas (1996) suggest that researchers ask themselves a number of questions to assist in their analysis:

1. What type of behavior is being demonstrated?

2. What is its structure?

3. How frequent is it?

4. What are its causes?

5. What are its processes?

6. What are its consequences?

7. What are people's strategies for dealing with the behavior?

MEMOING

Whilst coding data, the researcher can aid in the maximization of the validity and reliability of the modes of analysis process by writing *memos*. These are the ideas that occur to the researcher whilst coding the data, for example concerning explanation, theorizing, or other ideas about the data. They can be extremely helpful in trying to make sense of the data at a later date. Memos can be written directly on the transcripts, or else the researcher can keep a record of them elsewhere. Making memos as detailed as possible can help with later analysis.

Sport management coding example

As discussed, there is an abundance of literature published on qualitative research (e.g., Burns, 1997; Glaser & Strauss, 1967; Miles & Huberman, 1994; Sarantankos, 1998; Strauss, 1987; Strauss & Corbin, 1990); researchers advocate different approaches to coding and they employ a number of common steps. Initially, the sport management researcher should study their own transcripts to have a close familiarity with the material. It is during this process that all the concepts, themes, and ideas are noted to form major categories. For example, if interviews with sport organization stakeholders are concerned with establishing the causes and outcomes of the organizational change process occurring within a professional sport organization the initial *open coding* of the categories could include factors related to: (A) environmental disturbances; (B) internal adaptation; (C) organizational dynamics; and (D) culture. The coding of qualitative research in this fashion is important as it operates as a labeling, retrieval and organizational device. In this context the coding system becomes a "conceptual model" (Burns, 1997, p. 341).

Strauss and Corbin (1990), recommend that *axial coding* then be undertaken. This involves employing a set of procedures whereby data are put back together in new ways after open coding, by making a connection between categories. This results in a cumulative knowledge about relationships between that category and can subsequently lead to the development of sub-categories being created from the initial categories. The sport management researcher would therefore establish files for each of the new sub-categories. From the first four open-codes, eight sub-codes could be created: (1) external forces; (2) external competition; (3) internal change; (4) structural change; (5) political environment; (6) power relations; (7) organizational values; and (8) cultural conflict. This process would further add to the conceptual model as proposed by Burns (1997).

The sport management researcher could then make multiple copies of each segment of data, a copy would be filed under all categories and sub-categories to which it was relevant. With this system, when it is time for detailed analysis of a particular category or sub-category, all relevant data are readily available and there is no need to sift through the running record to find the relevant data segments. An additional advantage is that all items relevant to the same category or sub-category can be put side by side and compared. Hammersley and Atkinson (1983) indicate that data organization techniques play an important role in facilitating reflexivity – a core proponent of research: "They provide a crucial resource in assessing typicality of examples, checking construct-indicator linkages, searching for negative cases, triangulating across different data sources and stages of the fieldwork, and assessing the role of the researcher in shaping the nature of the idea and findings". (p. 173)

Memos can then be used initially to categorize the data and then provide a framework for the comparison of data (Strauss, 1987). Memos could be written on a file card that contains a number of references to the data and a conceptual category that this evidence suggests. The writing of memos can therefore act as a catalyst to spark ideas and allow the sport management researcher to see connections and implications that at first were not obvious. For example, the following interview transcript is used to demonstrate the link between the data to categories identified above. An interview participant was asked, "Do you believe your sport organization would have gradually evolved into a professional organization responsible for the management of a professional sport"?

> *… we wouldn't have changed if it had not been for what was happening outside the sport. We just couldn't ignore it if we were to survive. Previously we could ignore it as the environment was not that threatening to the game and indeed to those involved in the game, but with all that money being pumped into other sports and entrepreneurs trying to take over our sport if we didn't change we had no chance … our hand was forced.*

The memo on the file card attached to this transcript would indicate that these data were relevant to the category of environmental disturbances and the sub-category of external forces.

In respect to the comparison of data, details from transcripts could in the first instance be allocated to a category. For example, a question could be put to a number of interview participants involved in the interview process: "Do you believe the culture of your sport organization is changing"?

> *The culture of the organisation will never change … that's because most people are involved in sport for the same reasons I am involved and that's because we love the game. Its not about money for us, it's about doing something you enjoy doing and valuing why we do it. If we didn't we wouldn't be involved in the game there would be no such thing as an amateur player -we would all want to be professionals … why would you want to change the culture?*

For the purpose of the example, we then put the same question to another interview participant, who states:

> *Yes, the culture of the organisation is changing. People are starting to recognize that we need to change and that if we don't our sport will suffer as other sports take over the marketplace. So I think although some people might not like the idea of changing the culture they have accepted that it is inevitable and that we must.*

When analyzing this information a memo would then be attached indicating that the responses could be allocated to the initial category of culture. However, when revisiting the data further clarification is possible. It could be decided that the response given by both respondents provides examples that could be allocated to the sub-category of cultural conflict. A memo indicating this could therefore be attached to a file card of each transcript. Thus, by comparing the data within the initial category, and sub-dividing it further, a deeper understanding of the issues confronting the sport would start to emerge.

Finally, *selective coding* would then be undertaken (Miles & Huberman, 1994). As indicated previously, this is the process of selecting a core category and systematically relating it to the initial categories and sub-categories in order to validate the relationships that exist between them. This refinement process of linking the existing categories and sub-categories can therefore be geared toward generating precise themes that can form the structure for discussing the interview data.

TRIANGULATION

Denzin and Lincoln (1998) suggest that:

> *Qualitative research involves the studied use and collection of a variety of empirical materials - case study, personal experience,*

introspective, life story, interview, observational, historical, interactional, and visual texts-that describe routine and problematic moments and meanings in individuals' lives. Accordingly, qualitative researchers deploy a wide range of interconnected methods, hoping always to get a better fix on the subject matter at hand. (p. 3)

Qualitative research, therefore, exercises multiple methods, something that Denzin and Lincoln (1998, pp. 3–5) called *bricolage*. They referred to the qualitative researcher as a *bricoleur*, "a practical person who works with whatever strategies, tools, and materials are available to piece together an emergent solution to a puzzle or problem" (Bazeley, 1999, p. 279). It is an array of interpretative techniques that seek to describe, decode, translate and subsequently come to terms with the meaning, not the frequency (Van Maanen, 1983) of certain naturally occurring phenomena in the social world (Gilmore & Carson, 1996, p. 23).

Denzin and Lincoln (1998) introduced and then popularized this concept as *triangulation* into qualitative study. Triangulation involves examining the consistency of information generated by different data collection techniques, or by examining different data gathered by the same collection technique.

Triangulation has been generally considered as the way to reduce the likelihood of misinterpretation with the target to clarify meaning and verifying the repeatability of an observation or interpretation (Stake, 2000). By using multiple methods, for example, different kinds of data can emerge from the same topic so that it will involve more data that will likely improve the quality of the research (Denscombe, 1998). Albeit the initial aim of triangulation is to test the validity of qualitative research, recently its role has been put into practice to ensure comprehensiveness and encourage a more reflexive analysis of data (Pope & Mays, 2000). Seale (1999) suggests that "triangulation offers a way of explaining how accounts and actions in one setting are influenced or constrained by those in another" (p. 60). Silverman (1993) supports the idea by saying that this can assist "to address the situated work of accounts" more willingly than "using one account to undercut the other" (p. 158).

Burns (1997) postulated that triangulation leads to verification and validation of qualitative analysis in two ways: First, by examining the consistency of information generated by different data collection techniques, and second by examining the consistency of different information within the same technique. In other words, conforming to one method could have the tendency to bias the researcher's perspective of a "particular slice of reality being investigated" (Burns 1997, p. 325), but could be "neutralized when used in conjunction with other data sources, investigators and methods"

(Jick cited in Cresswell, 1994, p. 174). Denzin and Lincoln (1998, p. 46) identified four basic types of triangulation and are explained as:

- *Data-source triangulation:* The use of different types of data sources in a study, for example, time, space and person and each occurrence or social interaction is unique.

- *Investigator triangulation:* The use of different researchers or evaluators. The main purpose is to eliminate any bias inherent in using a single observer.

- *Theory triangulation:* The use of multiple perspectives to interpret a single set of data.

- *Methodological triangulation:* Involves the use of multiple techniques to study a single problem.

When analyzing data, ensuring that the triangulation methods above are covered will give the researcher an added measure of validity and reliability in the final reporting of results.

Sport management triangulation example

To provide an example of two of the above forms of triangulation, we return to our example of understanding organizational change within a professional sport organization. To ensure that the data collected are valid two triangulation techniques could be utilized. First, data-source triangulation could involve a comparison of data relating to the same phenomenon but derived from different phases of field work, and the accounts of participants located at different levels of the sport organization. Insofar as participants' accounts of organizational responses to environmental disturbances are concerned, the researcher would continuously reformulate and reiterate various questions and comments to consolidate or disconfirm their degree of validity or worth. This strategy would be employed across individual accounts, within the same account, and between accounts from individuals of differing managerial positions. For example, when discussing changing management practices a research participant could be asked: "How has the need for a more professional approach to management impacted on the organization?" A response could be:

> *Well, in a general sense it has impacted generally in a positive sense as the organisation as a whole is functioning more effectively and efficiently. We now have responsibility for specific tasks allocated to either a business unit such as marketing or an individual person who*

may oversee the organisation of a function that we are putting on. In this sense we have developed accountability as well as responsibility.

At a later date, the participant could be asked: "How do you establish a system that encourages a professional approach to management?" A response may be:

What we do is make people responsible for their function. What I mean is we tell them they have a certain amount of money to achieve certain objectives and that they are responsible for meeting those objectives. By doing this we make them accountable and make them recognize that their performance will be measured against this.

The same question would also put to another management member in a slightly varied way. For example, they could be asked: "Do you think you have a professional approach to management?" A response may be:

I have to, because the buck stops with me. I am given a certain amount of money and told what I have to achieve with it. I then delegate to other units within my area and tell them what they have to achieve with it. They answer to me if they don't achieve it but ultimately if we can't meet our business unit objectives I have to explain why.

This type of approach enables the researcher to recognize and consolidate key themes and concepts. In this case, the data indicate that professional management practices were being employed. This is highlighted by multiple responses that centered on delegation of responsibility and accountability.

Second, investigator triangulation between those involved in the research process could be used to determine whether inferences drawn were consistent. That is, the researcher would discuss the inferences drawn from the data collected with their supervisors. This provides greater validity to the findings as all parties need to support the conclusions drawn. These forms of triangulation provided a means of checking consistency and congruence of the findings.

CRYSTALLIZATION

Crystallization is proposed by Richardson (2000) to replace triangulation. Crystallization refers to the process of suspending the modes of analysis process in order to reflect on the analysis experience. Richardson (2000) states:

Rather, the central imaginary is the crystal, which combines symmetry and substance with an infinite variety of shapes, substances, transmutations, multidimensionalities, and angles of approach. Crystals grow, change, alter, but not amorphous. Crystals are prisms that reflect externalities and *refract within themselves, creating different colors, patterns, and arrays, casting off in different directions. What we see depends upon our angle or repose. Not triangulation, crystallization…Crystallization without losing structure, deconstructs the traditional idea of "validity" (we feel how there is no single truth, we see how texts validate themselves), and crystallization provides us with a deepened, complex, thoroughly partial, understanding of the topic. Paradoxically, we know more and doubt what we know. Ingeniously, we know there is always more to know. (p. 934)*

Commonly associated with research that embraces a postmodern frame, an integral part of the crystallization process is "immersion", where the researchers immerse themselves in the data they have collected by either reading or examining it in detail. By suspending this immersion, the researcher can "crystallize" – reflect on the analysis and attempt to identify and articulate patterns or themes noticed during the immersion process.

COMPUTER PROGRAMS FOR QUALITATIVE MODES OF ANALYSIS

Computer Assisted Qualitative Modes of Analysis Software (CAQDAS) can assist the sport management researcher in the modes of analysis process by searching, organizing, categorizing and annotating textual and visual data. Some programs can also support theory building through the visualization of relationships between variables that have been coded in the data.

Code-based Theory building software, and the earlier Code and Retrieve packages assist the researcher in managing the analysis of qualitative data, to apply thematic coding to chunks of data, thereby enabling the reduction of data along thematic lines (retrieval), limited searching tools and probably good memoing facilities. Code-based theory building software packages build on those tools and extend the collection of search tools allowing the researcher to test relationships between issues, concepts, themes, for example to develop broader or higher order categories, or at the other extreme, to develop more detailed specific codes where certain conditions combine in the data. Some of the programs enable the graphic visualization of connections and processes using mapping tools.

Some Textbase Managers have very sophisticated "content analysis" functions; creation of keyword co-occurrence matrices across cases, creation of proximity plots for identification of related keywords, charting and graph building facilities etc. Textbase Managers tend to offer more functionality than Text Retrievers and more possibilities to manage huge datasets in varied ways. One or two of the Textbase Manager packages now incorporate "thematic" qualitative coding functions which can be integrated with the range of content analysis tools, for example, the language based quantitative functions. They offer a comprehensive range of both qualitative and quantitative approaches to data within one software package. Examples of this type of software include QDA Miner with the add-on Wordstat module, and CISAID.

The purpose of CAQDAS packages is not to provide the researcher with a particular methodological or analytical framework from which to conduct the modes of analysis process. The sport management researcher should always remain in control of the interpretive process and decide which of the available tools within software can facilitate their own approach to analysis most effectively.

There are a number of well known packages. NUD*ST (Non-numerical Unstructure Data Indexing, Searching and Theorizing) allows the researcher to import data files which can then be coded and patterns and relationships identified by the computer. NUD*ST can also be used to deal with the analysis of photographs and other visual material.

Other software packages include ATLAS.ti, HyperRESEARCH, MAXqda, N6, NVivo 2, QDAMiner, Qualrus and Transana. The software packages range in the level of sophistication, and if intending to utilize a CAQDAS package, the sport management researcher should seek a package that has the tools that suit the research style, rather than just the package that offers the greatest functionality.

There are a number of issues related to the use of computer software for qualitative modes of analysis. First, although computer analysis may allow much quicker, and seemingly more objective analysis, the process of manually "tagging" specific quotations can often be considered desirable in that it gives you a "feel" for the data, and allows increased familiarity with the transcriptions. Second, as Dey (1993) notes: "the use of a computer can encourage a "mechanistic" approach to analysis" (p. 61). In this scenario, the roles of creativity, intuition and insight into analysis are eclipsed. The research analysis may then become a routine and mechanical process (Lee & Fielding, 1996). Third, much of the tagging that is carried out by such software requires words to be specified or coded beforehand by the researcher, which, given the wide range of possible answers, will be equally time consuming. Fourth, most of the available software only identifies the sentence within which a specific word or phrase occurs, and thus often fails to locate the context. Finally, the increased time incurred by manual tagging of transcripts is offset by the time required to develop competence in an appropriate computer software package. However, CAQDAS can also assist in the management of large quantities of text generated from transcripts or field notes by systematic storage, easy refinement of codes, and rapid retrieval of data. So, while CAQDAS can provide a powerful means through which to manage and manipulate the data more efficiently (Kelle, 1995; Lee & Fielding, 1995; O'Connell & Irurita, 2000) it is important to understand that a computer program does not do the analysis and coding for the researcher, and that data analysis remains the intellectual, interpretive and creative work of the researcher (Burnard, 1994).

Some of the packages, although extremely powerful, do take some time to learn, even with specialized instruction. The sport management researcher needs to weigh up the pros and cons of taking the time to learn such a package before deciding on a particular approach. If a sport management researcher is likely to be undertaking a considerable amount of qualitative research over a reasonable period of time, then it may be worthwhile learning one of the packages. On the other hand, if the researcher is engaged in a one-off piece of research, then we would recommend manual analysis.

The final decision on using CAQDAS is left to the confidence and expertise of the researcher. If a researcher does reject the use of CAQDAS for analysis, then it should not immediately be assumed that the quality of analysis is inferior. Provided the mode of analysis is carried out correctly then there should be little difference in the quality of analysis.

Research Brief

Title: Communicatively Constructed Stakeholders Identity: A Critical Ethnography of Cleveland Browns Fan Culture
Who: Hugenberg, B., Bowling Green State University
Hugenberg utilized critical ethnography to conceptualize fans as emotional stakeholders in the Cleveland Browns football organization. She preceded from a grounded theory orientation. Texts were collected via interview, participant observation and archival records. Fans were observed in a variety of settings. Cleveland Browns fans reported a narrative "Myth" of the "Cleveland Browns Way".

CONCLUSION

This chapter has explained the principles and techniques that should underpin modes of analysis. It began by discussing the phases of modes of analysis and an appropriate framework that can be used in organizing that analysis. It identified the importance of coding and provided a detailed discussion of open, axial and selective coding approaches to analyzing data and provided an example of how this might be undertaken. Triangulation and crystallization were then discussed and an example of how triangulation could be applied in the modes of analysis phase presented. Computer Assisted Qualitative Modes of analysis Software (CAQDAS) and how it can assist the sport management researcher in the modes of analysis process was discussed.

IN PROFILE - Associate Professor Paul M. Pedersen

Paul M. Pedersen is the Director of the Sport Management Doctoral Program at Indiana University (Bloomington, Indiana [USA]). Paul received his Ph.D. from Florida State University (FSU). With his background as a sportswriter and sports business columnist, at FSU Paul pursued a doctoral concentration in sport management in a program that allowed him to specialize in the study of sport communication. As a continuation of this focus, since the beginning of his academic career his teaching, research, and service activities pertain to the field of sport management and the specific segment of sport communication. Over the years, he has attempted to follow a vigorous research agenda in which he has published over 50 refereed scholarly articles in various outlets such as the *Journal of Sport Management, Journal of Sports Economics,* and *Sociology of Sport Journal.* Paul has researched, published, and presented on the activities and practices of many sport organization personnel, specifically those associated with the print media (i.e., newspaper sports editors and reporters) and affiliated with amateur sports (i.e., athletic directors, student-athletes). He has examined such areas as the symbiotic relationship between sport and the mass media, the management (activities; followership) of and promotion (success rates) within athletics, and gender and sport. The primary strand of his research agenda analyzes the activities and individuals within the sport communication segment of the sport industry. Paul's secondary research strand involves a broader examination of the field by developing the body of knowledge in sport management. It is Paul's desire to have these interrelated and interdisciplinary research streams producing scholarship

that has an impact on the academic (i.e., trends associated with scholarly publications and positions) and practical (i.e., more equitable media coverage) dimensions of the sport industry. Although he uses a range of approaches in the pursuit of his research agenda, the methodology Paul employs in an estimated half of his research is content analysis. The content analytic method – which, for valid, reliable, and replicable work, requires a lot of planning, intercoder reliability testing, and detailed coding – is a systematic research technique that is used to examine communication. Paul has applied this research methodology to issues in sport management (i.e., academic publications, job announcements) and sport communication (i.e., written coverage, media photographs). While much of his time has been spent collecting and coding data for research articles, Paul enjoys book writing. One of his graduate degrees is in history, so historical research is also an area of scholarly pursuit for him. One of his history books, *Build it and they will come: The arrival of the Tampa Bay Devil Rays* (1998), is an analysis of the sport and urban politics. His other history book is about a football coach and is titled, *Bobby Bowden: Win by Win.* A couple of his textbooks include *Strategic Sport Communication* (2007) and the upcoming *Contemporary Sport Management* (2010). In addition to researching, writing, and teaching, being an academician also involves service. For instance, Paul's service involves such aspects as leading doctoral dissertations, founding and leading the *International Journal of Sport Communication*, and being an associate editor, assistant editor, or editorial review board member of five national and international sport journals.

REVIEW AND RESEARCH QUESTIONS

The process of modes of analysis aims to provide the sport management researcher with the opportunity to make sense of the data so that evidence can be obtained which can then be used to answer the research question. With a basic understanding now of the modes of analysis process, attempt to answer the following questions:

- What are the three types of coding, and at what stage of the coding process would they be employed?

- Identify some advantages and disadvantages to the use of CAQDAS over completely manual modes of analysis processes.

REFERENCES

Bazeley, P. 1999. The bricoleur with a computer: piecing together qualitative and quantitative data. *Qualitative Health Research*, **9** (2), 279–287.

Biddle, S. J. H., Hanrahan, S. J., Sellars, C. N., (2001) Attributions: Past, present and future. In R. N. Singer, H. A. Hausenblas, & C. M. Janelle (Eds.), Handbook of Sport Psychology, (2nd Edition), pp. 444–471 , John Wiley & Sons.

Bleicher, J. 1980. Contemporary Hermeneutics: Hermeneutics as Method, Philosophy, and Critique. London: Routledge & Kegan Paul Books.

Bogdan, R. C. & Biklen, S. K. 1982. Qualitative Research for Education: An Introduction to Theory and Methods. Toronto: Allyn and Bacon.

Burnard, P. 1994. Using a database program to handle qualitative data. *Nurse Education Today*, **14** (3), 228–231.

Burns, R. B. 1997. Introduction to Research Methods. Melbourne: Longman.

Cresswell, J. W. 1994. Research Design: Qualitative and Quantitative Approaches. Thousand Oaks, CA: Sage.

Denscombe, M. 1998. The Good Research Guide: For Small-Scale Social Research Projects. London: Open University Press.

Denzin, N. K. & Lincoln, Y. S. 1998. Strategies of Qualitative Inquiry. Thousand Oaks, CA: Sage.

Dey, I. 1993. Qualitative Data Analysis: A User- Friendly Guide for Social Scientists. London: Routledge.

Frankfort-Nachimas, C. & Nachimas, D. 1996. Research Methods in the Social Sciences. London: Arnold.

Gadamer, H. G. 1976. Philosophical Hermeneutics. Berkeley: University of California Press.

Gilmore, A. & Carson, D. 1996. 'Integrative' qualitative methods in a services context. *Marketing Intelligence and Planning*, **14** (6), 21–26.

Glaser, B. & Strauss, A. 1967. The Discovery of Grounded Theory: Strategies for Qualitative Research. New York: Aldine.

Hammersley, M. & Atkinson, P. 1983. Ethnography: Principles in Practice. London: Tavistock.

Kelle, U. (Ed.). 1995. Computer-Aided Qualitative Data Analysis. London: Sage.

Krippendorf, K. 1980. Content Analysis: An Introduction to its Methodology. Beverly Hills, CA: Sage.

Lee, R. M. & Fielding, N. 1996. Data analysis: representations of a technology: a comment on Coffey, Holbrook and Atkinson. Sociological Research Online, 1 (4). Retrieved March 10, 2008 from http://www.socresonline.org.uk/socresonline/1/4/lf.html

Lee, R. M. & Fielding, N. G. 1995. Users' experiences of qualitative data analysis software. In: *Computer-Aided Qualitative Data Analysis: Theory, Methods and Practice* (Ed. by U. Kelle). London: Sage.

Miles, M. B. & Huberman, A. M. 1994. Qualitative Data Analysis: An Expanded Sourcebook. Thousand Oaks, CA: Sage.

O'Connell, B. & Irurita, V. 2000. Facilitating the process of theory development by creating a visual data analysis trail. Graduate Research Nursing, 1 (1). Article 1. Retrieved January 7, 2008, from http://www.graduateresearch.com/oconnell.htm

Patton, M. Q. 1990. Qualitative Evaluation and Research Methods, 2nd ed. London: Sage.

Pope, C. & Mays, N. 2000. Qualitative Research in Health Care. London: Blackwell.

Radnitzky, G. 1970. Contemporary Schools of Metascience, 2nd ed. Goteborg: Akademiforlaget.

Richardson, L. 2000. Writing: a method of inquiry. In: *Handbook of Qualitative Research* (Ed. by N. K. Denzin, Y. S. Lincoln), pp. 923–948, 2nd ed. Thousand Oaks, CA: Sage.

Ricoeur, P. 1974. The Conflict of Interpretation: Essays in Hermeneutics. Evanston, IL: Northwestern University Press.

Ritchie, J. & Spencer, L. 1993. Qualitative Data Analysis for Applied Policy Research. London: Routledge.

Sarantankos, S. 1998. Social Research. Melbourne: MacMillan.

Seale, C. 1999. The Quality of Qualitative Research. London: Sage.

Silverman, D. 1993. Interpreting Qualitative Data. London: Sage.

Stake, R. 2000. Case studies. In: *Handbook of Qualitative Research* (Ed. by N. K. Denzin, Y. S. Lincoln), pp. 435–454, 2nd ed. Thousand Oaks, CA: Sage.

Strauss, A. 1987. Qualitative Analysis for Social Scientists. New York: Cambridge University Press.

Strauss, A. & Corbin, J. 1990. Basics of Qualitative Research: Grounded Theory Procedures and Techniques. Newbury Park, CA: Sage.

Taylor, C. 1990. Philosophy and the Human Sciences. Cambridge: Cambridge University Press.

Thompson, J. B. 1981. Critical Hermeneutics: A Study in the Thought of Paul Ricoeur and Juergen Habermas. Cambridge: Cambridge University Press.

Maanen, Van 1983. Qualitative Methodology. Beverly Hills, CA: Sage.

Wynn, E. 1979. *Office Conversation as an Information Medium*. Unpublished doctoral dissertation, University of California, Berkeley.

PART 5

Selecting a Sport Management Research Method

Reflection in Sport Management Research

KEY TERMS

Reflection: a process incorporating a problem setting approach and learning by doing.

Critical reflection: constructive self-criticism of one's actions with a view to improvement.

Reflective practitioner: the learner who engages in a process of experience, reflection, restructuring and planning.

Reflecting-in-action: reflection on understandings that have been implicit in action, understandings which are criticized, restructured, and embodied in further action.

Reflection-on-action: enables workers to reflect on a critical incident from their own area of practice and identify specific learning that may have occurred as a result of the experience.

Single-loop learning: occurs when an error is detected and corrected without questioning or altering the underlying values of the system.

Double-loop learning: a hermeneutic activity of understanding and interpreting social situations with a view to their improvement, requiring people to question and challenge given value positions.

KEY QUESTIONS

The key questions raised in this chapter are as follows:

- What is reflection and reflective practice and its implications for sport management research?

- What is the relationship between critical reflection and sport management research and professional practice?

CHAPTER OVERVIEW

We begin this section of the book with a discussion on reflection. We do this because each research method discussed has embedded within it the need for critical reflection. In recent years, there has been considerable interest in the notions of reflection and reflective practice in a number of professions such as nursing, education and management. Edwards (1999) in his seminal work on the application of reflective practice to sport management research and practice raised our consciousness about the need for its application to be diffused into our research methods and daily sport management practice. Following this path mapped out by Edwards, this chapter discusses the importance and need for ongoing reflective practices to be mandatory in qualitative sport management research and professional practice.

REFLECTION

Historically Dewey (1933), who himself drew on the ideas of many earlier educators such as Plato, Aristotle, Confucius, is acknowledged as a key originator in the twentieth century to the concept of reflection. His basic ideas are seminal and indicate that reflection may be seen as the "hallmark of all intelligent action". Dewey perceives it to be an active and deliberate cognitive process involving sequences of interconnected ideas which take account of underlying beliefs and knowledge (Hatton & Smith, 1995).

Skilling (1999) argues that, for Dewey, the construct of reflection emanates from a cognitive perspective, one that focuses on logical reasoning, and involves an active analysis of beliefs and actions in search of meaning. Dewey's views of reflection are extended by experiential learning theory. Experiential learning theory emphasizes the central role that reflection on experience plays in learning, reinforcing the notion that ideas are constructed and reconstructed through experience, rather than existing as fixed and unchallengeable patterns of thought.

Kolb (1984) generated a model to illustrate these links between reflection and learning. He used the concept of the learning loop to develop a four-stage experiential learning model which includes (1) experience, (2) reflection, (3) generalizing or theorizing, and (4) planning. Kolb argues that ideal experiential learners are able to involve themselves in new experiences without bias, reflect upon experiences from multiple perspectives, integrate their observations into logically sound theories, and use these theories in problem solving. Kolb's theory says little about reflective observation and abstract conceptualization beyond defining them and positioning them within the learning cycle.

REFLECTIVE PRACTICE

Schön (1983 and 1987) extends the notions of reflection by rejecting the view that theory and practice should be viewed separately. Developing the term the *"reflective practitioner"*, Schön (1983), like Kolb, contends that the learner is engaging in a process of experience, reflection, restructuring and planning. Schön advances the notion of reflection by distinguishing between *reflection-in-action* and *reflection-on-action*.

Reflection-in-action

When reflecting-in-action, there is some puzzling phenomenon with which the individual is trying to deal. As they try to make sense of it, they also reflect on the understandings that have been implicit in action, understandings which "criticizes, restructures, and embodies in further action" (Schön, 1983, p. 5). Schon's "reflection-in-action" is also highly dependent on context. Matthews and Jessel (1998) argue that as a result:

> …*"reflection" becomes the process whereby such knowledge can be made more explicit so that it can be applied with some measure of control in the midst of an activity. This form of reflection may be achieved through framing likely contexts within which particular aspects of practice can be problematised and attended to and represented at a more conscious level, or "named". (p. 1)*

One group of professionals Schön studied are *managers*. Their reflection-in-action is basically similar to reflection-in-action in other professionals, but it also has special features of its own. This approach has particular relevance to sport managers. The phenomena on which managers reflect-in-action are the phenomena of organizational life. The manager draws on an existing body of organizational knowledge (i.e. notions of mission and identity, facts about the task environment), adapting it to some present concern. The manager also serves as an agent of organizational learning, modifying in his present inquiry the body of knowledge that will be available for future inquiry by the organization. Additionally, within an organization the manager operates in a unique "learning system" which may promote or inhibit reflection-in-action.

Schön's (1983) work represents a move away from strict theory toward a marrying of theory and practice, a move away from a hierarchical to a more equal relationship. It has also influenced the work of other researchers including Usher and Bryant (1987), who argue that Schön's idea of reflection-in-action can generate its own theory. The theory comes from being in a situation and shaping it through action selected from the results of reflection where "knowledge emerges dynamically from the dialectical interchange between the subject and his action in practice situations" (p. 206). As such, Usher and Bryant argue that:

> *the possibility therefore exists of a practice-derived knowledge, which is both experiential and rigorous. It can be seen as an alternative way to integrating theory and practice. Theory need not be abstract and remote from practice and the latter need not be intuitive and unsystematic. (p. 206)*

This implies that there is more than one kind of knowledge. Usher and Bryant (1987) argue that there are three kinds of knowledge: (1) *theoretical knowledge*, (2) *technical knowledge/knowhow* and (3) *practical knowledge/knowledge* of how to act appropriately in the world – but that practical knowledge is the most appropriate in a professional context. This is because practical knowledge always exists in a situation or context, its purpose to generate "informed and committed action" (p. 75), and it has an ethical dimension. The ethical dimension is of particular relevance to sport management research given the need for sports managers to consider clients and other interest groups, for Usher and Bryant argues:

> *practical knowledge, since it is concerned with appropriate action in the world, must consider "right" action. It is a kind of knowledge, which must inevitably take account of others, since those others are part of the situation. (p. 76)*

Usher and Bryant (1987) conclude that emphasizing practical knowledge bears both context and the practitioner's formalization of knowledge (through reflection). The implications for the professional status of the practitioner are important for Usher and Bryant claims that the practitioner will be seen as possessing wisdom, judgment and knowledge rather than merely being a technician. The ideas of Schön (1983) and Usher and Bryant (1987) have the potential to:

- Break down the dichotomy between theory and practice.

- Raise the status of practical knowledge.

- Draw on the experience of practitioners.

- Provide a model for the consideration of ethical considerations.

- Encourage a more reflective approach.

Freire (1972), Habermas (1973) and Mezirow (1978) had all been writing about reflection before Schön's work was published. Freire for instance, discussed the relationship between reflection and action and argued that congruences between the two are a form of praxis and there are certain similarities here to Argyris' (1976) and Schön's (1983) espoused theory and theory in use. Habermas had explored reflection in a variety of forms in his *"Knowledge and Human Interests"* in which he argues that self-reflection is a form of science, and here he combined critical sociology with Freudian analyses. Mezirow was influenced by Habermas and he produced a typology of reflection with seven different levels. Yet it was Schön's book, focusing as it does on the profession and professional practice which attracted most attention.

Reflection-on-action

Reflection-on-action enables researchers to reflect on a critical incident from their own area of practice and identify specific learning that may have occurred as a result of the experience. Reflection-on-action requires researchers to use what they had learned from the past situation in their current practice, enabling them to examine practice from a learning perspective. Argyris (1993) contributes to the discussion by differentiating between single-loop learning and double-loop learning. Single-loop learning, Argyris argues, occurs when "an error is detected and corrected without questioning or altering the underlying values of the system" (p. 9). Double-loop learning is a hermeneutic activity of understanding and interpreting social situations with a view to their improvement, requiring people to question and challenge given value positions (Cohen et al., 2000). Jolly (1999) argues that, whereas double-loop learning (correcting errors by firstly examining and altering the governing variables and then the actions) is necessary as a first step to a true improvement of practice, rather than just local adjustment (e.g., with engineers, their focus on technical skills), it ignores difficulties experienced in establishing group work or an inability to seek help with problems. Jolly builds on Cowan (1997) who extends Schön's work by embracing a third reflective loop: *reflection-for-action*.

Reflection-for-action

Reflection-for-action is anticipative: here the learner defines their aspirations and establishes priorities for subsequent learning (Jolly, 1999). Boud (1992) and Greenwood (1998) identify the importance of *reflection-for-action*, thinking through what one wants to do and how one intends to do it before one actually does it. "To fail to reflect before action may lead to error, in addition, and related to this, it allows an important opportunity for feedback to go begging" (Greenwood, 1998, p. 2).

REFLEXIVITY

Cowan (1997) by making explicit the notion of self-awareness, explicitly links reflective practice to *reflexivity* – intersections which are also often blurred and problematic. Jolly (1999) argues that Schön tends to use the terms "reflection" and "reflexive thinking" interchangeably. The idea of *"reflexive practice"*, as used by Schön (1987), relates to a tacit form of "knowledge-in-action" developed by skilled practitioners. Darling (1998) argues that reflection is related to self and improving future practice, whereas reflexivity is a pro-active tool to improve communication and provide insight, simultaneously, into priorities prior to reaction (cited in Jolly, 1999). Other writers integrate self-awareness into their perspectives of reflexivity by incorporating the Latin-derived dictionary definition: to turn back on oneself (Bourdieu & Wacquant, 1992).

Matthews and Jessel (1998), in their analysis of reflexive practice, contend that:

> … *we have to try to be self-aware in order to extend and further our understanding of situations … reflexivity is a resource to help us reveal our assumptions and their power constituents. Reflexivity can enable a better understanding of situations through a better understanding of ourselves, even though those understanding always contain a "fiction" or "story" … These understandings include experiences that relate to one's own self, beliefs, values, attitudes, assumptions, fears – those experiences that relate more centrally to the self than those which are relatively peripheral and relate to external things. (p. 1)*

Jolly (1999) argues that reflexivity can therefore be seen as the application of the fruits of reflection, and a higher-order skill. Jolly develops a model where the core from which reflection emanates and to which it returns in a never-ending loop. Reflection is now a tool in the continuous construction of reflexivity, with reflexivity a way of relating to the world and a basis for understanding and responding to experience.

CRITICAL THEORY AND REFLECTION

This increasing interest in reflection has been predominantly influenced by critical theory. Critical theory refers to a body of work that derives from the Frankfurt school, a body of work grounded in the critique of dominant ideologies. Critical theory seeks to look into what is promoted as the status quo of various social contexts, to discover and expose the forces that maintain them for their particular advantages. As human social constructions, knowledge and social existence emerge out of identifiable human interests that serve certain purposes, which may be seen as immutable and inevitable, thereby maintaining as unquestioned the advantages of the powerful elite they favor.

The promises of critical theory that are either implied or made explicit in the reflective practitioner processes, relate to the nature of critical theory as a philosophical position and as a process of theorizing. There is a liberatory intent in using radical critiques to transform the existing restrictive social order and conditions within the status quo into those that are based and enacted on the principles of equality, freedom and justice. The emancipatory critique of critical theory relies on systematic reflection and promises freedom from the distorted understandings, communication and activities of pre-existing social structures thereby providing possibilities for new ways of being and acting within them.

CRITICAL REFLECTION

Hatton and Smith (1995) argue that a key issue in regard to reflection is concerned with how consciously the one reflecting takes account of the wider historic, cultural and political values and beliefs in framing and reframing practical problems to which solutions are being sought – a process they identify as *"critical reflection"*.

Critical reflection, however, is also a term that is used loosely. For some, critical reflection can mean no more than constructive self-criticism of one's actions with a view to improvement (see Calderhead, 1989). Whereas for others (see McNamara, 1990), critical reflection implies considerations involving moral and ethical criteria, making judgments about whether professional activity is equitable, just and respectful of persons or not, as well as locating any analysis of personal action within wider socio-historical and politico-cultural contexts (Hatton & Smith, 1995). Boud and Walker's (1998) view, meanwhile, is that critical reflection accepts normal practice as being problematic.

Boud and Walker (1998) argue that any view of context in critical reflection must take account of the considerable theoretical contributions of critical social science, post-structuralism and post-modernism which have drawn attention to the ways in which our constructions of what we accept as reality are constituted, revealing features which are taken for granted and are normally invisible on a day-to-day basis. These features have a profound influence over who we are, what and how we think and what we regard as legitimate knowledge.

Boud and Walker (1998) also contend that this broader social, political and cultural context influences every aspect of learning, including reflective learning. Boud and Walker's view is, then, that critical reflection involves both a critical self-awareness and a critical awareness of context (or, in other words, discourse). These are concepts whose meanings are often blurred, intersecting and overlapping.

CRITICAL SELF-AWARENESS

Some researchers, including Skilling (1999), Jolly (1999) and Boud and Walker (1998) assume that reflexivity incorporates *critical self-awareness*. This understanding generates questions relating to the social and critical contexts involved in the processes of reflection and reflective practice. Matthews and Jessel (1998) argue for a social and intellectual unconscious and consciousness that needs to be examined, whereas Skilling (1999) and Boud and Walker (1998) discuss the need for critical self-reflection and Jolly (1999) identifies the critical component of his reflexive practice.

Critical self-awareness allows the dominant views within sport management to be expanded to encompass broader perspectives and differing ways of knowing. Being critical about the doctrines that dominate the field does not mean we reject all existing doctrines. It simply means that we remain open to other perspectives, theories, and concepts. Critical self-awareness requires a continued attention to the place from which we speak (Kelly, 2003) – as well as the need to make visible to ourselves who we are and what we are doing.

DIMENSIONS OF REFLECTION

Three aspects of reflection are apparent when the various current thoughts on it are taken as a whole. These aspects can be thought of as three dimensions: These include a dimension of (1) *time*, (2) *depth*, and (3) *orientation*. *Time* refers to when in relation to an experience reflection occurs. It can occur *antecedent to, concurrent with*, or *subsequent* to an experience. An example of reflection before or antecedent to an experience is Kolb's (1984) abstract conceptualization. Schön's (1983) reflection-in action illustrates reflection during or concurrent with experience. Both Mezirow's (1991) critical reflection and Kolb's reflective observation are instances of reflection that happens after or subsequent to an experience. These theorists all believe implicitly at least that timing of reflective activity is an important aspect of the process of reflection.

The second dimension, *depth*, refers to the level at which reflective inquiry transpires. Three different levels are evident here: *surface*, *subsurface*, and *core. Surface reflection* is reflection aimed at understanding the basic meaning of an experience, as in Kolb's (1984) reflective observation and Mezirow's (1991) content reflection. *Subsurface reflection* is that which penetrates below the surface to expose underlying assumptions and beliefs. Finally, *core reflection* not only surfaces underlying assumptions but subjects them to critical reassessment as well. Mezirow's critical reflection illustrates reflection at this level. Some theorists' conceptions of reflection comprise multiple levels, as Schön's reflection-in-action does (reflection-in-action can happen at all three levels). The distinction between different degrees of depth of reflection is apparent in current writing on reflection.

A third dimension apparent in thinking about reflection is its *orientation*. Orientation has to do with that which reflection is directed toward. Following Kegan's (1982) theory of human development, the two directions apparent in current theory can be called *object* (that which is other than the self) and *subject* (the self). Most discussions of reflection deal with "objects". This involves reflecting on problems to be solved, tasks to be mastered, people to be understood and so on. This type of reflection is apparent in everyone who writes about reflection. Significantly less common is reflection directed at "subject" or the self. Marsick's (1988) reflectively for self-understanding is illustrative of this aspect of reflection. Subsurface and core reflection may or may not be directed at the self.

Reflective practice processes

The discussion of these three dimensions indicates the way in which reflection is currently viewed. Roth (1989) provides a comprehensive summary of the reflective practice processes as highlighted in Table 7.1.

RATIONALE FOR REFLECTION IN RESEARCH

The research methods used to investigate a given phenomenon should be chosen based upon the nature of the phenomenon and the extent of existing knowledge about it.

Complex indeterminate context-bound social phenomena like reflection are best studied using what has been called "inquiry from the inside" (Evered & Louis, 1981), "direct research" (Mintzberg, 1979), or "naturalistic inquiry" (Marsick, 1991), or ethnographic research. In contrast to the

Table 7.1	A Summary of the Reflective Practice Processes
1.	Question what, why, and how one does things: ask what, why and how others do things
2.	Seek alternatives
3.	Keep an open mind
4.	Suspend judgment, wait for sufficient data, or self-validate
5.	Compare and contrast
6.	Seek the framework, theoretical basis, underlying rationale (of behaviors, methods, techniques, programs)
7.	View from various perspectives
8.	Identify and test assumptions (theirs and others, seek conflicting evidence)
9.	Put into different/varied contexts
10.	Ask "what if …?
11.	Ask for others' ideas and viewpoints
12.	Adapt and adjust to instability and change
13.	Function within uncertainty, complexity and variety
14.	Hypothesize
15.	Consider consequences
16.	Validate what is given or believed
17.	Synthesize and test
18.	Seek, identify and resolve problems ("problem setting", "problem solving")
19.	Initiate after thinking through (alternatives, consequences) or putting into context
20.	Analyze – what makes it work: in what context would it not?
21.	Evaluate – what worked, what didn't, and why?
22.	Use prescriptive models (behavioral models, protocols) only when adapted to the situation
23.	Make decisions in practice of the profession (knowledge created in use)

Sourced from Roth (1989, p. 32)

positivistic approach, which has historically characterized research of sport management development these approaches share the belief that organizational research should take a more involved, flexible, open minded and contextually aware stance. Because qualitative methods are ideally suited to realizing such a stance they are recommended for reflection. In addition to being useful for studying complex indeterminate phenomena in context, qualitative methods represent the most effective way to explore the social world from the perspective of the actors in that world.

Context of research methodology

The notion of *reflexivity*, in the context of research methodology, is clearly delineated. In research methodology, the term reflexivity identifies that researchers are inescapably part of the social world they are researching and that this social world is an already interpreted world by the actors: that they are both in the world and of the world (Cohen et al., 2000). In research methodology, the term reflexivity also suggests that researchers should acknowledge and disclose their own selves in the research:

> *... they should hold themselves up to the light, reflecting the understandings that they are acutely aware of the ways in which their selectivity, perception, background and inductive processes and paradigms shape their research as well as their obligations to monitor closely and continually their own interactions with participants, their own reaction, roles and biases. (p. 140)*

Reflexivity also underpins many of the research approaches such as action research, deconstruction, discourse analysis, ethnography and phenomenology which will be discussed in subsequent chapters.

REFLECTIVE RESEARCH IN SPORT MANAGEMENT

Reflective sport management research which draws upon the range of approaches outlined in this book has the potential to make significant contributions to practice. The purpose of research on reflection in sport management should be to build theory rather than prove theory. Given that what is proposed is exploratory theory-building research the research questions should be intentionally open-ended.

Drawing upon the critical theory approach that Smyth (1991) proposed there are a number of key principles that should underpin research utilizing reflection in sport management inquiry. Based upon his approach we see:

1. Reflection is founded on the belief that technical (knowledge) aspects of (sport management) practice is in a tentative and incomplete state. For example, the theory of sport management could all be described as technical knowledge. Reflection on this form of technical knowledge may lead to new knowledge.

2. Reflection is fundamentally about the practical aspects of practice. This practical knowledge is the "lifeworld" of sport management. This includes the complex array of routines, rituals, roles and rules that make up the everyday experience of sport management practice.

3. Reflection occurs best when it begins with the "lived experiences" of practitioners as they are assisted in the process of describing, informing, confronting and reconstructing their theories of practice.

4. Reflection is a process that is centrally concerned with challenging the dominant hegemonic beliefs and an ideology implicit in the way sport management is currently organized. Reflection in this way allows power and knowledge domains in sport management discourse to be available for scrutiny.

5. Reflection should not be restricted to practitioners reflecting individually upon their practice; there needs to be collective and collaborative dimensions to it as well. The outcome for such reflection is for professionals to draw upon the vast array of collective knowledge to exercise professional judgment as they act individually.

6. Reflection should not be restricted to examining only technical knowledge. It should also be possible to critically reflect upon the social, political and economic context of sport management practice.

CONCLUSION

This chapter has highlighted that reflection has come to be recognized as a core element of professional expertise. Reflection can refer to the ability to analyze one's own practice, the incorporation of problem solving into learning by doing, or the application of critical theory to the examination of professional practice. It has argued that reflection should be a key component of most qualitative research approaches.

IN PROFILE - Dr Allan Edwards

Dr Allan Edwards is a Faculty member at the University of Ulster, Belfast. His personal research interests lie in the areas of reflective practice, social capital, sport governance and research methods in Sport Management. Throughout his academic career, Edwards has championed the use of qualitative methodologies in the field of sport management. In his research, he has utilized a wide range of qualitative methodologies such as discourse analysis, critical ethnography, action research, narrative and deconstruction.

Almost a decade ago, his work on *Reflection in Sport Management* (1999) provided a challenge for sport managers to become reflective practitioners. More recently, he has pointed to the importance of reflection in the qualitative research process. Edwards believes that qualitative research allows researchers to explore the 'lived world' of sport management praxis and has challenged researchers to embrace a range of qualitative research methods to generate new theory in the field.

REVIEW AND RESEARCH QUESTIONS

1. The literature on the reflective practice often traces the roots of those ideas to the work of Schön (1983), although other commentators (i.e. Habermas, 1973; Kolb, 1984) have influenced its development. Identify how each author defines reflection and discuss its implications for sport management research and practice.

2. Reflective practice has the potential to bridge the theory-practice divide. Discuss this statement.

REFERENCES

Argyris, C. 1976. Theories of action that inhibit individual learning. *American Psychologist*, **September**, 638–654.

Argyris, C. 1993. Knowledge for Action. San Francisco: Jossy-Bass.

Boud, D. 1992. In the midst of experience: developing a model to aid learners and facilitators. In: *Striking a Balance* (Ed. by R. Harris, P. Willis). SA: Centre for Human Research Studies, University of South Australia.

Boud, D. & Walker, D. 1998. Promoting reflection in professional courses: *the challenge of context studies in Higher Education*, **23** (2), 191–206.

Bourdieu, P. & Wacquant, L. J. D. 1992. An Invitation to Reflexive Sociology. Chicago: University of Chicago Press.

Calderhead, J. 1989. Reflective teaching and teaching education. *Teaching and Teaching Education*, **5**, 43–51.

Cohen, L., Manion, L. & Morrison, K. 2000. Research Methods in Education, 5th ed. London: Routledge Falmer.

Cowan, J. 1997, June. Teaching science for tertiary students II: learning how to think like an engineer. Paper presented at the Stockholm Pre-conference Workshop.

Darling, I. (1998). Action evaluation and action theory: an assessment of the process and its connection to conflict resolution. pp. 1–6. The on-line conference on "The reflective practitioner." Dedicated to Donald Schön on ACTLIST. 1st of March to 3rd of April 1998.

Dewey, J. 1933. How We Think. New York: D.C. Heath.

Edwards, A. 1999. Reflective practice in sport management. *Sport Management Review*, **2** (1), 67–81.

Evered, R. & Louis, M. R. 1981. Alternative perspectives in the organizational sciences: inquiry from the inside and inquiry from the outside. *Academy of Management Review*, **6** (3), 385–395.

Freire, P. 1972. Pedagogy of the Oppressed. Harmondsworth, UK: Penguin.

Greenwood, J. 1998. The role of reflection in single and double loop learning. *Journal of Advanced Nursing*, **27**, 1048–1053.

Habermas, J. 1973. Knowledge and Human Interests, 2nd ed. London: Heinemann.

Hatton, N. & Smith, D. 1995. Facilitating reflection: issues and research. *Forum of Education*, **50** (1), 49–65.

Jolly, L. 1999, November. Challenging hegemony: reflections on reflection. Paper presented at the Teaching and Educational Development Institute (TEDI) Conference, Brisbane, Australia.

Kegan, R. 1982. The Evolving Self: Problem and Process in Human Development. Cambridge, MA: Harvard University Press.

Kelly, J. G. 2003. Science and community psychology: social norms for pluralistic inquiry. *American Journal of Community Psychology*, **31**, 213–217.

Kolb, D. A. 1984. Experiential Learning: Experience as a Source of Learning and Development. Englewood Cliffs. NJ: Prentice-Hall.

Marsick, V. J. 1988. Learning in the workplace: the case for reflectivity and critical reflectivity. *Adult Education Quarterly*, **38** (4), 187–198.

Marsick, V. J. 1991. Action learning and reflection in the workplace. In: *Fostering Critical Reflection in Adult-hood* (Ed. by J. Mizirow), pp. 23–46. San Francisco: Jossey-Bass.

Matthews, B. & Jessel, J. 1998. Reflective and Reflexive Practice in Initial Teacher Education: A Critical Case Study. London: Routledge.

McNamara, D. 1990. Research of teachers thinking: its contribution to educating student teachers to think critically. *Journal of Education for Teaching*, **16**, 147–160.

Mezirow, J. 1978. Educating for Perspective Transformation. New York: Colombia Teachers College.

Mezirow, J. 1991. Transformation Dimensions in Adult Learning. San Francisco: Jossey-Bass.

Mintzberg, H. 1979. An emerging strategy of direct research. *Administrative Science Quarterly*, **24**, 580–589.

Roth, R. 1989. Preparing the reflective practitioner: transforming an apprentice through dialectic. *Journal of Teacher Education*, **40** (2), 31–38.

Schön, D. A. 1983. The Reflective Practitioner: How Professionals Think in Action. New York: Basic Books.

Schön, D. A. 1987. Educating the Reflective Practitioner: Toward a New Design for Teaching and Learning in the Professions. San Francisco: Jossey-Bass.

Skilling, K. (1999). It's time to reflect on the benefits of reflective practice. Primary Educator, 7.

Smyth, J. 1991. Teachers as Collaborative Learners. Philadelphia: Open University Press.

Usher, R. S. & Bryant, I. 1987. Re-examining the theory–practice relationship in continuing professional education. *Studies in Higher Education*, **12** (2), 201–212.

CHAPTER 8

Action Research and Sport Management Research

OBJECTIVES

By the end of this chapter, you should be able to

- understand the basic concepts of Action Research

- identify different types of Action Research

- identify some practical methods associated with Action Research which can be applied to Sport Management

- consider some ethical challenges associated with Action Research

KEY TERMS

Action research cycle: The steps of Plan, Act, Observe and Reflect.

Emancipatory action research: a participatory, democratic process concerned with developing practical knowing in pursuit of worthwhile human purposes grounded in a participatory worldview. It seeks to bring together action and reflection, theory and practice, in participation with others, in pursuit of practical solutions to issues of pressing concern to people, and more generally, the flourishing of persons and their communities

Participatory action research: a type of action research that involves the participation of those who may be affected by the outcomes of research in decision-making in all stages of the research process. It is often used for liberationist inquiry or development research with disadvantaged communities

KEY QUESTIONS

The key questions raised in this chapter are as follows:

- What is "Action Research"?

- Which differing approaches to Action Research are most suited for application in the field of sport management research?

CHAPTER OVERVIEW

This chapter explores the various methodologies of Action Research, particularly Emancipatory and Participatory Action Research, both of which have features that make them applicable to the field of sport management research. Action Research in general is cyclic in nature, with the researcher working from within the organization to plan, act, observe, reflect and plan again based on the outcome of the first cycle. This chapter will provide some methods from which the sport management researcher can start the process of Action Research within a sport management organization.

INTRODUCTION

Action research is a generic term that covers many forms of action-oriented research. The array of approaches indicates diversity in theory and practice among action researchers and provides a wide choice as to what might be appropriate. Despite this diversity in approaches, there are common elements described by most action researchers.

Action research is usually described as cyclic, with action and critical reflection taking place in turn. In the cycle of "plan, act, observe and reflect" of action research, reflection is a key theoretical component. Reflection is used to review the previous action and plan the next one. The core steps have been articulated differently by different authors, such as Stringer's (1996) steps of looking at the situation, thinking about what is required and then taking action. Alternatively, the cycle popularized by Kemmis and McTaggart (1988) involves a spiral of cycles of:

- planning a change
- acting and observing the process and consequences of the change
- reflecting of these processes and consequences
- replanning
- acting and observing
- reflecting

The basic tenet in action research is that the social world can only be understood by trying to change it (McTaggart, 2002). As a result, the role of the scholar in action research contrasts with the roles of scholars in other forms of research because of the commitment to bring about change as part of the research act.

According to Carr and Kemmis (1986), the aims of action research relate to improvement and involvement. Involvement refers to the participation of practitioners in all phases of the action research cycle. Improvement refers to the situation in which a particular social practice takes place, the understanding practitioners have of their practice, the practice itself, or all of these. Reason and Bradbury (2001) claim that the primary purpose of action research is to liberate the human body and mind in the search for a better world. Several authors state that action research is a way of producing practical results for the people involved and is a knowledge-generation process that produces insights for both the participants and the researcher (Greenwood & Levin, 1998). According to Heron and Reason (1997) action research is similar to constructivist research methods, but it adds the important ontological components of co-operation and experiential knowing, affirming "the primary value of practical knowing in the service of human flourishing" (p. 274). This framework acknowledges self-reflection as part of a participatory worldview (Heron & Reason, 1997). These authors go on to state that "to experience anything is to participate in it, and to participate is both to mold and encounter; hence, experiential reality is always subjective-objective" (p. 278). Understanding this allows for appreciation of the lived experience and insights of all research participants or stakeholders of a system.

ORIGINS OF ACTION RESEARCH

The origins of action research can be traced to two independent sources, John Collier and Kurt Lewin (Reason & Bradbury, 2001). John Collier was commissioner of Indian Affairs from 1933 to 1945 and had the role of developing programs to improve race relations. He used the term "action research" to describe his collaborative method of researching important practical problems in order to be able to take effective action (French & Bell, 1990). Some authors attribute the origins of action research solely to the German social psychologist Kurt Lewin who used the term in the mid-1940s (Reason & Bradbury, 2001; Schwandt, 1997). His idea was that researchers would enter a situation, attempt change and monitor the results. Lewin's contribution to change in the workplace began shortly after World War 1 when at Harwood Manufacturing Company he helped to explore ways to enhance productivity by using action research methods in which workers participated in experimental changes in methods.

To Lewin (1948), action research was:

comparative research on the conditions and effects of various forms of social action and research leading to social action … (it is) a big spiral of steps, each of which is composed of a circle of planning, action and fact-finding about the result of the action. (p. 202)

When Lewin died in 1947, his action research theory was still being developed. Many people have contributed to the body of knowledge on action research. Some action researchers have emphasized experimentation, others have been concerned with feedback, planning, or learning and theory building. For example, the staff at the Tavistock Institute of Human Relations emphasized collaborative problem solving and joint learning. Lewin and his associates at the Center for Group Dynamics were more concerned with theory building and experimentation (Cunningham, 1993; Lewin, 1952a).

Kemmis (1995) continued to build on the action research approach and further identified five features of action research. These were as follows:

1. Action research is a social process: It deliberately explores the relationship between the realms of the individual and the social. It recognizes that "no individuation is possible without socialization, and no socialization is possible without individuation" (Habermas, 1972, p. 26).

2. Action research is participatory: It engages people in examining their knowledge (understandings, skills and values) and interpretive categories (the ways they interpret themselves and their action in the social and material world).

3. Action research is practical and collaborative: It engages people in examining the acts that link them with others in social interaction.

4. Action research is emancipatory: It aims to help people recover an awareness of and release themselves from the constraints of irrational, unproductive, unjust, and unsatisfying social structures which limit their self-development and self-determination.

5. Action research is critical: It aims to help people recover an awareness of and release themselves from the constraints embedded in the social media through which they interact. Their language (discourses), their modes of work, and the social relationships of power (in which they experience affiliation and difference, inclusion and exclusion – relationships in which, grammatically speaking, they interact with others in the first or second or third person).

Whilst there are a number of different recognized forms of Action Research, including Practical and Technical, Emancipatory and Participatory are two varieties of Action Research that have particular relevance and applicability to the field of sport management.

MODELS OF ACTION RESEARCH

There are a variety of commonly used models of action research which demonstrate both the diversity and the common elements of the approaches. Most models in the action research literature consist of anywhere from five to 14 steps (Barker & Barker, 1994; Cunningham, 1993; Greenwood & Levin, 1998; McTaggart, 2002; Lewin, 1948; Sapin & Wafters, 1990; Webb, 1989).

While the full range of action research models cannot be discussed in detail here, those developed by Lewin (1948), Greenwood and Levin (1998) and Gummesson (2000) are frequently referenced and provide representative examples of different approaches.

Lewin's original action research model consisted of the steps of planning, fact-finding and execution (Lewin, 1946, 1952b). One feature of the Lewinian approach is that the participants under investigation are to be involved in every stage of the action research cycle (Kemmis, 1988).

Greenwood and Levin (1998) highlight the diversity and complexity of the intellectual and political streams that feed into the different action research models and the different approaches to practice. They emphasize that there is no one right way to do action research and claim that what defines action research is the combination of research, action and democratization rather than adherence to a particular methodology (Greenwood & Levin, 1998). They observe that action research has five core characteristics: Firstly, action research is context bound and addresses real-life problems. Secondly, action research is inquiry where participants and researchers co-generate knowledge through collaborative communicative processes in which all participants' contributions are taken seriously. Thirdly, action research treats the diversity of experience and capacities within the local group as an opportunity for the enrichment of the research-action process. Fourthly, the meanings constructed in the inquiry process lead to social action and reflections on action lead to the construction of new meanings. Finally, the credibility validity of action research knowledge is measured according to whether actions that arise from it solve problems and increase participants' control over their situation.

Greenwood and Levin (1998) and Gummesson (2000) share similar views regarding the aims and values of action research. Gummesson prefers to use the term "action science" (Argyris, 1985), recognizing that the term "action research" has been inappropriately used at times to describe activities that do not demonstrate the core components of action research.

Gummesson (2000) is one of the few authors who refers to action research as being the most demanding and far-reaching method of doing case study research. He suggests that action science always involves two goals: to solve a problem for the participants and to contribute to science. During an action science project those involved – the researcher/consultant and client personnel – should learn from each other and develop their competencies. Gummesson notes that action science requires co-operation between the researcher and the client personnel, feedback to the parties involved, and continuous adjustment to new information and new events. Another characteristic of action science, according to Gummesson (2000), is that it is primarily applicable to the understanding and planning of change in social systems. He also maintains that there must be a mutually acceptable ethical framework within which action science is used.

An alternative model of action research is provided by Dick (2000a) who prefers the simple approach of action, critical reflection, action, critical reflection. For Dick (1993), there are two versions of action research: (1) action is the primary focus and research is a by-product; (2) research is the primary focus. Within both versions the researcher or consultant is employed by a client (a person or organization) to conduct research to change a problematic situation. The problem situation, the methodology, and goals are usually defined by the client or the researcher. The researcher conducts the interpretation of the data. Within both versions, the role of the researcher is that of a "change agent". For Dick convergent interviewing involves a cyclic nature, enables an ongoing interpretation of the data being collected.

More interviews are conducted until a clear picture has emerged. Within this cyclic process two kinds of patterns are sought: (1) "patterns of convergence or agreement"; (2) patterns of "discrepancy and disagreement". It is these patterns that help define the questions and the directions for each interview, and provide the researcher with "objective methods" for "refining subjective data".

EMANCIPATORY ACTION RESEARCH

Emancipatory action research, according to MacTaggart (1991), could be defined in two ways: First, as "[involving] a group of practitioners accepting responsibility for its "own emancipation" from the dictates of irrationality, injustice, alienation and unfulfillment". Second, as "the activity of a self-leading group aimed at developing new practices and/or changing the constraints with a shared radical consciousness" (p. 30).

According to MacTaggart (1991), emancipatory action research extends beyond the interpretation of meanings for participants to an understanding of the social, political, and economic conditions which allow meanings to be as they are. In terms of knowledge and human interests, emancipatory action research is clearly aimed at criticism and liberation through a process of critical reflection. The human interest served by such practices is that of "collective emancipation" (p. 30).

The main points of emancipatory action research, according to Carr and Kemmis (1986), that are of equal importance include:

- bridging the gap between theory and practice

- the epistemological understanding that the practitioners possess valid knowledge

- participation and equality of those involved within the situation

- practitioners critically reflecting on their own practices

- the empowerment of the practitioners

- democratically chosen actions are implemented

- communication, which implies dialogs between participants

- a cyclic process of planning, action, observation and reflection. (p. 17)

The methodology is chosen and implemented by the practitioners themselves, which implies it is situation specific. Thus, emancipatory action research is more than simple radical critique – it demands action.

Emancipatory action research in sport management relies on the equality of participants and democratically chosen outcomes. Meeting these ideals on a small scale may be possible; however, this may be more problematic on a larger scale within the sphere of social enquiry. Carr and Kemmis (1986) have contributed to the view that limits action research to a "narrow model of method" by not emphasizing the applicability of action research to a "large scale level".

Further, the process of critical self-reflection implies that the practitioner can move outside the ideologies and institutions and not have their reflection distorted by ideologies and institutions. However, the practitioner will, like the practices, not operate within a vacuum; hence it is unlikely that all the self-reflection will be free from ideological influences (MacTaggart, 1991).

Within the sphere of sport management emancipatory action research can serve the practitioners as an alternative to traditional methods of research and aid sport managers with improving their practices. This discussion will be taken up later in the chapter.

PARTICIPATORY ACTION RESEARCH

Participatory Action Research (PAR) had its beginnings in the 1950s in America; however it was not really taken seriously until the 1980s (Whyte, 1991). In PAR practitioners are co-researchers throughout; there is no external imposition of change. It is for this reason that PAR is credited with democratizing (van Manen, 1990) or proletarianizing science, that is, eschewing the traditional elitist view of research and researchers by providing practitioners with opportunities and tools to research and thereby improve their own practices. In addition, the very nature of PAR enables and encourages their development and continuous learning throughout the change process (Tripp, 1993).

To begin with, because they are involved in the research cycle from the outset practitioners' decision-making skills should be enhanced. Their involvement in diagnosis strategy development and implementation and ongoing evaluation should furnish them with decision-making opportunities. In addition, because problem diagnosis and strategy development is collaboratively agreed the interpersonal skills of practitioners should also be enhanced.

PAR seems to encompass facets of technical, practical and emancipatory action research. That is, first, it is usually defined as being participatory, yet the degree of participation and equality are not set. Second, there is usually a degree of facilitation, and third, the problem may be defined by the researcher (MacTaggart, 1989). Huang and Wang (2005) state that "participatory action research focuses on the development of knowledge through partnership and empowerment between the researcher and the community, and the creation of critical consciousness leading to necessary action and effective change" (p. 13). They also note that there has been a change in research methods, moving to more participatory approaches that value the input and experiences of everyone affected by and included within the organization.

REFLECTIVE PRACTICE AND ACTION RESEARCH

The action research models mentioned above include reflection as a step in the process. Reflective practice has developed as a specialty area of its own with its own body of knowledge and is not always associated with action research. Coghlan and Coghlan (2002) claims that it is the dynamics of the reflection cycle in action research that incorporates the learning process and enables action research to be more than everyday problem solving. The goal of reflection in action research is to create the possibility of new action, now informed by these insights and potentially transformed by the questioning of one's own assumptions and intentions (Watkins, 2000).

The stage of critical reflection in action research focuses on both the outcomes and process (Swepson, 1995). The reflection looks for both confirming and disconfirming evidence (Dick, 1999; Swepson, 1995) and for agreements and disagreements which need to be tested and explained. Dick (2000b) suggests that critical reflection underpins both action and understanding in action research by asking "what" questions and "why" questions. He comments that critical reflection that follows action and precedes planning identifies what has been learned from prior actions and can reinforce understanding.

CREDIBILITY AND RIGOR IN ACTION RESEARCH

Greenwood and Levin (1998) define credibility in action research as the arguments and the processes necessary for having someone trust the research results. One type of credibility is when knowledge generated by a group is credible to that group. This is fundamentally important to action research because of the collaborative nature of the research process. Another type is external credibility which is knowledge capable of convincing someone who did not participate in the inquiry that the results are believable.

Action research practitioners believe that only knowledge generated and tested in practice is credible, whereas the conventional social research community believes that credibility is created through generalizing and universalizing hypothetical and generic propositions (Greenwood & Levin, 1998).

The credibility of action research can be assessed in three ways (Greenwood & Levin, 1998): The first assessment is workability, that is, whether the actions taken in the action research process result in a solution to the problem. The second assessment of credibility is whether the inquiry is making sense out of the tangible results. The focus here is on examining how meaning is constructed through deliberative processes. Thirdly, the possibility of "transcontextual modeling" of situations is assessed. Meanings created in one context are examined for their credibility in another situation through a conscious reflection on similarities and differences between contextual features and historical factors. This is based upon the assumption of action research that a particular outcome is realized through a combination of environmental conditions, a group of people, and a variety of historical events, including the actions of the participants (Greenwood & Levin, 1998).

VALIDITY OF ACTION RESEARCH METHODS

Methods of establishing validity of the action research methodology are not widely established in the literature (Waterman, 1998). Action research is fluid, flexible, and very much contextually based. Therefore, validity rests on the goals and specific methods utilized for knowledge discovery or agreed upon by those involved in the process and are recognized as an acceptable approach for achieving the study goals. Mason (1996) states that qualitative Action Research rests on the researcher's ability to demonstrate that concepts "can be identified, observed, or "measured" in the way [the researcher says] they can" (p. 24).

One test of validity is the continuing action research process itself. Through the cyclical processes of reflection, planning, action and evaluation, there is created a "process of validation" (Winter, 1987). Some aspects of action research are difficult to validate because the processes that occur within the individual participants are not always clear. Processes can be intuitive, or occur on a subconscious level (Waterman, 1998). Altering perspectives are continuously sought to seek the reality of a situation. The test of validity in Action Research is not only change, but the process of attempted improvement. Indeed, taking no action (inaction) may be what participants agree upon. Waterman (1998) suggests three types of validity critique in action research; "dialectical, critical and reflexive validity" (p. 101). She also states that sometimes "researchers have to be patient, wait and nurture the situation before major change can occur" (p. 105). This is also relevant when organizational factors produce inhibition or resistance to change in learning approaches/strategies. Therefore, four types of validity are relevant: dialectical validity, reflexive validity, content validity, and most importantly, implementable validity; a type of validity identified by Argyris (2004).

Waterman (1998) discusses the tensions between practice, theory and research in action research as dialectical validity. She notes that there are often tensions that arise when moving from theory to practice and the seemingly simplistic models of action research belie the complexity of practice/research settings. She also acknowledges that synthesis of findings from various perspectives can be obtained over a period of time and even subconsciously. She recommends that the complexities of the research situation/context be revealed to aid the understanding of tensions between practice, theory and research.

Reflexive validity is achieved by the researcher reflecting on what was found in the research study. In contrast to traditional constructs about content validity, Reason (2003) avoids applying the term validity in action research because of "its reference back to positivist research which suggests that there is one validity" (p. 1). He explains that creating knowledge is a practical affair that is initiated by problems in practice. In his address, he quotes Rorty (1999) who suggests that: "We cannot regard truth as a goal of inquiry" (p. xxv). The purpose of inquiry is to achieve agreement among human beings about what to do, to bring consensus on the end to be achieved and the means to be used to achieve those ends. Inquiry that does not achieve co-ordination of behavior is not inquiry but simple wordplay.

CRITICISMS OF ACTION RESEARCH

Some of the criticisms of action research must be addressed. Badger (2000) concludes that action research is limited in its effectiveness as a strategy to manage change because of the lack of methodological rigor in this research method. She points to the fact that action research is not generalizable, and is basically a reflective, quality improvement strategy rather than research. There are also criticisms because there is no rigid methodology for action research. Each unique setting or organization requires a unique research method utilizing the researchers interpersonal and communication skills rather than a strict operationalized format (Badger, 2000). Issues of reliability and validity are also raised by Badger. Action research depends upon congruence of others' interpretations with that of the researcher to protect against bias and error. Bellman (2003) discusses this issue and also the debate about whether or not action research is scientific. She concludes that the most important aspect of validity in action research is "catalytic validity" (Lather, 1991 cited in Bellman, 2003). According to Bellman (2003), this "points to the degree to which research moves those it studies to understand the world and the way it is shaped in order to transform it" (p. 28). Regarding the lack of an ability to generalize, she states that this is not a problem, "because a unique, individual situation is being studied, but some findings may be generalizable to other similar settings" (p. 28).

ETHICAL ISSUES IN ACTION RESEARCH

Three major positions can be detected on the ethics of action research: First, there is a perception that it raises no additional or different ethical challenges to those raised by traditional research; Waterman (1995), for example, suggests that the same ethical principles apply (i.e., respect for participants, prevention of harm, assurance of confidentiality or anonymity, and maintenance of privacy). In such circumstances, action research is not ethical per se and it would be possible to have ethical traditional research and unethical action research.

Second, as a product of its inclusive and emancipatory nature, there is an implicit assumption within some elements of the action research literature that it is either in itself more ethical or more cautiously is undertaken on stronger ethical grounds than other less participatory forms of research (Williams, 1995). Within this context, a number of writers have proposed a range of rather idealistic and aspirational ethical guidelines: for example, Winter (1996) proposes the principles that action research should aspire toward including a situation of "transparency" where all participants should be involved in the formulation of a consensus on the nature of the research problem, the choice of methods, and subsequent data analysis. McNiff et al. (1996) identify "keeping good faith" as an ethical talisman and list various steps that would be involved in an "ethical" action research project, including: "negotiating access sensitively and honestly; promising confidentiality of information, identity and data; ensuring the right to withdraw; and keeping all informed at regular points in the work" (p. 24).

Third, beyond these aspirations, on the basis that by its nature action research is bound to encounter ethical issues, many have begun to provide a more thorough analysis of the ethical implications of activities associated with action research (Balogh & Beattie, 1987). Fundamentally, and contrary to the perception promoted above of an unproblematic relationship, Lincoln (2001) contends there has been to this point, little specific ethical guidance for action researchers and more significantly, she suggests that the complexity of this type of work raises ethical concerns not encountered in "conventional" research work; in other words a contrary view to that which suggests that action research is implicitly ethical.

Kemmis and McTaggart (1988) list a range of "principles of procedure" that have strong ethical components; these include the following:

- observing protocol;

- involving participants;

- negotiating with those affected;

- reporting progress;

- obtaining explicit authorization before observation starts;

- obtaining explicit authorization before files or data are examined;

- negotiating descriptions and others' point of view;

- obtaining explicit authorization before using quotations;

- negotiating reports for various levels of publication;

- accepting responsibility for maintaining confidentiality;

- assuming authorization has been gained, retain the right to report your work;

- making your principles of procedures binding and known.

They also offer a range of observations in getting started in action research, including participate yourself in the action research process; get organized when initiating the process; be content to start small; articulate the main theme and establish agreement around it; establish a time-line that sets the time period for the work; arrange for supportive work-in-progress discussions; be tolerant and supportive of all involved; be persistent about recording and monitoring; plan for the longer haul in bigger issues of change; register progress; write up throughout the project; be explicit about all progress made (Kemmis & McTaggart, 1988).

At the level of a practical "checklist" Titchen (1995) offers the following critical points:

1. Have data been collected from people who are likely to understand what the action researchers wanted to know?

2. Are the data collection methods appropriate for gaining the information required?

3. Have the researchers articulated the standards of rigor they set? How did they test these standards?

4. Do they make explicit how they used their bias constructively in the action and how they limited it to reduce distortion of inter-subjective and multiple realities?

5. Have they discussed the influence that their procedures have had on the participants' responses? Were any measures taken to prevent, or to respond to, problems?

6. Is there evidence that the researcher created a climate of openness with participants?

7. Does the evidence support the claims the researcher is making?

8. Has a rich description been provided to help the reader decide whether the research findings are useful, illuminating, relevant and applicable to their settings?

9. Do I, the reader, believe in and trust the outcomes of this study and see them as relevant? (p. 47)

Research Brief

Title: Action Research and Leadership
Who: Edwards, A.

Edwards was invited to work collaboratively within a sport organization to develop effective leadership skills with four (4) middle managers and the Chief Executive. He utilized an action research approach based on reflection, feedback, evidence and evaluation of previous actions and the current situation. Data were utilized to develop new plans of action in the light of that reconnaissance. Each cycle of the action plan cycle was utilized to inform future decisions and actions. The leaders of the Sport Organization specifically wanted the following:

- to lead the staff positively.
- to provide strategic direction throughout the sport organization.

- to develop a five-year organizational plan.
- to establish a organizational culture based upon corporate social responsibility.
- to develop the sport organization's profile.

Edwards used the following data collection methods:

- reflective interviews with staff.
- observing executive team meetings.

The process of research and action resulted in the leaders using the 'findings' of the action research – the theory – at the time of the research. Edwards concluded that a theory that 'fits' the complex, constantly evolving context in which sport organization leaders' work aligns well with the development process in action research.

APPLICATION OF ACTION RESEARCH IN SPORT MANAGEMENT

The notion of conducting action research within sport management organizations could be considered to be mutually antagonistic in many ways (McTaggart & Garbutcheon-Singh, 1988). This may be as a result of "hierarchical inertia" and technical procedure, where the purpose of the sport organization is correct and is consistent in the implementation of procedures. Institutional practices and the values of the organization can be questioned during the implementation of action research, and resistance can be expected. Changes brought about by conducting action research can be problematic for the sport organization and cause loss of credibility to those undertaking action research if they are seen to be radical (McTaggart & Garbutcheon-Singh, 1988).

Conducting research within one's own sport organization requires that the researcher has to balance the membership role he or she holds and hopes to continue to hold with the additional role of inquiry and research (Coghlan & Brannick, 2001). Coghlan and Brannick identify many issues in relation to conducting research in one's own sport organization. Apart from issues pertaining to conflicts between the objectives of academic supervisors and the researcher's workplace supervisor, there are issues of gaining access and approval for research, and building and maintaining support from peers and relevant sections within the organization. In some cases, gaining access to the organization is easier for an insider, but this is not always the case (Coghlan & Brannick, 2001). The researcher takes on an additional role to his or her conventional one, which is seen to both complicate and focus the investigation. The complication is due to the challenge of ensuring that the roles of researcher and staff member have clear and visible boundaries. The focus occurs due to a generally high presence of the researcher staff member within the research project (Bartunek & Louis, 1996).

Hart and Bond (1995) state that action research is particularly relevant to the development of solutions for improving practice. Evidence-based practice requires sport management practitioners to think about practice in a constructively critical manner, reviewing the best evidence to inform the process of change. Meyer (1999) argues that action research, by dealing with the realities of practice, is more likely to represent the "truth" as compared to other research methods. This is despite the fact that there have been several calls for action research approaches to be used in sport management settings. The work of Green (1997) and Wendy Frisby and her colleagues provide examples of how action research has been used in sport management settings. Frisby et al. (2005) employed five phases in their action research project that explored the provision and uptake of community-based recreation opportunities for low-income women in British Columbia, Canada. This resulted in the co-participation and co-construction of knowledge evident in the development of the research questions, the building of trust, collecting data, analyzing data, and communicating the results for action. It is clear that these works demonstrate the potential use for action research approaches in sport management settings.

Action Research Case Study

Who: Professor Keith Gilbert (University of East London), Dr Allan Edwards (University of the West of England).

What: Action Research in Sport Management Higher Education: Exploration of a Methodology for Program Evaluation.

Theoretical framework

Gilbert and Edwards utilized an Action Research methodology, collecting qualitative data to obtain stakeholder feedback to inform undergraduate sport management curricula in a UK University. The aim of the research was to identify stakeholder views about program content that prepares graduates for successful professional practice and employment. It also attempted to elucidate stakeholder views about weaknesses in the sport management program's curriculum. This approach was selected for the study because traditional program evaluation measures had been utilized to gather evaluative data for the university previously, but these fell short, by producing only multi year "insulated" feedback and no curricular change. Action research was seen to have the potential to create understanding, insight and awareness necessary for organizational learning and generate organizational momentum for evidence based programmatic changes.

Learning organizational concepts guided the research. Sport management undergraduates (eight), employer stakeholders (six) and faculty peers (four) engaged in focus groups to share strengths and weaknesses of the program under study. The data provided evidence of a program strong in teaching the necessary knowledge and competencies, but identified some weaknesses in the areas of teaching sport management roles and values.

Data collection methods

Action Research methods utilizing focus groups were used to collect data from stakeholders and then provide the faculty with data to inform curricular evaluation/planning. This cyclical process of gathering data included stakeholders as research partners and utilized collected information to change practice on the foundations of action research.

All focus groups were audio taped and transcribed verbatim by the researchers. Journaling was also employed. The researchers kept a journal to record thoughts, conceptual connections, feedback from colleagues, stumbling blocks, and "minutes" of applicable discussions with dissertation advisors, stakeholders and faculty peers. This information was used for reflection and to document process decisions over time. This activity added to the justification of the analysis and potential action steps in response to information obtained from research.

Data analysis techniques/presentation

Content data analysis was used for data analysis. The data analysis process began by transferring verbatim transcripts of the focus groups into the NVivo program. The next step was to begin coding the documents. Participants' own words were used for the codes. The codes were not exclusive; data were entered into multiple codes. This process was aided by the ongoing consultation with an expert in the use of the NVivo software. The conclusions drawn from this research informed future sport management curricular design.

Major findings

In summary, there was agreement by the faculty and stakeholder that the sport management program produced graduates who were capable in the basic, fundamental concepts of sport delivery. Stakeholders believed graduates had the necessary knowledge of sport management and the overall sport processes that are necessary for the novice sport manager. Nevertheless, there was a strong feeling from stakeholders that graduates were not critically reflective practitioners.

The overwhelming belief from focus group participants was that the program was a good sport management program. The graduates had information to share about specific program strengths. Some of these included: sport law, sport marketing and industry placement. Of significance were the themes about the weaknesses of the program that emerged. The students focused on weaknesses within the curriculum and a lack of communication with them from the Faculty. The research also revealed that community stakeholders wanted to be involved in program evaluation as they have a vested interest in the sport managers that are produced.

Given the above findings, action research was a seen as an effective methodology to engage stakeholders in the process to improve sport management curricula.

Suggestions for future research

The researchers proposed to continue to use focus groups to obtain evaluative feedback from sport management graduates and their employers and work toward having faculty involved in collecting this data so that there is greater ownership of evaluative data.

Case study research probes

1. What form of action research has been undertaken in this study? Support your answer with a justification.

2. How has the action research process facilitated ways in which the sport management curricula can be improved?

3. Identify ways in which you think this action research process could be improved.

CONCLUSION

Conducting Action Research within a sport management organization can be seen as problematic in relation to issues around conflict of interest, ethical considerations, and the positioning of the researcher in relation to membership of the organization. Despite this, there is evidence to suggest that action research, by dealing with the realities of practice, is more likely to represent the "truth" as compared to other research methods. The Emancipatory and Participatory models of Action Research would seem particularly applicable to the Sport Management field.

IN PROFILE - Associate Professor Berit Skirstad

Berit Skirstad is Associate Professor at the Norwegian School of Sport Sciences in Oslo, Norway. She established the study of sport management in Oslo in 1986, and since then she has been responsible for that area of study. She has attended all of the 16 conferences which have been organized by the European Sport Management Association (EASM) since the first conference in Groningen, in the Netherlands, in 1993, and since 2005 she has been the President of EASM. EASM recognises the importance of qualitative research and has scheduled a research methodology workshop that will focus on the use of qualitative research methods in sport management for the 2009 EASM Congress. Although Berit began as a very quantitative-oriented researcher, she finds herself today increasingly using qualitative methods in order to 'catch' alternative meanings of, for example, processes within organizations. While quantitative methods such as the use of questionnaires are useful in understanding aspects of the structural contexts of behaviour, qualitative methods offer a better understanding of the texture or 'feel' of relationships from the perspective of the participants. Such an understanding of the perceptions and subjective meanings held by people within organizations is essential for a fuller understanding of how organizations work. Berit considers it a sign of scientific maturity to have switched away from a reliance on exclusively quantitative methods towards the greater use of qualitative methods. She has used qualitative methods in investigating attitudes towards gender in sport organizations and the election process for leadership in those organizations. This has included action research, when she investigated and actively contributed to the abolition of gender testing by the International Olympic Committee. The use of qualitative methods such as interviewing and document studies enables the researcher to reach a level of understanding which would not otherwise have been possible.

REVIEW AND RESEARCH QUESTIONS

1. Distinguish between Emancipatory Action Research and Participatory Action Research.

2. List three examples of how you believe action research approaches could be used in sport management settings. You must include an example of emancipatory and participatory approaches.

3. Explain why reflective practice is such an important component of action research?

REFERENCES

Argyris, C. 1985. Action Science. San Francisco: Jossey-Bass.

Badger, T. G. 2000. Action research, change and methodological rigour. *Journal of Nursing Management*, **8**, 201–207.

Balogh, R. & Beattie, A. 1987. Performance Indicators in Nursing Education. London: University of London, Institute of Education.

Barker, S. B. & Barker, R. T. 1994. Managing change in an interdisciplinary inpatient unit: an action research approach. *Journal of Mental Health Administration*, **21** (1), 80–91.

Bartunek, J. M. & Louis, M. R. 1996. Insider/Outsider Team Researcher. California: Sage.

Bellman, L. 2003. Nurse Led Change and Development in Clinical Practice. London: Whurr.

Blaxter, L., Hughes, C. & Tight, M. 1996. How to Research. Thousand Oaks, CA: Falmer Press.

Bowling, A. 1997. Research Methods in Health. London: McGraw Hill.

Brown, L., Henry, C., Henry, J. & McTaggart, R. 1988. Action research: notes on the national seminar. In: *The Action Research Reader* (Ed. by S. Kemmis, R. E. McTaggart), pp. 337–353. Geelong: Deakin University Press.

Carr, W. & Kemmis, S. 1986. Becoming Critical: Education, Knowledge and Action Research. Victoria: Deakin University Press.

Coghlan, D. & Brannick, T. 2001. Doing Action Research in Your Own Organisation. London: Sage.

Coghlan, P. & Coghlan, D. 2002. Action research for operations management. *International Journal of Operations & Production*, **22** (2), 220–240.

Cunningham, J. B. 1993. Action Research and Organizational Development. Westport: Praeger.

Dick, B. 1993. You Want to Do an Action Research Thesis? How to Conduct and Report Action Research. Brisbane: Interchange.

Dick, B. 1999. Rigour without Numbers: The Potential of Dialectical Processes as Qualitative Research Tools. Brisbane: Interchange.

Dick, B. 2000a. Postgraduate programs using action research. Retrieved April 2, 2008, from. http://www.scu.edu.au/schools/gcm/ar/arp/ppar.html

Dick, B. 2000b. A beginner's guide to action research. Retrieved February 10, 2008, from. http://www.scu.edu.au/schools/gcm/ar/arp/guide.html

French, W. & Bell, C. H. 1990. Organisation Development: Behavioural Science Interventions for Organizational Improvement. Englewood Cliffs, NJ: Prentice Hall.

Frisby, W., Reid, C., Millar, S. & Hoeber, L. 2005. Putting "participatory" into participatory forms of action research. *Journal of Sport Management*, **19**, 367–386.

Green, B. C. 1997. Action research in youth soccer: assessing the acceptability of an alternative program. *Journal of Sport Management*, **11**, 29–44.

Greenwood, D. J. & Levin, M. 1998. Introduction to Action Research. California: Sage Publications.

Gummesson, E. 2000. Qualitative Methods in Management Research, 2nd ed. Thousand Oaks, CA: Sage.

Habermas, J. 1972. Knowledge and Human Interests. London: Heinemann.

Hart, E. & Bond, M. 1995. Action Research in Health and Social Care: Guide to Practice. Buckingham: Open University Press.

Heron, J. & Reason, P. 1997. Qualitative Inquiry. London: Sage.

Huang, C. & Wang, H. 2005. Community health development, what is it? *International Nursing Review*, **52** (1), 13–17.

Kemmis, S. 1988. A Study of the Batchelor College Remote Area Teacher Education Program: 1976–1988: Final Report. Geelong, Victoria: Deakin Institute for Studies in Education.

Kemmis, S. (1995). Research and communicative action. Paper presented at the Invited Address: National Forum of the Innovative Project, Melbourne. (May 26, 1995).

Kemmis, S., & McTaggart, R. (Eds.), 1988. The Action Research Reader. Geelong: Deakin University Press.

Lewin, K. 1946. Action research and minority problems. *Journal of Social Issues*, **2** (4), 33–46.

Lewin, K. 1948. Resolving Social Conflicts: Selected Papers on Group Dynamics. New York: Harper & Row.

Lewin, K. 1952a. Field Theory in Social Science. Great Britain: Tavistock Publications.

Lewin, K. 1952b. Group decision and social change. In: *Readings in Social Psychology* (Ed. by T. M. Newcomb, E. L. E. Hartley), pp. 459–473. New York: Henry Holt.

Lincoln, Y. S. 2001. Engaging sympathies: relationships between action research and social constructivism. In: *Handbook of Action Research* (Ed. by P. Reason, H. Bradbury), pp. 124–132. Thousand Oaks, CA: Sage.

MacTaggart, R. (1989, September). Principles for participatory action research. Paper presented at the 3rd Encuentro Mundial Investigacion Partipativa (The Third World Encounter on Participatory Research), Managua, Nicaragua.

MacTaggart, R. 1991. Action research: issues for the next decade. *Curriculum Perspectives*, **11** (4), 44–46.

Mason, J. 1996. Qualitative Researching. London: Sage.

McNiff, J., Lomax, P. & Whitehead, J. 1996. You and Your Action Research Project. London: Routledge.

McTaggart, R. 2002. The mission of the scholar in action research. In: *The Mission of the Scholar: Research and Practice* (Ed. by M. P. Wolfe, C. R. Pryor), pp. 1–16. London: Peter Lang.

McTaggart, R. & Garbutcheon-Singh, M. 1988. Fourth generation action research: notes on the 1986 Deakin Seminar. In: *The Action Research Reader* (Ed. by S. Kemmis, R. E. McTaggart), pp. 409–428. Geelong: Deakin University Press.

Meyer, J. 1999. Comparison of findings from a single case in relation to those from a systematic review of action research. *Nurse Researcher*, **7** (2), 37–59.

Reason, P. 2003. Pragmatist philosophy and action research. *Action Research*, **1** (1), 103–123.

Reason, P. & Bradbury, H. E. 2001. Handbook of Action Research. London: Sage.

Rorty, R. 1999. Philosophy and Social Hope. Harmondsworth: Penguin.

Sapin, K. & Wafters, G. 1990. Learning from Each Other. Manchester: The William Temple Foundation.

Schwandt, T. A. 1997. Qualitative Inquiry – A Dictionary of Terms. London: Sage.

Stringer, E. T. 1996. Action Research. California: Sage.

Swepson, P. 1995. Action research: understanding its philosophy can improve your practice. Retrieved March 4, 2008 from http://www.scu.edu.au/schools/gcm/ar/arp/philos.html.

Titchen, A. 1995. Issues of validity in action research. *Nurse Researcher*, **2** (3), 38–48.

Tripp, D. 1993. Critical Incidents In Teaching: Developing Professional Judgement. London and New York: Routledge.

van Manen, M. 1990. Researching Lived Experience: Human Science for an Action Sensitive Pedagogy. Basic Books: State University of New York.

Waterman, H. 1995. Distinguishing between "traditional" and action research. *Nurse Researcher*, **2** (3), 15–23.

Waterman, H. 1998. Embracing ambiguities and valuing ourselves: issues of validity in action research. *Journal of Advanced Nursing*, **28**, 101–105.

Watkins, K. E. 2000. Learning by changing: action science and virtual organization development. *Adult Learning*, **11** (3), 20–22.

Webb, C. 1989. Action research: philosophy, methods and present experiences. *Journal of Advanced Nursing*, **14** (5), 403–410.

Whyte, W. F. (Ed.), 1991. Participatory Action Research. California: Sage.

Williams, A. 1995. Ethics and action research. *Nurse Researcher*, **2** (3), 49–59.

Winter, R. 1987. Action-Research and the Nature of Social Inquiry. Professional Innovation and Educational Work. Avebury: Aldershot.

Winter, R. 1996. Some principles and procedures for the conduct of Action Research. In O. Zuberskerritt (Ed.), New directions in Action Research (pp 13–27). London: Falmer Press.

Autoethnography and Sport Management Research

OBJECTIVES

By the end of this chapter, you should be able to

- understand what defines autoethnographic research.
- discuss the principles that underpin the autoethnographic research process.

- identify the strengths and limitations of autoethnographic research.
- understand how autoethnography can be used in sport management research.

KEY TERMS

Autoethnography: Autoethnography is an autobiographical genre of writing and research that displays multiple layers of consciousness, connecting the personal to the cultural (Ellis & Bochner, 2000).

Author reflexivity: A critical analysis of one's own experiences of the social phenomenon under study that

works to locate the researcher as a living and breathing participant.

Crisis in representation: This argument suggests that autoethnographic researchers are blind to the effects of their research on those studied; that their pursuit of knowledge and understanding is self-serving and exclusionary.

KEY QUESTIONS

The key questions raised in this chapter are as follows:

- What is "autoethnography"?

- How can autoethnographic approaches to research be applied in sport management settings?

187

CHAPTER OVERVIEW

This chapter explores the emerging ethnographic research approach of autoethnography. It identifies and discusses the principles that underpin autoethnographic approaches to research in sport settings. It discusses the strengths and limitations associated with this approach and advocates that autoethnography is a viable methodology for sport management research. Although autoethnography has been applied in sociology of sport research it is yet to be applied to sport management research. It provides examples of how autoethnography has been used in a research setting and suggestions for its application to sport management settings.

INTRODUCTION

One way of understanding autoethnography is to deconstruct the components of the word. In this fashion *auto* refers to the self or the autobiographical (Reed-Danahay, 1997), *ethno* to a social group, and *graphy* to the process of researching and writing (Ellis & Bochner, 2000; Reed-Danahay, 1997).

As an outgrowth of the interpretive turn, autoethnography is considered a form of autobiographical narrative combining evocative writing and research that display multiple levels of consciousness, generally written in first-person (Denzin & Lincoln, 1994; Ellis, 2000, 2004). Autoethnography has been acknowledged as a method of inquiry since the mid-1970s and was shaped by the ideas of feminism, post-structuralism and postmodernism (Ellis & Bochner, 2000). Autoethnography has close ties to phenomenology and hermeneutics.

THE AUTOETHNOGRAPHIC RESEARCH PROCESS

Ellis and Bochner (2000) have advocated the use of autoethnography suggesting personal experience as an opportunity to move beyond a passionless and objective authoritative voice; autoethnography presents an opportunity to connect the personal to the cultural. The research becomes a personal account of experiences within and in relation to a particular culture that also draws on others' lived experiences; the completed text seeks to engage the readers and draws them into the experiences of the author and other participants. Ellis and Bochner suggest that autoethnography asks readers "to become co-participants, engaging the storyline morally, emotionally, aesthetically, and intellectually" (p. 745). Moreover, Ellis and Bochner characterize autoethnography as follows:

> *Autoethnography is an autobiographical genre of writing and research that displays multiple layers of consciousness, connecting the personal to the cultural. Back and forth autoethnographers gaze, first through an ethnographic wide-angle lens, focusing outward on social and cultural aspects of their personal experience; then they look inward, exposing a vulnerable self that is moved-by and may move through, refract, and resist cultural interpretations. As they zoom backward and forward, inward and outward, distinctions between the cultural and personal become blurred, sometimes beyond distinct recognition. Usually written in first-person voice, autoethnographic texts appear in a variety of forms: short stories, poetry, fiction, novels, photographic essays, personal essays, journals, fragmented and layered writing, and social science prose. In these texts, concrete action, dialog, emotion, embodiment, spirituality and self-consciousness are featured, appearing as relational and institutional stories affected by history, social structure, and culture, which themselves are dialectically revealed through action, feeling, thought, and language. (p. 739)*

There are several distinctions between type, meaning, methodological strategies, and application of autoethnography (Ellis & Bochner, 2000), ranging from personal narratives (Bochner, 2001) to autoethnographic performance (Slattery, 2001). Common among the more than 60 variations of autoethnographic application is the interconnectedness between the researcher and the research. Researcher emphasis varies between the self, the culture, and the form their research will take (Ellis & Bochner, 2000).

METHODOLOGY

Although gaining in acceptance, autoethnography is still a contested methodological approach (Ellis & Bochner, 2000; Holt, 2003; Sparkes, 2000). The use of self as the only data source can be problematic in this regard. Ellis (1995) argues that a story could be considered scholarly if it makes the reader believe the experience is authentic, believable, and possible. The intended purpose of autoethnography is to provide the opportunity for the reader and author to become co-participants in the recorded experience. There are also multiple warning signs, skills and difficulties that are experienced or needed in writing autoethnography (Ellis & Bochner, 2000). Researchers must be adept at identifying pertinent details, introspection, descriptive and compelling writing, and confronting things about themselves that may be less than flattering. Also, the researcher must handle the vulnerability of revealing oneself to a greater audience. The use of self as the source of data can be restrictive, yet a powerful aspect of unpacking the many layers involved in the study of a particular culture or social context. Tierney (1998) explains that autoethnography is intended to confront dominant forms of representation and power in an attempt to reclaim marginalized representational spaces.

Data collection

Autoethnography is as much about the written text as it is about the mode of collection. An autoethnographic account may take the form of creative nonfiction or creative fiction, it may appear in short story, poetry, personal essays or journal format – to name but just a few of the choices. The forms typically evolve as the research progresses and relate greatly to both subject matter and author intent (Ellis & Bochner, 2000; Sparkes, 2002). In autoethnographic data collection, all of the considerations of ethnographic field work are applicable as long as it adds useful information to the study. Interviews, artefacts, sketches, fieldnotes and photographs can all be part of autoethnographic research.

Ellis (1999) suggests the best place for a researcher to begin with autoethnography is a draft of their life story or "retrospective field notes on your life" (p. 675). This process is an in-depth account of the author's personal narrative. The author can write in chronological sequence of events, by degree of impact, draw links between the past and present, or if the experience is in the present tense, fully describe the events as they occur with regard to the above considerations for an in-depth account of the experience as it is being experienced.

Several scholars concur that what makes an effective autoethnography is a strong writing style that combines art and science together to produce a flowing and compelling narrative (Berger, 2001; Bochner, 2001; Ellis, 1999; Ellis & Bochner, 2000). In order to engage and bring the reader into the life of the research experience, the autoethnographer must write with conviction, artistic form, compelling language, and candidness (Bochner, 2001). Ellis cautions: "The self-questioning autoethnography demands is extremely difficult as is confronting things about yourself that are less than flattering" (p. 672).

Feldman (2003) has developed four criteria upon which autoethnography data collection are based:

1. Provide clear and detailed description of how we collect data and make explicit what counts as data in our work.

2. Provide clear and detailed descriptions of how we constructed the representation from our data. What specifics about the data led us to make this assumption?

3. Extend triangulation beyond multiple sources of data to include explorations of multiple ways to represent the same self-study.

4. Provide evidence that the research changed or evolved the educator and summarize its value to the profession. This can convince readers of the study's significance and validity (pp. 27–28).

Data analysis

In autoethnography, *reflective analysis* is an ongoing part of the data collection process (Ellis, 1999). The lived experience of the researcher is fundamental to understanding the experience as lived. The difficulty with this "anything goes" approach to *data analysis* is that it fuels the ongoing debate between traditional positivistic inquiry and contemporary qualitative research.

Methods of data analysis specifically utilized in autoethnography include *collaboration, emotional recall,* and *reflective field notes*.

Collaboration in autoethnographic research relates to understanding the phenomenon studied by those involved. On a concrete level, if participants are involved in the research process they can be repeatedly consulted throughout or brought together as a group to confirm, validate, alter or add to the data and the analysis process (Ellis, 1999). Ellis and Bochner (2000) assert that the analysis of data in autoethnography involves a process where the researcher *emotionally recalls* the events of the past. The researcher looks back on specific, memorable episodes and experiences paying particular attention to the emotions and physical surroundings during the recollection. Emotional recall is usually expressed through writing that includes thoughts, events, dialog, and physical details of the particular event.

Reflective filed notes are also a key element. In an autoethnography the analysis of data is an ongoing event, developing and crystallizing over time. With each re-reading of the personal reflexive journal, each examination of a written artifact, and with further introspection and self-analysis, the process and clarity of the research is enriched. These processes form the analysis of data in a qualitative study of an autoethnographical nature. The gathering and analysis of data go hand-in-hand as theories and themes emerge during the study. The reflection involved by the researcher consistently shapes and forms the articulation of the experiences of the researcher in a self-study.

Research Brief

Title: Autoethnography of Sport Managers
Who: Edwards, A., University of West England.
The purpose of this study was to describe and explain the perspectives of five (5) new sport administrators regarding the manner in which they view their emerging leadership roles and management responsibilities. An autoethnographic methodology was utilized in a manner that allowed personal experiences to contribute to the understanding of the emerging stories. Data were collected through personal interviews, group discussions, journal entries, reflective analysis and document analysis. The perspectives uncovered indicated that organizational socialization, role actualization, and job satisfaction were principle areas of reflection.

Validity and reliability

The inclusion of the lived experiences of others seeks to address issues of *validity and reliability*. Such considerations are often the crux of opposition toward autoethnographic research (Denzin, 1997; Sparkes, 2000). In the case of autoethnography, validity has been usefully defined by Ellis and Bochner (2000) as the seeking of "verisimilitude":

> *meaning that the work, evokes in readers a feeling that the experience described is lifelike, believable, and possible … [Validity might also be judged by] whether it helps readers communicate with others different from themselves, or offers a way to improve the lives of participants and readers, or even [the researcher's] own. (p. 751)*

In an apparent contradiction Ellis (2004) suggests that validity is still important in autoethnographic inquiry. She suggests several questions for assessing quality including the following:

1. Do the stories "ring true" to the audience?

2. Do the stories resonate with the lives of the researcher and readers?

3. Are the accounts plausible and coherent?

4. Does the author make claim to a single standard of truth or leave open the possibility of multiple interpretations and truths as is inherent in autoethnography?

5. Is the whole person taken into account?

6. Does the work communicate with others?

7. Is the resulting story useful in helping others?

Ellis (1999) also suggests that: "since we always create our personal narrative from a situated location, trying to make our present, imagined future, and remembered past cohere, there's no such thing as orthodox *reliability* in autoethnographic research" (p. 674). Despite this ethical and contextual dilemma, certain academic standards can be incorporated to satisfy positively both sides of the debate, while maintaining the integrity of the lived experience and the resulting research conclusions.

Reliability within an autoethnographic study can be sought through feedback from the other participants included in the research. Ellis and Bochner (2000) suggest that "when other people are involved, you might take your work back to them and give them a chance to comment, add materials, change their minds, and offer their interpretations" (p. 751). With inclusion of the "self" in the research, reliability is unorthodox as compared to traditional, positivist definitions that have previously been applied to qualitative research. To a certain degree, there must be some "letting go" of traditional, evaluative approaches to the notions of *validity and reliability*. As Holt (2003) argues:

> *Describing investigator responsiveness during the research process*
> *would be a constructive approach to validity, as opposed to the*
> *inclusion of evaluative checks to establish the trustworthiness of*
> *completed research (e.g., an external audit)… Constructive approaches*
> *to validity and reliability would be more appropriate criteria to judge*
> *autoethnography than the post-hoc imposition of evaluative*
> *techniques associated with the parallel perspective. (pp. 11–12)*

Finally, there has been argument that autoethnography is self-indulgent, narcissistic and academic "navel-gazing" (Sparkes, 2000). Autoethnographic research declares its intentions of including the personal, rather than proffering an "objective" epistemology that is likewise steeped in the personal. Regardless of perspective and paradigmatic positioning, Sparkes argues that there will be:

> *tensions, contradictions, conflicts and differences of interpretation*
> *about what the research should not cause undue anxiety … If*
> *autoethnography and narratives of self do nothing else but stimulate*
> *us to think about social issues in the sociology of sport, then they will*
> *have made a significant contribution to the field. (p. 38)*

Research Brief

Title: One Foot In: Student-Athlete Advocacy and Social Movement Rhetoric in the Margins of American College Athletics

Who: Broussard, W., University of Arizona

In "One Foot In: Student-Athlete Advocacy and Social Movement Rhetoric in the Margins of American College Athletics", the author explores student-athlete advocacy of black male student-athletes in revenue generating sports and educational and cultural reforms to NCAA policies and bylaws over approximately two decades (1985–2006). Throughout the dissertation, Broussard offers accounts (as digressive *excurses*) of his personal experiences as a student-athlete, instructor, and administrator in hopes of providing the reader snapshots of life within the well-guarded walls of college athletics.

These fragments, personal stories of importance which substantiate claims as well as contextualize his analytical approach, are also products of autoethnographic reflection.

TRUSTWORTHINESS IN AUTOETHNOGRAPHY

Ellis and Bochner (1996) remind us that autoethnographic writing reaches the traditional genre of realist writing that "construes the author as a neutral, authoritative, and scientific voice" (p. 19). Peshkin (2000) raises the idea of *Problematics* as counterpoint to interpretive decisions that were made by a researcher. Peshkin addresses the issue of researcher bias and asks us to problematize interpretive choices and decisions made by the researcher, stating in a clear, up-front manner that other decisions/interpretations could have been made during the research process.

In autoethnographic research, the author commits to researcher subjectivity and uses an introspective lens in writing personal narrative history, often confronting hidden emotional content. Sparkes (2002) has suggested that in autoethnography, "it is made clear that the author "was there" in the action, that the story is based on "real" people, "real" events, and "data" that were collected in various ways" (p. 3). Furthermore, a critical analysis of one's own experiences of the social phenomenon under study works to locate the writer/researcher as a living and breathing participant. Autoethnography is therefore not concerned with *generalizability*, but rather with understanding the unique experiences of cultural groups or members.

CRISIS OF REPRESENTATION

An area of continuing debate is the use of "I" in social science discourse (Piirto, 2002; Tierney, 2002). While Tierney (2002) endorses a change in qualitative research to support a more artistic narrative prose, he asserts that the continual reference to "I" in research writing, dominates the "other"; those whom we study and the contexts of their experience. He refers to this opposing dynamic as the "crisis of representation" that exists within field work and culture-bound research. "The crisis, of course, came about in large part because of epistemological issues pertaining to the nature of knowledge and representation" (p. 387). He also suggests that the assignment to "I" in autoethnographic research experience may silence the narrative voice of the participants. Furthermore: "given our human tendency to often overlook context and generalize "truths", our research conclusions, even the study itself, can positively or negatively affect the "I", the "other", and our respective communities" (p. 387).

AUTOETHNOGRAPHY AND SPORT MANAGEMENT

The use of narrative voice is a major strength of autoethnography. Rather than maintaining a disconnected objective position, the narrative and subjectivity of the researcher, fashion autoethnographic writing as "creative non-fiction" (Richardson, 2000). The reader is granted permission into the intricate life of another and in adding their own life experience the study becomes more personal and effective.

The effective and integral link in autoethnography is the researcher's emotional connectedness to the content, the described experience, and the author's vulnerability and conviction to a true account of the story and the process (Ellis, 1999). In reviewing the work, the reader becomes part of the story told as in fictional prose. Connecting with characters in the story, the reader introspectively evaluates their own constructions of reality, of self, and their interpersonal connections (Spry, 2001). In this literary context, the importance of narrative description of events and author reflections link the art (writing) and science (research) of autoethnographic discourse (Ellis, 1999).

In autoethnography, the researcher writes about the nature of the experience, the emotional affect of the experience, and their cognitive processes in understanding the experience. For example, Devine (2005) examined how the cultural structures which guide and control sport impact on the construction of an athlete's identity. Specifically, Devine utilized autoethnography and narrative inquiry to explore how her lived experiences in sport shaped her identity as a competitive female athlete. The work of Edwards as identified in an earlier Research Brief indicated that autoethnography research conveyed a deeper understanding of the experiences of sport administrators. Autoethnography is now an acceptable research approach in sport sociology mainly due to the work of Sparkes (2002); however, the opportunity exists for sport managers to embrace the approach.

Autoethnography Case Study

Who: Kurt Lindemann: Arizona State University

What: Living Out of Bounds, Pushing Toward Normalcy: Autoethnographic Performances of Disability and Masculinity in Wheelchair Rugby

Theoretical framework

Lindemann utilized autoethnography methods that invoke the author's experience in growing up the son of a wheelchair athlete. He utilized elements from what is generally called "postmodern" ethnography (Lindlof & Taylor, 2002), including fictive vignettes based on field work data and autoethnographic intrusions that both disrupt traditional reportage of field work and clarify his stance as a researcher in fieldwork.

Data collection methods

The data collection was based initially on the juxtaposition of the author's narratives with those of quad rugby players, as well with the autoethnographic interrogation of participant-observations, field notes, document analysis and interview data to provide a textured understanding of masculinity and disability through a performative voice. Lindemanns' field notes included autoethnographic musings that later became the foundation for extended performative interrogations of the researchers personal experiences growing up as a "child of disability".

Data analysis techniques/presentation

Lindeman began data analysis at the site of its collection, jotting memos and asides while writing scratch notes in the field (Emerson et al., 1995; Lindlof & Taylor, 2002). He then started formal data analysis through a process of open coding (Lindlof & Taylor, 2002) and employed the constant-comparative method (Strauss & Corbin, 1998), by which close readings allow themes to emerge from the data. He utilized ethnographic and semi-structured interviews to test thematic groupings in a process called member validation or member-checking. By posing tentative conclusions in interview questions, he was able to gauge how accurately themes reflected quad rugby members' understandings.

Major findings

The findings of this study highlight performed contestations of disability, gender, and sexuality. Male and female athletes' incongruous on-court displays emerged as a playing activity that aligned frames of meaning about athletic ability, the perceived invulnerability of the disabled sporting body, and the performativity of disability.

The conclusions drawn from this research were that employing a performative voice (Pollock, 1998) allowed for an interrogation of the scholarly literature and the researchers own findings, which illustrated the often partial understandings of disability able-bodied persons hold.

Suggestions for future research

Lindeman suggested that there is little scholarly research on disability in sport organizations (Colvert & Smith, 2000), and proposed that researchers should "pick up the threads" of this study and examine the ways in which sport organizations "culture" bodies (Trethewey, 2000).

Case study research probes

1. Describe how the autoethnographic research approach has been applied in this research?

2. How has the author demonstrated how the data collected is valid and reliable? If the author has not how could this be done?

3. Using the suggestions for future research as a reference point outline in one page how the autoethnographic approach could be applied in a sport management setting?

CONCLUSION

Although autoethnography is an emerging research approach that to date has not been applied to sport management it provides a new frame in which to understand the social world of sport management. It provides an opportunity for those who are working in the sport management field to use a research approach that will provide a partial understanding of the research issue under investigation. The sharing of these field experiences can only broaden and deepen our understanding of the complex issues that sport managers confront in their daily lives.

IN PROFILE - Professor Pirkko Markula

Pirkko Markula is currently a professor of socio-cultural studies of sport at the University of Alberta, Canada. Her research is embedded in qualitative methodologies and feminist, poststructuralist theory and has appeared in *Sociology of Sport Journal*, *Qualitative Inquiry*, the *Journal of Sport Management*, and the *Journal of Physical Activity and Aging*. Her work has focused on the commercial fitness industry in several cultural contexts (United States, New Zealand, UK, and Canada). Through an ethnography in the United States, her early work that derived from a Foucauldian perspective, illustrated how the creating fit, thin, toned, and young looking body was a central goal for the exercisers. At the same time, women became disciplined to work toward an unobtainable body shape. She has continued her Foucauldian work by interviewing mindful fitness instructors about their meanings regarding the construction of the ideal body through commercial exercise classes. Her other qualitative work includes textual analyses of how health informs current exercise practices. These data from the US, the UK, and New Zealand (popular fitness magazines, exercise and fitness course books, professional fitness publications) demonstrate that the quest for improved health has been turned into a disciplinary practice: either health is narrowly defined by the scientific discourse or health is conflated with appearance through a common nominator of thinness (to be thin is to be healthy and attractive). Exercise programs, consequently, are marketed through the dual benefits of 'looking good and feeling good.' Her most recent work engages autoethnography and performance ethnography as ways of representing research and as ways of creating change in the way fitness is currently popularized. She currently employs qualitative methodologies with Derridean and Deleuzian feminism to elicit transformation in the fitness industry. In her research, qualitative methods have served as a powerful tool to demonstrate, first, the need for change in the industry and second, as an opportunity to develop meaningful interventions into the industry practices. She co-authored, with Richard Pringle, *Foucault, Sport and Exercise: Power, Knowledge and the Transformation of the Self*; she edited *Feminist Sport Studies: Sharing Joy, Sharing Pain*, co-edited, with Jim Denison, *Moving Writing: Crafting Movement in Sport Research*.

REVIEW AND RESEARCH QUESTIONS

1. Provide an overview of the autoethnographic research process with particular emphasis on author reflexivity.

2. Explain why some individuals may question the value of using autoethnographic approaches in sport management research?

3. What benefits does autoethnography bring to sport management research?

REFERENCES

Berger, L. 2001. Inside out: narrative autoethnography as a path toward rapport. *Qualitative Inquiry*, **7** (4), 504–518.

Bochner, A. 2001. Narrative's virtues. *Qualitative Inquiry*, **7** (2), 131–157.

Colvert, A. L. & Smith, J. W. 2000. What is reasonable? Workplace communication and people who are disabled. In: *Handbook of Communication and People with Disabilities: Research and Application* (Ed. by D. O Braithwaite, T. L. Thompson), pp. 141–158. Mahway, NJ: Lawrence Erlbaum Associates.

Denzin, N. 1997. Interpretive Ethnography. Thousand Oaks, CA: Sage.

Denzin, N. K. & Lincoln, Y. S. (Eds.), 1994. Handbook of Qualitative Research. London: Sage.

Devine 2005. The Gift of Sport: An Autoethnographic Inquiry into Sport Culture and the Construction of Identity. Charlottetown: University of Prince Edward Island.

Ellis, C. 1995. Final Negotiations. Philadelphia: Temple University Press.

Ellis, C. 1999. Heartful autoethnography. *Qualitative Health Research*, **9** (5), 669–683.

Ellis, C. 2000. Creating criteria: an ethnographic short story. *Qualitative Inquiry*, **6** (2), 273–277.

Ellis, C. 2004. The Ethnographic I: A Methodological Novel About Autoethnography. Walnut Creek, CA: Altamira Press.

Ellis, C. & Bochner, A. P. 1996. Composing Ethnography: Alternative Forms of Qualitative Writing. Walnut Creek, CA: AltaMira Press.

Ellis, C. & Bochner, A. P. 2000. Autoethnography, personal narrative, reflexivity. In: *Handbook of Qualitative Research* (Ed. by N. K. Denzin, Y. S. Lincoln), pp. 733–779, 2nd ed. Thousand Oaks, CA: Sage.

Emerson, R., Fretz, R. & Shaw, L. 1995. Writing Ethnographic Fieldnotes. Chicago: University of Chicago Press.

Feldman, A. 2003. Validity and quality in self-study. *Educational Researcher*, **32**, 26–28.

Georgiou, D. & Carspecken, P. F. 2002. Critical ethnography and ecological psychology: conceptual and empirical explorations of a synthesis. *Qualitative Inquiry*, **8** (6), 688–706.

Holt, N. 2003. Representation, legitimation, and autoethnography: an autoethnographic writing story. *International Journal of Qualitative Methods*, **2** (1) Article 2.

Lindlof, T. R. & Taylor, B. C. 2002. Qualitative Communication Research Methods, 2nd ed. Thousand Oaks, CA: Sage.

Peshkin, A. 2000. The nature of interpretation in qualitative research. *Educational Researcher*, **29** (9), 5–10.

Piirto, J. 2002. The question of quality and qualifications. *Qualitative Studies in Education*, **14** (4), 431–448.

Pollock, D. 1998. A response to Dwight Conquergood's essay: 'beyond the text: towards a performative cultural politics.' In: *The Future of Performance Studies: Visions and Revisions* (Ed. by S. J. Dailey), pp. 37–46. Annadale, VA: National Communication Association.

Reed-Danahay, D. 1997. Auto/Ethnography: Rewriting the Self and the Social. Oxford: Berg Publishing.

Richardson, L. 2000. Writing: a method of inquiry. In: *Handbook of Qualitative Research* (Ed. by N. K. Denzin, Y. S. Lincoln), pp. 923–948, 2nd ed. Thousand Oaks, CA: Sage.

Slattery, P. 2001. The educational researcher as artist working within. *Qualitative Inquiry*, **7** (3), 370–398.

Sparkes, A. C. 2000. Fictional representations: on difference, choice, and risk. *Sociology of Sport Journal*, **19**, 1–24.

Sparkes, A. C. 2002. Telling Tales in Sport and Physical Activity: A Qualitative Journey. Champaign, IL: Human Kinetics.

Spry, T. 2001. Performing autoethnography: an embodied methodological praxis. *Qualitative Inquiry*, **7** (6), 706–732.

Strauss, A. & Corbin, J. 1998. Basics of Qualitative Research: Techniques and Procedures for Developing Grounded Theory. Thousand Oaks, CA: Sage.

Tierney, W. G. 1998. Life history's history: subjects foretold. *Qualitative Inquiry*, **4**, 49–70.

Tierney, W. G. 2002. Get real: representing reality. *Qualitative Studies in Education*, **15** (4), 385–398.

Trethewey, A. 2000. Revisioning control: a feminist critique of disciplined bodies. In: *Rethinking Organizational and Managerial Communication from Feminist Perspectives* (Ed. by P. M. Buzzanell), pp. 107–127. Thousand Oaks, CA: Sage.

Case Study in Sport Management Research

CHAPTER OVERVIEW

This chapter highlights that "case study", the term itself, has multiple meanings. It can be used to describe a unit of analysis/a choice of what is to be studied (Stake, 2000), which aims to describe and explain the phenomenon of interest (Zucker, 2001) or to describe a research method (Yin, 1994; Creswell, 1998; Scapens, 1990). This chapter argues that the use of case study as a research method, not a methodology, depends on both the nature of the research that could be descriptive, illustrative, explorative, evaluative, or explanative (Yin, 1994; Scapens, 1990) and the methodology (philosophical assumptions) that is used by the researcher (Scapens, 1990).

DEFINING CASE STUDY

The term case study is often used interchangeably with "field research", "qualitative research", "direct research", "ethnographic studies", or "naturalistic research". Yin (1994) defines a case study as: "an empirical inquiry that investigates a contemporary phenomenon within its real-life context, especially when the boundaries between phenomenon and context are not clearly evident" (p. 13). He argues that the case study "allows an investigation to retain the holistic and meaningful characteristics of real-life events" (p. 3). Stake (1995) focuses on the case as an object of study, derived from Smith's (1978) notion of the case as a bounded system. The case is "an integrated system", a "specific, a complex functioning thing" (p. 2) For Creswell (1998), a case study is an exploration of a bounded system which may be a program, an event, an activity, or a group of individuals. Similarly, Miles and Huberman (1994) define a case as "a phenomenon of some sort occurring in a bounded context" (p. 25). Merriam (1998) supports Stake's view, concluding that "the single most defining characteristic of case study research lies in delimiting the object of study, the case" (p. 27). Case study research also involves situating the research phenomena within their context: "The context of the case involves situating the case within its setting, which may be a physical setting or the social, historical, and/or economic setting for the case" (Creswell 1998, p. 61). Merriam (1998) further characterizes the case study as particularistic, descriptive and heuristic. Case studies are particularistic in that they "focus on a particular situation, event, program or phenomenon. They are descriptive in that they produce a rich, "thick" description of the phenomena under study" (p. 29).

CASE STUDY AS A RESEARCH METHOD

The case study approach can be characterized as the presentation and analysis of detailed information about single or multiple subjects, in relation to an event, culture or individual life. Through this analysis, the sport management researcher is able to obtain an in-depth understanding of the characteristics of cases in order to generate new insights.

Yin (2003) argues that the case study is neither "a data collection tactic nor merely a design feature alone, but a comprehensive research strategy which includes the logic of design, data collection techniques, and specific approaches to data analysis" (p. 14). Yin argues that case studies should benefit from the prior development of theoretical propositions to guide data collection and analysis. He defines the scope of the case study as an empirical inquiry that investigates contemporary phenomenon within its real-life context, "especially when the boundaries between phenomenon and context are not clearly evident" (p. 13). He further argues that case study inquiries cope with "technically distinctive situation in which there will be many more variables of interest than data points and therefore relies on multiple sources of evidence which need to be triangulated" (pp. 13–14).

Yin (1984) identifies four different applications for case studies:

1. To *explain*: the causal links in real-life interventions that were too complex for the survey or experimental strategies.

2. To *describe* the real-life context in which an intervention had occurred.

3. To *evaluate* an intervention in a descriptive case study.

4. To *explore* those situations where the intervention being evaluated has no clear, single set of outcomes.

Yin (2003) lists five components that are especially important for case studies: (1) a study's question; (2) its propositions, if any; (3) its unit(s) of analysis; (4) the logic linking the data to the propositions; and (5) the criteria for interpreting the findings (p. 21). When research is aimed at developing a theory rather than verifying one, then the use of the case study methodology is the most appropriate one. Moreover, the case study methodology suits both theory building and data analysis, as they interact with each other, through the multiple sources and flexible nature of the process of data collection.

Research Brief

Title: The Critical Success Factors of the Atlantic Coast Conference: A Case Study from the Perspective of Conference Leadership.

Who: Stroman, D., Capella University

Stroman utilized case study to investigate the Atlantic Coast Conference (ACC) which represents 12 Universities. She used critical success factor category analysis to identify 479 critical success factors in the planning areas of global, external, internal, temporal, risk, performance , culture and marketing as defined by ACC leadership. Structured interviews were used to discover that the ACC leadership, ACC culture, marketing and promotion, quality of institutions and ACC governance were the most important critical success factors for the conference.

EPISTEMOLOGICAL AND ONTOLOGICAL DIMENSIONS OF THE CASE STUDY

In their discussion of the epistemological and ontological assumptions that undergird case study methodology, Guba and Lincoln (1981) say that case study methodology operates within a naturalistic perspective whose epistemology assumes that there is interaction between the inquirer and the subject of his/her inquiry, and an ontology which assumes that reality in the situation being studied is "multiple, divergent and with inter-related elements" (Scott and Usher, 2004, p. 94). While acknowledging that we cannot fully know reality, although we can make judgments about it, Scott and Usher (2004) advise that these assumptions are important because of their implications about the relationship between the researcher's values, conceptualizations, knowledge frameworks and his/her construction of knowledge in the case study.

Generally, these assumptions associate the sport management researcher with the different ways by which he/she can gain some understanding of some aspects of the nature of reality in his/her research setting (the epistemological dimension), and the different ideas the researcher holds about the nature of reality in the research phenomenon (the ontological dimension). The implication of the epistemological assumption is that "the inquirer and his/her subject interact" (Scott and Usher, 2004, p. 94).

When the data is "analyzed", the use of the case study methodology allows the researcher to classify, compare and describe the findings, in a more meaningful way (Bouma, 2000; Perry et al., 1998, Shipman, 1997). For example, Perry et al. (1998) note that case studies allow for the: "...classification into categories and the identification of inter-relationships between these categories..." of the data acquired (p. 12).

This use of multiple sources of data has particular value, as it increases the construct validity of the research in question. Yin (1989, p. 42) notes that the use of multiple sources of evidence are, "...convergent lines of enquiry..." that allows a process of triangulation to take place (Bonoma, 1985; Parkhe, 1993) which Denzin (1978, p. 291) defines as: "...the combination of methodologies used in the study of the same phenomenon..." in an effort to verify the findings. Eisenhardt (1989) adds weight to Denzin's (1978) approach, arguing that: "...triangulation, made possible by multiple data collection methods ... provides stronger substantiation of constructs" (p. 291). Thus, using multiple sources of evidence makes the findings of the case study method both more convincing and accurate and thus shows that consistent levels of validity and generalizability were achieved (Bonoma, 1983; Shipman, 1997). In this way, it can be argued that the use of convergent interviewing, of data acquired from multiple sources, the use and analysis of multiple case studies, as a methodology, is as compelling as the use of other methods, such as surveys and the use of multivariate techniques (Parkhe, 1993; James & Champion, 1976).

Reynolds (1971) adds support arguing that: "…the best research design is one that does not require statistical analysis, because the results are so obvious that other scientists have high confidence in the results without considering statistical significance" (p. 27). James and Champion (1976), Pinfield (1986) and Eisenhardt (1989) all acknowledge that the use of the case study method allows the researchers to build on existing knowledge, to develop new concepts and hypotheses and to generate and, in appropriate circumstances, test the hypothesis. Furthermore, the case study methodology has been well established as a legitimate methodology in disciplines including; education, management and marketing.

WHAT THEN DEFINES A CASE?

Smith (1978) suggests that a case study is a "bounded system", there being a specific phenomenon as the focus of the investigation, such as: a particular athlete/player, an event, a process, a specific team or institution. Stake (1998) talks of a case being a functioning specific, having working parts and that we choose to study the case for a variety of reasons. A case may be studied because it is of particular concern, presents an issue or hypothesis or it may have intrinsic interest (Merriam, 1988).

In "defining the case" the sport management researcher needs to identify the unit of analysis – "what is it you want to be able to say something about at the end of the study" (Patton, 1980, p. 100)? Defining the unit of analysis helps in "binding" the case as so much information can be gathered that the researcher needs to decide to which body of knowledge they are wanting to contribute (Yin, 1994). A case study can use both quantitative and qualitative data; however, it is generally argued that a case study is associated with a qualitative method of research as opposed to the positivist approach of experimental, quantitative, controlled, laboratory-based research (Stenhouse, 1988). Case studies usually define their methods of data gathering as descriptive, qualitative, interpretive, particularistic, heuristic and naturalistic (Cohen et al., 2000).

CHARACTERISTICS OF A CASE STUDY

The "heuristic characteristic" of a case study enables the reader to have a greater understanding of the case. This may include new meaning or confirm what the reader already knows, it may explain the reasons for a problem, why something worked or not and it may provide further generalization or applicability (Merriam, 1988). The case study can allow insights into the why and how of phenomenon and illuminate new relationships between variables, perhaps adding to the theory.

The "characteristics" of a case study have been defined in a variety of ways. Stake (1995) uses the categories of intrinsic, instrumental and collective, while Merriam (1988) describes case studies as descriptive, interpretive and evaluative. Yin (1984) employs the terms exploratory, descriptive and explanatory. The similarities of the terms may be grouped thus: *intrinsic and descriptive, instrumental, interpretive and explanatory, and, exploratory and evaluative.*

Essentially *descriptive and intrinsic* case studies describe in detail a particular case without forming hypotheses, making judgments or pitting against a theory. As Stake (1995) states "...the study is undertaken because one wants better understanding of this particular case... not because the case represents other cases ... but because, in all its particularity and ordinariness, this case itself is of interest" (p. 88). The *descriptive* case can provide a basis for future comparison and theory building but it is not the primary reason for the study. *Instrumental, interpretive or explanatory* case studies are more about interpreting or theorizing about the phenomenon (Merriam, 1988). The interpretive, explanatory or instrumental case study is more likely to look at the "why" question and contain a far greater level of analysis and conceptualization than a descriptive case study. *Evaluative* case studies, according to Merriam (1988), involve "description, explanation and judgment" (p. 28). Although Yin (1994) does not ascribe evaluation as a specific type of case study he does state the value and place of case study in evaluative research because case studies can explain, describe, illustrate and explore to form judgments about a program, event or intervention.

TYPES OF CASE STUDY DESIGNS

Due to variability in the types of cases that may be studied, there are a number of case study designs that may be used. Each of these designs allows the sport management researcher to address a number of different questions in relation to the case under investigation. The following section is based on work by Willig (2001), who provides a useful categorization of the different types of case studies.

Intrinsic vs. instrumental case studies

Sport management researchers may choose to conduct case study research for the purpose of finding out more about the individual case. That is, the case is chosen purely for interest and for its particularity, rather than about the more general phenomenon or problem. This is called an intrinsic case study. By contrast, an instrumental case study selects a case of interest in order to understand more about a phenomenon. In this instance, the case develops models of a more general phenomenon. Rather than focusing on the case itself, instrumental studies examine a specific phenomenon within a particular case.

Descriptive vs. explanatory case studies

Case study research can also be defined as descriptive or exploratory. The descriptive case study is associated with describing how the phenomenon exists in the everyday world. An explanation of the phenomenon or an understanding of the relationships between variables is not made. Rather, the aim of descriptive case studies is to provide enough detailed description so that a better understanding of the phenomenon is made, and one is able to develop new insights. Unlike the descriptive study, the exploratory case study aims to not only provide a description of the case, but also attempts to provide an explanation of the phenomenon.

Single vs. multiple case studies

Case study research may be conducted using single or multiple participants. The single case design has frequently been chosen for rare or extreme cases. It has also proven effective when testing well-formulated theories. Therefore, the single case design is intrinsic in nature and is useful for testing the "applicability of existing theories to real world data" (Willig, 2001, p. 74). The multiple case study design differs from the single case in that it does not just test existing hypotheses, but allows the sport management researcher to generate new hypotheses. That is, through the comparison of individual cases, the sport management researcher has the opportunity to develop and refine these new formulations. Yin (1994) suggests that one may consider the multiple case design as multiple experiments. That is, the examination of each case modifies the emerging theory in some way. For example, if there is uniformity in the data derived from five cases, then there is compelling evidence for the initial proposal. However, if these cases are in some way contradictory, then the theory must be modified to accommodate for these differences. In this way, a replication logic is used and the study may be viewed similarly to how the positivist deals with contradictory experimental findings. Therefore, multiple case studies are often considered to yield more impressive data, and the overall study is therefore regarded as being more robust.

SELECTION OF CASES FOR STUDY

Case studies, and qualitative research generally, however, do not aim to be statistically representative in the manner of the formal random samples typical of quantitative studies. Rather, case studies "draw a purposive sample, building in variety and acknowledging opportunities for intensive study" (Stake, 2000, p. 446). Purposive sampling, or criterion-based selection, (Maxwell, 1996; Ritchie et al., 2003) bases the selection of study settings and participants on features and characteristics that will enable the researcher to gather in-depth information on the areas of research interest. This form of sampling is therefore purposeful and strategic (Maxwell, 1996), with considerations of convenience and ease of access to study situations and participants given only secondary importance.

USING THE CASE STUDY METHODOLOGY TO BUILD A THEORY

According to Mintzberg (1979), for a researcher to effectively build a theory, it needs to be clearly specified as to what kind of data are to be collected and how that data are to be systematically gathered. For as Eisenhardt (1989) states: "The definition of the research questions, within a broad topic, permit the researcher to specify the kind of organization to be approached…and the kind of data to be gathered" (p. 536). This is in line with Yin's (1989, 1993) thinking, which confirms the importance that the research question plays in the overall design of the research. However, what about the role of developed theory or the lack of one, within the research design? While Eisenhardt (1989) is not wholly in favor of developing a theory prior to the data collection phase, Yin (1989) argues that: "…theory development prior to the collection of any case study data is an essential step in doing case studies" (p. 36). Yin (1989) notes that there are a number of steps in the process, which include the following:

- developing a theory from the reviewed literature
- then defining the relationship between the variables within the theory

- then defining the units of analysis

- the process of analysis and

- the criteria for interpreting the findings. (pp. 33–35)

By doing so, one can be assured of the robustness of the findings, once they have been interpreted and the soundness of the research design as a whole (Yin, 1989, 1994). In contrast to Yin (1989), Eisenhardt (1989) argues that: "...investigators should formulate a research problem and possibly identify some of the potential variables, with some reference to extant literature" (p. 536). Eisenhardt further elaborates, noting that: "...the investigator should avoid thinking about specific relationships between variables and theories as much as possible, especially at the outset of the process...since such attempts will bias and limit the findings" (p. 536). Similarly, Eisenhardt sets out a way of approaching this process, suggesting that: "the research problem is formulated. From which only some of the variables are identified. This allows for an appropriate research design to be chosen, allowing the data to be specified and synthesized to then, build a theory/model" (p. 537).

Through the work of Stake (1995), Hamel (1993) and Eisenhardt (1989), a clear vision of the activities needed to conduct a useful case study emerges. These activities include:

1. Determination of the object of study: it is important to outline the aims and construct tentative hypotheses.

2. Selection of the case: the researcher must select a case pertinent to the object of the study which could be fully investigated.

3. Building of the initial theory through a literature review: enhance the validity, generalizability and theoretical level by tying the emergent theory to existing literature.

4. Collecting and organizing the data.

5. Analyzing the data and reach conclusions: the ultimate goal is to uncover patterns, determine meanings, construct conclusions and build theory.

DATA COLLECTION IN CASE STUDIES

Unlike some other forms of research, the case study approach does not employ any particular methods of data collection or data analysis, but uses a range of techniques appropriate to the given context. A case study may employ a wide variety of data collection methods. Generally, case studies will use qualitative methods of data collection and analysis such as interviews (unstructured and/ or structured), observations, ethnography, use of documents and written material. The sport management researcher is often a participant observer and plays a part in the data collection as they establish relationships and become part of the "furniture". The sport management researcher brings his or her own subjectivity and interpretations of reality that can enable the readers to create their own reality or interpretation of the case. Merriam (1988) states, "because the primary instrument in qualitative case study research is human, all observations and analyses are filtered through one's worldview, one's values, one's perspectives" (p. 39). The sport management researcher will provide the rich description of the context in order to try and capture as much of a holistic picture as possible, identifying any number of variables. A case study may run over a long period of time. For instance, if the case study is of a particular program or group then the study may follow the program or group for a number of years depending on the purpose of the study.

ANALYZING THE DATA

When using the case study methodology, Patton (1990) advises that each case should be written up as a "…holistic and comprehensive narrative" (p. 338). Yin (1989) suggests, rather than supplying every detail, it is better to provide a summation of the key findings using the pattern matching approach. However, as Yin (1989) then notes, all the data need to be available for other researchers to review and so, all the data are available.

This process, although conducted separately, involves four steps. These are as follows:

Step 1: The sport management researcher must immerse themselves in the data for the case (interviews and journals) through numerous readings.

Step 2: The sport management researcher must commence data reduction through coding emerging themes.

Step 3: Once the data are coded, the sport management researcher begins data interpretation.

Step 4: Once all case studies are analyzed and written up, they are then compared by the sport management researcher for similarities and differences.

Research Brief

Title: Beyond Child Labour in Pakistan's Soccer Ball Industry: Hard Times in Imperial Space
Who: Khan, F.R., Mc Gill University
Articulating a case study of the Sialkot soccer ball labour project in Pakistan (1995–2003) the study explores the communication constraints that are faced by weak actors in interorganizational domains located in the developing world. Relying on both written documents and field interviews, especially with women stitchers at village level, a typology of communication constraints is developed. The case study permits an investigation of contemporary transnation activism and the unintended consequences of this activism.

ADVANTAGES OF CASE STUDY APPROACH

Marshall and Rossman (1995) and Yin (1994) state that when the main purpose of the research project is exploratory, then a case study approach is an appropriate strategy. More specifically, Yin (1994) asserts that the case study is appropriate for exploratory analysis when investigating contemporary phenomenon within its real-life context, and when the boundaries between the phenomena and the context are not clear. Furthermore, case studies are the strategy of choice when the focus is on understanding the dynamics present within single settings, and when existing theory seems inadequate (Eisenhardt, 1989).

The second key factor which influenced the use of a case study is related to the nature of what was being studied. As stated previously, the study of knowledge transfer is complex and involves examination of human factors such as perception, feelings and impact of culture. Easterby-Smith et al. (1991) indicate that: "research problems in case study investigations often involve an understanding of managerial perceptions or culture where meanings are socially-constructed rather than being value-free" (p. 24).

A further advantage of the case study approach relates to style and structure A case study approach can permit: "flexible and opportunistic data collection methods that allow additions to questions during interviews" (Easterby-Smith, 1994, p. 532). Torraco (1997) believes that case studies more than any other method offer the greatest potential for revealing richness, holism and complexity in events. Adelman et al. (1983) believe the advantages of case study research to be that it is strong in reality, allows generalization either about an instance or from an instance, recognizes the complexity of social truths, and represents the discrepancies or conflicts between the viewpoints held by participants. Dick (1990) contends that case research deals with the world on its own terms by enabling a greater depth of description. Stake (1983) suggests that case studies are valuable because they utilize the reader's knowledge and experience.

Lincoln and Guba (1985) outline the advantages in the following way:

1. The case study provides a grounded assessment of context. It represents an unparalleled means for communicating contextual information that is grounded in the particular setting that was studied.

2. The case study provides the "thick description" so necessary for judgments of transferability.

3. The case study is an effective vehicle for demonstrating the interplay between inquirer and respondents.

4. The case study builds on the researcher's tacit knowledge, presenting a holistic and lifelike description. Readers of a case study report receive a measure of vicarious experience.

5. The case study is the primary vehicle for and is best suited to emic inquiry. That is that, the naturalistic inquirer tends toward a reconstruction of the respondents' constructions (emic) while positivistic inquirers tend toward a construction that they bring to the inquiry a priori (etic) (pp. 359–360).

LIMITATIONS OF CASE STUDY BASED RESEARCH

While case study based research has many advantages, it is also subject to a number of limitations, which will now be addressed. There are five limitations usually ascribed to the use of the case studies methodology, these are as follows:

1. It can result in overly complex theories.

2. It can be difficult to ensure external validity.

3. It can be difficult to conduct, effectively and efficiently.

4. That no single approach can be deemed sufficient for the development of a sound theory.

5. The high risk of researcher bias. (Parkhe, 1993; Bailey, 1992; Yin, 1994).

The first of these limitations is that it can result in overly complex theories, which results in a loss of parsimony (Eisenhardt, 1989; Parkhe, 1993). This can be overcome by the careful development of prior theories, coupled with specific questions about the theories. Parkhe supports this, arguing that: "…this should be less of a problem in executing the research program … when the research is guided by an initial, tentative framework that attempts parsimoniously to tie core variables into an integrated theoretical system" (p. 255).

The second, common limitation is that of external validity, that is, can this case be generalized beyond itself into the wider situation? Black and Champion (1976) and Parkhe (1993) contend that the use of multiple data sources, such as case studies and other data, coupled with the use of pattern matching and cross-case analysis in the multiple cases, using a theoretical replication logic, is as compelling and scientifically meaningful as the use of surveys and multivariate statistical analysis. For as James and Champion (1976) argue: "…the researcher does not regard case study findings as conclusive proof of anything…neither does the survey researcher" (p. 92).

The third common limitation of case study research is that it can be difficult to conduct, due to unforeseen logistical problems (Bedeian, 1989; Parkhe, 1993). This limitation is not insoluble as the case study protocol acts as a guide to ensure that the case study is conducted consistently, in an appropriate manner (Yin, 1994). The fourth limitation is that the use of case study based research is insufficient to completely develop a coherent and cogent theory (Parkhe, 1993). However, this is not a limitation of case based research alone, for as Parkhe (1993) states: "…no single approach to theory development … is self-sufficient and capable of producing a well-rounded theory that simultaneously maximizes the research quality criteria of construct validity, internal validity, external validity and reliability" (p. 255). The fifth and final limitation is that of researcher bias (Bailey, 1992; Parkhe, 1993). To overcome this problem and perception, Bailey (1992) argues that: "…a good case-researcher must be able to step away from preconceived notions…"" and view the data, and subsequent findings, objectively and not subjectively" (p. 52).

In conclusion, while it can be argued that case study based research has some major limitations, which can be interpreted as a lack of objectivity, rigor or even precision, this does not mean that they cannot be overcome (Yin, 1989, 1994; Perry, 1998).

VALIDITY, RELIABILITY, AND GENERALIZATION

The use of the terms *validity and reliability* is deemed to be inappropriate in case study research in the qualitative paradigm (Sandelowski, 1996;

Bergen & While, 2000). Theoretical generalizations and explanatory theories are viewed as valid outcomes in case study research even though they are considered a weak basis for generalization in the empirical sense. It is argued by case study researchers that generalization is a redundant concept for case study research and analysis is based on the "categorical aggregation of instances" (Bergen & While, 2000). More is learned about the "particular" and the interpretation of these particulars is through an analytical generalization. A case study may be transferable to other people in other sporting organizations and the terms of transferability and "fittingness" are more complementary terms that can apply to case study research, in that persons and settings can be essentially similar and recognizable (Rolfe, 1998; Yin, 2003).

Rather than validity the term "authority" is preferred to acknowledge the reasonableness and authenticity of the research, and there can also be a "shock of recognition" when the case study method is used (Rolfe, 1998). Through the objectification of a practice or the subjectivation of individuals to examination a collective effect on individuals can be revealed. This collective effect on individuals finds them having similar experiences when in similar contexts.

Another criticism or debate about validity of case study research is the notion of generalization. Can and should we generalize from a single case? There appears to be three particular discourses pertaining to generalization. The first is skeptical of the ability of a single case to influence general applicability and confirm grand narratives.

The second aligns the generalization to a theory rather than a population (Firestone, 1993). It is the importance of the relationship between the data and the theory or concepts that can strengthen the theoretical tenets. "When one generalizes to a theory, one uses a theory to make predictions and then confirm [or refine, or disrupt, or refute] those predictions" (Firestone, 1993, p. 17). Although generalization is not an aim of case study research, the case study may have applicability to other cases or persons in similar situations or sport organizations. In case study analysis, as well as comparing with other case studies, the analyst seeks out patterns that are compared with other units of data, leading to the identification of recurring themes and replication. A strict cycle of analysis is undertaken on the units of analysis and each separate data piece within the same case (within-case analysis) that is then compared with the results of other cases (cross-case analysis). This cycle of analysis leads to analytical generalizations (cross-case synthesis) and the results of case study research can be viewed as "mirroring" other similar cases in their natural setting (Yin, 1994, 2003; Cowley et al., 2000).

CASE STUDY AND ETHICS

Because of the intense nature of involvement and participatory observation by the researcher in a case study over a prolonged period of time there is the possibility of revealing or encountering issues that could be harmful to the participants (Ball, 1984; Stake, 1995). The risk of exposure and embarrassment to the participants can be high and it remains the responsibility of the sport management researcher to ensure that the participants are comfortable with all stages of reporting, be it interview transcripts, anecdotal evidence, initial interpretations or the final public document. Merriam (1988) in her summary of ethical considerations concludes:

> ... the burden of producing a study that has been conducted and disseminated in an ethical manner lies with the individual investigator ... the best that an individual researcher can do is be conscious of the ethical issues that pervade the research process, from conceptualizing the problem to disseminating the findings. (p. 184)

Case Study Example

Who: Sean Phelps, Florida State University

What: The Creation and Development of an International Sport Federation: A Case Study of the International Triathlon Union from 1989–2000.

Theoretical framework

Phelps utilized the case study method to analyze what, if any, influence the International Olympic Committee and other organizations had on the International Triathlon Union as it rapidly went from creation, to recognition, and inclusion of the sport on the competition program of the Olympic Games. Using Institutional Theory as the framework, this study looked at identifying the various isomorphic influences exerted upon the International Triathlon Union as the organization moved toward its Olympic goal. While institutional theory describes why organizations move toward homogeneity, typically by three traditional isomorphisms, this study also looked at the variables of leadership and culture to see if they might also influence the direction of this international federation. Additionally, interaction between all the isomorphic influences and variables was also considered. Through use of qualitative methodology incorporating heuristic inquiry and a constructionist philosophy, a variety of pressures, both internal and external, was seen to be exerted on the newly formed international federation.

Data collection methods

By combining heuristic inquiry, phenomenology, and a historical review, as a methodological approach, Phelps explored what transpired over five years development of the ITU. Both primary and secondary data were used to explore and examine what influences were experienced by the ITU as it was created and developed into the international federation for the sport. Primary sources of data included interviews and correspondences with some of the founders of the International Triathlon Union as well as members of other organizations that have been involved with ITU representing national governing bodies.

Data analysis techniques/presentation

This research utilized both primary and secondary data. After collecting the data, content analysis took place. Phelps examined themes and patterns from all the data collected. It was through the triangulation of the data, reviewing all the interview transcripts, historical documents, and field notes from observations that these themes and patterns began to appear. These themes were then coded to help make sense of the plethora of material under review. The conclusions drawn from this research were specific major instances of influences that confronted the ITU and their subsequent impact on development.

Major findings

In summary, this research found that unlike previous studies in sport management that attributed change in organizations due to mimetic isomorphism, the largest influence being exerted upon the International Triathlon Union was that of coercive isomorphism, in a variety of forms. The International Olympic Committee and the Olympic Charter provided the direction the founders of the new international federation had to take.

Phelps found that while coercive isomorphism was the primary influence in how the founders of the International Triathlon Union determined the direction of the organization, there were examples of mimetic and normative influences.

Suggestions for future research

Phelps suggested that future research within this area is vast and involves pristine territory. He argued that International sport federations and their companion national governing bodies have not received the attention by North American researchers when compared to studies incorporating larger professional leagues and major university athletics. According to Phelps, the application of institutional theory in a setting with more than one agency pushing for homogeneity, and possibly in different directions, is seen as an outgrowth of this study.

Case study research probes

1. Discuss how the case study design has been used in this research?
2. What are the advantages of using a case study approach in this research?

CONCLUSION

The aim of case study research is generalizing to theoretical propositions but not to populations. Sport management case studies may be epistemologically in harmony with experiences of others, and a natural basis for generalization. Although the case study method is valuable to sport management, it is infrequently used as a method in sport management research. Encouragement for its use in sport management research as a method is given to investigate the day-to-day observations and interventions that constitute sport management practice. The benefits of using case study include: the research can be conducted in the natural setting; and because of this it is grounded or embedded and this allows for rich description (Yin, 2003). Case study as a research method can and does provide rich narrative data gathered by a variety of both qualitative and quantitative methods. Bounding or defining the case strengthens the methodology, design and validity. Inherent in the characteristics of case study is the sport management researchers' depth of interest and focus on the specificity or uniqueness of the case. This makes possible or allows for a detailed study of all aspects of an individual case or cases.

IN PROFILE - Dr Alison Doherty

Dr Alison Doherty is Associate Professor in Sport Management at the School of Kinesiology, Faculty of Health Sciences, The University of Western Ontario. Her research focuses broadly on the management of nonprofit sport, and community sport volunteerism, group dynamics, and organizational capacity in particular. She has used both quantitative and qualitative designs equally, as well as incorporating concurrent and sequential mixed-methods approaches. Specific qualitative designs she has used include content analysis, policy analysis, and single and multiple case studies. Case study design was used in several different projects to examine in depth particular phenomena in nonprofit sport organizations; specifically, the implementation of a strategic sponsorship process, board conflict, the adoption and implementation of innovation, and organizational capacity. These projects enabled her students, colleagues and herself to gain rich insight into the nature and mechanisms of these organizational aspects by focusing on just one, or a few, particular cases. Case study design is still gaining acceptance in the sport management field, and it can only make further inroads as a viable approach if it is conducted systematically and soundly. A lot of Dr Doherty's qualitative work has also been based around field research comprising personal and focus group interviews. In addition to these traditional designs, she has relied on the rich information that open-ended questions can provide as part of a closed survey instrument. She believes that there is great merit in the use of qualitative data to answer certain research questions. Not every research problem warrants a qualitative design, nor should the researcher assume that a qualitative approach should be used in every case. Dr Doherty finds qualitative research particularly effective to gain insight into a relatively unexplored area, in order to better understand it before developing a further qualitative or quantitative design. It is also particularly useful for better understanding a phenomenon that has been tapped into by quantitative research, and by other researchers. Students and researchers should be well versed in both broad research perspectives, in order to recognize their respective merits, and how and when each approach is used most effectively, and to understand how they may complement each other.

REVIEW AND RESEARCH QUESTIONS

It has been highlighted in this chapter that the case study approach can be characterized as the presentation and analysis of detailed information about single or multiple subjects, in relation to an event, culture or individual life. Through this analysis, the sport management researcher is able to obtain an in-depth understanding of the characteristics of cases in order to generate new insights. With an understanding of the case study approach, attempt to answer the following questions:

1. Identify the process a sport management researcher would follow to design a case study approach?

2. Provide an example of how a case study approach could be used in a sport management setting, identify the limitations that may exist and how those limitations may be overcome?

REFERENCES

Adelman, C., Jenkins, D. & Kemmis, S. 1983. Rethinking case study: notes from the second Cambridge conference (pp. 1–10). Case Study Methods, 2nd ed. Waurn Ponds: Deakin University Press.

Bailey, M. T. 1992. Do physicists use case studies? The thoughts on public administration research. *Public Administration Review*, **52** (1), 47–54.

Ball, S. 1984. Beachside reconsidered; reflections on a methodological apprenticeship. In: *The Research Process in Educational Settings: Ten Case Studies* (Ed. by R. Burgess), pp. 69–96. London: Falmer.

Bedeian, A. G. 1989. Management, 2nd ed. Chicago: The Dyrden Press.

Bergen, A. & While, A. 2000. A case for case studies: exploring the use of case study design in community nursing research. *Journal of Advanced Nursing*, **31**, 926–934.

Black, J. A. & Champion, D. J. 1976. Methods and Issues in Social Research. New York: Wiley.

Bonoma, T. 1985. Case research in marketing: opportunities, problems, and a process. *Journal of Marketing Research*, **12**, 199–208.

Bonoma, T. V. 1983. Get more out of your trade show. *Harvard Business Review*, **Jan–Feb**, 75–83.

Cohen, L., Manion, L. & Morrison, K. 2000. Research Methods in Education, 5th ed. London: Routledge/Falmer.

Cowley, S., Bergen, A., Young, K. & Kavanagh, A. 2000. Generalising to theory: the use of a multiple case study design to investigate needs assessment and quality of care in community nursing. *International Journal of Nursing Studies*, **37** (3), 219–228.

Creswell, J. W. 1998. Qualitative Inquiry and Research Design: Choosing Among Five Traditions. Thousand Oaks, CA: Sage.

Denzin, N. K. 1978. Sociological Methods: A Sourcebook. New York: McGraw-Hill.

Dick, B. 1990. Convergent Interviewing. Brisbane: Interchange.

Easterby-Smith, M. 1994. Evaluating Management Development, Training and Education, 2nd ed. Brookfield: Gower.

Easterby-Smith, M., Thorpe, R. & Lowe, A. 1991. Management research: an introduction – action research case study. *British Journal of Management*, **11** (2), 103–119.

Eisenhardt, K. M. 1989. Building theories from case study research. *Academy of Management Review*, **14** (4), 532–550.

Firestone, W. A. 1993. Alternative arguments for generalizing from data as applied to qualitative research. *Educational Researcher*, **22** (4), 16–23.

Guba, E. G. & Lincoln, Y. S. 1981. Effective Evaluation. San Francisco, CA: Jossey-Bass.

Hamel, J. 1993. Case Study Methods. Newbury Park, CA: Sage.

James, A. B. & Champion, D. J. 1976. Methods and Issues in Social Research. Melbourne: John Wily & Sons.

Lincoln, Y. S. & Guba, E. G. 1985. Naturalistic Inquiry. Newbury Park, CA: Sage.

Marshall, C. & Rossman, G. B. 1995. Designing Qualitative Research. Newbury Park, CA: Sage.

Maxwell, J. A. 1996. Qualitative Research Design: An Interactive Approach. Thousand Oaks, CA: Sage.

Merriam, S. B. 1988. Case Study Research in Education: A Qualitative Approach. San Francisco: Jossey-Bass.

Merriam, S. B. 1998. Qualitative Research and Case Study Applications in Education. San Francisco: Jossey-Bass.

Miles, M. B. & Huberman, A. M. 1994. Qualitative Data Analysis: A Sourcebook of New Methods, 2nd ed. Thousand Oaks, CA: Sage.

Mintzberg, H. 1979. An emerging strategy of "direct" research. *Administrative Science Quarterly*, **24**, 580–589.

Parkhe, A. 1993. "Messy" research, methodological predispositions, and theory development in international joint ventures. *Academy of Management Review*, **18** (2), 227–268.

Patton, M. Q. 1980. Qualitative Evaluation Methods. Thousand. Oaks, CA: Sage.

Patton, M. Q. 1990. Qualitative Evaluation and Research Methods. Newbury, Cal: Sage.

Perry, C. 1998. Processes of a case study methodology for postgraduate research in marketing. *The European Journal of Marketing*, **32** (9/10), 785–802.

Perry, C., Riege, A. & Brown, L. 1998. Realism rules OK: scientific paradigms in marketing research about networks. Conference Proceedings of the 28th Australian and New Zealand Marketing Academy. Dunedin: University of Otago.

Pinfield, L. 1986. A field evaluation of perspectives on organisational decision making. *Administrative Science Quarterly*, **31**, 365–388.

Reynolds, P. 1971. A Primar in theory construction. Indianapolis: Bobbs-Merrill.

Ritchie, J., Lewis, J. & Elam, G. 2003. Designing and selecting samples. In: *Qualitative Research Practice: A Guide for Social Sciences Students and Researchers* (Ed. by J. Ritchie, J. Lewis). London: Sage.

Rolfe, G. 1998. The theory–practice gap in nursing: from research-based practice to practitioner-based research. *Journal of Advanced Nursing*, **28**, 672–679.

Sandelowski, M. 1996. Using qualitative methods in intervention studies. *Research in Nursing & Health*, **19**, 359–364.

Scapens, R. W. 1990. Researching management accounting practice: the role of case study methods. *British Accounting Review*, **22**, 259–281.

Scott, D. & Usher, R. 2004. Researching Education: Data methods and theory in education inquiry. London: Continuum.

Shipman, M. 1997. The Limitations of Social Research. London: Longman.

Smith, L. M. 1978. An evolving logic of participant observation, educational ethnography and other case studies. In: *Review of Research in Education* (Ed. by L. Shulman), pp. 316–377. Itasca., IL: Peacock.

Stake, R. 2000. Case studies. In: *Handbook of Qualitative Research* (Ed. by N. K. Denzin, Y. S. Lincoln), pp. 435–454, 2nd ed. Thousand Oaks, CA: Sage.

Stake, R. E. 1983. The case study method in social inquiry. In: *Evaluation Models – Viewpoints on Educational and Human Services Evaluation* (Ed. by G. F. Madaus, M. Scriven, D. Stufflebeam), pp. 279–286. Boston: Kluwer-Nijhof Publishing.

Stake, R. E. 1995. The Art of Case Study Research. Thousand Oaks, CA: Sage.

Stake, R. E. 1998. Case studies. In: *Strategies of Qualitative Research* (Ed. by N. K. Denzin, Y. S. Lincoln), pp. 86–109. Thousand Oaks, CA: Sage.

Stenhouse, L. 1988. Case Study Methods. In I. P. Keeves (Ed.), Educational research, methodology and measurement: an international handbook (pp. 49–53). Oxford: Pergamon Press.

Sutton, R. I. & Staw, B. M. 1995. What theory is not. *Administrative Science Quarterly*, **40**, 371–384.

Torraco, R. J. 1997. Theory building research methods. In: *Human Resource Development Research Handbook: Linking Research and Practice* (Ed. by R. A. Swanson, E. F. Holton), pp. 114–138. San Francisco: Berrett-Kohler.

Willig, C. 2001. Memory work. In: *Introducing Qualitative Research in Psychology: Adventures in Theory and Method* (Ed. by C. Willig). Buckingham: Open University Press.

Yin, R. 1984. Case Study Research: Design and Methods, 1st ed. Beverly Hills, CA: Sage.

Yin, R. 1989. Case Study Research: Design and Methods (Rev. ed.). Beverly Hills, CA: Sage.

Yin, R. 1993. Applications of Case Study Research. Newbury Park, CA: Sage.

Yin, R. 1994. Case Study Research: Design and Methods, 2nd ed. Thousand Oaks, CA: Sage.

Yin, R. K. 2003. Case Study Research, Design and Methods, 3rd ed. Newbury Park: Sage.

Zucker, D. 2001. Using case study methodology in nursing research. *The Qualitative Report*, **6** (2).

CHAPTER 11

Deconstruction and Sport Management Research

OBJECTIVES

By the end of this chapter, you should be able to
- understand the basic concepts of deconstruction.
- identify the implications of the use of deconstruction methodology in sport management.

KEY TERMS

Différance: This French neologism is, on the deconstructive argument, properly neither a word nor a concept; it names the non-coincidence of meaning both synchronously and diachronically, and also describes the process within which meanings are produced or defined by interpreters of the literature by an infinite number of deferrals to other linguistic, political, social and philosophical meanings so that no meaning is the ultimate truth.

Trace: The idea of *différance* also brings with it the idea of *trace*. A trace is what a sign differs/defers from. It is the absent part of the sign's presence. In other words, through the act of *différance*, a sign leaves behind a *trace*, which is whatever is left over after everything *present* has been accounted for. According to Derrida, "the trace itself does not exist" (Derrida, 1976, p. 167) because it is self-effacing. That is, "[i]n presenting itself, it becomes effaced" (p. 125). Because all signifiers viewed as *present* in Western thought will necessarily contain traces of other (absent) signifiers, the signifier can be neither wholly present nor wholly absent.

Écriture: In deconstruction, the word *écriture* (usually translated as *writing* in English) is appropriated to refer not just to systems of graphic communication, but to all systems inhabited by *différance*. A related term, called *archi-écriture*, refers to the positive side of writing, or writing as an ultimate principle, rather than as a derivative of *logos* (speech). In other words, whereas the Western *logos* encompasses writing, it is equally valid to view *archi-écriture* as encompassing the *logos*, and therefore speech can be thought of as a form of writing: writing on air waves, or on the memory of the listener or recording device, but there is no fundamental dominance at work.

Logocentrism: In critical theory and deconstruction, logocentrism is a phrase coined by the German philosopher Ludwig Klages in the 1920s to refer to the perceived tendency of Western thought to locate the *center* of any text or discourse within the logos (a Greek word meaning *word*, *reason*, or *spirit*). Jacques Derrida used the term to characterize most of Western philosophy since Plato: a constant search for the "truth."

Sign: What is written.

Signifier: Is the visual mark, acoustic expression, or sound-image of the sign.

Signified: The concept of mental image associated with the sign.

CHAPTER OVERVIEW

This chapter explores the controversial methodology of deconstruction – which many critics claim is not a legitimate methodology. Deconstruction seeks to locate and identify multiple interpretations within texts and to then dislocate the dominant discourse by examining the language and structure of the text – by what has been selected, and not selected, to create the structure. In sport management literature, deconstruction can facilitate further scholarly discussion by challenging the legitimacy and validity of those precepts and ideas generally accepted within the sport management academic community to be irrefutable. This chapter will provide an introduction and overview to the concept of deconstruction and provide some suggestions as to possible frameworks from which to start the process of deconstruction in the reading of sport management literature.

DEFINING DECONSTRUCTION AS A METHODOLOGY

Deconstruction has its modern origins in the discipline of philosophy and the work of Jacques Derrida, who proposed it as a strategy for challenging some of the taken-for-granted ideas that have permeated philosophical thought since the time of Plato. Derrida employed the strategies of deconstruction in his earliest writings in the 1960s, particularly in his seminal work *Of Grammatology* (Derrida, 1976), where he de-constructs philosophical texts by (amongst others) Plato, Kant, Hegel, Heidegger and Rousseau. However, Derrida's refusal to privilege philosophical texts, indeed, his questioning of philosophy as a discipline in its own right, ensured that deconstruction was quickly adopted by other disciplines, particularly literary theorists. Deconstruction is often associated with postmodernism, although Derrida never (as far as we are aware) used the term or regarded himself as a postmodernist.

One of the difficulties that many readers have with deconstruction is its slipperiness, its unwillingness to be pinned down and precisely defined. We can see its elusive nature in Derrida's constant refusal to offer a definition.

For example, a number of quotes that illustrate its elusiveness are offered below:

> *Deconstruction doesn't consist in a set of theorems, axioms, tools, rules, techniques, methods ... There is no deconstruction, deconstruction has no specific object (Derrida, 1996, p. 218).*

> *Deconstruction is not a method and cannot be transformed into one (Derrida, 1991, p. 273).*

> *It must also be made clear that deconstruction is not even an act or an operation (Derrida, 1991, p. 273).*

And, ultimately,

> *What is deconstruction? Nothing, of course! (Derrida, 1991, p. 275)*

Derrida's theories are concerned with language, meaning, philosophy and politics.

Derrida saw the binary oppositions in Western thought as pervading intellectual and cultural life, and grouped these under the term "logocentrism" which describes the orientation of thought around a word. Part of this theory was that in Western philosophy, the first terms in the binary pairs took on positive value and legitimacy: such pairs include presence in presence/absence, reason in reason/emotion, and public in public/private. Derrida also invented other terms including his word *differance* which attempts to describe the process within which meanings are produced by interpreters by infinite deferrals to other linguistic, political, social and philosophical meanings so that no meaning can be irreducibly distilled to a pure essence.

To construct something is to build it from selected materials. To "deconstruct" is to reverse the process. "Deconstruction" is not *destruction* as it does not destroy the existence of anything; rather, it is "deconstruction": a discovery of the materials selected, and those not selected, to create the structure. Deconstruction facilitates the questioning of the theoretical and moral limits possessed by the structure imposed by the selected materials used to create it. Derrida (1995) says: "it is the breakdown that lays bare the functioning of the machine as such" (p. 348).

Within a research framework, deconstruction takes an author's own criteria for privileging their own work, and then de-constructs the text by pointing out how the author violates their own system of privilege. Deconstruction examines texts and demonstrates how the legitimacy of any claim to an external metaphysical grounding (beyond the text itself) is supported by only the linguistic and rhetorical, perhaps sophisticated, strategies of the author. The purpose of deconstruction, then, is to subvert the attempt to get closure around knowledge production – the attempt to silence other voices by illicitly claiming to possess a superior awareness of "truth". The subversive impulse makes deconstruction polemical, a political act designed to critique and dismantle intellectual elitism.

What deconstruction attempts to destroy is the claim of any rule-bound system of knowledge production to unequivocally dominate another, the attempt to close off the scholarly conversation by privileging one's own discourse over others. Deconstruction takes an author's own system of grounding and reveals their intellectual position. Norris (1982) says: "Derrida refuses to grant philosophy the kind of privileged status it has always claimed as the sovereign dispenser of reason" (pp. 18–19).

Derrida's theories of deconstruction and "differance" are a valuable tool for exploring the paradoxes, biases, and contradictions in social and organizational behavior, and by extension, into the field of sport management research. According to Derrida, deconstruction informs us that multiple interpretations of texts are always possible despite their appearance of fixity they have assumed in our minds.

Many current theories of sport management are infused with unexamined commitments to particular moral and social orders. Thus, the practice of sport management and theorizing about that practice are always and already informed by ethics which help to *create* the material conditions of human lives. To deny the value-laden-ness of one's theorizing is to deny responsibility for the consequences of one's theories. Deconstruction can be utilized to bring those value commitments to the surface and lead sport management researchers to question their research on *ethical* grounds. Deconstruction can also be utilized to subvert the pretensions of positivism as a higher order theory of knowledge production.

METHODS

It has often been the case that "deconstruction" has been presented and defended by its best proponents as neither a traditionally constituted philosophical system tending toward its own coherence and closure, nor an easily reproducible, stabilizable method of inquiry or analysis (Wortham, 1998). Derrida himself refused to characterize deconstruction as a method, referring to it at different times as an "experience" or a "movement". It has in innate exploratory nature. The experience of deconstructing a text is to "work through the structured genealogy of its concepts ... to determine from a certain external perspective that it cannot name or describe what this history may have concealed or excluded, constituting itself as history through this repression in which it has a stake. The goal of the deconstructor is to challenge the text's claims to coherence, neutrality and objectivity.

Then what can be perceived as deconstruction's methodology? Often in the literature that attempts to explain Derrida's approach it is described as a "disturbance" which we then conceptualize in our typical intellectual mind frame as though it were an experience of a movie, as in, "oh my, that was disturbing"! Deconstruction is not a compartmentalized disturbance that one leaves within the text.

How are these ideas to be translated into action? Deconstruction cannot be sought in an instruction manual. It is not a method to be followed regardless of context, discourse and purpose. Derrida's theoretical notions inform us of the broad purpose of deconstruction and of a general outline of its practice but there is no one way to "do" it. Derrida's writings supply "some general rules, some procedures that can be transposed by analogy, but these rules are taken up in a text which is each time a unique element and which does not let itself be turned totally into a method. Each deconstructive inquiry is unique as reading is a mixed experience of the other in his or her singularity as well as philosophical content, information that can be torn out of this singular context.

The challenge of deconstruction is that it locates its understanding within a "language game" of textual analysis, and discovers multiple interpretations within texts (signifiers) which challenge meaning and identity. Deconstruction seeks to extrapolate signs and significations from a text which operate within written texts but conform to language as their regulated function (Derrida, 1976). In this language game, the text acts as a signifier in which language becomes a chain of significations and the author is seen as inscribed within the text. Basically, this implies that multiple interpretations of the text are valid, and in Derrida's terms, "Il n'y a pos hors-texte" (p .158) – there is nothing outside the text.

By questioning the organizing principles of canonical texts, Derrida aimed to place these principles in new relation to each other, suggesting the possibility that interpretations can be debated rather than suppressed. Thus, deconstruction is used not to abolish truth, but to question how these interpretations evolve from texts and how they are employed to systematically support categories of thought and communication. The implications of a deconstructive reading are therefore not limited to the language of the text itself but can be extended to the political and social context in which the text is placed. This allows the reader to understand the extent to which the objectivity and persuasiveness of the text is dependent on a series of strategic interpretations.

Research Brief

Title: Power Relation in a Professional Sports Franchise
Who: Edwards, A. & Skinner, J. (2001), Journal of Football Studies, 4(1) 69–81
Edwards and Skinner utilized the theoretical lens provided by Foucault's (1977) discourse of power in deconstructing the function of power structures in a professional sport franchise. They argued that if power relations operate at the level of the body, and exist in action, then they should be observable in the microlevel practices of sport organizations. The study was concerned with the possibility of deconstructing power relations through observations gained through workplace experience in a sport franchise. Edwards and Skinner utilized reflective reconstruction and analysis of critical incidents from workplace experiences as the way to elaborate power dimensions in the sport franchise.

DECONSTRUCTION IN SPORT MANAGEMENT RESEARCH

Within sport management research, the *meta-narrative* (dominant paradigm or discourse) of evidence-based practice (EBP) sets itself in opposition to other "narratives" which offer alternative stories about the lived world. This meta-narrative is privileged over other narratives. In other words, the meta-narrative establishes the rules according to which all other narratives are judged. We can see this quite clearly in the widely accepted "hierarchy of evidence" (Evans, 2003), which privileges the findings from "hard" quantitative research over other forms of evidence such as "soft" qualitative research and reflections on practice. The meta-narrative is therefore very difficult to challenge, because it sets the criteria by which any challenges are to be judged.

Some sport management researchers may argue that the EBP school of sport management research exercises undue influence on the production of sport management knowledge. The continued influence of EBP is due to many factors; among them: (1) sport management scholars' unwillingness to critically examine the political, ontological, metaphysical and epistemological assumptions that underlie research, and (2) specific institutional arrangements for the production and dissemination of sport management knowledge (i.e., scholarly journals and conferences) which form a "market" for sport management research that is driven by factors beyond the intellectual competence of the research. Thus, sport management research is less expansive and less intellectually rigorous than it could be because of the biopolitical control (Hardt & Negri, 2000) of EBP. The aim of deconstruction is thus to "undermine the framework" on which the meta-narrative is built. Rather than critiquing EBP, deconstruction focuses on the legitimacy of the criteria that EBP has privileged, and which in turn privilege EBP itself.

The use of deconstruction shows that EBP is not supported by hard research evidence; that the generation and application of research findings to practice is itself open to the distortions of memory. Second, deconstruction is concerned with language and the way that it is often distorted by the dominant discourse to its own ends. So, for example, it demonstrates how the word "evidence" has been used to provide a logical, empirical facade to research-based practice. Third, deconstruction attempts to break down dichotomies in which one term is favored over its opposite by the dominant discourse. The most obvious example is the way in which EBP has been set up in opposition to reflective practice, as Edwards (1999) highlights below:

Evidence-Based Practice	Reflective Practice
Based on hard research	Based on personal anecdote and intuition
Objective and unbiased	Biased due to fallible human memory
Based on truth	Based on fiction

Drawing on the initial deconstruction discussion above, it is possible to identify some strategies from which to begin the process of deconstruction. These are highlighted in Table 11.1.

Table 11.1	Strategies from Which to Begin the Process of Deconstruction
Strategy	**Sport Management Example**
Dismantling a dichotomy – exposing it as a false distinction	The opposition of evidence-based practice and reflective practice
Examining silences – what is not said	Which groups were not surveyed
Attending to disruptions and contradictions, places where the text fails to make sense	Does the language support the assertion or reality of the situation. For example, in reading sport management policy documents, does the language support the conclusions?
Focusing on the element that is most alien to a text or a context as a means of deciphering implicit taboos – the limits to what is conceivable or permissible	"Facts", "evidence" and "theory" in sport management policy should never be examined independently of hegemonic beliefs.

(*continued*)

Table 11.1 Strategies from Which to Begin the Process of Deconstruction *continued*	
Strategy	**Sport Management Example**
Interpreting metaphors as a rich source of multiple meanings	What figures of speech/symbolism innate to sport management can have multiple meanings?
Analyzing "double-entendres" that may point to an unconscious subtext, often sexual in content.	Challenging the oppressiveness of the "hidden agenda" contained in oral and written text.
Separating group-specific and more general sources of bias by "reconstructing" the text with iterative substitution phrases	Positivist theory and the empirical tradition are not entitled to the kind of epistemic privilege and authority that they have enjoyed in silencing other kinds of sport management research. For example, What knowledge is represented in sport management journals?
Exploring, with careful "reconstructions" the unexpected ramifications and inherent limitations of minor policy changes	Understanding that policy is not merely theoretical but has practical, material implications for those people who live within the confines of oppressive discourses within the document.
Using the limitations exposed by "reconstruction" to explain the persistence of the status quo and the need for more ambitious change programs	"The sport manager" is a subject position for participants to occupy. Why is it that only those who occupy the subject position may be (re)presented in the discourse?

By introducing deconstruction to sport management, it is possible to subvert the pretensions of positive theory as a theory of knowledge production. Therefore, by supporting deconstruction it is possible to hold positive theory intellectually accountable and to make clear the fact that knowledge production is always shaped by political, ontological and epistemological assumptions.

The challenge of deconstruction as a research approach is that no one *narrative* is considered dominant or superior over another. As such deconstruction is often viewed as more a form of critique than of conclusive analysis.

Deconstruction Case Study

Who: Dr James Skinner (Griffith University), Associate Professor Bob Stewart (Victoria University) & Dr Allan Edwards (Griffith University)

What: Interpreting Policy Language and Managing Organizational Change

Theoretical framework

Skinner, Stewart and Edwards utilized Derrida's (1976, 1978, 1981, 1982) postmodern theories of deconstruction and "differance" to analyze organizational change in rugby union during the 1990s. Specifically, the research aimed to examine the ways in which internal policy and planning documents produced were formulated, and subsequently interpreted by the many volunteer officials at the local and community level. Derrida's constructs provided a framework within which to explain the potential for policy and planning documents to produce fragmented organizational outcomes. This approach to the interpretation of texts proved a valuable tool for exploring the paradoxes, biases, and contradictions in social and organizational behavior.

Data collection methods

The data collection was through semi-structured interviews with individuals at differing functional levels within rugby union. Audio taping allowed the researchers to preserve the rapport they had developed and concentrate fully on the interviewees' responses and use these as a basis for further questioning. All interviews were carried out in person and interviewees demonstrated a willingness and openness in their responses to the questions posed. The interview data were supplemented by content analysis of policy and planning documents developed.

Data analysis techniques/presentation

Derrida's (1976, 1978, 1981, 1982) postmodern theories of deconstruction and "differance" were utilized as a tool for exploring the paradoxes, biases, and contradictions in social and organizational behavior in rugby union. The researchers interpreted the interview data through this lens and policy documents through the qualitative technique of latent content analysis to provide more subjective information on such areas as motives, attitudes and values as text. In this way, themes were identified.

The analysis of data showed that policy and planning documents were not only interpreted differently at the different functional levels within rugby union's management, but when used to guide change, often met resistance that was not anticipated. The ambiguity of these documents therefore complicated the organizational change process because organizational sub-units frequently gave meanings to the text that were not intended by senior management.

Major findings

In summary, the philosophical praxis of "deconstruction" and the interrelated concept of "differance" were used to highlight the ways in which the policy and planning documents produced by rugby administrators produced multiple meanings. It was established that what is significant within any text, and why it is significant, depended upon who was reading the text and in what context it was being read. In this case, the differing interpretation of the planning documents contributed to fragmented outcomes, and undermined the organizational change process.

Although the findings of this research support the work of other sport management change scholars who have indicated that sporting organizations will invariably resist change if it is seen as a perceived threat to the status quo, it extended our understanding of how resistance to change can be mobilized through the interpretation of policy documents by volunteer management. Despite policy and planning documents being developed by management to guide change, the differing interpretations of these documents at the local/club level reduced their effectiveness in managing the change agenda. This created ongoing tensions that slowed the whole change process, and forced management to re-consider their change strategies.

This study confirms that the management of organizational change is fraught with difficulty, and requires more than a set of policy documents and vision statements to secure the desired outcome. In this case, the policies and plans were frequently re-interpreted to defend/maintain traditional values and practices.

Suggestions for future research

Although historical approaches encourage us to constantly challenge our own understandings about organizational change, the test is whether they can reveal and predict the real nature of this change. Skinner, Stewart and Edwards believe that deconstruction provided a framework within which to explain the potential for policy and planning documents to produce fragmented organizational outcomes. It is suggested that the application of this deconstructive approach to other sporting organizations could further enhance our understanding of the complex phenomena of organizational change.

Case study research probes

1. Do you think that the research approach of deconstruction has provided insights into the organizational change process that positivist approaches could not achieve? If so, how, if not, why?

2. How do you think Derrida's concept of "difference" has been used in this research?

3. How could the outcomes of this research be used to inform sport managers who are facilitating an organizational change process?

CONCLUSION

This chapter has explored and examined the concept and method of Deconstruction. A controversial methodology since the 1960s, with numerous critics and proponents, deconstruction nonetheless has facilitated a vibrant and ongoing discourse by challenging long held tenets and beliefs by a comprehensive analysis of language and text. Researchers in sport sociology, notably Cole, Garber and Andrews, have utilized Derridean concepts as strategies to deconstruct issues such as sexual and gender politics, racial difference, and even drug-taking in sport. Deconstruction has its origins in philosophy, but we argue that it is useful and relevant as a way of challenging the dominant paradigm of any discipline, including sport management.

IN PROFILE - Associate Professor Maria Hopwood

Maria Hopwood is Associate Professor Public Relations in the Faculty of Humanities and Social Sciences at Bond University on Queensland's Gold Coast. Her research interest is sports public relations which means that her work is recognized by the disciplines of both public relations and sports management. She has published in Corporate Communications: An International Journal, The International Journal of Sports Marketing and Sponsorship, Sport Marketing Europe and in leading edited texts in the sports marketing field. She is a regular conference presenter at international conferences and sits on the Editorial Boards for *Public Relations Review* and *The International Journal of Sports Communication*. Maria joined Bond University in 2006 following 20 years' lecturing at the University of Teesside in North East England. Having worked extensively in consultancy with professional English sports organizations such as Durham County Cricket Club and Middlesbrough Football Club, Maria is now enjoying experiencing the Australian approach to sport. Maria's research into sports public relations began when working on the thesis component of her Master of Science degree in Public Relations at the University of Stirling in Scotland. Her research interest was into whether and how English County Cricket clubs were implementing public relations. The lack of previous research into sports public relations and the nature of the research meant that this study relied predominantly on qualitative research as it was concerned with process rather than the outcomes of products and because reflexivity was an important dimension. Qualitative research continues to predominate in her work because much of what she does requires that she talks to people and frequently adopts the role of participant observer. She also strongly agrees with Daymon and Holloway's (2002) observation that there is an increasing awareness in contemporary public relations and marketing communications of collaborative dialog and that qualitative research has the potential to enable this to be achieved.

REVIEW AND RESEARCH QUESTIONS

Deconstruction seeks to locate and identify multiple interpretations within text which challenge meaning and identity. With a basic understanding now of deconstruction as an alternative to the more traditional methodologies associated with sport management research, attempt to answer the following questions:

- Is there any place within sport management research for deconstruction? Provide 2 examples.

- Identify those key features of the frameworks suggested here that you believe would enable an effective "deconstruction" of a sport management text.

REFERENCES

Daymon, C. & Holloway, I. 2002. Qualitative Research Methods in Public Relations and Marketing Communications. London: Routledge.

Derrida, J. 1976. Of Grammatology (G.C. Spivak, Trans.). Baltimore: John Hopkins University Press.

Derrida, J. 1978. Writing and Difference. London: Routledge & Kegan Paul.

Derrida, J. 1981. Dissemination. London: Athlone Press.

Derrida, J. 1982. Margins of Philosophy (A. Bass trans.). Chicago: University of Chicago Press.

Derrida, J. 1991. Letter to a Japanese Friend. In P. Kamuf (Ed.), A Derrida Reader: Reading Between the Blinds (pp. 270–276). New York: Harvester Wheatsheaf.

Derrida, J. 1995. Points: Interviews 1974–1994 (P. Kamuf, Trans.). Stanford: Standford University Press.

Derrida, J. 1996. Deconstruction and Pragmatism. New York: Routledge.

Edwards, A. 1999. Reflective practice in sport management. *Sport Management Review*, **2** (1), 67–81.

Evans, M. 2003. Gender and Social Theory. Philadelphia: Open University Press.

Foucault, M. 1977. Discipline and Punish: the birth of the prison. London: Penguin.

Hardt, M. & Negri, A. 2000. Empire. Cambridge, MA.: Harvard University Press

Norris, C. 1982. Deconstruction: Theory and Practice. London and New York: Methuen.

Wortham, S. M. 1998. Counter-Institutions: Jacques Derrida and the Question of the University. New York: Fordham University Press.

Discourse and Critical Discourse Analysis in Sport Management Research

OBJECTIVES

By the end of this chapter, you should be able to
- understand the basic concepts of discourse, discourse analysis and critical discourse analysis.

- identify the implications of the use of discourse analysis and critical discourse analysis methodology in sport management.

KEY TERMS

Discourse: Discourse refers to the attitudes, rules, "ways of being", actions and language used to construct a particular knowledge. Language, power, and knowledge are joined. Discourse ultimately serves to control not just *what* but *how* subjects are constructed. There is no just one discourse but a polyvalence of discourses that are simultaneously occurring and sometimes even contradicting each other.

Discursive practices: Discursive practices are the translation of discourses into social action; they are the enactment of discourse.

KEY QUESTIONS

The key questions raised in this chapter are as follows:
- What is "Discourse", "Discourse Analysis" and "Critical Discourse Analysis"?

- What are the implications for utilizing discourse analysis in the field of sport management research?

CHAPTER OVERVIEW

This chapter explores the methodology of discourse, discourse analysis and critical discourse analysis and their possible applications to the field of sport management research. Discourses are the conversations and the meanings behind those conversations of groups of people who hold certain ideas and beliefs in common. In the context of sport management research, the analysis of discourses can provide new and exciting insights into the reasons behind the adoption of certain sport policies, and the acceptance of certain research outcomes as "truth". This chapter will provide an introduction and overview to the concept of discourse and provide some suggestions as to possible frameworks from which to start the process of discourse analysis in the reading of sport management literature.

DEFINING DISCOURSE AND DISCOURSE ANALYSIS

The notion of "discourse" has been influenced by Michel Foucault's analyses of society and social practice (Foucault, 1991). Foucault developed the concept of "discourse" by which he meant the *"different ways of structuring areas of knowledge and social practice"*. By "discourse" Foucault is not referring to language alone or to a linguistic concept connected to speech or writing but to sets of enunciative (speakable) statements that recur in talk and texts of all kinds and in different historical periods, and contexts, where they take on different configurations (Foucault, 1972). Discourses are made up of a limited number of statements that are linked together in a single (loosely unified) linguistic formation and for which specific conditions of emergence and existence can be found.

The concept of "discourse" has been refined over time and, according to Shapiro (1987), "discourse" can be "any systematic or disciplined way of constituting subjects, objects, and relationships" (p. 365). There are, of course, a variety of alternate ways of defining the notion of discourse. Parker (1992), for example, defines discourse as *"a system of statements which construct an object"* (cited in Burr, 1995, p. 48). For Burr (1995) Discourse Analysis, is, "the analysis of a ...text in order to reveal either the discourses operating within it or the linguistic and rhetorical devices that are used in its construction" (p. 184).

For Fairclough (1996), discourse actively constitutes or is involved in constructing society in its various dimensions. Fairclough maintains that discourse *"constitutes the object of knowledge, social subjects and forms of "self", social relationships, and conceptual frameworks"* (p. 39). In addition to the notion of discourse, the notion of "discursive practices" developed by Foucault describes the linguistic practices and the use of socially charged language to produce dominant fields of knowledge. Foucault's analysis highlights the struggle between dominant social, cultural and political power groups within society. Foucault's position was that as a result of this struggle a discourse is not either true or false; rather, truth is simply the effect of power relations that create and constitute a prevailing form of truth and meaning (Fairclough, 1996).

For Foucault (1972) discourses and discursive practices do not consist of one statement, text, action or point of origin but appear across a range of texts and conducts and in various forms. He stipulates that discourses consist of a hypothesized unity that is always provisional. "We must conceive of discourse as a series of discontinuous segments whose tactical function is neither uniform or stable" (p. 124). Discourses, then, do not refer to a single object formed once and for all. Thus, a different discourse, enabled by a different episteme (a historically specific way of thinking or knowing) can emerge and dislocate an existing one, producing a modified or new discursive formation, knowledge and practice.

Discourses, then, are disciplinary and productive in that they enable and constrain fields of knowledge and inquiry, govern what can meaningfully be said and talked about, done and thought within those fields (Foucault, 1972, 1981). They are functional (Potter & Wetherell, 1987), inhibiting and productive (Hook, 2001), and rhetorical and persuasive (Billig, 1991). Discourse theory asks why this version of things, why this particular utterance or "reality" exists without implying an underlying hidden "truth". And it considers the functionality of discourse in terms of the status of the speaker and the sociocultural, historical, spatial, and institutional contexts (such as sport organizations) from which statements are made or discourses spoken.

> *We must grasp the statement in the exact specificity of its occurrence; determine its condition of existence, fix at least its limits, establish its correlations with other statements that may be connected with it, and show what other forms of statement it excludes ... The question ... might be formulated in this way: what is the specific existence that emerges from what is said and nowhere else? (Foucault, 1972, pp. 30–31)*

Discourse analysis is not without challenge. Jacobs (1999) outlines three major areas of theoretical criticism namely, *relativism, the privileging of "agency" over "structure"* and, finally, the *problem of bias*. In a rebuttal of this criticism, we argue that discourse analysis is not a *method* through which the "truth" is revealed, rather discourse analysis is a technology that provides a consistent and rational explanation of sport management discourse positions.

THE OPERATION OF POWER

For Foucault discourses are about productive and disciplinary power. Power functions in and through discourse and their practice; discourses are where relations of power are exercised and enacted (Fairclough, 1989; Parker, 1992).

Foucault (1984) stipulates that he uses the word "power" as a shortcut to his intended expression of "relations (or capillaries) of power" that are to be found in all social fields, in all institutional apparatus and technologies, in bodies, conducts, gestures, and in all human relations be they, for instance, love relationships, sexual, economic or institutional relationships. Although unevenly distributed, power is everywhere. In short, "power is not an evil [negative and repressive] but involves strategic games" (p. 18).

According to Foucaultian theory, discourses do more than designate things and "it is this "more" that we must reveal and describe" (Foucault, 1972, p. 54). His theory posits that it is through the discursive generation of knowledge that sustains certain "regimes of truth" and rules out others that power is made operative (Foucault, 1977, 1978, 1980, 1983). Discourse, then, is the point of juncture between knowledge and power. That is, through discourse both knowledge and power are inextricably linked and set in motion; "both directly imply one another" (Foucault, 1977, p. 27). For Foucault discourses are about productive and disciplinary power. Power functions in and through discourse and their practice; discourses are where relations of power are exercised and enacted.

> [T]here is no power relation without the correlative constitution
> of a field of knowledge, nor any knowledge that does not presuppose
> and constitute at the same time power relations. (Foucault, 1977,
> p. 27)

By "power" Foucault is not merely referring to sovereign or ruling class power, political structure, government or the "master-slave" interface (though these are certainly aspects) but to any "reality" that is supporting (and supported by) types of knowledge (Foucault, 1980).

DISCURSIVE PRACTICES AS METHODOLOGY

Discursive practices are the translation of discourses into social action; they are the enactment of discourse. They are the discursively inscribed, ordered regularities of behavior that underscore discourses as social action (Fairclough, 1989). Discourses, then, are made intelligible from the behavioral patterns manifest in the discursive practices that discourses (constructed knowledges) give rise to (Wetherell et al., 2001). In this way, discursive practices have been defined as the "institutionalized use of language". (Davies & Harre, 1990). According to discourse theory, as we inevitably engage with and enact (as well as further produce) discourses through practising them, we are being constituted and disciplined at the same time. As Davies and Harre (1990) suggest, "among the products of discursive practices are the very persons who engage in them" (p. 43).

While a discursive perspective and method of analysis likewise do no more than tell (different) stories, the truth claims, know-hows, power and politics of those stories and their relations to technologies of regulation are (hopefully) different in as much as they can generate knowledges that are unhinged from "Truth". As such discourse theory can be seen as a useful theoretical framework and analytic approach for a critical re-appraisal of the discursive domain of sport management.

DISCOURSE ANALYSIS CRITERIA

Potter and Wetherell (1987, 1995), Parker (1992), Fairclough (1996), Burr (1995) and Roe (1994), all of whom have developed methods of discourse analysis, provide some guidelines for discourse analysis.

According to Potter and Wetherell's (1987) stages of how to analyze discourse, the selection of participants, collection of records/documents, conduction of interviews, transcription, coding, and final data analysis, should be approached in a particular way when doing discourse analysis. In outlining principles for analysis, it must first be noted that there was no "how to" or "step-by-step" guide utilized when performing discourse analysis in the conventional sense that method is typically understood. However, it is still possible to employ some general guidelines when approaching the data. Fairclough (1996) utilizes critical discourse analysis (CDA) guidelines which will be discussed later through a more detailed discussion of CDA.

CRITIQUE OF DISCOURSE ANALYSIS

Critics accustomed to the positivist paradigm within which much research takes place may assert that discourse analyses are too subjective, relying almost entirely upon the particular researchers reading of a text. Discourse analysis theory openly acknowledges the inevitability of a theoretical position being context and observer specific. Indeed, the role of discourse analysis as a critical tool requires that the researchers' particular perspective be made explicit.

There are a few ways of validating one's assertions in discourse analysis. The extensive use of the actual textual material used in the analysis is important for it allows others to assess the researchers' interpretations and follow the reasoning process from data to conclusions. In discourse analysis, the text is not a dependent variable, or an illustration of another point, but an example of the data itself. Another powerful criterion of validity is whether an analytic scheme can make sense of new kinds of discourse and generate new understandings. Evidence of other interpretations and cognitive processing are also important as they provide a deeper insight into how text can assist in creating different perceptions of the world for others.

It should be clearly understood that the analysis of discourse analysis does not only involve simply the cataloging and observation of patterns, but also includes a critical dimension. The very characteristic that defines discourse as a poststructural activity is its goal in identifying cultural hegemony and the manner by which it is reproduced.

DISCOURSE ANALYSIS AND SPORT MANAGEMENT

When applied to sport management, the discourse analyst should consider the historical, sociocultural, spatial and institutional context within which the discourse was assembled, legitimized and disseminated.

The process of a Foucaultian style discourse analysis involves careful reading of entire bodies of text and other organizing systems (such as taxonomies, commentaries and conference transcriptions) in relation to one another, in order to interpret patterns, rules, assumptions, contradictions, silences, consequences, implications and inconsistencies (Weedon, 1987).

The product identifies and names language processes and social practices that people use to construct their understanding of social life, that necessarily serves either to reproduce or challenge the distribution of power as it currently exists (Weedon, 1987).

The potential contribution of a Foucaultian style discourse analysis to the discipline of sport management is twofold: First, discourse analysis would provide an approach suitable for addressing such notions as

1. the taken-for-grantedness of specific sport management practices;

2. the history of sport management practices;

3. the vested interest of authorized voices;

4. the rules of evidence used to formulate and structure discussions;

5. the rules by evidence used to produce explanations and the rules of which topics are dismissed from inquiry.

Examples of questions that could guide this form of discourse analysis include

- Who are considered the leading authorities in sport management and why?

- What discourses are contained in sport management texts and journals?

- How do we justify sport management as a discipline?

- When you submit an article on sport management to be published, what changes are commonly made and by whom?

A second area in which discourse analysis can contribute to the discipline is by providing a way to analyze power in sport management. Examples of issues that would benefit greatly from the power perspective provided by discourse analysis, include the discourses of theory, professionalism, practice, gender and sport management communication to name only a few. An examination of these issues would contribute to the further development of sport management as an academic discipline.

With respect to sport management, Foucaultian analysis can illuminate the mechanisms and techniques used by sport management to legitimize its own knowledge claims and the various, often competing, discourses embedded in sport management knowledge. They can reveal the nature of the interplay between sport management "experts" and practitioners. For example, in sport management the technocratic discourse operates in such a way as to limit the sport mangers' perception of the nature of management practice. The power afforded to the technocratic/managerial discursive framework is such that it is very difficult for sport management practitioners to move away from a management approach to a reflective practitioner. As such the discursive formation of the managerial model both legitimizes this approach to sport management practice and limits other forms of possibility.

The product of a discourse analysis includes a description of the internal rules and ideological elements of a particular discourse, plus documentation of the "conditions of its existence". Questions that would illuminate the conditions of existence for the discourse of sport management theory, for example, would include the following:

1. What kinds of practices or discourses had to be in place before the discourse of sport management theory could be constructed?

2. What social practices and power arrangements are necessary for the discourse of sport management theory to continue?

3. What implicit rules are there in the discourse of sport management theory that help to validate its existence?

In such analysis, there is a dynamic relationship between power and "truth" where truth is a product of dominant discursive frameworks shaped and defined by power, whilst power is legitimated on the basis of expert ownership of such "truth". For example, the scientific/management model is regularly described as neutral and value-free. So hegemonic is this notion of objectivity, that the underlying relations of power embedded in "true" concepts such as objectivity and neutrality are not exposed. Foucault extends the conceptualization of power from the realm of the ideological, to figuring in the very production of the instruments for the formation and accumulation of knowledge. In such an analysis, knowledge is not identical to ideology but in fact precedes ideology. Further, dominant discourses figure in both the development and the continuation of social truths.

From Foucault's (1978) perspective, all discourses are merely perspectives. If one discourse has more value than another, this is not because of its intrinsic properties as truth but because of the role that discourse plays in constituting practices. Discourses produce not "truth" but "truth effects" (i.e. they organize and constitute the world in particular ways). These effects are not contingent on whether the discourse is oppressive or liberating. Any discursive regime (and human existence is unthinkable without one) implies a particular exercise of power. Power not only represses but it also makes possible the knowledge that constitutes culture – any culture. Foucault argues for the power effect of knowledge rather than its truth value. The notion of ideology critique is misleading in that it promises a truth not distorted through the effects of domination. For Foucault such a notion is an impossibility.

Discourse analysis draws attention to the discursive construction of sport management knowledge and practices; the point is not to replace one set of categories with another, but to focus on differences and marginality, thus expanding different theoretical understandings and facets of experience. Poststructural sport management discourses of inquiry do not propose a new "paradigm" in the sense of value-free truth seeking, the concern is with "intertextualism", which involves the generation of new positions to resist or question existing discourse.

Clearly, there are numerous ways in which discourse analysis has been applied in various contexts whether it be for critical social commentary, empowerment, or to further reform agendas. However, for the purposes of sport management we are particularly interested in Foucaultian analysis.

MAPPING THEORIES OF DISCOURSE

It is not argued in this book that all the approaches to textual, conversational and pictorial analysis are, in fact, similar or interchangeable. Indeed, there are certain ways in which they are divergent. Silverman (1993), for example, argues that discourse analysis and CDA are different from Ethnomethodology and Conversation Analysis (CA) in that the former two analytic approaches possess the following three features:

1. They are concerned with a far broader range of activities, often related to more conventional social science concerns (e.g. gender relations, social control, etc.).

2. They do not always use analysis of ordinary conversation as a baseline for understanding talk in institutional settings.

3. Discourse analysis [and CDA] work with far less precise transcripts than CA. (p. 121)

To highlight some major similarities and differences in these analytic approaches a number of key perspectives associated with these different theories of discourse are summarized in Table 12.1. As is shown, the various approaches differ somewhat in the way they view some features of the social world.

Table 12.1 Mapping Theories of Discourse

Theories of Discourse	Ethno-Methodology/CA	Discourse Analysis	Foucaultian Discourse Analysis	Critical Discourse Analysis	Social Semiotics
Key founding claims	Interaction is an ordered achievement	Discourses constitute the social world	Institutions construct subjects as objects of knowledge	Linguistic forms are constitutive of ideological positions	Texts and talk constitute cultural signifiers and social signs
View of the social world	The world is orderly and constituted through talk and texts	The world is interactively constituted through discourses	Technologies of the self and regimes of truth constitute the social world	The world is interactively constituted through discourses	The world is interactively constituted through talk and texts
Key notions and concepts	Sequential organization; membership categorization devices	Discourses are both shaped and constrained by social structure	Social regulation; disciplinary power; panopticism	Discourses have major ideological effects; intertextuality	Multi-modality; information value; salience; framing
Main forms of Language analyzed	Printed and spoken materials; both mundane and institutional talk and texts	Printed and spoken materials	Mostly printed materials, in particular historical documents	Printed and spoken material	Printed, spoken and visual materials
Concept of context	Context is realized within and through texts and talk	Interactions are contextually situated and influential on what happens	Social institutions are contexts that work to regulate he populace	Institutional contexts influence positioning practices	Context both shapes and is shaped by textual signifiers
Relationship of language to thought	Language normatively writes and talks social worlds into being	Language shapes and determines ought	Language is related to regimes of truth that embody thought	Language shapes and determines thought	Language signifies thought through a system of signs
How "power" in language is conceptualized	Power is written or talked into being, and has to be evidenced in the data	Power is everywhere and enacted within and through texts and talk	Power is everywhere, evidenced in regimes of truth	Power is embedded within identifiable grammars	Power is enacted through the inclusion and placement of components
What analysis can reveal	How social members manage their interactions	The operation of powered structural constructions	Institutions at work	Social/ideological grammars	Systems of social signs

CRITICAL DISCOURSE ANALYSIS (CDA)

The discussion of CDA presented in this section represents an attempt to introduce this methodology in a way that makes it more easily accessible to sport management researchers who wish to undertake a more critical form of discourse analysis. The section begins with a description of the history of the application of CDA and identifies its main protagonists in order to provide a comprehensive background to the use of CDA for sport management researchers interested in utilizing this methodology. It then outlines the particular approach to CDA offered by Fairclough (1992, 1995, 2003), which is applicable to the analysis of sport management research. This section concludes with an example of how a critical discourse analysis of a particular sport management-related policy problem.

CDA is a relatively new method of discourse analysis, which initially grew out of the work of a group of linguists at the University of East Anglia in England in the late 1970s and was first recognized as a distinct methodology in the late 1980s (Blommaert & Bulcaen, 2000; Threadgold, 2003). The development of CDA was largely led by Norman Fairclough, Ruth Wodak and Teun van Dijk, who remain some of the main protagonists of the method (Blommaert & Bulcaen, 2000). CDA is located within the critical social sciences, and critical social theory has greatly influenced its development (Chouliaraki & Fairclough, 1999). The theoretical underpinnings of CDA bring together a wide variety of critical social theories, the Frankfurt school, and other neo-Marxist scholars (Blommaert & Bulcaen, 2000). Collectively these theories have influenced many facets of CDA including the way *power* is conceptualized. Most importantly, they have influenced the way that those utilizing a CDA analysis understand the nature of discourse as "an instrument in the social construction of reality", and the functioning of discourse as both constitutive of and constituted by social practices (Blommaert & Bulcaen, 2000; Phillips & Jorgensen, 2002).

It is the connection between "the social and the linguistic" which characterizes the analysis undertaken through CDA (Chouliaraki & Fairclough, 1999). The development of CDA was influenced by a branch of linguistics called "critical linguistics", which became prominent in the late 1970s (Teo, 2000). The analysis practiced by critical linguists aimed at investigating more than just the content of discourse, which was a narrow focus that they viewed as problematic within other modes of linguistic analysis such as conversation analysis (Fairclough, 1995). *Conversation analysis* concerns itself with the "micro", textual organization of discourse but ignores the "macro" influences of social practices on the construction of discourse (Fairclough, 2001).

Unlike *conversation analysis*, CDA pays equal attention to both these micro and macrolevels of discourse and, as will be discussed shortly, adds to this a focus on the "meso" level of discourse practices. CDA privileges critical social theories while also offering a methodological approach that sets out an analysis which includes an examination of how discourse is formed at a micro-textual level. In this way, CDA seeks to perform at both a theoretical and a methodological level, positioning itself as an improvement and challenge to approaches that privilege either theory or method to the exclusion of the other (Chouliaraki & Fairclough, 1999). CDA thus works to mediate between pure linguistic analysis such as that of conversation analysis on one side, and poststructuralist studies of discourse on the other. The application of CDA seeks to explain this link.

What it is about "critical discourse analysis" that is deemed to be "critical" and therefore separates it from "discourse analysis"? As discussed above, some strands of discourse analysis are viewed by the protagonists of CDA as being too descriptive. The use of the term "critical" signifies a departure from this by indicating an analysis that focuses on exploring the "ideological underpinnings of discourse that have become so naturalized over time that we begin to treat them as common, acceptable and natural features of discourse" (Gee, 2004; Teo, 2000).

CDA has positioned itself as "critical" in relation to other forms of discourse analysis, which, while utilizing methodologies that are technically strong, do not engage with the way that social structures, or more generally power, create and effect the operation of discourse (Gee, 2004; Teo, 2000). CDA attempts to examine the processes of power and how these processes use discourse in subtle, yet controlling ways (Fairclough, 2001). Discourses are therefore, viewed as being instrumental in the reproduction of power within a given social situation (van Dijk, 1993).

For critical discourse analysts, language is not viewed as powerful in and of itself, but is given power as a result of how it is used, who uses it and the context within which this usage takes place (Wodak, 2001). Discourses do not merely reflect social practices, but are integral to the constitution of power through these practices in order to achieve certain ends (Jäger, 2001). It is therefore crucial that language is not analyzed out of context, but is situated within the specific context of social practices of which it is a part (Fairclough, 2001).

As with discourse analysis, more generally, CDA cannot be seen as a single methodology, but rather as a collection of methodological approaches which center around an analysis that attempts to link the linguistic and the social (Weiss & Wodak, 2003). The methodology varies between researchers, as to the nature of the research questions being asked and according to the particular discursive event under examination.

FAIRCLOUGH'S APPROACH TO CDA

Fairclough is one of the main protagonists of the CDA method and his approach fits well with an analysis of policy issues, textual analysis and public relations related to sport management practice. For Poynton (2000), Fairclough's approach to discourse analysis is important because of its ability to move between the minutiae of a multistranded descriptive technology and some of the most productive frameworks for understanding social life as developed in broadly poststructuralist theories. For Fairclough (1995, 2003) there are three aspects that need to be considered when looking at a text. These are, first, the context in which the text is produced; second, the way it is received and, finally, the details of the text itself. These aspects of the discourse can be understood through analyzing the discourse at three levels: the sociocultural level, the discourse practice level and the textual level (Fairclough, 1995). An analysis of these three levels provides a comprehensive discussion of the texts being studied as opposed to analysis confined solely to either the social level or discourse level.

There is no set questioning through which a CDA analysis takes place. The questions asked in an analysis of a particular text depend on the research aims and the nature of the debate under analysis (Fairclough, 2003). Fairclough (1992) suggests that a research project which utilizes CDA should focus its analysis on "moments of crisis" in which the data can reveal the "manipulative strategies" through which identities and institutions create and retain their power (Teo, 2000). The identity of the sport management practitioner acts as a "moment of crisis" in the debate around a changing skill mix in the sport workforce. An analysis of the discourses surrounding the sport management practitioner identity can be used to reveal these manipulative strategies and point to possible approaches to practice. This analysis thus has a practical goal of suggesting an appropriate policy response to this conflict over sport management practice.

A NOTE ON BIAS

Similar to criticisms, mentioned previously in the critique of discourse analysis, critics of CDA have commented that CDA researchers read what they want to find in the texts they analyze (Schegloff, 1997; Stubbs, 1997). This is a common criticism made against critical social scientists in many disciplines and is not necessarily seen as a criticism by CDA researchers. Far from being a problem for CDA however, Chouliaraki and Fairclough (1999) suggest that this is one of the important understandings of a critical discourse analysis. They comment that CDA takes the view that any text can be understood in different ways – a text does not uniquely determine a meaning, though there is a limit to what a text can mean. Different understandings of the text result from different combinations of the properties of the text and the properties (social positioning, knowledges, values, etc.) of the interpreter.

When sport management researchers use a CDA analysis, it is important they acknowledge the bias inherent in any research methodology but minimize this bias through the use of a consistent methodological approach. The sport management researcher needs to analyze the utterances of all speakers within the debate, using the same questioning, and to be up-front concerning overt personal biases. For example, if a sport management practitioner were undertaking this analysis, it would be important that he or she acknowledge this so that the research could be understood in light of this influence.

Research Brief

Title: Yao Ming and Masculinity in Middle America: A Critical Discourse Analysis of Racial Representations in NBL Game Commentary.
Who: Lavelle, K.L., Wayne State University
Lavelle studied the rhetorical construction of Yao Ming (7 foot 6 inches tall Chinese basketball player), specifically how representations of him function as a clash of cultures and a statement on notions of masculinity, where race is one element, in the National Basketball Association. This study was derived from the literature that talks about how race and ethnicity can shape how players are rhetorically constructed during game commentary. Lavelle utilized *critical discourse analysis* to examine 15 game commentaries quantitatively and qualitatively. The qualitative analysis data consisted of a thematic analysis of players, focusing on a comparison between of how players were described. Lavelle concluded that the depictions of Yao reinforce his role as a model minority.

CDA AND SPORT MANAGEMENT

Critical discourse analysis presents a structured methodology for analyzing any text and is useful for sport management researchers who require a set approach to the analysis of discourse. The utility of the textual analysis offered by CDA lies in the depth that it can add to issues related to sport management practice. CDA brings in the multiple layers which shape a text and therefore assists researchers to examine discourse in the context of both the social environment in which the text is produced and the nature of the textual form in which the discourse is presented. Critical discourse analysis can be put to a variety of uses in sport management research, and ultimately the goal of a CDA analysis depends on the research project for which it is being used.

CDA RESEARCH IN ACTION – REVIEWING SPORT POLICY

One area in which Critical discourse analysis could have particular relevance within the sport management research domain is Sport Policy. Policies can be broadly defined and include directives for action, or the responsibilities for action and the processes guiding the implementation of action. Policies include, for example, widening participation, equity, drug control and so on.

According to Grimley (1986), policy can also be seen as: "an expression of values by a politically dominant group" (p. 20). When considered from this perspective, policy loses some of its innocence as a neutral conveyor of procedures and undertakings to be implemented for the common good of a sport organization and can be viewed as a vehicle which promotes the values, understandings and ultimately the interests of a particular group. When sport policy impacts on the practice of sport management it is essentially a political exercise, in that from a number of possibilities certain views will be chosen and enshrined in policy documents.

The reading of policy documents as texts that represent certain views of reality can inform critical discourse analysis. The way in which policies are developed, represent reality, are spoken about and thought about, is the product of dominant discursive frameworks or discourses by which we mean certain ways of thinking or talking about reality (Foucault, 1977). These dominant discourses are themselves the product of social, historical and other structural influences. The development and maintenance of such dominant discursive frameworks shapes the way in which sport managers and others think about sport management and the practice of sport management.

Thus, what is not said or embodied in policy that shapes sport management is of as much interest as what is present or said. When considered from a critical discourse analysis perspective such as proposed here, policy can be viewed as a vehicle that promotes the ideology of a certain group.

Policy analysis as a field of study has suffered from an uncertain identity and vagueness of conceptualization. Critical discourse analysis aims to expose sources of domination, repression and exploitation that are entrenched in, and legitimated by policy. Thus a policy analysis goes beyond analyzing the content and implementation of policies to examine how those policies reflect certain understandings of reality in the first instance. Policy analysis is therefore overtly political in that it attempts to expose favored values and social arrangements and the sources of power and control underpinning them and hegemonic technologies that restrain human consciousness and emancipation.

One focus of such an analysis is upon the policy as text, incorporating an analysis of the values, interests and assumptions characterized through the scope, intentions, and language of the policy document. The questions raised related to "whose needs, values and preferences are represented" and "on what basis are (they) validated as being appropriate and good"? Thus, analysis of the language used in the text of the policy unveils the underlying values, assumptions and ideologies that underpin the policy. However, a focus solely upon the language and text of policy can become technical and functionalist if it fails to consider the processes associated with policy development and implementation. Further, text is always produced in social settings where a great deal more than language is present. A discourse approach must of necessity take account of the processes of text (policy) production as well as the actual test (policy) itself. This involves investigation and examination of the processes by which the need for policy is determined and communicated, and the processes by which policy is developed (i.e. policy committees and how these committees are constituted and conducted), implemented and reviewed.

Therefore, in viewing sport management focused policy documents as constituted by certain discourses a critical discourse analysis requires analysis of the relationship between texts, processes in the development of those texts and the social conditions in which the texts are produced and operate. This analysis of social conditions must consider both the immediate conditions of the situational context, and the seemingly more remote yet ever present conditions of the institutional and social structures within which the policy is constituted. Thus, in relation to sport policy, it is necessary to not only examine the text of the policy, but also the structural aspects of policy development (i.e. the relationship between processes of production and implementation).

From a critical discourse analysis perspective text (policy) is viewed as an outcome of historical and political conditions. Thus, a CDA approach to policy analysis requires examination of the social milieu surrounding text (policy) production in order to illuminate the nature of the relationships between processes of text (policy) production, and how they are constituted through and constitutive of dominant ideologies.

It should be clear that it would be incomplete to describe the evolution of sport policy in a particular context without considering the social structure of the culture from which the sport policy arises. Some questions that could be asked in such an inquiry include. What factors gave rise to the sport policy? What power relations were at work in the politics of sport policy development? Were there equity issues involved? What political issues have influenced sport policy?

In reviewing the preceding discussion of CDA, this section has presented an introduction to the use of critical discourse analysis for sport management research, including its background and recent use in sport management research. Like discourse analysis discussed previously, the methodology of CDA provides an approach for a structured analysis of the discourses surrounding debates about sport management practice.

Discourse Case Study

Who: Lane Robert Mandlis, University of Alberta

What: The (Re)Presentation of "The Boxer": A Discursive Analysis and Deconstruction (2005)

Theoretical framework

Mandlis interrogates different aspects of the representation of boxing and boxers. Using discourse analysis and specific Derridian deconstructive ideas, he examines how the dominant understanding of the boxer is constructed and reified in popular culture. He concludes by delving into queer theory and how the dominant discourse about boxing allows for a queer reading of all boxers.

Data collection methods

Mandlis utilized discourse analysis to study boxing, because he wished to show that what is (re)presented as the true version of the boxer is a social construction that is held in place by oppressive hegemonic discourses. In uncovering the processes that legitimate one representation over another, Mandlis attempted to open a dialog about boxing in order to allow for a richer, more complex understanding of these athletes and their sport. The data collection was based on data from primary and secondary sources. A broad cross section of literature on boxers was selected as the primary source.

Data analysis techniques/presentation

Discourse analysis allowed Mandlis to examine how language constructs phenomena, not how it reflects and reveals it. The subject "the boxer", then is not only represented by the way in which it is spoken about, but the actions and behaviors of the person in the subject position are constrained (both limited and enabled) and constituted by the language used. This representation, then, constitutes the "how" of the boxer: the way in which the boxer comes to be understandable as a "what."

Major findings

In summary, this research found that the production of "the boxer" is a totalizing identity that results in a discourse that seems to unproblematically incorporate all participants in the sport. This discourse acts to constrain who may or may not be understood as "the boxer". Discourse analysis offered Mandilis a way to expose the structures that produce and maintain the trope of the boxer. Because the constraints on boxers and would-be-boxers occur from many different angles, this research attacks the discourse from different directions.

Suggestions for future research

This research suggested many avenues of research for the future. Mandlis asks researchers to explore women's experience in, and the construction of their identities through sport, particularly boxing.

Case study research probes

1. How and why has discourse analysis been used in the research by Mandlis?

2. What are the advantages using discourse analysis for this type of research?

CONCLUSION

The discipline of sport management exists in universities worldwide without a long history of allegiance to an established philosophical perspective or social theory. Sport management is therefore in the enviable position of having a widely informed choice among philosophical approaches as models for teaching, practice and research.

The application of discourse analysis as a methodology for sport management inquiry provides the discipline with the opportunity to construct alternative perspectives on power/knowledge. Such an addition to sport management inquiry would therefore seem justified.

IN PROFILE - Associate Professor Russell Hoye

Dr Russell Hoye is an Associate Professor in the School of Sport, Tourism and Hospitality Management, LaTrobe University, Australia. Dr Hoye is a board member of the Sport Management Association of Australia and New Zealand (SMAANZ) and an editorial board member of *Sport Management Review, International Journal of Sport Policy*, and the *Australian Journal on Volunteering*. Dr Hoye's areas of expertise include corporate governance, organizational behavior, volunteer management and sport policy, all areas that utilize both quantitative and qualitative research methods. His research interests focus on examining how governance is enacted with sport organizations, how volunteers engage with and are managed by sport organizations, and the effects of public policy on sport. He has published papers on these topics in journals such as *Nonprofit Management and Leadership, Sport Management Review, and the European Sport Management Quarterly*. He has also written books based on research that utilized qualitative research methods, including *Sport and Social Capital* (2008)

and *Sport Governance* (2007) both published with Elsevier. Dr Hoye has employed qualitative research methods to explore questions such as the distribution of leadership within the boards of sport organizations, the nature of the working relationships between boards and CEOs, the perceptions and attitudes of volunteers toward recruiting recognition schemes and other management systems used by sport organizations, as well as organizational culture. These methods included the use of unstructured and semi-structured interviews, interpretation and analysis of interview transcripts using coding techniques, and content analysis of organizational documents. Dr Hoye continues to use qualitative research methods because it enables a more robust analysis of the causes of phenomena to be undertaken and it facilitates a deeper understanding of the issues by the researcher as they interact directly with their research subjects. Above all, doing qualitative research is challenging and exciting and brings an authentic real sense of reality to doing research in sport management.

REVIEW AND RESEARCH QUESTIONS

Discourses are conversations and the meanings behind those conversations. Discourse analysis seeks to understand the sociocultural, historical, institutional and spatial environments that led to the creation of those discourses and the way in which these discourses influenced outcomes. With a basic understanding now of discourse, discourse analysis and critical discourse analysis attempt to answer the following questions:

- Is there any place within sport management research for discourse analysis? Provide two examples.
- Identify those key features of critical discourse analysis that would have particular relevance for the field of sport management research.

REFERENCES

Billig, M. 1991. Ideology and Opinions. London: Sage.

Blommaert, J. & Bulcaen, C. 2000. Critical discourse analysis. *Annual Review of Anthropology*, **29**, 447–466.

Burr, V. 1995. An Introduction to Social Constructionism. London: Routledge.

Chouliaraki, L. & Fairclough, N. 1999. Discourse in Late Modernity. Rethinking Critical Discourse Analysis. Edinburgh: Edinburgh University Press.

Davies, B. & Harre, R. 1990. Positioning: the discursive production of selves. *Journal for the Theory of Social Behavior*, **20** (1), 43–63.

Fairclough, N. 1989. Language and Power. London: Longman.

Fairclough, N. 1992. Discourse and Social Change. Cambridge, UK: Polity Press.

Fairclough, N. 1995. Critical Discourse Analysis: The Critical Study of Language. New York: Longman.

Fairclough, N. 1996. A reply to Henry Widdowson's 'Discourse analysis: a critical view'. *Language and Literature*, **5** (1), 49–56.

Fairclough, N. 2001. The dialectics of discourse. *Textus*, **XIV** (2), 231–242.

Fairclough, N. 2003. Analyzing Discourse: Textual Analysis for Social Research. New York: Routledge.

Foucault, M. 1972. The Archaeology of Knowledge. London: Tavistock.

Foucault, M. 1977. Discipline and Punish. (A. Sheridan, Trans.) London: Allen Lane.

Foucault, M. 1978. Politics and the study of discourse. *Ideology and Consciousness*, **3**, 7–26.

Foucault, M. 1980. Power/knowledge selected interviews and other writings, 1972–77 (C. Gordon, Trans.). New York: Harvester Wheatsheaf.

Foucault, M. 1981. The order of discourse. In: *Untyping the Text* (Ed. by R. Young), pp. 48–78. London: Methuen.

Foucault, M. 1983. The subject and power. In: *Beyond Structuralism and Hermeneutics* (Ed. by D. Dreyfus, P. Rabinow, M. Foucault), pp. 208–226, 2nd ed. Chicago: University of Chicago Press.

Foucault, M. (1984). The ethic of care for the self. An interview with Michel Foucault (January 20, 1984).

Foucault, M. 1991. Governmentality. In: *The Foucault Effect: Studies in Governmentality* (Ed. by G. Burchell, C. Gordon, P. Miller), pp. 87–104. Hemel Hempstead: Wheatsheaf.

Gee, J. P. 2004. What is critical about critical discourse analysis? In: *An Introduction to Critical Discourse Analysis* (Ed. by R. Rogers), pp. 19–50. Mahwah, NJ: Lawrence Erlbaum.

Grimley, J. 1986. Critical educational policy analysis: a discussion of perspectives. *Australian Journal of Teacher Education*, **11** (2), 19–25.

Hook, D. 2001. The disorders of discourse. *Theoria*, **1** (97), 41–68.

Jacobs, G. 1999. On how to construct conflicts and how (not) to resolve them. *Document Design*, **1** (2), 135–137.

Jäger, S. 2001. Kritische Diskursanalyse. Duisberg: DISS.

Parker, I. 1992. Discourse Dynamics: Critical Analysis for Social and Individual Psychology. London: Routledge.

Phillips, L. & Jorgensen, M. W. 2002. Discourse Analysis as Theory and Method. London: Sage.

Potter, J. & Wetherell, M. 1987. Discourse and Social Psychology: Beyond Attitudes and Behavior. London: Sage.

Potter, J. & Wetherell, M. 1995. Discourse analysis. In: *Rethinking Methods in Psychology* (Ed. by J. Smith, R. Harré, R. van Langenhove), pp. 80–92. London: Sage.

Poynton, C. 2000. Linguistics and discourse analysis. In: *Culture and Text: Discourse and Methodology in Social Research and Cultural Studies* (Ed. by A. Lee, C. Poynton), pp. 59–80. Sydney: Allen & Unwin.

Roe, E. 1994. Culture as Deficit: A Critical Discourse Analysis of the Concept of Culture in Contemporary Social Work. Durham: Duke University Press.

Schegloff, E. A. 1997. Whose text? Whose context? *Discourse & Society*, **8**, 165–187.

Shapiro, M.J. (1987). Educational theory and recent political discourse: a new agenda for the left? Teachers College Record, Winter.

Silverman, D. 1993. Interpreting Qualitative Data: Methods for Analysing Talk, Text and Interaction. London: Sage.

Stubbs, M. 1997. Whorf's children: critical comments on critical discourse analysis. In: *Evolving Models of Language* (Ed. by A. Wray, A. Ryan), pp. 100–116. Clevedon: Multilingual Matters.

Teo, P. 2000. Racism in the news: a critical analysis of news reporting in two Australian newspapers. *Discourse & Society*, **11** (1), 7–49.

Threadgold, T. 2003. Cultural studies, critical theory and critical discourse analysis: histories, remembering and futures. *Linguistik Online*, **14**, 5–37. Retrieved January 10, 2008 from http://www.linguistik-online.de/14_03/index.html.

Van Dijk, T. 1993. Principles of critical discourse analysis. *Discourse & Society*, **4** (2), 249–283.

Weedon, C. 1987. Feminist Practice and Poststructuralist Theory. Oxford: Blackwell.

Weiss G. & Wodak R. (Eds.). (2003). Critical Discourse Analysis: Theory and Interdisciplinarity. Basingstoke: Palgrave Macmillan.

Wetherell, M.,Taylor, S. & Yates S.J. (Eds.). (2001). Discourse as Data: A guide for Analysis. London: Sage.

Wodak 2001. The discourse-historical approach. In: *Methods of Critical Discourse Analysis* (Ed. by R. Wodak, M. Meyer), pp. 63–95. London: Sage.

CHAPTER 13

Ethnography and Sport Management Research

OBJECTIVES

By the end of this chapter, you should be able to

- understand the basic concepts of ethnography.
- differentiate between traditional ethnography, and ethnographical research underpinned by critical and postmodern theories.

- identify the implications of the application of critical and postmodern methodologies to ethnographical research in sport management.

KEY TERMS

Thick description: a description that explains not just the behavior, but its context as well, such that the behavior becomes meaningful to an outsider.

Participant observation: the researcher is immersed in the day-to-day lives of the people, or conducts one-on-one interviews with members of the group.

Critical ethnography: a perspective through which a qualitative researcher can frame questions and promote

action. Critical ethnography goes beyond a description of the culture to action for change, by challenging the false consciousness and ideologies exposed through the research.

Postmodernism: term applied to a wide-ranging set of developments in fields of research, which are generally characterized as either emerging from, in reaction to, or superseding, modernism.

KEY QUESTIONS

The key questions raised in this chapter are as follows:

- What is "Ethnography"?
- What are the implications for applying critical and postmodern theories to ethnographical research

processes being undertaken in the field of sport management?

CHAPTER OVERVIEW

This chapter explores the qualitative research approach of Ethnography. Whilst traditional ethnography has been applied to the field of sport for many years, from the late 1990s sport researchers began to embrace ethnographic frameworks underpinned by critical and postmodern theories. The benefit for sport management researchers in applying critical and postmodern thought to ethnographic approaches is that it sharpens their own critical consciousness. This chapter will provide an introduction and overview to the concepts of ethnography, and provide some examples of critical and post-modern frameworks from which ethnographic researchers can approach the field of sport management.

ORIGINS OF ETHNOGRAPHY

Ethnography has its roots in social anthropology and emerged in the late nineteenth and twentieth centuries when famous anthropologists such as Malinowski (1922), Boas (1928) and Mead (1928), while seeking cultural patterns and rules, explored several non-western cultures and the lifestyles of the people within them. Sociologists and the Chicago School of Sociology also had an influence on ethnographic methods, immersing themselves in the culture (LeCompte & Preissle, 1993). From the pioneering beginnings at the Chicago School of Sociology in the 1920s and 1930s, a division occurred between ethnography as practiced by social scientists and ethnographic methods used by anthropologists.

FEATURES OF ETHNOGRAPHY

Hammersley (1990) points out that the term ethnography typically relates to social research, which comprises most of the following characteristics, in that:

- people's behaviors are studied in everyday context, rather than under experimental situations developed by the investigator.

- data are collected from various sources, with observation and interviews being the primary aspects.

- data are gathered in an "unstructured" manner in that it does not follow a plan. This does not imply that the research is unsystematic, rather data is collected in as raw a form, and on as wide a front, as feasible.

- the focus is commonly a single setting or group and on a small scale.

- data analysis entails interpretation of the meanings and functions of human actions and is primarily conducted in the form of verbal descriptions and explanations. (p. 1)

TRADITIONAL ETHNOGRAPHY

Ethnography is a qualitative research methodology aimed at describing and analyzing the practices and beliefs of cultures and communities. Most contemporary definitions of ethnography are compatible with Denzin's (1997) notion that ethnography is: "that form of inquiry and writing that produces descriptions and accounts about the ways of life of the writer and those written about" (p. xi). Ethnography attempts to articulate authentic representations of the complexity and richness of people's lives through narratives or tales of oral and life histories.

Traditionally, ethnography has been associated with the fields of sociology and anthroplogy, and the works of such researchers as Malinowski and Evans-Pritchard in social anthropology. The works of traditional ethnographic researchers such as Margaret Mead and Gregory Bateson were built upon in the post war years (Tedlock, 2000) and extended into the 1970s. Individuals such as Becker, Greer, Hughes, Strauss, Gusfield and the Spindlers were prominent. This "modernist phase" of rigorous qualitative research attempted to formalize qualitative methods in order to make them as rigorous as its quantitative counterpart (Denzin & Lincoln, 2000).

Ethnography from the 1970s to the mid-1980s was described by Smith (1987) as being in a state of "zesty disarray", with the boundaries between the social sciences and the humanities difficult to define. At this time, ethnography was characterized by the researcher observing behavior within the context of its setting, and eliciting from those observed the "structures of meaning which inform and texture behaviour" (Wilcox, 1980, p. 2). However, although offering some insight into the day-to-day reality of human life, such ethnography only provided the perspective of an interested observer. Ethnographic practice was being driven by a diverse and competing range of methodologies borrowed from phenomenology, symbolic interactionism, ethnomethodology, Marxism and feminism. Changes in these parent disciplines and the linguistic turn in the mid-1980s created a "crisis of representation". This crisis focused attention on the writing practices of ethnographic researchers. As a consequence, new models of truth, method and representation were sought as issues of difference, particularly gender, race and class took center stage in understanding how research was presented. In an attempt to make sense of this "crisis" a period of "experimental writing" emerged in the 1990s. This was shaped by the emergence of postmodernism in ethnographic research. This approach was deemed to be particularly useful in adding greater theoretical weight to ethnographic research as the "epistemologies from previously silenced groups emerged to offer solutions to representational concerns" (Denzin & Lincoln, 2000, p. 17). The notion of the grand narrative was being challenged by what was seen as the need for "more local, and small-scale theories fitted to particular problems and particular situations" (p. 17).

METHODOLOGY OF TRADITIONAL ETHNOGRAPHY

As with all research, there are critical decisions to be made concerning the selection of participants whose sport management practices or accounts are to be studied. There are a number of approaches that can be followed:

Expedient selection – selecting those readily available, who are interested or engaged in relevant activities, show characteristics of interest to the study, or perceive problems relevant to the terms of the study.

Purposeful selection – these are selected because they are taken to represent instances of best or worst cases, clusters of cases, variations commonly encountered, typical cases, or special interest. For example, there are those sport organizations that have cultures that indicate a poor level of treatment and respect for women which is reflected in the behaviors of players and other stakeholders. These sport organizations could be used as case examples of the hegemonic sport and sport management practices that exist in some sport organizations.

Probability selection – selected on the basis of knowledge of the larger population to which the researchers wish to generalize the findings. This may involve random selection or stratified-random selection in which random choice occurs through a proportional selection from within predetermined groupings, in proportions that directly reflect the prevalence of those groupings within the larger population relevant to the study.

Ethnographic studies can vary in their structures. They may be:

- Single site, "single shot" studies, where one site is studied.

- Multi-site, single "shot".

- Longitudinal (single or multiple).

- Cumulative, sequentially building on one another over time, with the questions and methods increasingly refined.

One of the strengths of ethnographic research is the flexibility of its conduct. In traditional approaches to studying social phenomena, we typically find the development of the hypothesis, the selection of an appropriate sample of people, the prior development of assessment or codable instruments or materials, the collection of data, and the drawing of inferences concerning the findings.

Ethnographers use many of the following steps, particularly interview and participant observation, but draw attention to the fact that, as a researcher becomes more immersed in the research site, the use of particular materials, the pursuit of hypotheses developed prior to entering the site, and the nature of what may be inferred from the findings will all have a highly interactive effect on one another. Some of the practices ethnographers use include the following:

- Direct, first-hand observation of daily behavior. This can include participant observation.

- Conversation with different levels of formality. This can involve small talk to long interviews.

- Detailed work with key consultants about particular areas of community life.

- In-depth interviewing.

- Discovery of local beliefs and perceptions.

- Problem-oriented research.

- Longitudinal research. This is continuous long-term study of an area or site.

- Team research.

- Case studies.

CRITICISMS OF TRADITIONAL ETHNOGRAPHY

Criticisms of ethnography largely center around issues of representation and legitimation. Can ethnographers really capture lived experience? It is argued, such experience is brought into part largely through the texts written by the researcher. The ethnographic account provided by a researcher is, and always remains, a representation of his or her own understanding of what is going on in the field. Despite the researcher's attempts to "bracket" their own personal beliefs and understandings, there is no unfiltered way of directly representing the experiences of those studied. This insight counteracts the intentions of those interpretive ethnographers who see the aim of ethnography as being the true, accurate, and reliable representation of the meanings and intentions of the people studied in the field. In other words, there is no ethnographic account that is "thick" enough to bridge the ultimate gap between meaning and representation. While the researcher may describe their initiation into the field, the subsequent identified social or cultural patterns are presented as objective descriptions, untainted by either the ethnographers' presence or the rhetorical decisions made.

As Marshall (1989) noted in his critique of objectivism in research, "such a presentation of the world as an external reality implies that it can be observed objectively and impartially by any person" (p. 104). The ethnographic picture and the researcher are positioned as independent entities. This style of narrative realism presents fieldwork as an essentially rational activity rather than a social and political undertaking.

In positioning the researcher as a neutral gatherer and hence the presenter of truth, traditional ethnographies are seen to deny the notion that knowledge is constituted within social relations. The researcher is not understood to be implicated in the production of the knowledge that purportedly belongs to the informants. Whilst the context of the research may be understood as socially constituted, the researcher is presented as a neutral tool. Sport management researchers need to recognize this shortcoming and acknowledge that the researcher's interactions within the organization may influence internal perceptions of the sport organization. At the same time, the researcher's presence may also contribute to organizational members developing a broader understanding of sport practices and/or their sport organization.

The second assumption being critiqued is the criteria employed for evaluating and interpreting qualitative research. This critique calls for a rethinking of terms such as validity, generalizability and reliability. In the practical realities of contemporary qualitative research, these issues become blurred, with researchers taking on the requirements to legitimate any representation in terms of some specific set of criteria that permits the researcher (and reader) to make links between the text and the world that is being written about.

Critics of traditional ethnography are also concerned about the exclusion of power from the field of study. Recent interpretive analyses have drawn attention to the role individuals play in the construction and maintenance of "meaning" in social systems, and hence constitute "a vast improvement" upon work by positivists and structural functionalists; however, it fails to address the power relations between these individuals. Traditional ethnographic description uncritically represents versions of perceived realities without locating its stories within a framework of political and social explanation. Far from intentionally enlightening the subjects of an ethnography or giving them the means to understand and alter their circumstances, traditional ethnographic practice has historically involved subjective, anthropological description in which the subject of ethnography is observed by an authoritative, yet sympathetic observer (Hammersley, 1992; Weedon, 1987).

While qualitative research has not been universally embraced in the general discipline of management, it is gradually evolving into a more accepted practice in the specific discipline of sport management. The following sections explore the concept of ethnography's use as a qualitative research methodology in sport management, underpinned by critical and postmodern theories. Ethnography inspired by these theories can be seen to address some of the criticisms and weaknesses of traditional ethnographic thought. Embracing ethnographic research designs underpinned by critical and postmodern thought can significantly advance the understanding of sport management practice and organizations.

ETHNOGRAPHY AND SPORT MANAGEMENT: THE INFLUENCE OF CRITICAL THEORY

The influence of critical theory on ethnography constitutes an alternative to traditional ethnographic research. As well as emphasizing the inherently ideological nature of the social sciences and their part in governing contemporary capitalism, critical theoretical approaches to ethnography have attempted to reconstruct the conceptual practices that comprise ethnography.

Anderson (1989) describes critical ethnography as a form of representation and interpretation of social reality, which is one of the many methodological experiments that have grown out of new genres of research. Thomas (1993) suggests that critical and conventional ethnography share many common characteristics, such as a reliance on qualitative interpretation of data, core rules of ethnographic methods and analysis and a preference for theory derived directly from fieldwork (following on from Glaser & Strauss, 1967). However, Thomas (1993) believes that there are several characteristics that differentiate critical from traditional ethnography.

Thomas (1993) suggests traditional ethnography refers to the tradition of cultural description and analysis that displays meanings by interpreting meanings. Critical ethnography however, refers to the reflective process of choosing between conceptual alternatives and making value-laden judgments of meaning and method to challenge research, policy and other forms of human activity, critical ethnography is conventional ethnography with a political purpose. Therefore, critical ethnographic researchers share a concern with social inequalities and social theory, including the nature of social structure, power, culture and human agency (Carspecken, 1996).

Critical theoretical approaches to ethnography are concerned with the power struggles permeating human interactions and the construction of social reality. One of the main goals of such ethnography is to expose the hidden mechanisms through which humans and institutions make oppression and domination seem natural and/or unavoidable. By showing that social reality is not "natural" but largely socially constructed, critical ethnographers hope to empower people subjected to oppression (on the basis of social class, race, ethnicity, gender, sexual orientation, age and religious preferences) to engage in the reconstruction of less discriminatory social realities (e.g. as it happened in the feminist and Black Power movements of the 1960s and 1970s, in the USA).

Simon and Dippo (1986) argued that for work to be critical it must meet three fundamental requirements:

1. The work must employ an organizing problematic that defines one's data and analytical procedures in a way consistent with its project.

2. The work must be situated, in part, with a public sphere that allows it to become the starting point for the critique and transformation of the conditions of oppression and inequitable moral and social regulations.

3. The work must address the limits of its own claims by a consideration of how, as a form of social practice, it too is constituted and regulated through historical relations of power and existing material conditions. (p. 197)

Examples of critical theoretical approaches to ethnography that address hegemonic practices that affect women in sport and sporting organizations can be seen in the work of Birrell and Theberge (1994), Edwards et al. (2000), Lenskyj (1994), Markula (1995), and Sykes (1996). In an analysis of their leadership experience of women, Edwards et al. conducted a critical ethnography of the dominant practices and discourses that exist within sporting organizations that can restrict and inhibit the potential for women sport mangers to manage effectively. In the context of the research by Edwards et al., empowerment of the marginalized (such as women) was not a product of the work of the researchers who, as the "transformative intellectuals", assisted participants to realize the falsity of their views, and to adopt the use of the researchers critical discourse or that of a new shared reality. Rather, empowerment involved the research participants in an exploration of the politics of production of their knowledge. By examining the political nature of their sport organizations the possibility for enhanced insights into the hegemonic practices that existed was achieved.

Critical theoretical approaches to ethnography also provide an alternative to traditional forms of research designed to improve sport management practices within their environment. However, despite the advantages of utilizing such ethnographic approaches critical theoretical approaches stop short of allowing or enabling the researcher to assist the empowerment process. Although ethnography inspired by critical theory talks about the empowerment of individuals involved in the research process and alerts us to particular types of issues of injustice, it does not actively involve the researcher in empowering the research participants' understanding of the research issue under investigation. Ethnography underpinned by postmodern thought claims to do this.

Research Brief

Title: The experiences of African American Student Athletes at a Predominantly White National Collegiate Athletic Association (NCAA) Division 1 Institution: A Critical Ethnography
Who: Arnold, D., Washington State University
Intercollegiate athletics has been a place of courage and accomplishment as well as a source of frustration, disappointment, and despair for African Americans. Student athletes have historically struggled against the discrimination that has been a part of intercollegiate sport. This critical ethnography utilized semi-structured interviews and observations with five African American student athletes to describe and then analyze the college experiences of these African American student athletes. A key finding of this study is that African American student athletes' primary strategy for coping with their experiences at a Predominately White Institutions (PWI) is to develop a common 'Black students culture'. The respondents' narratives reflected a shared cultural understanding of 'Black student culture' based on the following dominant themes: (a) spirituality and a focus on religion, (b) family commitment and a belief in the power of a college education, (c) Black consciousness in a White-privileged world, (d) struggle for self-appraisal and the need to build an identity, and (e) planning ahead for the 'American Dream'. The study concluded with recommendations for proactive steps that predominantly White institutions and the National Collegiate Athletic Association (NCAA) can take to enhance the educational experiences of African American student athletes.

ETHNOGRAPHY AND SPORT MANAGEMENT: THE INFLUENCE OF POSTMODERNISM

The contribution of ethnography influenced by postmodern thought to empirical work on organizational behavior to date has been minimal. According to Kilduff and Mehra (1997), this is because organizational researchers have tended to neglect or reject the critiques of academic enquiry offered by those who write from a postmodern perspective. They suggested that this might be because the import of postmodernist approaches for organizational studies is unclear. Indeed the term postmodern is itself vaguely understood: it is often equated with deconstruction (Linstead, 1993), and is generally viewed as a nihilistic enterprise that offers nothing beyond a cynical skepticism (Codrescu, 1986). Postmodern writings are therefore derided for their unintelligibility (Thompson, 1993), and dismissed for reducing research to textual analysis (Giddens, 1987).

Postmodernists also claim that fundamental socio-historical changes cannot be adequately explained by modernist theories and, therefore, new conceptual schemes are required. Postmodernists favor social analysis that incorporates local, contextualized and restricted conceptual strategies that focus on explicitly practical or moral interests. Local narratives are preferred to grand narratives, telling local stories rather than articulating general theories.

Ethnography influenced by postmodernism, as in critical theoretical approaches to ethnography, challenges the content and form of dominant models of knowledge, and also produces forms of knowledge through breaking down disciplinary boundaries and giving voice to those not represented in dominant discourses (Giroux, 1992). However, when the tenets of postmodernism are applied to ethnography, ethnography underpinned by postmodern thought, we believe it moves beyond ethnography inspired by critical theory in that the presence of the researcher is encapsulated in the research. The researcher is actively involved not only in the research process, but also in the empowerment of the research participants' understanding of the research issue under investigation.

To achieve this, Kilduff and Mehra (1997) argue that postmodern researchers, in pursuit of conventional wisdom, could mix and match various perspectives of research styles for esthetic effect in order to contrast with tradition. This freedom to combine styles of discourse follows from the belief that no method grants privileged access to truth and that all research approaches are embodied in the cultural practice that postmodernists seek to make explicit (Smircich & Calas, 1987).

Paramount in the postmodern shift is a re-examination of the values, beliefs, and practices perpetuated by elites that serve to suppress the expression of minority viewpoints. The importance of finding a single totalitarian truth or commonality is replaced by the realization that multiple truths exist simultaneously and that the real issue is not what the truth is but which one is being allowed to be heard. By focusing attention on social processes like power and conflict which operate below the surface of an individual's awareness, postmodernism challenges the monopoly of currently dominant orthodoxies. Skinner (2001) utilized postmodern theory in his ethnographic research to examine the impact of environmental jolts and disturbances on the strategic direction and culture of rugby union in Australia. Skinner suggested that the application of postmodern principles to an ethnographic study would allow for a critical examination of which values, beliefs and practices being promoted by senior rugby union managers were reflective of all organizational members. The importance of finding a single totalitarian truth or commonality was replaced by the realization that multiple truths about the ramifications of the change process may exist simultaneously. Through this examination Skinner focused on the social processes of power, control and conflict to determine whether a fragmentation of values and beliefs about how the sport should be managed in the new era of professionalism existed. As a result, the perceived wholeness and interconnectedness that is meant to accompany the change process was re-examined, as individuals were able to tell their own stories, to identify their own concerns, and present their own opinions about the outcomes of the change process.

According to Packwood and Sikes (1996), what postmodernism has to offer is a focus on the narrative of the individual and the acknowledgment of the situated, partial nature of knowledge claims within the context of the shifting and often contradictory nature of reality. In other words, the meta-narratives that comprise single explanations for the occurrence of a phenomenon are to be deconstructed into micro-narratives of the individuals. This approach serves a dual purpose in sport management research. First, it allows the voices of those dispossessed by meta-narratives to be heard. In a sporting organization space could be given to the voices of volunteers and not just to the management alone. Second, it allows the taken-for-granted truths and realities of those meta-narratives, in relation to the complexities of organizational behavior, to be made problematic and therefore verified (Skinner et al., 1999). Consequently, sport management researchers should be cautious of broad universal claims about the complex organizational nature of sport organizations and remain open to diverse interpretations through the inclusion of alternative representations. Postmodern approaches to sport management research therefore involve a search for the non-obvious, the counterintuitive, the surprising, the ambiguous, the contradictory, and the chaotic reality of sport practices or the organizational nature of sport organizations.

In scientific research, there is a search for wholeness and interconnectedness rather than the fragmentation of phenomena. In sport management research, modern methods of scientific examination and expert-driven discourse can be supplanted by postmodern methods of conversation that allow the emergence of multiple realities and the realization of the limitations of currently dominant research paradigms. The postmodern approach in sport management research can therefore view the narrative as a dialogical production of a co-operatively evolved polyphonic text. In other words, it can be representative of the differing views that exist among sports fans, or that exist in sporting organizations. Utilizing this approach will allow the sport management researcher to capture the passionate views of a diverse cross section of sports fans on one hand, or on the other hand, the fractured and chaotic organizational reality of sport organizations. Such an approach will only benefit sport management research.

Regardless of the strong arguments for adopting a postmodern approach to research, Clifford (1986) raised concerns that centered on the dual crisis of legitimation and representation. This relates to the problems of defending representations of research participants as legitimate rather than merely as constructions of the researcher. She suggests that this is a particular problem for postmodern research approaches that deliberately set out to take participants' stories through increasing levels of abstraction.

Silk and Amis (2000) in their ethnographic work based on the Kuala Lumpur 1998 Commonwealth Games alluded to the postmodernist concerns of "legitimation" and "representation" raised by Parson's and the realization that social researchers are part of the world they study. Silk and Amis suggest that these concerns spread across numerous facets of the research process and can include issues surrounding the gathering of data in respect to whose voice is heard and whose voice is excluded, through to the actual writing of the research paper, recognizing it is how each participant's story is interpreted and whose interpretation is given priority and weight that can shape the outcomes of the research.

A fundamental implication of the application of postmodern thought to traditional ethnographical research is the unavoidable process of critical self-appraisal that it imposes on sport management research. Postmodernism compels sport management researchers to examine their theoretical accomplishments, question their epistemological assumptions and continually challenge the appropriateness of their methodological procedures. In sum, ethnographic research that embraces postmodern thought must address the methodological concerns raised through postmodern inquiry. These include the following:

- Acknowledgment of the researchers' values, interests, interactions and interpretations within the research process.

- Acknowledgment of the reasons for undertaking research.

- Research is a mutually participative, creative process, wherein the "voice" of the participants is valued and recognized in the research process.

- Acknowledgment is made of the authorial self as intrusive, but as indispensable to the research process.

- Encouragement is given to facilitate and allow individuals to tell their own stories, to identify their own issues and find their own solutions beyond the activities of the researcher.

Research Brief

Title: Inventing the Tradition: Cowboy Sports in a Post-modern Age
Who: Hightower, M., University of Virginia
Hightower utilized ethnographic research protocols to investigate Cowboy Sport subculture amongst 'Old Dominion Cowboys' in Virginia. He collected data through participant observation at a number of events. Hightower's coded data revealed 15 themes. He then analyzed the themes in the context of American character formation, frontier history, western genre of entertainment, collective memory studies and sport sociology to situate Cowboy Sports in a social and historical context.

FIVE TASKS IN ETHNOGRAPHICAL RESEARCH DESIGN

According to Spradley (1980) there are five tasks in ethnographic research design, although appearing sequential are actually cyclical in design

1. Selecting an ethnographic project.

2. Collecting ethnographic data.

3. Analyzing ethnographic data.

4. Asking ethnographic questions.

5. Writing the ethnography.

All are important components of ethnographic research and below is a brief synopsis of what Spradley (1980) considers the important key elements within each task of ethnographic research design.

Selecting an ethnographic project

It is important to consider the scope of the investigation. Within a single organization – such as a sport organization – it is possible to narrow the scope of the investigation and focus on perhaps several social situations. For example, the sport management research could focus on those social situations that provide insights into relationships between players and coaches. It is important however that the researcher does not bring pre-conceived ideas about these relationships. Although our own biases and belief systems cannot be totally removed it is important that when selecting a project to recognize if you have the ability to undertake the project objectively.

Collecting ethnographic data

Ethnographic projects are predicated on the notion of participant observation. In a sport organization you will observe the activities of a variety of people (athletes, coaches, sport managers, sponsors, etc), the physical characteristics of the organization and get a feel for the atmosphere within that organization. Throughout the study the types of observation the researcher observes will change. For example, the sport management research is likely to move through a cycle where they begin with "descriptive observation" – trying to get an overview of the social dynamics of the organization. After recording and analyzing this data the research would then move to more "focused observations" – looking at specific types of interactions between players and coaches. After further analysis the sport management researcher will then narrow the investigation further and make "selective observations". It is important to note however that even as your observations narrow the sport management researcher should continue to make general descriptive observations until the research is completed.

Analyzing ethnographic data

Analyzing data is not completed when you only have large amounts of data. The process of question-discovery is the key to ethnographic inquiry. It is important that the sport management researcher does not come into the organization with specific questions. As a sport management ethnographer it is important to analyze the data that has been gathered through the participant observation process to discover questions. It is necessary to analyze the data regularly – that is, after each phase of the fieldwork.

Asking ethnographic questions

Asking ethnographic questions signals the start of the ethnographic field-work. This seems self-evident when as a researcher you are conducting an interview but it is important to note that simply observations and fieldnote entries require the asking of questions. For example, if we are analyzing the interactions between players and coaches, assume all players and coaches are having a debriefing after losing a vital game. During the debriefing a number of players leave the room in an inappropriate manner, others give an opinion, others sit quietly, others argue among themselves about their performance and some challenge the coaches about their comments. The behaviors of the coaches also vary. The head coach speaks in an aggressive manner to some players and in a supportive manner to others, some assistant coaches are quiet while others clearly express their disappointment in the performance of some players. Here you have answered several implicit questions, questions you have asked without realizing it:

1. What types of interactions occur in match debriefings after a loss?

2. How do players react?

3. How did the coaches react?

4. Do players argue with each other over their performance?

There are a range of questions that could be asked through observing this process. It is important to remember though that there are three major kinds of ethnographic questions that can lead to different types of observations in the field. As with the data collection, questioning in ethnography begins with "descriptive questions". In the case of the match debriefing the sport management researcher may ask: "who is present", "what are they doing"? What is the physical setting of this situation? Further into the study, after using these kinds of questions that guide your observations, and after analyzing the initial data, the sport management ethnographer would move to a combination of "structural questions" and "contrast questions". These types of questions will assist the researcher in making more focused observations.

Writing the ethnography

This last major task in the research cycle takes place toward the end of the research. Writing is part of the analysis process as well as a means of communication, which can lead to new questions and observations and occurs toward the end of the research cycle. Burns (2000) states that the most distinctive element is the emphasis on reflexivity: description and analysis of the research process itself, reporting extracts from the data – which gives the reader an opportunity to assess the study, especially when quotations from the data are utilized to support arguments. Those however who begin their writing early in their research find that writing is embedded within the research cycle.

VALIDITY IN ETHNOGRAPHY

Data collection and analysis strategies used by ethnographers in ethnographic studies maintain high internal validity (Burns, 1997) for various reasons. Firstly, the long-term living relationship with participants in the setting allows continual data analysis and comparison to "refine constructs and to ensure the match between scientific categories and participant realities" (p. 324). Secondly, interviews with informants, which constitute a primary ethnographic data source, must be solely derived from experience or observation and "are less abstract than many instruments used in other research designs" (p. 324). Thirdly, the researcher's role as participant observer, in order to acquire the reality of life experiences of participants, is found in the natural settings. Fourthly, ethnographic analysis embodies a process of ethnographer self-monitoring – known as disciplined activity, in which the researcher continually questions and re-evaluates information and challenges his/her own opinions or biases.

Finally, Hammersley (1990) advocated that although replication is not always possible in natural sciences and may not be feasible in ethnography, it does not therefore "detract from the validity of ethnographic findings" (p. 10). Furthermore, ethnographers utilize methods designed to secure that their findings are not idiosyncratic – for instance by comparing information from other sources, a term known as triangulation. Triangulation is employed to enhance validity (Burns, 1997; Hammersley, 1990).

RELIABILITY IN ETHNOGRAPHY

The degree of reliability in ethnographic research is based on replication of the study, and that two or more individuals can have comparable explanations by conforming to categories and procedures in the study (Burns, 1997). Although replication in natural sciences is not always achievable (due to changes in the setting or behaviors of members), the possibility to replicate ethnographic findings does not undermine assessments of their validity, though it may make the task more difficult. Burns (2000) states that qualitative research does not pretend to be replicable. The researcher "purposely avoids controlling the research conditions and concentrates on recording the complexity of changing situational contexts" (p. 417).

The threat to reliability in ethnographic studies can be overcome in the following ways: Ethnographers can (i) provide a profile for the research together with major question(s) they wish to address, (ii) describe their views on the question(s) and explain the research assumptions and biases, and (iii) explain the data collecting process in view of timing and parameters of the study, interviews, relationships with members and categories to be developed for analysis (Burns, 1997). The quality of data is also improved when the participant observer establishes and sustains trusting and co-operative relationships with people in the field. In a sense, validity and reliability are closely associated issues that "acquire a distinct character for the methodology of participant observation" (p. 325).

TRUST AND INTEGRITY IN ETHNOGRAPHIC RESEARCH

There are no definite guidelines for researchers to gain trust and integrity in ethnographic research and, according to Neuman (1994), "a genuine concern for and interest in others, being honest, and sharing feelings are good strategies" (p. 342). The researcher's long-term period in this study interacting with members, listening and understanding their concerns, their verbal and non-verbal language and acknowledging their cultural rules helped to develop rapport, trust, integrity and cooperation. This degree of relationship between the researcher and members is very helpful in obtaining "accurate and dependable information" (Jorgensen, 1989, p. 70) and checking of data was undertaken with informants.

ETHICAL PRINCIPLES

Informants are human beings who have interests, concerns and problems and researchers' values are not necessarily similar to informants. As field-work is an essential component of ethnography, researchers in the field frequently confront conflicting values and a broad range of possible choices. For example: "How will I use the data collected and will I tell the informants how it will be used" (Spradley, 1979, p. 79). Therefore, ethnographers need to protect the physical, social and psychological welfare and to honor the dignity and privacy of their informants. Ethnography also entails interaction with other people such as sponsors and gatekeepers, who may have the power to grant or withhold permission to conduct interviews. The researcher must also safeguard the artefacts that are collected.

DATA COLLECTION METHODS

There are several different information-gathering techniques that are used in ethnography – observing, listening, asking and examining materials – which are conducted during fieldwork in order to survey the setting, which includes the nature of the language, kinship ties, historical data and function of the culture (Fetterman, 1989). The key to fieldwork "is being there" (Fetterman, 1989) for the purpose of observation, asking "seemingly stupid yet insightful questions" (p. 19), taking notes and recognizing that cultural influences are created from what individuals say, do and act (Fetterman, 1989; Neuman, 1994; Spradley, 1979).

Postmodern Ethnographic Case Study

Who: Lisa Swanson, University of Maryland

What: Soccer Fields of Cultural [Re]-Production? An Ethnographic Explication of the 'Soccer Mom'.

Theoretical framework

Swanson examined the cultural practices of "soccer moms" as a segment of America's privileged, suburban, upper middle class. She employed a multi-faceted ethnographic approach to generate a substantial body of empirical data.

In analyzing specific class practices, Swanson relied on Pierre Bourdieu's sociological theories related to the interplay between "habitus" and several forms of capital (economic, cultural, and social) within various cultural fields. She provided an analysis of the ways in which the subjects reproduce their class status in and through the cultural experiences of their children.

Data collection methods

Swanson studied the everyday experiences of women whose children participate in competitive youth soccer programs. She attended soccer practices and games to observe and immerse herself in the culture, carried out unstructured, thematic interviews of "soccer moms" in an attempt to gain an emic perspective, and ultimately compared and contrasted "soccer moms" private reality with the public's view of their white, middle class, maternal role. Data collection procedures included fieldwork, participant observation, survey, and both structured and unstructured interviews. The results of this research shed light on the complexities of the "soccer mom" role by problematizing the taken-for-granted assumptions about upper-middle class women. An interpretive analysis of the rich, ethnographic data gathered was informed by Pierre Bourdieu's theories on culture and class reproduction, specifically in terms of intersecting experiences of social class and gender.

Data analysis techniques/presentation

Swanson followed a five-stage framework for analyzing unstructured, qualitative data; she did this while continuously reflecting back upon theoretical work by Bourdieu. The five interconnected stages comprising the framework were familiarization, identifying a thematic framework, indexing, charting, and finally mapping and interpretation. These stages were developed with the understanding that the researcher has the ability to conceptualize his or her own data and how best to relate the interpretive process. Overall, following this five-stage framework enabled Swanson to develop a written analysis rich in the words of her subjects.

Major findings

In summary, the research found that women fought for an identity separate from the stereotypical "soccer mom". They made their distinctions by emphasizing that they did not get very caught up in the competitions and played a very nurturing, yet undervalued role. According to Swanson, the mothers, as agents, responded to the demands of the broader social structure. The subjects played a self-sacrificing role, as most of them left careers to raise their children.

Swanson argues that research like this study is essential, as women's current expected mothering practices can ultimately be understood as an issue of wellness. She argues that examination and awareness of the nuances of the field through studies such as this one, can contribute to an examination and restructuring of suburban, upper-middle-class, mothering practices.

Suggestions for future research

Swanson indicated that similar studies of upper-middle class "soccer moms" would help to ascertain if this is truly a unique group of subjects whose understanding of their role in their children's sport experience differs from other team mothers. She added that mothers of various social class backgrounds could be studied with the intention of comparing and contrasting habitus and lifestyle choices. She indicated that an obvious follow-up study to the current research would be an ethnography of mothers of football (not soccer) playing children, since the results of this study indicated a strong contrast between the subjects' perceptions of these two autumn season team sports.

Another direction of future research that Swanson suggests is the production of a more complete picture of what is happening among all the individuals involved in youth sport organizations. An intense focus, including one-on-one interviews with the fathers would develop insight into whether or not both parents share in their habitus and lifestyle choices for their children. She added that a grand scale project could produce a great overview into the inner workings of dominating classes reproducing their habitus in their children through sport.

Whilst Swanson was focused solely on the mothers' production and maintenance of their boys in soccer, she did at times encounter data regarding their girls' experiences with sport – particularly in relation to food and exercise. She is convinced a future study on parents of girls in youth sport could produce a very interesting and telling study of the maintenance of the female body.

Finally, Swanson believed that one of the significant contributions of her research is the ethnographic approach to the research. She argues that ethnography is a powerful and effective approach by which to expand our knowledge of the various meanings and identities represented within culture.

Case study research probes

1. What challenges did this ethnographic approach provide for the researcher?

2. How does this ethnographic approach provide insights that may have not been possible through the application of other research approaches?

3. Would this ethnographic approach differ from a postmodern ethnographic study of change in a sport organization?

CONCLUSION

Traditional ethnography's approach to such areas of study as sport management has a number of criticisms and weaknesses. More recent discourses such as critical and postmodern theories can be applied to the ethnographic method to broaden the field of ethnography by accentuating awareness of research practices, drawing attention to the role of power relations in the construction of reality, problematizing the role of the researcher as subject, and providing the potential to empower the research participants' understanding of the research issue under investigation.

In endeavoring to emulate rigorous standards of research sport management researchers should be encouraged to take more methodological "risks" and embrace more eclectic research approaches. Critical and postmodern research approaches offer these opportunities. Moreover, if sport management researchers embrace critical and postmodern thought it provides them with a theoretical framework to question the social, historical and political forces that play a role in shaping social reality.

IN PROFILE - Professor Tim Crabbe

Tim Crabbe is currently a professor of the sociology of sport and popular culture at Sheffield Hallam University, UK. His work has been strongly influenced by participatory action research approaches and has appeared in the *British Journal of Sociology*, the *International Review for the Sociology of Sport*, *International Journal of Sport Management and Marketing* and *Leisure Studies*. His research has principally focused on the use of sport as an agent of social change and development with a particular focus on 'race', 'deviance' and young people. Adopting an approach informed by the cultural studies perspective pioneered at the Centre for Contemporary Cultural Studies at the University of Birmingham, his early work was concerned to better understand the cultures of racism pervading English football through an ethnography of four professional football clubs and their fans. This work was motivated by and mobilized around a high profile campaign of action to tackle issues of prejudice within the game. This commitment to participatory action research, or praxis, is driven by an iterative inquiry process that balances collaborative problem solving actions with data-driven analysis and research to understand underlying issues which can then be used to review and guide further action. This is an approach which challenges traditional research methods, by moving beyond reflective knowledge created by outside 'experts' to a more active

moment-to-moment and involved process of theorizing, data collection and inquiry which is itself used to inform new emergent structures. These principles have since been mobilized around a growing body of work focused around the use of sport as an agent of *social* development. A series of considerations of sport based social interventions targeted at disadvantaged groups in the UK and India over a 10-year-period have helped to inform shifts in sport based social policy toward the use of sport as an engagement tool in wider processes of personal social development. Most recently, this has culminated in Tim's involvement in the foundation of the social research co-operative Substance which specializes in the development of self evaluation techniques designed to enable delivery agents to better represent the value and impact of their work through the collapsing of false dichotomies between qualitative and quantitative evidence and the enabling of an evidence based process of learning and development. He co-authored, with Les Back and John Solomos, *The Changing Face of Football: Racism, identity and multiculture in the English game* and, with Tony Blackshaw, *New Perspectives on Sport and 'Deviance': Consumption, performativity and social control*; he co-edited, with Adam Brown and Gavin Mellor, *Football and Community in a Global Context: Studies in Theory and Practice*.

REVIEW AND RESEARCH QUESTIONS

Ethnography is a qualitative research methodology aimed at describing and analyzing the practices and beliefs of cultures and communities. With a basic understanding now of ethnography, attempt to answer the following questions:

1. Is there any place within sport management research for ethnography underpinned by critical and postmodern theories?

2. Identify those key features of the critical and postmodern theories suggested here that you believe would advantage the sport management researcher?

REFERENCES

Anderson, G. L. 1989. Critical ethnography in education: origins, current status, and new directions. *Review of Educational Research*, **59** (3), 249–270.

Birrell, S. & Theberge, N. 1994. Feminist resistance and transformation in sport. In: *Women and Sport: Interdisciplinary Perspectives* (Ed. by M. Costa, S. Guthrie), pp. 361–376. Champaign, IL: Human Kinetics.

Boas, F. 1928. The Dynamics of Cultural Transmission. New York, NY: Morton.

Burns, R. B. 1997. Introduction to Research Methods, 3rd ed. Melbourne: Longman.

Burns, R. B. 2000. Introduction to Research Methods, 4th ed. Melbourne: Longman.

Carspecken, P. F. 1996. Critical Ethnography in Educational Research: A Theoretical and Practical Guide. New York and London: Routledge.

Clifford, J. 1986. Introduction: partial truths. In: *Writing Culture* (Ed. by J. Clifford, G. Marcus), pp. 1–26. Berkeley, CA: University of California Press.

Codrescu, A. 1986. A Craving for Swan. Columbus: Ohio State University Press.

Denzin, N. 1997. Interpretive Ethnography. Thousand Oaks, CA: Sage.

Denzin, N.K., & Lincoln, Y.S. (Eds.). (2000). Handbook of Qualitative Research 2nd ed. Thousand Oaks, CA: Sage.

Edwards, A., Skinner, J. & O'Keefe, L. 2000. Women sport managers. *International Review of Women and Leadership*, **6** (2), 48–58.

Fetterman, D. 1989. Ethnography: Step by Step. Newbury Park, CA: Sage.

Giddens, A. 1987. Structuralism, Poststructuralism and the Production of Culture. Cambridge: Polity Press.

Giroux, H. A. 1992. Border Crossing: Cultural Workers and the Politics of Education. New York: Routledge.

Glaser, B. & Strauss, A. 1967. The Discovery of Grounded Theory: Strategies for Qualitative Research. New York: Aldine.

Hammersley, M. 1990. Reading Ethnographic Research: A Critical Guide. New York: Longman.

Hammersley, M. 1992. What's Wrong with Ethnography: Methodological Explorations. London: Routledge.

Jorgensen, D. L. 1989. Participant Observation. Newbury Park, CA: Sage.

Kilduff, M. & Mehra, A. 1997. Postmodernism and organizational research. *Academy of Management Review*, **22**, 453–481.

LeCompte, M. D. & Preissle, J. 1993. Ethnography and Qualitative Design in Educational Research, 2nd ed. New York: Academic Press.

Lenskyj, H. 1994. Women, Sport and Physical Activity: Selected Research Themes. Gloucester, Ontario: SIRC.

Linstead, S. 1993. From postmodern anthropology to deconstructive ethnography. *Human Relations*, **46**, 97–120.

Malinowski, B. 1922. Argonauts of the Western Pacific. New York: Dutton.

Markula, P. 1995. Firm but shapely, fit but sexy, strong but thin: the postmodern aerobicizing female bodies. *Sociology of Sport Journal*, **12**, 424–453.

Marshall, J. D. 1989. Foucault and education. *Australian Journal of Education*, **33**, 99–113.

Mead, M. 1928. Coming of Age in Samoa. New York: Dell.

Neuman, D. L. 1994. Social Research Methods: Qualitative and Quantitative Approaches. Boston: Allyn & Bacon.

Packwood, A. & Sikes, P. 1996. Adopting a postmodern approach to research. *International Journal of Qualitative Studies in Education*, **9** (3), 335–346.

Silk, M. L. & Amis, J. 2000. Institutional pressures and the production of televised sport. *Journal of Sport Management*, **14** (4), 267–292.

Simon, R. & Dippo, D. 1986. On critical ethnographic work. *Anthropology and Education Quarterly*, **17**, 195–202.

Skinner, J., Stewart, B. & Edwards, A. 1999. Amateurism to professionalism: modelling organizational change in sporting organizations. *Sport Management Review*, **2** (2), 173–192.

Skinner, J. L. (2001). *Environmental Turbulence and its Impact on Strategic Change and Organisational Culture: The Case of the Queensland Rugby Union*. Unpublished doctoral dissertation, Victoria University, Melbourne, Australia.

Smircich, L. & Calas, M. 1987. Organizational culture: a critical assessment. In: *Organizational Communication* (Ed. by F. Jablin, L. Putnam, K. Roberts, L. Porter), pp. 228–263. London: Sage.

Smith, D. 1987. The Everyday World as Problematic: A Feminist Sociology. Boston: Noreastern University Press.

Spradley, J. 1979. The Ethnographic Interview. New York: Holt, Rinehart and Winston.

Spradley, J. P. 1980. Participant Observation. New York: Holt, Rinehart & Winston.

Sykes, H. 1996. Constr(i)(u)cting lesbian identities in physical education: feminist and poststructural approaches to researching sexuality. *Quest: Journal of the National Association for Physical Education in Higher Education*, **48** (4), 459–469.

Tedlock, B. 2000. Ethnography and ethnographic representation. In: *Handbook of Qualitative Research* (Ed. by N. K. Denzin, Y. S. Lincoln), pp. 455–486, 2nd ed. Thousand Oaks, CA: Sage.

Thomas, J. 1993. Doing Critical Ethnography. Newbury Park, CA: Sage.

Thompson, P. 1993. Postmodernism: fatal distraction. In: *Postmodernism and Organizations* (Ed. by J. Hassard, M. Parker), pp. 183–203. Newbury Park, CA: Sage.

Weedon, C. 1987. Feminist Practice and Poststructuralist Theory. London: Blackwell.

Wilcox, K. 1980. The Enthnography of Schooling: Implications for Educational Policy Making (Project report 80-A10). Institute for Research on Educational Finance and Governance.

CHAPTER 14

Emerging Ethnographies in Sport Management Research: Netnography, Ethnodrama and Phenomenography

CHAPTER OVERVIEW

This chapter will discuss some emerging ethnographical methodologies and demonstrate how they can be situated in the sport management research field. Netnography, Ethnodrama, and Phenomenography may appear on the surface to have little relation to sport management research; however this chapter will briefly cover each of these methodologies and discuss their potential applications to the field of sport management.

NETNOGRAPHY AND SPORT MANAGEMENT RESEARCH

What is netnography?

Kozinets (1998) defines netnography as "a written account resulting from fieldwork studying the cultures and communities that emerge from online, computer mediated, or Internet-based communications, where both the fieldwork and the textual account are methodologically informed by the traditions and techniques of cultural anthropology" (p. 6).

The Internet is a home to a vast number of online communities whose members, from all corners of the world meet in chat rooms, forums and via email mailing lists to discuss common interests – be it in tapestry, animal husbandry, Star Trek, or sport. Blogs, wikis and bulletin boards are also web formats that can host online communities. By their nature, many of these online communities are not open for public scrutiny, with only members having access to archives, online information and access to other members. For the sport management researcher interested in pursuing a netnographical approach, this would necessitate joining a particular online community, as gathering research purely by external observation is unlikely to be as successful.

A key distinction between netnography and traditional ethnography is the fact that netnography: "is based primarily upon the observation of textual discourse, an important difference from the balancing of discourse and observed behavior that occurs during in-person ethnography" (Kozinets, 2002, p. 7). This raises a host of issues, primarily: how does the netnographer determine the trustworthiness – not to mention the age, gender, race, etc. – of their informants?

Kozinets (2002) explains that netnography seems "perfectly suited to the approach of G.H. Mead (1938) in which the ultimate unit of analysis is not the person, but the behaviour of the act" (p. 7). In other words, while traditional ethnography observes people, netnography studies "conversational acts", including "the act, type and content of the posting, the medium, and so on" (p. 7).

This approach in fact turns a potential problem of netnography (lack of access to informants' nonverbal cues, including their physical appearance) into a potential asset. If, as mentioned above, ethnographic studies always reflect "differences and similarities between participants and scholars in terms of class, gender, race, culture or subculture, educational background, age, etc." (Seiter et al., 1989, p. 227), then netnography's tendency to obscure these variables may produce research uncomplicated by issues of class, gender and race. Most Internet and Usenet posts betray no information about the poster's age, gender or race. Therefore, the focus of netnography is on what is written, not on who does the writing. It is suggested that one way for dealing with netnography's reliance on textual discourse as opposed to observed behavior is simply to develop an understanding of the online community and its leaders, its rank-and-file members, its rhetorical style, and its codes and mores. After extensive exposure, a netnographer will develop a sense of whether a particular posting is valid and reliable. As Kozinets (1998) suggests, netnographers must always be aware that "the limitations and requirements of producing and communicating textual information obviously structure virtual relationships in many ways, including: eliminating and simulating physicality and body (e.g., body language has been virtually replaced by (deliberately) shared (emot)icons), privileging verbal–rational states and skills over nonverbal–emotional ones, and allowing more "pre-editing" of expressed thoughts and thus more opportunities for strategic self-presentation efforts" (p. 3). He adds that in the end, good netnography is built on the same foundation as good ethnography: "persistent observation, gaining rapport and trust, triangulating across sites and sources, using good interview techniques, and researcher introspection" (p. 7).

Ethics and netnography

Research ethics may be one of the most important differences between traditional ethnography and netnography. Ethical concerns over netnography turn on contentious and still largely unsettled concerns about whether online forums are to be considered a private or a public site, and about what constitutes informed consent in cyberspace (see Paccagnella, 1997). In a major departure from traditional methods, netnography uses cultural information that is not given specifically, and in confidence, to the sport management researcher. The sport consumers who originally created the data do not necessarily intend or welcome its use in research representations.

Advantages and limitations of netnography

Compared to surveys, experiments, focus groups, and personal interviews, netnography is a far less obtrusive method. It is conducted using observations in a context that is not fabricated by the sport management researcher. Netnography also is less costly and timelier than focus groups and personal interviews. It is a naturalistic and unobtrusive technique – a nearly unprecedented combination.

The limitations of netnography draw from its more narrow focus on online communities, its inability to offer the full and rich detail of lived human experience, the need for researcher interpretive skills, and the lack of informant identifiers present in the online context that leads to difficulty in generalizing results to groups outside the online community sample. Sport management researchers wishing to generalize the findings of a netnography of a particular online group to other groups must apply careful evaluations of similarity and consider using multiple methods for research triangulation. Netnography is still a relatively new method, and awaits further development and refinement at the hands of a new generation of Internet-savvy ethnographic sport management researchers.

Applications of netnography to sport management research

The sport management researcher interested in applying netnographical methodologies to their research first needs to determine whether or not a viable and functioning online community exists from within which to conduct the research study. A search of Yahoo groups, which claims to host millions of online groups, fails to find a single hit with the keyword search "sport management". "Management" secures over 63 000 results.

The sport management researcher must obviously first focus on who are the target participants for the research study. If sport managers themselves are the desired participants, then it is likely that another source will need to be found other than Yahoo groups. The question then needs to be asked whether sport managers are likely to utilize online forums, groups, etc. to exchange information, share resources, seek solutions to problems from other sport managers, and even vent to others with a shared interest/profession. If no online community exists for the target participant group, then the sport management researcher may even consider establishing such a group, although the time involved to cultivate members, build trust, and establish a network of members beyond a localized area would probably be prohibitive. One of the advantages of online communities is their ability to link people with a shared interest who would otherwise never have connected due to differences in culture, language and geographical distance. The sharing of information, opinions and even life stories from seemingly disparate groups of people who may on the surface have only one obscure thing in common can make for a rich source of data for the budding netnographer.

Whilst online communities of sport managers may be few and far between (or even completely missing), the netnographer will still find a rich source of potential research participants among the possibly millions of online groups dedicated to particular sports, sporting teams, and individual athletes. Membership of these groups will vary, from die-hard fans to the merely curious fan looking for a specific piece of information, to support teams, and family and friends of athletes looking for an easy way to maintain contact and share information.

Depending on the particular focus of the research study, online communities have the potential to offer the sport management researcher access to a pool of participants eager and willing to share information and their opinions. The very fact of their active membership in a particular online community demonstrates their interest in the topic. Active participation in discussions within the community demonstrates the willingness of members to share information.

The sport management researcher will need to proceed with caution however, as long standing online communities will usually take action against perceived "lurkers" or "trolls" (by eviction from the community), and will need to take the time to build trust within the community. This may involve being completely upfront about the purpose of the researcher's membership of the community.

Research Brief

Title: Wrestling with the Audience: Fan culture on the Internet

Who: Weisberg, D.E., Northwestern University

Weisberg utilized the methodology of netnography. This study considered the culture of the 'Internet Wrestling Community', a segment of the professional wrestling audience that pursues an aspect of its fandom online. The research questions that guided this research were (1) What are the Internet Wrestling Community's beliefs and attitudes about itself and its relationships with offline fans and the wrestling industry? (2) Do online fans believe that they are 'better' fans than offline fans? (3) Does the Internet Wrestling Community want to be catered to by the wrestling industry? (4) How much 'power' do Internet wrestling fans believe they wield, relative to the industry and offline fans? (5) To what degree do online fans feel that they and offline fans have similar tastes and attitudes about the wrestling product? To answer these questions, the study's primary data consisted of postings culled from the Usenet group rec.sport.pro-wrestling and from wrestling-related Web sites. These data were supplemented with open-ended telephone interviews with prominent members of the Internet Wrestling

Continued

Community. The data reveal several results that challenge traditional theories of Internet fan communities. This study found significant evidence of ambiguity among Internet wrestling fans in two distinct but related areas. Individually, while many users credit the Internet for enhancing their experience as wrestling fans, many others surprisingly report that heavy Internet use has diminished their enjoyment of wrestling. Collectively, the Internet Wrestling Community is also struggling to negotiate its relationships with the wrestling industry and with casual wrestling fans. Some fans suggest that the Internet offers the wrestling industry a free, naturally occurring focus group comprised of the most reflective, reflexive, critical, knowledgeable, loyal and articulate segment of the audience. These fans see themselves as 'opinion leaders' in a variation of the two-step flow model of media consumption by catering to the refined tastes of the hardcore fans, the industry will produce a stronger product that will in turn attract the casual, mass audience. Other fans remain dubious of this model; they insist that the wrestling industry should not pay too much attention to its online fans.

ETHNODRAMA AND SPORT MANAGEMENT RESEARCH

What is ethnodrama?

The term ethnodrama represents a recent trend in ethnography to present research as a performance text. This ethnographic genre has other labels as well – ethnoperformance, and performance and reflexive anthropology (Denzin, 1997, p. 91).

Ethnodrama allows an actor to embody the experience of another, an action that in itself is interpretive. In other words, we have the text that represents lived experiences and then, the performer who represents these experiences before an audience. The actor and members of the audience then become cultural critics as they represent/view a reality that has been deconstructed through the editing and performance process. Therefore, the purpose of an ethnodrama is not to entertain, but to encourage critical thinking and questioning. Denzin (1997) outlines five forms of performance text:

1. dramatic texts (rituals, poems, and plays meant to be performed);

2. natural texts (transcriptions of everyday conversations);

3. performance science texts (fieldwork notes and interviews);

4. improvisational; and

5. critical ethnodramas (the merging of natural script dialogs with dramatized scenes and the use of composite characters).

According to Saldana (2005), Ethnodrama consists of "dramatised, significant selections of narrative collected through interviews, participant observation, filed notes, journal entries, and/or print and media artefacts such as diaries, television broadcasts, newspaper articles, and court proceedings"

(p. 2). Coffey and Atkinson (1996) go further to say that the "idea of ethnodrama is to transform data (dialog, transcripts, etc.) into theatrical scripts and performance pieces" (p. 126).

The primary function of ethnodrama is to tell the stories of the participants, as true to their words and actions as possible. As Saldana (2005) says, ethnodrama maintains "close allegiance to the lived experiences of real people while presenting their stories through an artistic medium" (p. 3). The goal of ethnodrama, however, is to "investigate a particular facet of the human condition for purposes of adapting those observations and insights into a performance medium" (p. 1).

Ethnodrama and the research process

Given that qualitative research lends itself to note taking, observations, interviews, transcripts, coding, triangulation, etc. and the transformation, selection, interpretation and perceptions of the researcher, it would be safe to say that these methodological approaches and issues transfer into the ethnodrama research design.

Scripting an ethnodrama

The process of scripting an ethnodrama means incorporating as much verbatim narrative as possible (Mienczakowski & Morgan, 1993). This allows the performance text to attempt to create a high degree of "vraisemblance" or "semblance of truth" (Mienczakowski, 2001). By inviting "informants" to validate the research by attending scripting sessions, rehearsals, group readings, and preview performances, Mienczakowski used feedback from the "informants" to edit and rewrite the script. Postperformance discussions with the audience also allow the researcher to "renegotiate" the ethnodrama's meaning after every performance. This high level of communication and cooperation between researcher, informant, and audience make Mienczakowski's approach reflexive, polyvocal and accessible to a broad audience.

The role of the audience in an ethnodrama

The ethnodrama is the culminating piece to research. In recent years, various researchers have recognized that they are pursuing the same ends – voicing the marginalized experience – albeit through different lenses. In the late 1980s and early 1990s, sociologists began turning ethnographic research into performances while theater artists began to turn to ethnographies for performance material (McCall, 2000).

The next step is to develop the material beyond its ethnodrama format into a Theater-In-Education (TIE) program. TIE is an effective educational tool that invites audience members to interact with the characters on stage in a variety of ways and often through creative drama methods. For example, the audience members may become a part of the scene being acted out, or may be allowed to interview characters to learn more about their lives. The audience can give the characters advice, which may in turn influence the outcome of the play. The actors can also freeze a scene, allowing the audience the chance to analyze the conflict, and rewind it to playback the same scene for further clarification. The TIE program often involves its audience physically as well as mentally. This involvement is intrinsic to the plot and the students become an essential part of the action, either as participants, or as critical observers whose opinions are sought and valued. In the work of Mienczakowski one finds a form of TIE techniques. During an after-performance discussion, Mienczakowski's (2001) performers "rework scenarios, reinterpret events, and thereby reconstruct and negotiate the individual's understanding of the play's outcomes" (p. 361).

Ethical concerns and limitations of ethnodrama

According to Saldana (2005), "theater's primary goal is neither to educate nor to enlighten. Theater's primary goal is to *entertain* ..." (p. 141). This poses a dilemma for the ethnodramatist. Is it possible for ethnodrama to be widely accepted as a valid and viable methodology for data presentation or is it just entertainment?

There are also ethical concerns surrounding the participants themselves, relating to issues of confidentiality and anonymity. It is essential, therefore, that all participants consent to all the content in the performance, and that they are fully aware of the implications of being in the performance, if that is the approach taken (Saldana, 1998, 2005).

The role of the sport management researcher in an ethnodrama

The application of theatrical devices to data bring into question the sport management researcher's role in the ethnodrama (Denzin, 1997). Is the sport management researcher a participant? How much influence does the sport management researcher have on the data collected, selected and shaped into a performance? Has the data selection been influenced by dramatic merit or is the accuracy of the participant's story the primary concern? Can it be both? Is it valid to have the sport management researcher's narrative or commentary placed within the performance script? (Denzin, 1997; Saldana, 2005). Therefore, whose truth it is and to whom does it belong?

Ethnodrama and sport management research

Ethnodrama has the potential to demonstrate that the embodiment of human experience through artistic means can enhance the understanding of the experiences of sport managers, and can situate the experience within a recognizable context that also has the facility to satisfy the "entertainment" component of theater.

The personal reflections of a sport manager, especially one with connections to high profile clubs, teams, or athletes, will have the voyeuristic component that will attract a certain audience membership, as well as the educational component that other sport managers, sporting purists, and a wider segment of society will find attractive.

Having dealt with those ethical implications and possible conflicts of interest of the researcher discussed earlier, the sport management researcher has the opportunity to use ethnodrama to discover, discuss and explore previously untouched areas of sport management by creating a "real world" presentation of the "real life" experiences of sport managers in such a way that will engage the audience in critical reflection and debate on the issues and situations presented in the ethnodrama.

PHENOMENOGRAPHY AND SPORT MANAGEMENT RESEARCH

What is phenomenography?

Phenomenography is a process that is concerned with identifying peoples' ideas about a phenomenon, rather than proving that the actual phenomenon exists. Through this approach the researcher begins to formulate an understanding of the specific ways in which these understandings form similarities and differences amongst people. Phenomenography attempts to identify and describe, as faithfully as possible, the individual's conceptions of some aspect of reality (Sandberg, 1995). In this way, it attempts to bring all conceptions to light and tries to describe them. The phenomenographer seeks to understand, systematize and order these conceptions in relation to each other, thus arriving at a view of the whole picture of the phenomenon, by describing the range of variation among its subjects (Svensson, 1994). For Bruce (1997), phenomenography is able to:

- provide direct descriptions of a phenomenon;

- describe conceptions in a holistic and integrated way;

- capture a range of conceptions, due to its focus on variations in people's experiences;

- produce descriptions of conceptions which are useful in teaching and learning;

- focus on groups of people, rather than on individuals (p. 5).

Phenomenography was recognized as a research approach in the 1970s at the University of Gothenberg where the focus of study was to examine *what* people learn rather than *how* or *why* they learn (Saljo, 1988). It is the *what* question that differentiates phenomenography from other ethnographies. Marton and Booth (1997) believe that phenomenography also looks at how:

> ... *people handle problems, situations, the world, we have to understand the way in which they experience the problems, the situations, and the world that they are handling or in relation to the way they are acting. Accordingly, a capability for acting in a certain way reflects a capability of experiencing something in a certain way. The latter does not cause the former, but they are logically intertwined. You cannot act other than in relation to the world as you experience it. (p. 117)*

Phenomenographic research

Phenomenographic research is centered on the variation in experiencing phenomena, and describing phenomena as others see them (Hasselgren & Beach, 1997). The variations in experiences are teased out from individual conversations, and used to exemplify different "categories of description", which are collectively expressed as "conceptions". Conceptions have been variously described as a "way of seeing something, a qualitative relationship between an individual and some phenomenon" (Johansson et al., 1985, p. 236), as the ways in which individuals experience the meaning of something (Svennson, 1994), and as "people's ways of experiencing a specific aspect of reality" (Sandberg, 1997, p. 203). The central aim of phenomenographic research is its attempt to uncover and describe qualitatively different ways people perceive, experience and understand various aspects of phenomena in the world as they see it. Phenomenography is therefore primarily concerned with identifying and understanding the relationship between the person and the phenomenon being studied.

Phenomenography and sport management research

The methods for conducting phenomenographical research will vary depending on the phenomena under investigation. The researcher will research and adopt those methods appropriate to the research study. This said, in phenomenography, sport management researchers should try to describe, analyze and understand how people think about particular phenomena. This is not about describing how reality "is", but how reality is perceived by that person. For the sport management researcher, the opportunities are boundless. For example, the following could be considered:

- How does the sport manager perceive their organization's performance in the hosting of a major sporting event?

- How does the sport manager evaluate their performance as manager of a major sporting event?

- Did the sport manager identify problems in the event that were not recognized elsewhere?

Phenomenographic approaches can be utilized in sport management research but have not been applied to date. The challenge for sport management researchers is to engage with the method and demonstrate that new sport management knowledge can be generated from this approach.

CONCLUSION

The three research methodologies discussed in this chapter may have different output and appearance, but they are related in their connection to ethnography and its focus on the experience of the research participant. In many ways, these are research approaches that will be taken on by the next generation of sport management researchers. The discipline can only benefit by sport management researchers embracing these new and emerging ethnographies to understand sport management practice.

IN PROFILE - Dr Robert Rinehart

Dr Robert Rinehart received his Ph.D. at the University of Illinois, Urbana-Champaign, in sociology of sport. He studied with John Loy, Susan Greendorfer, Synthia Sydnor, and Norman Denzin. He has been affiliated with Idaho State University; CSU, San Bernardino; Washington State University, and is currently an Associate Professor at the University of Waikato in the Department of Sport and Leisure Studies. He would characterize the body of his research as ethnographic in nature. The threads of his research have been, recently, alternative sport forms (including 'minor' and non-dominant sports) and the use of fiction and fictional methodology to enhance research opportunities – particularly, how performative types of ethnographies may begin to answer questions regarding lived experience and affective behaviors. He believes that narrative itself is a key both to engaging audiences (in the broad sense), that narrative as text can be discussed in a variety of meaningful ways that help us to understand broader questions of how individuals may become involved in sport, why they may persevere in sport, why they may leave sport – in short, narrative in its many incarnations may allow us to see a variety of responses to how and why people enter into physical activity.

REVIEW AND RESEARCH QUESTIONS

Ethnography is a qualitative research methodology aimed at describing and analyzing the practices and beliefs of cultures and communities. Each of the emerging ethnographies discussed in this chapter embraces this as a basic tenet whilst adopting a unique methodological approach that has significant relevance to sport management research. With a basic understanding now of these emerging ethnographies, attempt to answer the following questions:

- Is there any place within sport management research for netnography?

- Discuss the positive and negative features of an Ethnodramatical approach to a Sport Management Research question.

- Provide other examples of how phenomenographic approaches to sport management research could be applied.

REFERENCES

Bruce, C. 1997. The Seven Faces of Information Literacy. Adelaide: Auslib Press.

Coffey, A. & Atkinson, P. 1996. Making Sense of Qualitative Data: Complementary Research Strategies. Thousand Oaks, CA: Sage.

Denzin, N. K. 1997. Interpretive Ethnography: Ethnographic Practices for the 21st Century. Thousand Oaks, CA: Sage.

Hasselgren, B. & Beach, D. 1997. Phenomenography: A 'Good for Nothing Brother' of Phenomenology? *Higher Education Research and Development*, **16** (2), 191–202.

Johansson, B., Marton, F. & Svensson, L. 1985. An approach to describing learning as change between qualitatively different conceptions. In: *Cognitive Structure and Conceptual Change* (Ed. by L. West, A. Pines). New York: Academic Press.

Kozinets, R. V. 1998. On netnography. Initial reflections on consumer investigations of cyberculture. In: *Advances in Consumer Research Vol. 25* (Ed. by J. Alba, W. Hutchinson), pp. 366–371. Provo, UT: Association for Consumer Research.

Kozinets, R. V. 2002. The field behind the screen: using netnography for marketing research in online communities. *Journal of Marketing Research*, **XXXIX**, 61–72.

Marton, F. & Booth, S. 1997. The learner's experience of learning. In: *The Handbook of Education and Human Development: New Models of Learning, Teaching and Schooling* (Ed. by D. R. Olson, N. Torrance), pp. 534–563. Oxford: Blackwell.

McCall, M. M. 2000. Performance ethnography: a brief history and some advice. In: *Handbook of Qualitative Research* (Ed. by N. K. Denzin, Y. S. Lincoln), pp. 412–433, 2nd ed. Thousand Oaks, CA: Sage.

Mienczakowski, J. 2001. Ethnodrama: performed research – limitations and potential. In: *Handbook of Ethnography* (Ed. by P. Atkinson, A. Coffey, S. Delamont, J. Lofland, L. Lofland), pp. 468–476. London: Sage.

Mienczakowski, J. & Morgan, S. 1993. Busting: The Challenge of the Drought Spirit. Brisbane: Griffith University Reprographics.

Paccagnella, L. 1997. Getting the seats of your pants dirty: strategies for ethnographic research on virtual communities. *Journal of Computer-Mediated Communication*, **3**, (1). Retrieved January 10, 2008 from http://jcmc.indiana.edu/vol3/issue1/paccagnella.html.

Saldana, J. 1998. Ethical issues in an ethnographic performance text: the dramatic impact, the juicy stuff. *Research in Drama Education*, **3** (2).

Saldana, J. 2005. Ethnodrama: An Anthology of Reality Theatre. Walnut Creek CA: Alta Mira Press.

Saljo, R. 1988. Learning in educational settings: methods of inquiry. In: *Improving Learning: New Perspectives* (Ed. by P. Ramsden). London: Kogan Page.

Sandberg, J. 1995. Are phenomenographic results reliable? *Nordisk Pedagogik*, **15**, 156–164.

Sandberg, J. 1997. Are phenomenographic results reliable? *Higher Education Research and Development*, **16**, 203–212.

Seiter, E., Borchers, H., Kreutzner, G. & Warth, E. 1989. Don't treat us like we're so stupid and naive: toward an ethnography of soap opera viewers. In: *Remote Control* (Ed. by E. Seiter, H. Borchers, G. Kreutzner, E. Warth), pp. 223–247. New York, NY: Routledge.

Svensson, L. 1994. Theoretical foundations of phenomenography. In: *Phenomenography: Philosophy and Practice* (Ed. by R. Ballantyne, C. Bruce), pp. 9–20. Brisbane: Queensland University of Technology.

CHAPTER 15

Ethnomethodology and Sport Management Research

CHAPTER OVERVIEW

This chapter seeks to explore a qualitative research methodology that aims to study, understand and articulate how people make sense of themselves and each other in everyday life – ethnomethodology. Simply stated, ethnomethodology is a form of discourse analysis (refer to the chapter on Discourse Analysis). In the field of sport management research, ethnomethodology has to date been largely ignored. In this chapter, we explore some of the basic tenets of ethnomethodology and how these can be applied to the field of sport management research in useful and practical ways that can facilitate the development of practices that enhance sport management education. This will aid in the positive development of praxis within the sport management community that can enhance in a positive way the experience and engagement of members of the sport management community.

WHAT IS ETHNOMETHODOLOGY?

The term "ethnomethodology" was coined by Garfinkel (1967), and was designed originally as a general label for a range of phenomena associated with the use of mundane, everyday knowledge and reasoning by ordinary people (Heritage, 1984). The term now generally refers to the study of a particular subject matter: the body of common-sense knowledge and the range of procedures and considerations by means of which the ordinary members of society make sense of, and find their way about in, and act on the circumstances in which they find themselves. (Heritage, 1984). At the heart of the ethnomethodological perspective is the "lived order".

According to Goode (1994) The term "lived order":

> ... calls our attention to both the contingent and socially structured ways that societal members construct/enact/do/inhabit their everyday world. Ethnomethodologists have generally noted that the lived orders of the everyday world are both relied upon and ignored by societal members. Every American English speaking adult, for example, knows in incredible detail, and as a matter of practical production and recognition, the structures involved in taking turns in conversation, or in supplying the necessary "continuers" to allow conversation to proceed. In this sense, the everyday orderliness is known. But, it is not known in a way that is conscious and reportable. (pp. 127–128)

The paramount concern of ethnomethodology is everyday social practice, as constructed through social interaction among participants. As a way of viewing and understanding social interaction, ethnomethodology studies the specific interactions among participants and acknowledges that interactions are actually agents for constituting social order and reality. Gubrium and Holstein (2000) suggest that ethnomethodologists focus on how members actually "do" social life, aiming in particular to document how they concretely construct and sustain social entities, such as gender, self and family.

Five concepts are central to ethnomethodology; these are as follows:

1. *Indexicality:* The meaning of a word – indeed of all words – is dependent on its context of use. Context means, literally, the actual sequence of individual talk-in-interaction. Thus, words and context give an utterance sense (Coulon, 1995). This model of understanding – that sense is recovered from utterances in context and that context is focused on sequence – is central to ethnomethodology.

2. *Reflexivity:* This is the process in ordinary conversation by which we build up meaning, order and rationality by both describing and producing action simultaneously. Reflexivity is a radical concept. It asserts that while we are talking – the meaning, the order, and the rationality of what we are doing are being produced. "To describe a situation is to constitute it... "Doing" an interaction is telling it" (Coulon, 1995, p. 23).

3. *The documentary method of interpretation:* The meaning of a word is indexical, but at the same time we seek patterns to compensate for this indexicality of language and which make sense (Coulon, 1995). "Every experience of the actor occurs within a horizon of familiarity and pre-acquaintanceship" (Schutz, 1962, p. 7). Even the unfamiliar is grasped against this background. Garfinkel's (1967/1999) notion of the documentary method of interpretation is theorized as a circular process in which an individual in conversation sees an utterance as "evidence" and mentally compares this with an underlying pattern to make sense of it. Garfinkel writes: The method consists of treating actual appearances as "the document of", as "pointing to", as "standing" on behalf of a presupposed underlying pattern. Not only is the underlying pattern derived from its individual documentary evidences, but also the individual documentary evidences, in their turn, are interpreted on the basis of "what is known" about the underlying pattern. Each is used to elaborate the other. (p. 78)

   Garfinkel (1967/1999) illustrates the documentary method with an experiment and goes on to show that every area of sociological investigation uses the documentary method. For example, an interviewer reviewing or editing transcripts who has to decide "what the respondent had in mind" (p. 79) and a researcher "historicizing a person's biography" (p. 95), which is known as "the biographical method" today (Tierney, 2000, p. 539), has to select and organize what has happened in the past to provide a relevant account of the present and possibly the future. Garfinkel (1967/1999) describes his demonstration of the documentary method as being designed to "catch the work of fact production" (p. 79).

4. *The notion of member:* The term *member* is used in ethnomethodology to describe a member of a group who has mastered the natural language of that group and does not have to think about what he or she is doing as the routines of everyday social practice are known. It is certainly not a social category (Coulon, 1995). Since this term was coined in the late 1960s, the notion has been developed substantially. For example, Shotter (1993, p. 135) describes a culture's "sensus communis" as a process in which "socially shared identities of feelings" are created in a flow of activity between members.

5. *Accountability:* Accountability for Garfinkel (1967/1999) means that "the activities whereby members produce and manage settings of organized everyday affairs" are "observable-and-reportable" (p. 1). By this he means that the social world is able to be described, understood, reported on and analyzed as it is revealed in the practical actions of people (Coulon, 1995). This social world is constantly being constructed by members' talk-in-interaction.

METHODOLOGY

According to Schegloff (1991), the basic task of the ethnomethodologist is "to convert insistent intuition, however correct, into empirically detailed analysis" (p. 66). Lee's (1991) five principles of ethnomethodology summarize the analyst's position.

First, an ethnomethodologist suspends belief or acceptance of social relationships between categories of people (Hilbert, 1992; Psathas, 1995). For example, matters of cause and effect relationships or power relationships are set aside until such time as those relationships are made relevant and accomplished by the members themselves as they interact. An ethnomethodologist understands that members continually display the "lived" reality of their relationships and their world to themselves and to others.

Second, the ethnomethodologist's task is to treat interactive situations as scenes that are jointly and sequentially produced by all participants. Mundane talk-in-interaction occurs within a framework that assumes "that utterances which are placed immediately next to some prior are to be understood as produced in response to or, more loosely, in relation to that prior" (Heritage, 1984, p. 261). Therefore, what a turn at talk *is* (e.g., a question), is ascertained in how it is heard as the sequence of talk continues, hence its joint and sequential accomplishment.

Third, the ethnomethodologist sets aside formats of talk or interaction that given participants *would* or *should* use in favor of the structures of talk and interaction that they *do* use (Cuff & Payne, 1984; Psathas, 1995; Schegloff, 1995).

Fourth, the assumption that the orderliness of social structures and social organization is achieved in the day-to-day ordinary activities of members and will, therefore, be available in the details of everyday events, is maintained by the ethnomethodologist. It documents what the members orient to as normal, unremarkable, and to use Garfinkel's (1967) description, "unnoticed".

Finally, and following on from the aforementioned point, the ethnomethodologist understands that, for members of a society, that society's traditions, customs and mores are not sequestered from the talk and interaction, nor do they limit and constrain what those members do and say. Rather, a society's culture is embedded in and built by everyday courses of action.

WHAT DEFINES "DATA" FOR THE ETHNOMETHODOLOGIST?

Ethnomethodology is premised upon the fact that social structures are locally produced and locally maintained through the interactive, practical activities of members (Garfinkel, 1967). It attends to the interpretive procedures through which members are able to make continuous sense out of everyday activities as they occur. For ethnomethodologists, members' methods, that is, their utterances, practices, interpretations and accomplishments, are necessarily foregrounded in investigations of social organization. What this means for ethnomethodological research is that the theoretical apparatus of ethnomethodology proposes a particular theory of *data*. Data can be captured on tape (especially videotape) and this permits repeated analysis and availability for other researchers.

The ethnomethodological approach to research, in the early stages of its development, used conversation in naturally occurring forms (i.e. everyday conversations), consequently the approach became known as Conversation Analysis (or CA). CA studies have documented the features of the talk and the sequential procedures used by participants to achieve courses of action (Dwyer, 1997). More recent ethnomethodological investigations, such as those of Drew and Heritage (1992) have turned to "institutional talk" or the talk that occurs naturally in institutional settings, for example, law courts, medical clinics, schools. These students have broadened the field of ethnomethodological analyses and have resulted in the use of the term Talk-In-Interaction (or **TII**). Drew and Heritage referred to **TII** as the principle means for lay persons to pursue their utilitarian goals, and the central channel for the conduct of daily work-related activities of many professional persons and institutional representatives. Interviews fit neatly into this category of **TII**.

In ethnomethodological studies, people's *reports* of what they did or did not do and say in a particular situation cannot be substituted for *what* they did or did not do. Similarly, interviews of interactants about a particular incident cannot stand in the place of observations, recordings and transcriptions of the incident. This is not to say reports and interviews are not potentially interesting data *per se*. For example, in the case of interviews of sport managers about organizational practices, the interviews would count as data in the question of what sport managers say in interviews about what they do in their organizations, but they would not count as data that answers the question of what those sport managers do in their organizations.

THE ANALYTIC TOOLS OF ETHNOMETHODOLOGY

The key analytic tools of Ethnomethodology are Conversation Analysis (CA) and Membership Categorization Devices (MCDs).

CA is characterized by three main features or assumptions: first, interaction is structurally organized; second, contributions to interaction are contextually oriented; and third, as a result of these two characteristics, no order of detail in interactions can be dismissed as disorderly, accidental or irrelevant (Heritage, 1984). These features are the basic foundations on which conversation analysis is built.

The basic tenets of CA still pertain to the analysis of institutional talk in that there is an emphasis on revealing the orderly nature of such talk through the analysis of sequential practices such as turn taking, and through the use of membership categorization analysis (MCA) to identify how participants position themselves and each other within and through their talk as institutional members. This broadening of ethnomethodology's field of analysis has led to the realization that it is not conversation but "talk-in-interaction" that is the broader and more inclusive characterization of the phenomena of study.

CA then, as a branch of Ethnomethodology examines order as it is produced through talk in an achieved manner *in situ,* accomplished in and through the actual practices of social members. So it is that in such ways the institutions of home and sport organizations, and institutional identities of parents, coaches, and athletes/children, and their inter-institutional relationships are actively talked into being.

CA adheres to the ethnomethodological tenet to refrain from taking an analytic position on what "really happened", concentrating instead on how it is that *members* decide such matters (Cuff et al., 1990) and adopting what Garfinkel and Sacks (1986) have called "ethnomethodological indifference" in describing the formal structures of interaction while "abstaining from all judgments of their adequacy, value, importance, necessity, practicality, success, or consequentiality" (p. 166). The structural, sequential, and publicly available natures of conversation are essential tools used in the analysis of conversation and the interaction of members engaged in the conversation and by extension the implications of this conversation to social structure and relevance.

The MCD is an analytic tool which describes the culturally available sets of categories into which we commonsensically divide persons. These categories are fundamental sense-making resources for members in everyday interaction. Within an interaction there is a "selection problem" in categorizing persons as every person is an incumbent of more than one category in more than one device. The analyst's task then, is to discover the procedural basis by which members engaged in making selections, that is, resolve the question of which membershipping devices and categories are "relevantly correct" (Speier, 1971). Given this, Sacks (1974) developed "rules of application". The "economy rule" or "reference satisfactoriness rule" (p. 219) holds that "if a member uses a single category from any membership categorization device, then they can be recognized as doing "adequate reference to a person" (p. 219). This accounts for the fact that reference to a person can often be achieved with a single categorisztion. This is not to say that more than one category reference may not or cannot be used, but that a single category can be referentially adequate; for example, it may be possible to identify a person by saying that she is a "sport manager" or a "athlete". Secondly, the *"consistency rule"* or "relevance rule" holds: that if a category from some device has been used to categorize a first member of the population, then that device is available to categorize further members of the population.

Some membership categories can be used and heard commonsensically as going together, such as husband/wife, parent/child, teacher/student, and so on. Such associations of categorizations or MCDs are known as "standardized relational pairs" (Silverman, 1993, pp. 111–112). In the field of sport management research, such relational pairs could be coach/athlete. One way of approaching textual and conversational data to document the ways in which members achieve social order is by using membership categorization analysis (MCA). Such an approach "affords a way of examining how social structures are articulated in the talk-in-interaction of everyday life" (Hester & Eglin, 1997, p. 157). A summary of the terminology used in MCD analysis is highlighted in Table 15.1.

Table 15.1   Membership Categorization Devices (MCDs)
Category: any person can be labeled in many "correct" ways
MCD: categories are seen as grouped together in collections
Economy rule: a single category may be sufficient to describe a person
Consistency rule: if one person is identified from a collection, then a next person may be identified from the same collection
Duplicative organization: when categories can be heard as a "team" hear them that way
Category-bound activities: activities may be heard as "tied" to certain categories
Standardized relational pairs (SRPs): pairs of categories are linked together in standardized routine ways

RIGOR

The essential problem for ethnomethodological research is not operationalizing some theory, as in the case of cognitive constructionism, but in making the world able to be investigated in terms of the phenomena that the theory of ethnomethodology specifies (Benson & Hughes, 1991). This places a methodological constraint on the researcher in that nothing can be assumed to be known about the phenomena specified in advance of investigating the world through the theory. Benson and Hughes suggest that "to do otherwise would transgress the requirements of rigor in failing to establish that the world can be investigated by the theory to produce findings about the phenomena. Rigor, then is adhering to the methodological election to treat the social order as a member's accomplishment through and through" (p. 129).

Research Brief

Title: Toward an Alternative Theory of Self and Identity for Understanding and Investigating Adherence to Exercise and Physical Activity.
Who: McGannon, K.R., University of Alberta.
Mc Gannon developed an alternative theory of self and identity grounded in a view of language that prioritizes the process and outcome of language and how it is tied to discursive, cultural, social, and institutional practices. Feminist post-structuralism 'ethnomethodology', and narrative psychology were combined to theorize women's self and identity (i.e. who they are) and implicitly, exercise behavior as a collection of conversations they have with themselves and others or more specifically as narratives/stories spoken from subject positions within larger discourse(s).

POSSIBLE APPLICATIONS OF ETHNOMETHODOLOGY TO SPORT MANAGEMENT RESEARCH

Conversational practices are instrumental to human sociality, and enable the construction of social reality. This construction extends to institutions whereby restrictive codes of conduct, which establish the context and content, serve to distinguish it from everyday talk. In the context of sport communication and public relations the sports interview is one such institution, which involves the construction of turn taking through sequence design, lexical choice, and asymmetry. Additionally, the sports interview requires firstly, the management of success in order to maintain the loser's "face" and secondly, the use of text to sustain the opposition's sporting abilities. Heritage (1997) provides "tools" to analyze sport interviews such as: "sequence organization, turn design, lexical choice, and asymmetry which may provide an insight into the institutional practices of the sports interview" (p. 164).

Another area of investigation could involve the role of women in sport management. Little research has been conducted on the impact of psychosocial development (how women grow, develop and are socialized) and its influence on their career choices, specifically their decision to be involved in sport management. This type of research could explore the psychosocial developmental experiences and critical factors leading women to choose sport management as a career option. This effort is significant for the following reasons:

1. Discovering and understanding the factors that lead women to study sport management.

2. Increasing the overall number of women sport managers.

3. Hearing the stories of how other women made their choices to become sport managers, will provide affirmation to those in the profession and motivation to others to make this career choice.

Ethnomethodology may also draw Bourdieu's (1973) conceptions of "habitus, cultural and symbolic capital". Bottomley (1991) claims that, within one's everyday world, power relations are both structured and symbolically formed, giving meaning to everyday practice. From this perspective the sport manager engages in action that supports power within the sport organization but at the same time may resist oppression. The dialectics of oppression and resistance become obvious in the taken-for-granted terrain of practice. The power relationship in sport organizations can be analyzed using the ethnomethodological tools of CA and MCD.

Ethnomethodology can also treat social interactions such as sporting team training sessions primarily as organized interactional events. The goal of ethnomethodology is to explore how people coordinate their everyday courses of action in and through the routines of their talk, without pre-empting what the structure of those routines might look like. Ethnomethodology can be useful in exploring the cultural practices we see in sporting clubs and sporting teams and examining how they are embedded in and built by the everyday discourses and conversations that occur between members.

Ethnomethodologists understand this shared common-sense and experienced world to be constituted by orderly social practices evidenced in texts and talk. The task of ethnomethodologists is to investigate the recurrent practices found within members' interactions that constitute their shared common-sense worlds, and make them orderly.

In ethnomethodological studies, people's *reports* of what they did or did not do and say in a particular situation cannot be substituted for *what* they did or did not do. Similarly, interviews of interactants about a particular incident cannot stand in the place of observations, recordings and transcriptions of the incident. This is not to say reports and interviews are not potentially interesting data *per se*. For example, in the case of interviews of sport managers about their management practices, the interviews would count as data in the question of what sport managers say in interviews about what they do, but they would not count as data that answers the question of what those sport managers actually do when "managing" the sport organization.

Jones (1989) locates the meaning of critical ethnomethodology in the ways in which power relationships are mediated through social structures and how and why these relationships become lived out in everyday practices and understandings. As we will see in the following case example ethnomethodological resources can be used to analyze closely the activities of members in meetings, to show how they do the work of policy making and therefore to clarify the questions that can be asked about the doing of this policy making work.

Ethnomethodology Case Study

Who: Dr Allan Edwards (University of the West of England) and Dr Keith Gilbert (University of the West of England)

What: Beyond the Divide: Relations between Sport Managers and Academics in a Collaborative Research Partnership.

Theoretical framework

The notion of "partnership" dominates contemporary sport organization improvement and reform agendas. Edwards and Gilbert utilized on ethnomethodological resources to develop understandings about how the participants accomplish partnership work through their talk-in-interaction. Most discourse about partnerships between sport organizations and universities historically relates to the apparent divide between practice and theory, between practitioner and academy. Edwards and Gilbert investigated the meeting talk between groups of sports managers and academics as they plan and report on a collaborative project aimed at improving practices in the sport organization.

Whereas most research investigating sport organization and university partnerships addresses the outcomes of such partnerships, or attempts to describe and advocate for ideal partnerships, Edwards and Gilbert considered the actual interactional work of the participants as they engage in the everyday and ongoing activities of partnership. It showed how partnerships are constructed through talk and activity. Instead of considering the partnership as a predetermined and pre-existing phenomenon, this study adopted the view that the work of partnership is an ongoing accomplishment through the activity of the participants. In this way, Edwards and Gilbert showed the local social order of a partnership as it was built, maintained and transformed through the interactional work of the participants. Both the institutional setting and the participants' enactment of partnership work contributed to the establishment of the social and moral order of the partnership.

Data collection methods

The data collection drew on ethnomethodological resources of conversation analysis and membership category analysis, and applied them to demonstrate the interactional resources used by the participants as they accomplished, through collaborative talk-in-interaction, the work of the partnership, and thus the partnership itself. Focus group discussions were conducted and were recorded for later analysis. This study contributed to understandings and issues relating to practitioner or insider research.

Data analysis techniques/presentation

The specific focus was the talk of partnership that occurred in meetings between members of sport organizations and of the university. These meetings were audio-recorded, transcribed, and analyzed using the techniques and procedures of conversation analysis and membership category analysis. These methodological resources revealed the social and moral orders at work.

Edwards and Gilbert indicate that the ethnomethodological resources, particularly conversation analysis and membership category analysis, could be used to analyze in close detail the social interactions of participants in the institutional talk of meetings. In showing how the social and moral orders of partnerships are revealed and by offering understandings of the pragmatics of sport organization and university partnership, the social structure of sport organization and university partnerships was explicated.

Major findings

In summary, Edwards' and Gilbert's research identified four partnership themes:

1. *Levels of expertise*: the construction of expertise as an accomplished and demonstrated feature of the talk-in-interaction of partnerships;

2. *Interactional management of partnership*: the partnership itself as a social activity accomplished through the interactional activities of the participants;

3. *Leadership*: the management of leadership through the interactional activity of the participants in the partnership;

4. *Talk as an agent of understanding*: the activity of talk-in-interaction, accomplished through the social and moral work of the participants as they assemble their activities of partnership through the agency of talk, specifically through the institutional talk of meetings.

Edwards and Gilbert claim the study offered analytic tools for uncovering the interactional resource of the participants through one example of what a sport organization and university partnership can be like. Epistemologically, Edwards and Gilbert explored and exposed sport organization and university partnerships. It showed how the work of partnership "can" be accomplished by participants, rather than attempt to claim how it "should" be done.

Suggestions for future research

Edwards and Gilbert proposed that by undertaking this kind of work, sport managers can move beyond the practice/theory divide and build a profession based on investigation, evidence and shared understandings. Such work, they argued, opens the door to exploring and undertaking new ways of investigation as well as privileging participants' own accounts of how they do their everyday business as social actors.

They suggest sport managers can be involved in innovative practitioner based partnership research across a range of sport management organizations such as community sport councils, government agencies and National governing bodies. Finally, they propose that sport management scholars should engage with the ethnomethodological research process to improve their reflective understanding of the sport management working environment.

Case study research probes

1. How does ethnomethodology provide a research lens to develop understandings how participants can accomplish the partnership work through their talk-in-interaction?

2. In the context of this research what has ethnomethodology offered that other research approaches could not provide?

3. What are the potential problems you might confront using ethnomethodology in the context of this research?

CONCLUSION

This chapter has introduced the research method of ethnomethodology. The method aims to study, understand and articulate how people make sense of themselves and each other in everyday life. Simply stated ethnomethodology is a form of discourse analysis. Ethnomethodology is offered as a contribution to an emerging body of scholarship that is directed at promoting a more rigorous and theoretically informed understanding of the conduct and reporting of ethnographic fieldwork. It clearly has unexplored potential in the field of sport management research.

IN PROFILE - Professor Paul De Knop

Paul De Knop has a Ph.D. in Physical Education at the Faculty of Physical Education of Vrije Universiteit Brussels (VUB), Belgium. He graduated in leisure studies at the same university and earned a Masters Degree in Sports Sociology and Sports Management from the University of Leicester (UK). He is a full time professor at the VUB and dean of the faculty of Physical Education. In October 2008 he was elected as the rector magnificus of the VUB. He was chairman of the board of BLOSO (Flemish sports administrative body) (from 1999 until 2006), chairman of the RAGO (Council of the Community Education of Flanders) since 2002, and deputy chief of cabinet to the Flemish minister of Sport since 2004. Furthermore, he is co-ordinator of a "Top Level Sport and Studies" program at the Vrije Universiteit Brussel and project manager of two sport centers. His teaching includes areas of sport, leisure and physical education from a socio-pedagogical perspective. Research interests are: youth and sport, sport and ethnic minorities, sport and tourism, sport management, quality in sport and sport policy. He has used qualitative research in studies related to: (1) ethics and qualitative aspects of youth sport; (2) sport for underprivileged youth; (3) sport for Islamic minority girls; (4) motives of sport tourists; (4) benchmark of top level sport success; (5) top level sport students at university; (6) competencies of sport managers; (7) sport policy and strategic planning; and (8) evaluation of physical education programs. Professor De Knop strongly endorses the use of qualitative research in sport management as qualitative data can provide a deep insight into the research issue under investigation.

REVIEW AND RESEARCH QUESTIONS

1. When deciding whether to use ethnomethodology as a research approach what should the sport management researcher consider?

2. How can ethnomethodology be applied by sport management researchers in their everyday work?

REFERENCES

Benson, D. & Hughes, J. 1991. Method: evidence and inference – evidence and inference for ethnomethodology. In: *Ethnomethodology and the Human Sciences* (Ed. by G. Button), pp. 109–136. New York: Cambridge University Press.

Bottomley, G. 1991. Representing the "second generation": subjects, objects and ways of knowing in intersections. Gender/Class? Culture? Ethnicity Edward Elgar Publishing.

Bourdieu, P. 1973. Cultural reproduction and social reproduction. In: *Knowledge, Education and Cultural Change* (Ed. by R. Brown), pp. 71–112. London: Tavistock.

Coulon, A. 1995. Ethnomethodology. Thousand Oaks, CA: Sage.

Cuff, E. C. & Payne, G. C. F. 1984. Perspectives in Sociology, 2nd ed. London, UK: Allen & Unwin.

Cuff, E. C., Sharrock, W. W. & Francis, D. W. 1990. Perspectives in Sociology, 3rd ed. London: Unwin Hyman.

Drew, P. & Heritage, J. 1992. Analyzing talk at work: an introduction. In: *Talk at Work* (Ed. by P. Drew, J. Heritage), pp. 3–65. Cambridge: Cambridge University Press.

Dwyer, B. (1997). *The Local Accomplishment of Institutional Membership: Interactive Variations in the Enactment of Childhood for School.* Unpublished doctoral dissertation, Griffith University, Brisbane, Australia.

Garfinkel, H. 1967/1999. Studies in Ethnomethodology. Englewood Cliffs, NJ: Prentice-Hall.

Garfinkel, H. & Sacks, H. 1986. On formal structures of practical actions. In: *Ethnomethodological Studies of Work* (Ed. by H. Garfinkel), pp. 160–193. London: Routledge.

Goode, D. 1994. A World Without Words. Philadelphia: Temple University Press.

Gubrium, J. & Holstein, J. 2000. Analyzing interpretive practice. In: *Handbook of Qualitative Research* (Ed. by N. K. Denzin, Y. S. Lincoln), pp. 487–508, 2nd ed. Thousand Oaks, CA: Sage.

Heritage, J. 1984. Garfinkel and Ethnomethodology. Cambridge, MA: Polity Press.

Heritage, J. 1997. Conversation analysis and institutional talk: analyzing data. In: *Qualitative Analysis: Issues of Theory and Method* (Ed. by D. Silverman), pp. 161–181. London: Sage.

Hester, S. & Eglin, P. (Eds.). 1997. Culture in Action: Studies in Membership Categorization Analysis Washington DC: International Institute for Ethnomethodology and Conversation Analysis and University Press of America.

Hilbert, R. A. 1992. The Classical Roots of Ethnomethodology: Durkheim, Weber, and. Garfinkel. Chapel Hill: University of North Carolina Press.

Jones, F. M. 1989. The organization of tea leaf readings and the reader–client relationship. In: *The Interactional Order: New Directions in the Study of Social Order* (Ed. by D. T. Helm, W. T. Anderson, A. J. Meehan, A. W. Rawls), pp. 186–209. New York, NY: Irvington Publishers.

Lee, J. R. E. 1991. Language and culture: the linguistic analysis of culture. In: *Ethnomethodology and the Human Sciences* (Ed. by G. Button), pp. 196–226. Cambridge: Cambridge University Press.

Psathas, G. 1995. Conversation Analysis: The Study of Talk-in-Interaction. Thousand Oaks, CA: Sage.

Sacks, H. 1974. On the analyzability of stories by children. In: *Ethnomethodology: Selected Readings* (Ed. by R. Turner). Harmondsworth: Penguin.

Schegloff, E. 1991. Reflections on talk and social structure. In: *Talk and Social Structure: Studies in Ethnomethodology and Conversation Analysis* (Ed. by D. Boden, D. H. Zimmerman), pp. 44–70. Berkeley: University of California Press.

Schutz, A. 1962. The Problem of Social Reality. The Hague, Netherlands: Martin Nijhoff.

Shotter, J. 1993. Conversational Realities: Constructing Life through Language. London: Sage.

Silverman, D. 1993. The machinery of interaction: Sacks' lectures on conversation. *Sociological Review*, **41** (4), 731–752.

Speier, M. 1971. Some conversational problems for interactional analysis. In: *Studies in Interaction* (Ed. by D. Sudnow). New York: Free Press.

Tierney, W. G. 2000. Undaunted courage: life history and the postmodern challenge. In: *Handbook of Qualitative Research* (Ed. by N. K. Denzin, Y. S. Lincoln), pp. 537–553, 2nd ed. Thousand Oaks, CA: Sage.

CHAPTER 16

Gender Theories and Sport Management Research

KEY TERMS

Feminism: theories and philosophies concerned with issues of gender difference and which advocate for women's rights and interests.

Feminist theory: Feminist theory extends feminism into theoretical and philosophical grounds. It aims to understand the nature of inequality and focuses on gender politics, power relations and sexuality. While generally providing a critique of social relations, much of feminist theory also focuses on analyzing gender inequality and the promotion of women's rights, interests, and issues.

Standpoint theory: A standpoint is a position from which a human being views the world, and influences how they construct their position in the world. Standpoint theory recognizes how the views of marginalized individuals within a mainstream society can present a more balanced and objective account of the world.

Queer theory: calls into question "essential" sexed, gendered, and sexual identities, striving to destabilize discursive constructions of sexuality that come to be accepted as "natural" and that maintain a dominant/subordinate power relationship.

KEY QUESTIONS

- Is there a distinctive Feminist Methodology?

- What are three types of "difference" in feminist theory?

- What is Queer Theory?

CHAPTER OVERVIEW

This chapter explores gender research methodologies, in particular feminist and queer theories. The first section outlines how Feminist research methodologies emerged from the political activism of the women's movement of the 1960s and 1970s, with the aim of securing equality and ending discrimination against women. It suggests that whilst some researchers would argue against the existence of a distinct feminist methodology, the philosophical and theoretical tenets of feminist theory strongly influence and inform research practices that can be defined as distinctly "feminist". It argues that while feminist methodologies are still in an evolving and emerging state, the developing recognition of the importance of difference and the need to empower and give voice to research participants offers the sport management researcher scope to investigate issues specifically related to gender, and the impact these issues may have on the sport management environment. The second section of this chapter discusses Queer theory and calls into question "essential" sexed, gendered, and sexual identities, striving to destabilize discursive constructions of sexuality that come to be accepted as "natural" and that maintain a dominant/subordinate power relationship. We discuss how queer theory has the potential to be inclusive of race, gender, sexuality, and other areas of identity by calling attention to the distinctions between identities, communities, and cultures, rather than ignoring these differences or pretending that they don't exist

FEMINIST THEORY AND SPORT MANAGEMENT RESEARCH

Origins of feminist theory

Feminist theory has its origins in the political activism of the 1960s and 1970s, generally referred to as the second wave of feminism, the first wave being centered mainly in the suffrage movement of the late nineteenth and early twentieth centuries. The second wave of feminism, put simply, sought equality and an end to discrimination. Although the activism of the 1970s has been somewhat tempered, feminism, as an academic focus, has thrived throughout the 1980s and 1990s, and into the twenty first century, co-existing alongside what has been called the third wave of feminism, which arose as a result of perceived failures of the second wave. This third wave of feminism, with its origins in the 1980s, seeks to challenge existentialist definitions of femininity and accepted views of what is or is not good for women. Also recognizing the importance of voices other than white middle-class women, the third wave of feminism has introduced into feminist research theory the important concepts of difference, and difference amongst women, specifically in relation to race, class and culture.

The concept of difference as being essential to Feminist research since the 1980s has been articulated by Evans (1995). Evans describes three differences: equality, difference, and difference within or among women. Equality looks at differences in such things as division of labor (and wages for labor), resources, political voice, and to some extent the sexualization of women's bodies. Difference looks at the stereotyped ideas of masculinity and femininity, and difference among women looks to a different understanding of women's place in the world with a recognition of the importance of the voices of women of color, disabled women, lesbians and women from different cultures including the third world.

Is there a feminist methodology?

It is difficult to define a single feminist epistemology or methodological approach because there are many branches of feminism, and both discourse and practices surrounding feminist research methodologies and epistemologies are complex and contested. Van Zoonen (1994) notes "the issue of what exactly constitutes feminist research has been a subject of debate since the late 1970s" (p. 127). Indeed there has been little agreement among feminist scholars as to what feminist methodology is, or whether there is an explicit set of feminist research tools distinct from those employed by other researchers.

Reinharz (1992) notes in her introduction to *Feminist Methods in Social Research*, "feminists have used all existing methods and have invented some new ones as well. Instead of orthodoxy, feminist research practices must be recognized as a plurality. Rather than there being a "woman's way of knowing," or a "feminist way of doing research," there are women's *ways* of knowing" (p. 4). Feminist researchers and theorists have found it a challenge to define "feminist research" in part because of this plurality. While attempts to define feminist methodology have been debated, one consistent concern is the connection between the researcher and the research. Feminist research contends there exists a reciprocity that must be acknowledged and articulated.

Research Brief

Title: Embodied Coherence, De(con)structive Selves: Personal Narratives, Self Stories, and Taekwondo
Who: Johnson, C.R., University of Iowa
Johnson utilized a feminist poststructuralist positioning to explore the creation of narratives, or 'self-stories', of Taekwondo practitioners. Johnson's purposes were twofold: first, to examine the self-stories of people who practice Taekwondo, which, she suggests, is a sport that offers a particularly unique set of narratives to draw from in constructing a 'self'; second, to examine the methodological and epistemological usefulness of using a feminist poststructuralist perspective within a field that has been slow to move past postpositivist frameworks.

METHODOLOGY

Some researchers believe that Feminism is not a research method per se but rather a philosophical stance which can be used to underpin the research. Acker et al. (1991) propose three principles which underlie feminist research. They are (a) knowledge produced by the research should be useful for the participants, (b) the research method should not be oppressive, and (c) the research method should be reflexive allowing for reflection on both the intellectual traditions and the progress of the study.

Hammersley (1992) agrees that there is no distinct feminist methodology but identifies themes that mark a definition. These themes include the following:

1. the significance of gender;

2. the rejection of hierarchical relationships in research that can occur between the researcher and research participants; and

3. the research has an aim of emancipation (p. 187).

Nielsen (1990) details five epistemological and methodological commitments of feminist research, which are as follows:

1. For research to be considered feminist it must not only focus on gender but it must also make women's experiences central to the research and seek to understand the way in which women make sense of concepts relevant to the research.

2. "Women's ways of knowing" is a twofold process: In the first instance, the research must value women's ways of knowing by encouraging women to describe their own experiences and must respect their truths. But secondly, researchers must address their own experiences and knowledge and as van Zoonen (1994) terms it, "radically politicize the research process" (p. 130) by reflexively interrogating their own role, standpoint epistemologies, research praxis and position of power.

3. A focus on "feminist synalytics" which she describes as a blend of analysis and synthesis to facilitate new understanding that supersedes "the usual male-defined definitions".

4. "Revolutionary pragmatism" – a call for research that is of practical value and which is the basis for a call for change.

5. "Methodological integrity" – the necessity to utilize diverse methods and perspectives.

Numerous theorists such as Reinharz, for example, describe feminist research as multi-methodological. Reinharz (1992) goes on to identify further themes in feminist methodology which include the following:

1. using a multiplicity of research methods;

2. the research should be informed by feminist theory;

3. the research is transdisciplinary;

4. the research has the aim of influencing change; and

5. the research aims to represent diverse views of the women interviewed (p. 240).

The purpose of feminist research is to create a social system that represents equality, as well as question the status quo, challenge existing social systems, challenge old and create new personal choices related to health/life choices, and shift the balance of power (Wuest, 1994). Enang (1999) asserts that feminist methodology provides the flexibility that is required to comprehend women's views and their experiences. According to Wuest (1994), "A major goal of feminist research is seeing the world through the eyes of "the other" for the purpose of emancipation" (p. 578). Streubert-Speziale and Carpenter (2003) add that feminist researchers strive to see the world from the women being studied and attempt to be analytical in examining the issues and advocate for improving the lives of those being studied. Using feminist theory moves the concept of emancipation closer and specifically addresses women's lives. Standpoint theory has evolved from this discussion.

STANDPOINT THEORY

Feminist standpoint theory assumes that there is no single objective truth and that class, race, gender, and sexual orientation structure a person's understanding of reality. To survive, less powerful groups must be attuned to the culture of the dominant group. In fact, these individuals have the potential for a more complete and less distorted view of social reality precisely because of their disadvantaged position (Nielsen, 1990). By living out their lives in both the dominant culture and in their own culture, members of stigmatized groups can develop a type of double vision, and hence a more comprehensive understanding of social reality (Hartsock,

1987, 1998; Westkott, 1990). This standpoint, however, must be developed by appropriating one's experiences through intellectual and political struggles against gender, race, class, and sexual orientation inequalities (Allen & Baber, 1992; Harding, 1987; Hartsock, 1987, 1998). The location of oppressed groups vis-a-vis their oppressors creates the potential for critical social analysis, but such a standpoint only emerges through consciousness raising experiences, such as those utilized by the feminist movement of the 1960s and 1970s. Practically, feminist standpoint research utilizes a variety of methodologies (e.g., both qualitative and quantitative approaches) to engage research participants (typically members of oppressed groups) in reflection on how their gender, race, social class, and sexual orientation shape their experiences in the social world. In addition, feminist standpoint researchers must reflect upon (and share with their readers) how their own social group status influences their interpretations of their data, which leads us to a discussion of the importance of the researcher in feminist research.

THE ROLE OF THE FEMINIST RESEARCHER

Most researchers recognize that they bring a unique history, connection, value, and interpretation to the research they are conducting, and this then becomes an important and vital part of the research process. Gergen (1988) agrees, saying that "feminist meta-theory and methodology would thus incorporate the tenet that the investigator and the subject are interdependent" (p. 90). Harding (1987) also discusses the importance of positioning by the researcher. The researcher is located in the "same critical plane" as the subject. Class, race, culture, gender, beliefs, and assumptions of the researcher provide important and real information. The articulation of the researcher's unique relationship to the research not only identifies the limitations of the research, but will also strengthen the quality of the findings.

FEMINIST APPROACHES TO RESEARCH

Just as there is debate as to the existence of a distinct and definable feminist research methodology, it is also impossible to define a specific method of set of techniques which are uniquely feminist (Riger, 1992). Feminist researchers draw on a range of qualitative research methods depending on what will best suit the research subject or topic.

Reinharz (1992) notes that some "feminist methods" do appear new and unique (e.g., consciousness raising as a method of inquiry, group diaries, multiple person stream-of-consciousness narratives, associative writing), but only because their application is new to recognized academic endeavors, which have traditionally relied on experimental and survey designs. These "new" methods typically bring women together and collect data within those groups. It is perhaps more accurate therefore, to speak of "feminist approaches to research" or "feminist methodologies" as opposed to "feminist methods".

The interview method has remained central to feminist inquiry but has also been the subject of debate (Oakley, 1981; Ribbens, 1989; Cotterill, 1992; Webb, 1993). Empowering methods such as *reflexivity*, *critique* and *dialog* are used to promote the participant's increased awareness of power imbalances inherent in the area of interest. Value is placed on *mutuality* in which, as Hall and Stevens (1991) describe, participants are assumed to be truth-tellers. Researcher–participant relationships, in research other than feminist, are more commonly noted for their power inequalities and these are seen as creating situations in which women are unlikely to feel comfortable when talking about what is really important to them. *Mutuality* should be designed to foster a sense of jointly working toward some understanding of and potential change to the area under study (Hall & Stevens, 1991).

RELIABILITY AND VALIDITY WITHIN FEMINIST ANALYSIS

Reliability is often considered to mean repeatability – the ability to yield the same results from a repeated trial in a different setting. As this denies the unique nature of the human experience and its contextual relatedness, neither *repeatability* nor validity are seen as appropriate to feminist research, as the purpose is not to acquire information that will automatically have relevance to other settings.

Rigor

Hall and Stevens (1991) describe a series of criteria by which feminist researchers can plan rigorous studies and evaluate their own efforts. Their criteria are reflexivity, credibility, rapport, coherence, complexity, consensus and relevance.

Because a feminist researcher makes no effort to remain detached or aloof from the discussion and actively dialogs with the participant, a degree of rapport is established. A sense of trust, sensitivity and shared purpose developed, which Hall and Stevens (1991) following Oakley (1981) would suggest gives confidence that the research adequately reflects what is significant to the women in the study.

If at the conclusion of the research participants are able to read the report and recognize the faithful representation and interpretation of their particular reality, then it is a valid representation of the data they provided.

Feminist ethical concerns

Feminists have been critical of the traditional scientific approaches for treating the researched in ways which could be described as unsafe, unjust and oppressive. There is a long history of manipulation, exploitation and deception of the subjects of research.

For feminist researchers there are complex ethical issues, including the risk of exploitation, the need for empowerment of the participants and the experience had by participants in the course of contributing to research. Issues of authorship, collegial relationship and the presentation of findings present ethical challenges which are not similarly viewed by non-feminist researchers. For knowledge to emerge which is not oppressive, it should be developed through dialog rather than one-sided questioning. Thompson (1992) summarizes ethical concerns in feminist research into two areas. She believes we should first ask if the research is either exploitative or empowering of participants and others, and then ask how oppressive objectification of participants can be avoided given that any method has the potential to be oppressive. Meeting these ethical concerns is not simple or straightforward, and feminist researchers have sometimes reported the challenges of carrying out completely ethical research on feminist terms (Maguire, 1987).

FEMINIST THEORY AND SPORT MANAGEMENT

Feminist research has bridged a diversity of methods, content areas and epistemologies. Considerable impact has been made on both women's lives and the wider society by the knowledge and critique generated by such research. An important shift has occurred in that the research has moved from being *about* women to being *for* women, but there is no certainty yet as to how effective the research is *for* women. This is pertinent when considering the utilization of feminist research within the sport management research community. This is both an academic community and very much an applied and practical discipline and, as such, the debate is important but the outcomes and applicability of the research for practice are paramount.

Because of the essentially applied nature of the discipline of sport management, issues of equality, difference and postmodernist challenges to feminist research have not been overwhelmingly present in the small amount of feminist research in the sport management literature. Sport management feminist researchers such as Frisby (2005) have long recognized the need for the ongoing development of a strong research culture.

Sport management as a practice discipline focuses on working alongside individuals in a wide range of contexts and situations. These situations can include local club settings through to major international events. The range of people that sport managers work with is also extremely diverse, from able-bodied athletes to disabled athletes, able-bodied spectators to disabled spectators, and in a range of locations and settings each with their own specific requirements, difficulties and expectations. Sport managers also need to be able to deal with crisis situations resulting from sudden accidents or injuries, or other issues arising from health and illness. For knowledge to have value to sport management, it must offer explanation or illumination of the human experience in ways which allow growing reflection on the quality and applicability of sport management practice.

Feminist research has traditionally been informed by a political vision of change and ultimately of equity, and most recently by the recognition of differences in women and the need to recognize those different voices. Historically, women have often been omitted from research, the assumption often being that a male perspective would be inclusive of women (Boulding, 1992; Miles, 1989). Just as often women's lives and experience have been distorted and misconstrued within much of positivist research (Fonow & Cook, 1991). Feminist research has much to offer the sport manager.

Feminist approaches to research also enable the sport management research to be located within "situated knowledge" (Haraway, 1988), specifically that of a feminist embodied knowledge as opposed to the (unattainable) disembodied, "objective" positioning favored in traditional orthodoxies. It removes the necessity to adhere to the highly structured methods of data collection attendant upon the pursuit of objective and neutral research which in turn has allowed a greater range and degree of freedom in methods of data collection. This has enabled a broader set of knowledges surrounding the research topic to be included and ultimately provided a fuller understanding of the subject being researched.

Feminist research also encourages "the interpretive understanding of human experience" (Denzin & Lincoln, 2000) and is "a situated activity that locates the observer in the world ... qualitative researchers study things in their natural settings, attempting to make sense of, or to interpret, phenomena in terms of the meanings people bring to them" (p. 3). This type of research is well suited to the field of sport management.

Qualitative research also endorses the utilization and collection of a variety of empirical materials – case study; personal experience; introspection; life story; interviews; artefacts; cultural texts and productions; observational, historical, interactional, and visual texts (Denzin & Lincoln, 2000) as recommended by feminist researchers. Each of these can be used to provide different perspectives on the research topic and when several are used in conjunction, can facilitate a deeper overall understanding.

Within a feminist research framework which emphasizes pluralism, diversity and difference and exhorts sport management researchers not to homogenize their research findings but rather to retain even contested meanings between participants as important (Angrosina & Mays de Perez, 2000) the challenge for sport management researchers is how to claim legitimacy for their findings. While it is not possible for sport management researchers to divorce themselves totally from their own standpoint epistemologies and that different sport management researchers with different life histories and perspectives can produce differing accounts, that is not to say that all possible accounts are "equally useful, credible or legitimate" nor is it necessary to "descend into a relativism" in which all accounts are valid or "anything goes" (Smith & Deemer, 2000). Hammersley theorizes that the two key elements of validity are plausibility and credibility. In the case of plausibility, some claims will be self-evidently plausible while others will need to supported with evidence. With regard to credibility, he argues that this should be judged by examining relevant factors such as "the nature of the phenomena concerned, the circumstances of the research.

Recent sport management related feminist research studies have covered a diversity of topics. Brown (2007) utilized socio-legal, legal geographic, and feminist sports theory to examine increased participation of women in elite sport in a patchwork case study on four nations: Canada, the United States of America, the Islamic Republic of Iran, and Australia. Scrogum (2005) explored the experiences of 14 women who play rugby. Women took part in three focus groups to discuss their experiences in rugby and the meanings they attributed to them. Although not explicitly utilizing feminist theory Farrell (2006) investigated female consumption of women's basketball through the voices and perspectives of female spectators of men's basketball.

From a theoretical perspective, two studies provide a valuable starting point for research from a feminist perspective. Firstly, *Sport and Traditions of Feminist Theory* (Burke, 2001) involves a philosophical examination of the opportunities that are offered to females who seek authority in sporting participation, by an examination of the ideas that emanate from various streams of feminist thought. Secondly, in *Getting girls in the game: A qualitative analysis of urban sport programs* (Cooky, 2006) discusses three of the four major theoretical approaches to the study of sex/gender: feminist interaction theory, feminist structural theories of the gender order and feminist theories of the cultural/symbolic order, including the foundations and concepts of the approach and how the theories can help elucidate understandings of girls and women in sports.

QUEER THEORY

What is queer theory?

Although difficult to define as it is ever evolving, queer calls into question "essential" sexed, gendered, and sexual identities, striving to destabilize discursive constructions of sexuality that come to be accepted as "natural" and that maintain a dominant/subordinate power relationship (Halperin, 1995; Jagose, 1996). Queer theory claims diversity through its inclusiveness of any subject who somehow deviates from normative definitions of (sexual) desire (Giffney, 2004) and who may choose to claim "queer" as an identity label. In academia, when applying a queer lens, Green (2002) has suggested that one works to reveal "queer cracks in the heteronormative façade (i.e., "queering"), and "decentering" those regimes of "normality" that bear on the sexual and gender status quo" (p. 522).

Queer theory is a contested term that is sometimes used as a catchall for marginalized sexual groups, or as a radical new theory that has emerged out of *lesbian and gay studies*. Queer theory has been critiqued by some as not being inclusive of other forms of difference, for example, race or gender. Gamson (2000) argues that "queer studies is largely a *deconstructive* enterprise, taking apart the view of a self-defined by something at its core, be it sexual desire, race, gender, nation, or class" (p. 348). He goes on to say, "Queer marks an identity that, defined as it is by a deviation from sex and gender norms either by the self inside or by specific behaviours, is always in flux" (p. 349).

The distinction between queer identity and queer theory is important. We understand queer as a way of reading an action, behavior, or characteristic, so that queer can remain a fluid, dynamic term. Beemyn and Eliason (1996) write that queer theory must "be flexible enough to accommodate all people who identify as queer" (p. 3). Beemyn and Eliason go on to argue that, "queer theory has the *potential* to be inclusive of race, gender, sexuality, and other areas of identity by calling attention to the distinctions between identities, communities, and cultures, rather than ignoring these differences or pretending that they don't exist" (p. 165). Krane (2001) argues that queer theory has moved beyond lesbian and gay studies because, "queer theory seeks to avoid privileging one component of identity over another" (p. 404). This may also be the opinion of Tierney (1997) who sees queer theory as seeking "to interrogate terms such as gender and race so that the norms of our lives are reconfigured" (p. 37).

Queer theory calls into question understandings of identity categories and operations of power; it seeks to destabilize accepted gender and identity constructs through individual acts of resistance/subversion. Queer theory also claims diversity through its intended inclusion of gay, lesbian, bisexual, transgendered and transsexual persons, and really any subject (even heterosexual) that somehow deviates from normative definitions of (sexual) desire; it purports to be inclusive of any one who feels marginalized from the norm – be it a result of sexuality, intellect, culture, etc. (Giffney, 2004).

Development of queer theory

It is useful at this point to explore the evolution of "queer" in order to place it historically. It has been written that queer theory evolved specifically as an academic discourse in reaction to gay/lesbian studies that were thought to be too liberal and too accepting of falsely constructed norms of sexuality (Duggan, 1992; Jagose, 1996). Critics of gay/lesbian studies suggest that within the gay/lesbian movement, there was racial, class, ability, and gender privilege (i.e., it was all about white, middle-class males). In that regard, queer theory seeks to avoid such hierarchy, theorizing that sexual acts/desire should not equal sexual identity, and even further, that sexual identity is a false construct created to categorize deviant behavior and to promote a dominant sexuality. Individuals come to recognize themselves as subjects within, or opposed to, dominant discursive constructions.

To this point in time we have sought to present what queer theory is, and at the same time what it is not (in relation to gay/lesbian studies), queer theory is not without its critics. While some writers argue that queer theory is actually too inclusive because it renders difference invisible, others argue that it is not inclusive enough. Walters (1996) critiques "queer theory" because she feels that it "erases lesbian specificity and the enormous difference that gender makes, evacuates the importance of feminism, and rewrites the history of lesbian feminism and feminism generally" (p. 843). Goldman (1996) argues, "existing queer theory, despite attempts to avoid normativity, harbors a normative discourse around race, sexuality, and class" (p. 179). These critiques suggest that queer theory in practice has not lived up to the potential. Goldman (1996) proposes an alternate direction for queer theory saying, "if queer theory is to truly challenge the "normal," it must provide a framework in which to challenge racist, misogynist, and other oppressive discourse/norms, as well as those that are heterosexist and homophobic" (p. 174).

Critics of queer theory suggest that it fails to consider the reality of structural power (class, patriarchy, race/ethnicity, ability) and further that it has simply re/named and then re/constructed typical power relations despite its claims of diversity (Kirsch, 2000). This is a result of a queer theory that attempts to be too encompassing. In particular, lesbian feminist theorists postulate that by virtue of exclusion from specific articulation, lesbians become invisible as do queers of color, differently-abled queers, etc: "Queer's totalizing gesture is seen as having the potential to work against lesbian and gay specificity, and to devalue those analyses of homophobia and hetero-centrism" (Jagose, 1996, p. 112).

Butler (1991) maintains that she is "permanently troubled by identity categories" and finds them to be "invariable stumbling-blocks" (p. 14). The critique of identity pervades queer theory. Butler promotes identities as multiple, contradictory, fragmented, incoherent, disciplinary, unstable, fluid, "hardly the stuff that allows a researcher to confidently run out and study sexual subjects as if they are coherent and available social types" (Gamson, 2000, p. 256). As queer theory has increasingly taken social constructionist insights and added a poststructuralist critique of the unified, autonomous self, the lesbian and gay subject has become increasingly hard to recognize, not to mention research.

Sport and queer theory

Queer theory as a *theoretical framework* works and encourages the decon-struction of dominant ideology, the taken-for-granted state-of-being espoused by and through heteronormativity. We should not devalue the theoretical insights of queer because of potential political shortcomings. It remains useful to turn a queer lens on different social milieus in order to continue to deconstruct hegemonic notions of sexuality and the various meanings associated with such socially constructed categories of gay/lesbian/bisexual, etc. Critics suggest that this is not enough that queer theory is too theoretical and removed from reality. Suggestions have been made to work toward a blending of queer theory and gay/lesbian studies, at least in terms of recognizing structural influences such as socio-economic status (Duggan, 1992; Green, 2002; Kirsch, 2000; Messner, 1996), and by acknowledging the institutionalization of sexuality that shapes the lives of those whom we study.

Although not yet used in a sport management context queer theory as a research method has been applied in sport studies. Davidson and Shogan (1998) urge scholars to consider a queer theoretical perspective that would deconstruct sexuality and dominant ideologies within sport. More recently, Abdel-Shehid (2005) has explored the possibility of analyzing sport through a queer lens, and more specifically of deconstructing black masculinity, its link to heterosexuality and the sexualization of black athletes. Abdel-Shehid has proposed that deconstructing sport using "black queer theory" would engage questions of visibility and recognition and would provide an alternative reading of sport culture and black masculinity.

Research Brief

Title: Transgressing the Closets: Female Coaches Negotiations of Heteronormativity in Sport.

Who: Kauer, K.J., University of Tennessee

Kauer utilized queer and poststructuralist theories to investigate how lesbian, gay, bisexual, and transgendered coaches must negotiate their identities through a continuum of hegemonic or transgresssive discourses. As previous literature indicates, female coaches with non-hegemonic sexualities have been threatened, fired, harassed, and silenced within the context of sport. Male hegemony in sport perpetuates the production and management of heterosexism and heteronormativity in order to maintain a privileged status in sport. Queer and feminist poststructuralist theories posit that identity cannot be reduced to an essential core, and that subjectivity is fragmented, fluid, and contextual. Further, such frameworks elicit an interrogation of compulsory heterosexuality and the deconstruction of oppositional binary systems of gender and sexuality that are inherently hierarchical. Kauers' study is designed to explore the ways in which 'out' lesbian coaches transgress the heteronormative boundaries of sport. Further, this study explores the notion of political agency of 'out' lesbian coaches and how they effect social change.

Poststructuralist Feminist Case Study

Who: Larena Hoeber: The University of British Columbia

What: Putting Organizational Values into Practice: Gender Equity for Athletes in a Canadian University

Theoretical framework

The purpose of this study was to understand and critique the meanings and practices of gender equity for athletes from the perspectives of administrators, coaches, and athletes in a Canadian university. Hoeber utilized a post-structuralist feminist lens to emphasize the local meanings and the production of gendered knowledge to encourage a critique of the embeddedness of dominant discourses in organizational cultures, and provide strategies for uncovering alternative meanings and organizational practices. This was accomplished through case studies of four sport programs that varied in terms of structure and history in one athletic department.

Data collection methods

Hoeber utilized four data collection methods, field notes, document analysis, observations, and in-depth interviews. Data were collected from interviews with administrators, coaches, and athletes, observations of practices and competitions, and analysis of related documents and field notes. Hoeber recorded field notes in research journals throughout the data collection and analysis processes to chronicle information relevant to the study. Reflexivity is one strategy that qualitative researchers use to illuminate and confront their assumptions, emotions and reactions, realizing that they influence the interpretations of the researcher. Espoused values were identified in organizational documents, such as policy statements, mission statements, and internal and external communications, and compared with other sources of data to reveal consistencies, gaps, or contradictions. Observations of team practices and competitions helped Hoeber to appreciate the culture and institutional conditions of the sport programs and to witness firsthand if and how gender equity was manifested in organizational practices. Finally, in-depth interviews with administrators, coaches, and athletes associated with the four sport programs provided Hoeber with detailed insight into their understandings of the meanings and practices.

Data analysis techniques/presentation

Hoeber utilized ongoing and concurrent processes, including organizing, managing, reading, reviewing, memoing, reflecting, describing, coding, categorizing, making comparisons, and developing the final account. Initially, she analyzed the data by converting documents (i.e., mission statement, athletic department policy document), field notes, and interview transcripts to electronic documents and reviewing them. Analyzing data early on in the research process allowed her to build on and revise emergent patterns and themes as she continued to collect additional data and review the literature. After Hoeber had collected most of the data, she analyzed them through the formal processes of deconstruction, content analysis, coding, and categorizing.

The data in field notes were compared to data collected by other methods through the process of deconstruction that consisted of uncovering hidden meanings and silences and challenging dominant understandings. The documents (mission statement, policy documents, news releases, and operating budgets) were separately analyzed using content analysis and deconstruction. Observational notes were content analyzed and themes were developed as to the extent to which gender equity was observed in various cultural manifestations. Finally, interview transcripts were coded and categorized.

Major findings

The findings revealed multiple but narrow meanings of gender equity that were not fully implemented into organizational practices. Overall, respondents were complacent about changing the status quo and used a variety of arguments to justify the observed gaps between meanings and practices. While it was assumed that gender equity had been achieved because the total number of men's and women's teams was similar, a number of inequities in terms of funding, promotion, and treatment were observed. The findings challenged the assumptions that there are unitary and widely shared understandings of organizational values and that espoused organizational values are fully put into practice.

Suggestions for future research

Hoeber suggests that to move further with a gender equity agenda, discussions in sport organizations must be initiated to disrupt existing discourses and develop new ways of addressing and implementing this organizational value. She reveals several potential directions for future research. First, the experiences of administrators, coaches, and athletes with respect to the intersection between gender and other subjectivities and to examine implications for policies and practices is an important area of study. This can be accomplished by contextualizing the backgrounds of key stakeholders, including those who decline to participate in such studies. While she provided detailed information about the athletic department and the case study sports to situate the findings future research in this area should include more thorough descriptions about the respondents and their identities.

Second, her research is one example of more critical and reflective research in sport management as she encourages more sport management researchers to consider conducting their research from this perspective as it would heighten their sensitivity to the arbitrariness of dominant discourses. For example, more work needs to be undertaken to challenge the myth of revenue generating status that some men's teams maintain. With little evidence to support this claim, it remains a common and unquestioned justification of inequities in athletic departments.

Third, she recommends that future work examine the informal manifestations of the organizational culture such as informal practices (e.g., networking), norms (e.g., social interactions, humor), and artifacts and symbols (e.g., physical configurations, jargon) as these also contribute to the gendered structure of sport organizations. Additionally, the informal and formal rules of the game are manifested in these along with the formal work practices under examination in this study. As well, identifying that gender inequity is embedded in the informal aspects of organizational cultures, which makes it appear to be a normal and expected part of university athletics, would help to disrupt the apparent and preferred consensus and harmony that currently exists.

Fourth, studying the gendering of organizational practices, values, and cultures could be more adequately addressed by using more time intensive and culturally sensitive research designs, such as ethnography. Being immersed in a setting over a longer period of time would also provide the researcher with the opportunity to develop a more sensitive understanding of the historical and social contexts, observe and witness seemingly normal and mundane situations in the institutional conditions, and interview those who appear ambivalent to or openly resentful to the research topic.

A final recommendation was to conduct multiple interviews with each respondent and observe multiple practices over many years. This is seen by Hoeber as especially important given that changes to gender equity take time. Longitudinal research could critically examine this truth rule.

Case study research probes

1. Why do you think Hoeber has employed a poststructuralist feminist lens for this research?

2. What strategies would you employ to reduce potential bias that may occur due to the gender of the researcher?

CONCLUSION

Gender theories have much to offer the sport management researcher. The overarching goal of feminist research is to identify the ways in which multiple forms of oppression impact women's lives and empower women to tell their stories by providing a respectful and egalitarian research environment. To this end, multiple methodologies are used to obtain the best outcome, which has led to claims that there is no feminist research methodology as such. Feminist researchers would argue that it is the philosophical and theoretical underpinnings of feminism that define the methodology as distinctly feminist. Similarly, sport management researchers who apply "queer theory" as a research lens are provided with a method to question understandings of identity categories and operations of power. Gender researchers aim to strengthen connections between researchers and participants by giving voice to marginalized sections of society and conducting research in a nonhierarchical, caring research environment. Research conducted in this way has much to offer the sport manager, as issues of empowerment and the potential for change are an essential part of the research process. Research can be, and should be, a setting for consciousness raising and social change. Gender scholarship demonstrates to the sport management community how the process of research can be redefined as a setting for and agent of change.

IN PROFILE - Professor Cara Aitchison

Cara Aitchison has a background in the disciplines of geography and sociology, where qualitative research has become increasingly important since the 'cultural turn' in the early 1990s. Cara has taken these disciplinary perspectives and associated epistemologies and methods into her research in leisure, sport and tourism studies. For Cara, qualitative research is about literally 'giving voice' to research participants and her research has addressed ways in which leisure, sport and tourism can both exacerbate and ameliorate social exclusion related to the identities of class, gender, disability, 'race' and religion. Cara recently moved from a research Professorship in Human Geography into the management role of Dean of the Faculty of Education and Sport at the University of Bedfordshire. The university's mission to widen access and participation in education mirrors Cara's own research interests in social inclusion and, interestingly, some of her management practice now draws on her own learning from the implementation of qualitative research. Over the years Cara has undertaken a range of what Cara refers to as 'theoretically-informed applied

research' projects that have developed multi-method, multi-phased approaches to methodology. The most interesting projects have been those that gave voice to groups not used to 'speaking out' including Muslim women in sport and young disabled people in leisure who have participated in focus groups and kept diaries of their sport and leisure participation. Whilst much of her theoretical work has evolved from qualitative empirical research Cara's experience of undertaking applied research has demonstrated that policy-makers and practitioners are more readily persuaded by reports that combine qualitative and quantitative research. This, in turn, has helped Cara's to reflect on her own theoretical research and to contribute to the 'rematerialization' of social science; an approach that advocates giving equal consideration to structural/material/economic realities and cultural/symbolic/social realities. Building on this perspective, Cara's research has examined the ways in which the structural and the cultural interact to produce, legitimize, contest and, potentially, rework power relations within what Cara has termed 'the social-cultural nexus'.

REVIEW AND RESEARCH QUESTIONS

With a basic understanding of feminist and queer theories, attempt to answer the following questions:

- Do the advantages of Feminist theory for sport management research outweigh the possible disadvantages?

- How important is the gender of the researcher in Feminist research? What are some of the issues a sport management researcher should be aware of before undertaking a Feminist approach?

- Provide examples of how "queer theory" could be applied to sport management research.

REFERENCES

Abdel-Shehid, G. 2005. Who da man? Black Masculinities and Sporting Cultures. Toronto: Canadian Scholars.

Acker, J., Barry, K. & Esseveld, J. 1991. Objectivity and truth: problems in doing feminist Research. In: *Beyond Methodology: Feminist Scholarship as Lived Research* (Ed. by M. Fonow, J. Cook). Bloomington & Indianapolis: Indiana University Press.

Allen, K. R. & Baber, K. M. 1992. Ethical and epistemological tensions in applying a postmodern perspective to feminist research. *Psychology of Women Quarterly*, **16**, 1–15.

Angrosino, M. & Mays de Perez, K. 2000. Rethinking observation: from method to context. In: *Handbook of Qualitative Research* (Ed. by N. K. Denzin, Y. S. Lincoln), pp. 673–703, 2nd ed. Thousand Oaks, CA: Sage.

Beemyn, B. & Eliason, M. (Eds.). 1996, Queer Studies: A Lesbian, Gay, Bisexual, and Transgender Anthology. New York: New York University Press.

Boulding, E. (Ed.). 1992. New Agendas for Peace Research: Conflict and Security Reexamined. Boulder, CO: Lynne Rienner

Brown, D. M. 2007. Communicating Design: Developing Web Site Documentation for Design and Planning. Berkeley, CA: Peachpit.

Burke, M. (2001). *Sport and Traditions of Feminist Theory*. Unpublished doctoral dissertation, Victoria University, Melbourne, Australia.

Butler, J. 1991. Gender Trouble: Feminism and the Subversion of Identity. New York, NY: Routledge.

Cooky, C.A. (2006). *Getting Girls in the Game: A Qualitative Analysis of Urban Sport Programs*. Unpublished doctoral dissertation, University of Southern California.

Cotterill, P. 1992. Interviewing women. *Women's Studies International Forum*, **15** (5/6), 593–606.

Davidson, J. & Shogan, D. 1998. What's queer about studying up? A response to Messner. *Sociology of Sport Journal*, **15** (4), 359–366.

Denzin, N. K. & Lincoln, Y. S. 2000. *Handbook of Qualitative Research*. Thousand Oaks, CA: Sage.

Duggan, L. 1992. Making it perfectly queer. *The Socialist Review*, **22** (1), 11–31.

Enang, S. (1999) *The Childbirth Experiences of African Nova Scotia Women*. Unpublished master's thesis, Dalhousie University, Halifax, Nova Scotia, Canada.

Evans, J. 1995. Feminist Theory Today: An Introduction to Second-Wave Feminism. London: Sage.

Farrell, K. 2006. HIV on TV: conversations with young gay men. *Sexualities*, **9** (2), 193–213.

Fonow, M. M. & Cook, J. A. 1991. Back to the future: a look at the second wave of feminist epistemology and methodology. In: *Beyond Methodology: Feminist Research as Lived Research* (Ed. by M. M. Fonow, J. A. Cook), pp. 1–15. Bloomington: Indiana University Press.

Frisby, W. 2005. The good, the bad, and the ugly: critical sport management research. *Journal of Sport Management*, **19**, 1–12.

Gamson, J. 2000. Sexualities, queer theory, and qualitative research. In: *Handbook of Qualitative Research* (Ed. by N. K. Denzin, Y. S. Lincoln), pp. 347–365, 2nd ed. Thousand Oaks, CA: Sage.

Gergen, K. J. 1988. Feminist critique of science and the challenge of social epistemology. In: *Feminist Thought and the Structure of Knowledge* (Ed. by M. Gergen), pp. 27–48. New York: New York University Press.

Giffney, N. 2004. Denormatizing queer theory: more than (simply) lesbian and gay studies. *Feminist Theory*, **5** (1), 73–78.

Goldman, R. 1996. Who is that queer queer? Exploring norms around sexuality, race, and class in queer theory. In: *Queer Studies: A Lesbian, Gay, Bisexual, and Transgender Anthology* (Ed. by B. Beemyn, M. Eliason), pp. 169–182. New York: New York University Press.

Green, A. 2002. Gay but not queer: toward a post-queer study of sexuality. *Theory and Society*, **31**, 521–545.

Hall, J. M. & Stevens, P. E. 1991. Rigor in feminist research. *Advances in Nursing Science*, **13** (3), 16–29.

Halperin, D. M. 1995. Saint-Foucault: Towards a Gay Hagiography. New York: Oxford University Press.

Hammersley, M. 1992. What's Wrong with Ethnography: Methodological Explorations. London: Routledge.

Haraway, D. 1988. Situated knowledges: the science question in feminism and the privilege of partial perspective. *Feminist Studies*, **14** (3), 575–599.

Harding, S. 1987. Feminism and Methodology. Bloomington: Indiana University Press.

Hartsock, N. 1987. Rethinking modernism. *Cultural Critique*, **7**, 187–206.

Hartsock, N. C. M. 1998. The Feminist Standpoint Revisited and Other Essays. Boulder, CO: Westview.

Jagose, A. M. 1996. Queer Theory: An Introduction. New York: New York University.

Kirsch, M. 2000. Queer Theory and Social Change. London: Routledge.

Krane, D. 2001. Disorderly progress on the frontiers of policy evaluation. *International Journal of Public Administration*, **24** (1), 95–123.

Maguire, P. 1987. Doing Participatory Research: A Feminist Approach. Amherst, MA: University of Massachusetts.

Messner, M. 1996. Studying up on sex. *Sociology of Sport Journal*, **13**, 221–237.

Miles, A. 1989. Feminism: From Pressure to Politics. Montreal: Black Rose Books.

Nielsen, J. M. 1990. Feminist Research Methods: Exemplary Readings in the Social Sciences. Boulder, GO: Westview Press.

Oakley, A. 1981. Interviewing women: a contradiction in terms. In: *Doing Feminist Research* (Ed. by H. Roberts), pp. 30–61. London: Routledge and Kegan Paul.

Reinharz, S. 1992. Feminist Methods in Social Research. Toronto, ON: Oxford University Press.

Ribbens, J. 1989. Interviewing – an "unnatural situation?". *Women's Studies International Forum*, **12** (6), 579–592.

Riger, S. 1992. Epistemological debates, feminist voices: Science, social values, and the study of women. *American Psychologist*, **47**, 730–740.

Scrogum, J. (2005). *Binaries and Bridging: A Feminist Analysis of Women's Rugby Participation*. Unpublished master's thesis. University of North Carolina at Greensboro.

Smith, J. K. & Deemer, D. K. 2000. The problem of criteria in the age of relativism. In: *Handbook of Qualitative Research* (Ed. by N. K. Denzin, Y. S. Lincoln), pp. 877–896, 2nd ed. Thousand Oaks, CA: Sage.

Streubert Speziale, H. J. & Carpenter, D. R. 2003. Qualitative Research in Nursing. Advancing the Humanistic Imperative, 3rd ed. New York: Lippincott, Williams, and Wilkins.

Thompson, D. 1992. Against the dividing of women: lesbian feminism and heterosexuality. *Feminism & Psychology*, **2**, 387–398.

Tierney, W. 1997. Academic Outlaws: Queer Theory and Cultural Studies in the Academy. London: Sage.

Van Zoonen, L. 1994. Feminist Media Studies. London: Sage.

Walters, S. D. 1996. From here to queer: radical feminism, postmodernism, and the lesbian menace. *Signs*, **21**, 831–869.

Webb, C. 1993. Feminist research: definitions, methodology, methods and evaluation. *Journal of Advanced Nursing*, **18**, 416–423.

Westkott, M. 1990. Feminist criticism of the social sciences. In: *Feminist Research Methods: Exemplary Readings in the Social Sciences* (Ed. by J. M. Nielsen), pp. 58–68. Boulder, CO: Westview Press.

Wuest, J. 1994. A feminist approach to concept analysis. *Western Journal of Nursing Research*, **16** (5), 577–586.

CHAPTER 17

Grounded Theory and Sport Management Research

KEY TERMS

Symbolic interactionism: The theory that the most distinctive aspects of human behavior are a product of the fact that man alone is a symbol-manipulating animal – that man has developed conventionalized signs which have become organized into language which, in turn, is the vehicle for the transmission of culture and which provides the major means for carrying on social interaction

Theoretical coding: is dealing with conceptual codes, which are derived from the open codes and form the link between the data and the theoretical findings.

Theoretical sampling: the process of choosing new research sites, participants or targets, based on an analysis of the data already collected, and the theories gleaned from that data.

KEY QUESTIONS

The key questions raised in this chapter are as follows:

- What is Grounded Theory?

- What are some of the strengths of the Grounded Theory method for Sport Management research?

- What are some of the weaknesses of the Grounded Theory method for Sport Management research?

CHAPTER OVERVIEW

This chapter explores the research approach of grounded theory. It examines the debates surrounding the application of grounded theory to research and identifies and discusses the principles that underpin grounded theory approaches to research in sport management settings. Despite some identified weaknesses in the grounded theory approach, it argues that there are certainly some distinct advantages in the approach for the sport management researcher. It is suggested that the grounded theory approach is compatible with the aims of sport management researchers because it enables the researcher to capture and explicate on a theoretical level the complexity of organizational situations and processes.

DEFINING GROUNDED THEORY

Grounded Theory was originally developed and refined by Glaser and Strauss. Their book, *The Discovery of Grounded Theory: Strategies for Qualitative Research* (1967), presents their strategies for qualitative research to the area of human science research. In doing so, Glaser and Strauss shared their notion that this was a "beginning venture in the development of improved methods for discovering grounded theory" (p. 1). Also their basic position in contrast to logical deduction theory building from a priori assumptions, was "that generating grounded theory is a way of arriving at theory suited to its supposed uses" (p. 3). Thus, theory building is based on the accumulation of data that reflect the experiences of the researcher, rather than the research being used to test or prove a prior formulated theory.

The theoretical assumption that underpins grounded theory is symbolic interactionism. In his theory of symbolic interactionism, Blumer (1969) identified three basic tenets:

1. People act or react to other people or things depending on what those people or things mean to them.

2. These meanings are derived from communication between individuals.

3. These meanings are modified, accepted and established via an interpretative process engaged in by individuals (cited in Denzin & Lincoln, 1994, p. 124).

The sport management researcher utilizing the grounded theory of qualitative research therefore must understand the world and their interpretation of it, as the research participants understand it (Marshall & Rossman, 1995).

Grounded theory aids the researcher seeking to study social phenomena in a range of different fields, in its natural setting. For the sport management researcher, this could be a study of athletes at a competition, specific consumers attending a sporting event, or even the management team within a sporting organization. The researcher will engage in a data collection process of field observation, in-depth interviews and document analysis (Glaser & Strauss, 1967). Following analysis of one set of data, the researcher then decides what data to collect next and where to find them from other participants, sites, and/or events or incidents. Therefore, the grounded theory researcher develops the theory as it emerges in this ongoing process – referred to by Glaser and Strauss, as "grounding" the theory in the data. Because of this continual "grounding" process, the theory accurately reflects the data.

It takes a researcher both time, and the ability to think conceptually about the data in order to develop a grounded theory. Wilson (1989) asserts that the time is essential to allow for both a component of creativity and comprehensive analysis of the data, the end result of which is a theoretical explanation of the phenomenon being studied. This theoretical explanation is enough to provide differing accounts while at the same time allowing generalizations.

THE GROUNDED THEORY DEBATE

The literature provides discussion of an *ongoing debate* initiated by the original researchers and augmented by differing schools of thought on the "correct" method and interpretation of grounded theory. The method of grounded theory as originally proposed by Glaser and Strauss (1967) has more recently been presented in densely codified and structured format (Strauss & Corbin, 1990). However, this later version has been criticized by Glaser (1992) on the grounds that it deviates from the original method in that it is orientated toward "forcing" the data into a codified frame rather than allowing the theory or concepts to emerge from the data. This debate is further elaborated on by Kendall (1999) who states that Strauss and Corbin (1990) perceived the need to address what they viewed as the limitation caused by a lack of detail in the literature surrounding the processes involved in generating meaningful theories grounded in qualitative data. The main criticism of their approach is the apparent contradiction of the original assumptions, in particular the emphasis on conceptual description rather than emergent theory. Kendall (1999) proposes that the crux of the issue in differences between the two approaches is the use of axial coding. There is no argument regarding the importance of coding (Glaser, 1978, 1992; Strauss & Corbin, 1990) in that it is essential to transform the raw data into theoretical constructions of social processes. Glaser and Strauss (1967) and Glaser (1978) describe two types of coding, substantive or open and theoretical coding, whereas Strauss and Corbin (1990) articulate three types, open, axial and selective coding.

While the versions of open coding are espoused to be similar (Kendall, 1999) there are nonetheless, differences. The controversy was created when Strauss and Corbin (1990) added "axial" coding to the coding process, which they define as a set of procedures whereby data is put back together in new ways after open coding has occurred, by making connections between the categories. Specifically, conditions, contexts, action and interactional strategies and consequences are articulated. Glaser (1978) emphasizes the need to allow codes and theoretical underpinnings to "freely" emerge. It would appear that Glaser's (1978) main concern with axial coding is the act of placing labels on the codes which should be guided by conceptual interests emergent from the data, and not interpreted as belonging to, or being representative of particular scheme as proposed in Strauss and Corbin's (1990) paradigm model. Glaser (1978) identifies 18 coding elements which could be used to guide the researcher to connect categories. These elements are not exclusive and therefore, because there is no pre-set framework, there is an increased guarantee of a unique emergence of the data, rather than fitting it to a framework (Kendall, 1999). In a counterclaim, Strauss and Corbin (1990) argue that their process allows the researcher to be guided by a more complex, systematic and accurate method. The key difference in the two approaches was formalized when Strauss co-published a text on grounded theory (Strauss & Corbin, 1990). Glaser went public with allegations that the method espoused in this text was not true to the original notion of grounded theory, and he articulated two major reasons for this: (1) researchers are required to ask questions of the data which varies from the original purpose to ask "what is the main concern or problem and what accounts for most of the variation in processing the problem? and (2) a preconceived framework for asking questions of the data is used rather than allowing the categories to emerge from the data itself.

GROUNDED THEORY METHODOLOGY

The essential features of the grounded theory methodology are firstly that the data itself is used to identify and interrelate the abstract concepts which drive theory and secondly that the resultant theory is the product of the data collection and analysis process. As previously mentioned, this is the process whereby the data drives the theory and is what Glaser and Strauss (1967) refer to as "grounding" the theory in the data. Because of this continual "grounding" process, the theory accurately reflects the data.

Eaves (2001) states also that one aim of grounded theory methodology is not only to study processes, but also assume that making theoretical sense of social life through a systematic study is itself a process.

Although Glaser and Strauss (1967) did not specifically articulate the basic tenets of grounded theory, subsequent theorists have articulated such tenets as follows:

1. The theory must be generated from praxis.

2. The theory must be interesting and useful, or have what is called "grab".

3. The resultant theory must fit, that is, demonstrate relevance and be able to explain, predict and be modified by the social phenomenon under study.

4. Data collection and analysis are undertaken simultaneously, that is both processes are interwoven with the concepts and propositions which emerge guiding the subsequent data collection.

5. The substantive theory should be able to transcend a particular setting and extend to a wider scope of circumstances.

6. The emergent theory must be able to incorporate other theories, rather than existing in opposition.

7. The approach of grounded theory presumes the possibility of discovering fundamental patterns in all social life, specifically the emergency of variability of the core category of basic social processes (Wilson, 1989).

In addressing all of these tenets, what results is a theoretical explanation of the phenomenon which

1. fits the substantive area under study;

2. is appropriately dense and thereby provides an adequate variational account;

3. abstract enough to allow generalization; and

4. allows for a degree of control over structures and processes seen in the everyday account of the phenomenon (Wilson, 1989).

Additionally, grounded theory methodology assumes that discovery of a core category(ies) and a core process (substantive theory) is the ultimate focus of grounded theory studies (Eaves, 2001).

ASSUMPTIONS UNDERPINNING GROUNDED THEORY METHOD

Eaves (2001) was able to identify seven assumptions about the method from Glaser's and Strauss' writings. These assumptions are as follows:

1. Grounded theory method assumes the emergence of a substantive theory from the research process, rather than verifying pre-existing theories. According to Glaser and Strauss (1967), the development of theories that are grounded on data is an important process that many social scientists ignored.

2. The systematic application of grounded theory method analytical techniques (constant comparative analysis) lead progressively to more abstract theories.

3. A third assumption, therefore, is that the process and products of grounded theory studies are shaped from data rather than a preconceived theoretical framework.

4. Grounded theory methodology assumes that discovery of a core category(ies) and a core process (substantive theory) is the ultimate focus of grounded theory studies. For instance, a basic social process (BSP) is one type of core category that provides the building blocks of a theory (Glaser, 1978).

5. The aim of grounded theory methodology is not only to study processes, but also to assume that making theoretical sense of social life through a systematic study is itself a process.

6. Rigor of the related study is enhanced by simultaneous data collection and analysis in a grounded theory study.

7. Finally, theoretical sampling in the grounded theory method maximizes the coverage of variations within the phenomenon being studied.

According to Glaser and Strauss (1967), the major *uses* of grounded theory include the following:

- Preliminary, exploratory and descriptive studies, where little research has been done and further investigation may be required.

- The provision of a different perspective in areas where a substantial amount of research utilizing other research methodologies has been completed.

- The clarification and explanation of some of the major components of a social and psychological process, for example, implementing change.

- The sharpening of sensitivities to the problems, dilemmas, and issues that are facing people who work in some area of social life, for example, sport managers implementing change.

- The prediction and explanation of behavior, thus allowing understanding and control over some situations.

THE GROUNDED THEORY METHOD

Annells (1997a,b), asserts that the following 10 *elements* are essential to any approach utilizing the grounded theory method. These are presented in no particular order:

1. the asking of theoretically orientated questions;

2. theoretical coding – this includes open, theoretical and selective coding;

3. constant comparative analysis;

4. theoretical sensitivity;

5. memoing;

6. theoretical sampling;

7. theoretical saturation;

8. identification of a core category(ies), for example, a BSP (Glaser, 1978);

9. the development of a theory from the core category(ies) (the core process);

10. the grounding of theory upon data through data-theory interplay.

We shall now discuss some of these elements.

Method

The first step in the grounded theory method, following the identification of the phenomena to be studied, is the collection of data. The data can be collected in a number of ways – field observations, in-depth interviews and document analysis (Glaser & Strauss, 1967). Interviews can be a useful technique when little is known, and there are no assumptions about the phenomena being examined. The analysis of the data can be seen as a concurrent process that should occur simultaneously with the data collection and the construction of the emerging theory – this process is the constant comparative method.

Constant comparative method

In the constant comparative method, each piece of data or item of information gleaned from the data collection process is repeatedly compared with all other data, so that theoretical concepts are generated that will include as much behavioral variation as possible. The purpose of comparative analysis is to determine the accuracy of data collected, establish the generality of a fact, specify a concept, and thereby generate a theory (Glaser & Strauss, 1967).

Coding

Glaser (1998) described coding as assigning categories to incidents in the data. He explained that incidents were identified in a phrase or a sentence in the interviews. Joint coding and analysis lifted the data from an empirical or descriptive level to a conceptual or theoretical level (Glaser, 1978). The path from the empirical to conceptual level was not linear but creative in nature, and Glaser (1978, 1998) warned of using pathways that were too prescriptive. Coding is carried out on three levels: *Open coding, theoretical coding and selective coding*. These coding methods will now be described.

Open coding

Glaser (1978) described open coding in detail. Open coding was defined as "running the data open" or coding "different incidents into as many categories as possible" (p. 56). He stated that data collection and open coding were completed when no new properties of categories or the same properties were identified in further interviews.

Theoretical coding

Glaser (1978) described theoretical coding as dealing with conceptual codes, which were derived from the open codes and formed the link between the data and the theoretical findings. Theoretical codes form the basis for the theoretical findings and are important that they emerge from the data and not from extraneous sources (Glaser, 1998).

Selective coding

In selective coding, as described by Glaser (1978), the researcher "selectively code[s] for a core variable and cease[s] open coding" (p. 61). Once the core category is identified the researcher delimits their coding and data collection to gather properties related to the core variable only.

Theoretical sensitivity

It is the ability of the researcher to move beyond the mere description of the data to see theoretical possibilities, to see the variables in the data and recognize the meanings attributed to them by the participants in the study that Glaser and Strauss (1967) referred to as theoretical sensitivity. This sensitivity can guide the researcher to recognize and conceptualize a theory as it emerges from the data – thus ensuring that the theory is "grounded" in the data.

Memoing

Memos are an essential part of data analysis in the grounded theory method. They are the "theorizing write-up of ideas about codes and their relationships as they strike the analyst while coding" (Glaser, 1978, p. 83). Another goal of memo writing, according to Glaser, was to allow the researcher the freedom to develop ideas as they arise because the contents of the memos do not have to be in logical order. The analysis, through the use of memos, can then be justified because it is grounded in the data.

Theoretical sampling

Following an analysis of the most recent set of data, the researcher decides what data to collect next, and where to collect it from. The theory is developed as it emerges from the data.

Theoretical saturation

Data collection is complete when saturation is reached. Theoretical saturation occurs when no new or relevant data seem to emerge regarding a category, the category is well developed with a variation of its properties and dimensions, and the relationships among categories are well established and validated (Strauss & Corbin, 1998).

The core category

The end product of developing theory is the core category (Glaser & Strauss, 1967). Glaser and Strauss describe the emergence of a "core category" as follows: As categories and properties emerge, develop in abstraction, and become related, their accumulating interrelations form an integrated central theoretical framework – *the core of the emerging theory.*

This "core of the emerging theory" is, therefore, not only the substantive theory, but also is more commonly known as the "core category". The emergence of a core category occurs after extensive analysis of the data using the constant comparative method. The purpose of a core category is to conceptualize the basic social psychological process; or the basic social problem which is addressed by the theory. Glaser (1978) states that: "the core category must account for most of the variation in a pattern of behaviour" (p. 93). Glaser further suggests that for a core category to be effective it must be central, stable, complex, integrative, incisive, powerful and highly variable.

The mandate of **grounded theory** is to strive for the verification of its resulting hypothesis which is attained as part of the research method. Grounded theory aims to be a rigorous method through the provision of detailed and systematic procedures for data collection, analysis and theorizing, along with the quality of the emerging theory (Strauss & Corbin, 1994). More specifically, the most important criteria for maintaining and determining rigor in a grounded theory study is following the systematic grounded theory process and procedures.

These include those that comprise the constant comparative method: concurrent collection of data and analysis; theoretical sampling; theoretical sensitivity; and memoing (Glaser & Strauss, 1967; Strauss & Corbin, 1990). Four central criteria for a good grounded theory are that it should:

1. reflect the phenomenon being studied;

2. be easily understood by both the researcher and those involved in the phenomenon;

3. provide generality and applicability to a diverse range of contexts;

4. provide control by stating the condition which the theory applies.

Strauss and Corbin (1990) provide their own interpretation of criteria for rigor in response to their re-worked version of grounded theory which was primarily to allow for a more structured way to undertake grounded theory. These criteria include plausibility; generalizability; concept generation;

systematic conceptual relationships; density; variation; and the presence of process and broader conceptions.

Research Brief

Title: A Qualitative Analysis of Revenue Producing Sport Student Athletes' perceptions of the national Collegiate Athletic Association (NCAA)

Who: Brett III, M.J. The Ohio State University

Brett's examination of the NCAA's history reveals that the association was formed primarily to protect the health, safety, and welfare of student athletes. However, aside from the initial reforms to the game of football, many critics of the Association contend that the NCAA has focused more on commercial gains than the needs of their student athletes. The study utilized grounded theory to investigate varsity student athletes in revenue producing sports: (a) general perceptions of the NCAA and (b) whether these perceptions match the NCAA's stated purposes and goals

ISSUES RELATED TO SEARCHING THE LITERATURE IN THE GROUNDED THEORY METHOD

According to Stern (1985), in grounded theory research, a detailed pre-study literature search is disadvantageous for three reasons: (1) the search may lead to pre-judgment and affect premature closure of ideas and research inquiry; (2) the direction may be wrong; and (3) the available data or materials used may be inaccurate. In other words, some knowledge of the literature is required, yet an exhaustive review before data collection may increase the chance of a researcher's bias or pre-conceptions which may lead to insufficient interpretation of the phenomenon.

Although a detailed pre-study literature search is disadvantageous in grounded theory research, the question of just how much literature review or reading is sufficient before commencing a ground theory study still remains a matter of debate. A criticism of not conducting an extensive literature review is that without doing this the researcher may not be able to identify gaps in existing research or the implications of research already conducted in the topic. The researcher may not know how extensive the phenomenon has been researched and whether or not the use of a grounded theory method might add to the existing knowledge about it. However, when the researcher considers literature as a slice of data (Glaser & Strauss, 1967) that is concurrently used to compare with the emerging categories from the data, it makes sense that more relevant and appropriate literature specific to the emerging categories will be used to rigorously complete the analysis. The use of literature as a slice of data for the analysis of emerging categories from data minimizes the risk of the researcher's pre-conceptions about these categories. Furthermore, in a grounded theory study, technical (academic) and non-technical (common publications and media reports) literature are also used as slices of data during the process of constant comparative analysis. These data trigger new questions and further data collection, and provide the basis of verification for the researcher to draw conclusions, until data saturation occurs (Strauss & Corbin, 1998).

THE ROLE OF THE RESEARCHER IN GROUNDED THEORY

Issues of validity and truth rely on the interpersonal skills of the researcher to obtain the perspective of the participant, as the researcher is the instrument, or conduit for, receiving and interpreting the narrative. Importantly, therefore, the researcher should utilize the following stratagems: acknowledgment of involvement and subsequent "inseparability" from the research; use of the first person; use of reflexive accounts about the research process and decisions made.

Strauss (1978) alerts the researcher to the fact that they can shape the interview by the way they probe for detail, clarity or explanation, and non-verbal gestures and associated responses. The grounded theory researcher has to consider specific strategies when interviewing to suit grounded theory methods. Specifically, how to ask questions and what to ask based on: (a) what is being said in the interview; (b) questions predetermined as dictated by theoretical sampling; and (c) the development of hypotheses or relational statements (Glaser & Strauss, 1967; Strauss & Corbin, 1990). The grounded theory researcher "conducts" the interview in a highly alert state – the interview although tape recorded and transcribed is a one off opportunity to engage with the source of data and participate in the collection of data which could be missed without an in-depth awareness of what is being said, the nuances of the narrative and an understanding of what questions to ask.

Additionally, where the researcher is relying on observation, they need to be alert to nuances in behavior and reactions of those being observed, and to accurately record the evidence they are observing, so that the next stage of the comparative analysis and theoretical sampling process can effectively occur.

Research Brief

Title: Toward an Understanding of the Needs of Sport Spectators with Disabilities

Who: Grady, J.M., Florida State University

The purpose of this study was to assess the needs of sport consumers with disabilities attending live sporting events. Three research questions guided this exploratory study. The first research question sought to identify the physical and service needs of sport consumers with mobility impairments attending a live sporting event. The second research question investigated whether the needs of sport consumers with mobility impairments attending a live sporting event were being met. The third research question examined what could be done differently by a service provider to enhance the experience of a consumer with a mobility impairment. A grounded theory methodology was used to develop an understanding of the needs of people with disabilities in stadia. Through the use of focus group and in-depth interviews with six male sport consumers with mobility impairments, as well as observations at sports venues and in-depth interviews with facility personnel, an understanding of the needs of people with disabilities attending live sporting events emerged.

GROUNDED THEORY AND SPORT MANAGEMENT RESEARCH

In Grounded Theory, the theories relevant to a particular event, situation or phenomena emerge from the data following a continual process of comparative analysis. As such, it is particularly applicable to research areas that have been ignored or even not identified at all. It does not require a pre-formulated theory for testing, and as such allows the sport management researcher great scope to investigate, observe, interview – and then to engage in the methodology of grounded theory to draw sometimes surprising or unexpected theories from the data collected at the site of the phenomena under study.

The core activities in the grounded theory method, the continual interplay of comparative analysis and theoretical sampling, require the study of a phenomena "in action" or "in situ" as the theories develop and evolve over a period of time as the sport management researcher engages continually with the phenomena and the data collected from it. As the theories are generated from praxis, grounded theory is therefore particularly relevant for the sport management researcher. In addition to developing the theories, grounded theory enables the sport management researcher to go beyond a mere description or statistical analysis of the phenomena, to describe the how and the why, and situate the phenomena within specific contexts. As sport management often functions in complex social and physical situations and with a wide variety of human interactions both internal and external to the sport management event or organization, grounded theory can provide a useful and functional approach to the sport management researcher.

The case study is a frequently used research and reporting tool of the sport management researcher, and grounded theory works to enhance the strengths of the case study. Grounded theory ensures that the data are collected in the setting in which the case study is set, and can be gathered in a variety of ways including observation and interviewing. Additionally, as the sport management researcher engages in the processes of comparative analysis and theoretical sampling, the issues being investigated or studied in the case study can be reviewed and clarified at many different times over the duration of the study. In a sport management setting, a case study looking at operational issues with a sport management organization can utilize grounded theory methods to look at attitudes and performance over a period of time, and the grounded theory method can facilitate the development of theories that before the start of the study, had not even been considered.

A variety of data collection methods often utilized by the sport management researcher are intrinsically suited to the grounded theory method. Observations, interviews, questionnaires, document analysis, and even the sport management researcher as active participant in the research process are all methods familiar to the sport management researcher, and which suit the method of grounded theory. Grounded theory gives the researcher the opportunity to observe and eventually formulate unanticipated results and theories derived from the data collected.

Despite the advantage of grounded theory in enabling the sport management researcher to insinuate himself/herself into the research study to facilitate a greater understanding of participants and their view of the phenomena being studied, the limitations of the sport management researchers' knowledge and analytic ability in relation to the phenomena can also lead to questions about the validity or reliability of the emergent theories derived from the data. As each sport management researcher may have a unique perspective on the phenomena being studied, and their levels of theoretical sensitivity will vary, it can be difficult to replicate the findings generated from a grounded theory study.

Theorists also disagree on the importance of cultural difference in the grounded theory method. Whilst Glaser (1978) did not believe that variables such as age, sex, race, etc. should not be considered relevant until the relevance emerged from an analysis of the data, other researchers such as Barnes (1996) believe that the responses of participants should be analyzed from the participant's own cultural perspective, given that language is the symbolic representation of the participant's views and ideas, and these views and ideas are shaped by the cultural context from which the participant and by extension, the sport management researcher, operates.

Three recent studies provide an indication of the application of grounded theory to various sport management contexts. Sotiriadou et al. (2003) examined the impact of the Australian Federal Government involvement with sport policy on the sport development processes at a national level. In doing so, she explored the roles of the key sport development players and the ways sport policies shape sport development processes. Sotiriadou et al. (2003) utilized constant comparison and coding of data from the Annual Reports of 35 National Sporting Organizations in Australia.

Dunphy (2006) investigated the perceptions of the two parties associated with an event bid: the event bidders and the event owners. The event management research also compared and contrasted the international findings with the New Zealand findings and a model of the event bidding process (Targeted Model). Using the grounded theory methodology, common success factors and a model of the event bidding process emerged from the data. A common success factor that was frequently mentioned by event owners and event bidders included the need for government support.

From a sport marketing perspective Jones and Bee (2003) examined (1) what it means to be a sport fan, (2) the factors and conditions that influence an individual to become a sport fan, and (3) how sport fans interpret sport-related events. Grounded theory methodology was selected as a means of exploring this previously unexamined phenomenon. Jones' study relied on interpretations of interviews with 14 highly committed sport fans and excerpts submitted by sports fans on two popular sport-related websites (www.SportingNews.com and www.ESPN.com). Perhaps the most comprehensive application of grounded theory is illustrated in Roy's 2004 study outlined below in the case study example.

Research Brief

Title: Mapping Cultural Dimensions in Australian Sporting Organisations
Who: Aaron C.T. Smith, La Trobe University; David Shilbury, Deakin University
Sport Management Review, 2004, **7**, 133–165
The aim of this study was to identify a set of dimensions that could describe the cultures of Australian sporting organizations. The population for this study included Australian National Sport Organizations (NSOs), State Sport Organizations (SSOs) and clubs participating in national league competitions. Smith and Shilbury utilized theoretical sampling to select the eight sport organizations that formed the study. Data were collected via 24 in-depth interviews. This study revealed 12 dimensions and 68 sub-dimensions of culture, which may be used to begin the process of mapping sport cultures. These results reveal some unique sport dimensions with no single existing dimensional model that captures the collective elements revealed in this study. The unique dimensions revealed in this study include 'Rituals', 'Symbols', 'Size', 'History and tradition', with support for these dimensions found within the sub-dimensional codes. This suggests that the dimensions recorded here might provide a useful launching pad for future studies on sport culture.

Grounded Theory Case Study

Who: Robert Joseph Edmund Roy, Simon Fraser University

What: A Grounded Theory Approach to the Extension and Revision of Scanlan's Sport Commitment Model

Theoretical framework

Roy utilized a qualitative, hermeneutic approach to expand the sport commitment model (SCM). He incorporated concepts from diverse theoretical backgrounds to provide a richer, more complex understanding of the factors that affect sport enjoyment and sport commitment. Roy also enhanced the generalizability of the model by extending it to athletes actively competing at the intercollegiate, national, international, or Olympic level. They competed in the following sports: wrestling, basketball, soccer, football, track and field, and triathlon.

Data collection methods

All participants engaged in a semi-structured interview lasting between 60 and 90 minutes. Verbatim transcripts were subjected to inductive content analysis via the constant comparative method.

Data analysis techniques/presentation

The study utilized a hermeneutical approach to examine sources of sport commitment and sport enjoyment. The data were organized with the aim of interpreting raw quotes to create a thematic hierarchy based on the researcher's conceptual repertoire, clinical experience, and experiential knowledge of sport. This was conducted through an iterative process of interpreting and reinterpreting the data, each time with an increased and more differentiated understanding. To prepare for the analyses, each transcript was read while the corresponding interview was played on audiotape. This was done to re-familiarize the researcher with the participant, and to take note of any verbal inflections, emphases, or affective cues that would not be evident on the transcript.

Major findings

This study generated a series of eight thematic hierarchies representing the participant sample's reported sources of sport commitment. Five of these hierarchies corresponded to the original constructs of the SCM. They were Enjoyment, Involvement Alternatives, Investments, Social Constraints, and Involvement Opportunities. These hierarchies also included a number of component themes that served to explicate and differentiate these constructs. The remaining three hierarchies reflected superordinate constructs proposed for addition to the model. They are Transcendence/ Teleology, Transformation, and Adaptive Functioning/Coping. The end result was a richer, denser, more complex theoretical model that can now be tested using positivistic, quantitative methodologies.

Suggestions for future research

Roy hoped that the results of his study would provide useful detail for future revisions of the sport commitment model. In this regard, he recommended that future researchers apply the SCM procedure to the current results, and particularly to the three new higher-order constructs.

Case study research probes

1. How has a grounded theory approach been used in this research?

2. What insights has a grounded theory approach provided that a positivist approach could not have?

CONCLUSION

Despite some identified weaknesses in the grounded theory approach, there are certainly some distinct advantages in the approach for the sport management researcher. The grounded theory approach is generally compatible with the aims of sport management researchers because it enables the research to capture and explicate on a theoretical level the complexity of organizational situations and processes. Because by its nature grounded theory requires a basis in praxis, the organizational elements and participants can recognize and relate to the aims of the sport management researcher following this particular methodology. Finally, and probably most importantly, because the continual process of comparative analysis facilitates the emergence of theories grounded in the data, some theories may emerge which lead to the investigation of new areas, and also give a refreshed perspective to previously researched areas.

IN PROFILE - Professor David Shilbury

David Shilbury is the Foundation Chair in Sport Management and a former Head of the School of Management and Marketing at Deakin University in Melbourne, Australia. Professor Shilbury's academic qualifications include a Ph.D. (Monash University), an M.Sc. (Sport Management, UMASS) and a B. App. Sc. (Rec.) from the former WA College of Advanced Education. David has published widely in the leading journals in the field and is co-author of two leading textbooks; *Strategic Sport Marketing* and *Sport Management in Australia. An Organisational Overview*. Professor Shilbury's research interests focus on sport governance, sport development and strategy. Recently, he supervised Ph.D. research examining the impact of social expectations on ethical governance within AFL clubs, a study exploring the sport development practices of Australian national sporting organizations (NSOs) and a study aimed at enhancing the strategic capability of New Zealand NSO boards. Two of the three studies used variants of grounded theory although each relied on quite different data sources. The study of AFL club directors relied on interviews as the primary data source, whilst the study of NSO development practices used annual reports over a four year period from 35 NSOs. In both instances, grounded data analysis relied on the use of NVivo software and key

principles of grounded theory including Open and Axial coding, comparative analysis, conceptual saturation and theoretical sampling. Action research formed the basis of the third study, and given the focus on governance was timely in that the field has identified a need to directly observe board behavior in a way that is not possible through traditional quantitative approaches. The central research question in this study was – 'how can boards of NSOs build their strategic capability?' A constructivist-interpretative paradigm underpinned the approach, with the Ph.D. student working with each of the three NSOs to identify how strategic capability could be enhanced. On reaching agreement with each NSO, the researcher designed an intervention and monitored the results which were gleaned from interviews, focus groups, workshops, video and audio recording of meetings and a final evaluation interview. A written data template was devised to record key information in a standardized manner, supported by researcher memos highlighting key incidents and reflections at relevant points in the study. Action research is founded on the premise that change and research are not mutually exclusive and that dual foci on improving practice and developing theory are possible (Coghlan & Brannick, 2001). This was the goal in this study.

REVIEW AND RESEARCH QUESTIONS

Grounded theory is a qualitative research methodology that by a continual process of comparative analysis and theoretical sampling results in the identification of theories situated within the phenomena being studied, and which are drawn from the data itself – or "grounded" within the data being analyzed. With a basic understanding of grounded theory, attempt to answer the following questions:

- Do the strengths of Grounded Theory for sport management research outweigh the possible weaknesses?

- How important is the role of the researcher in grounded theory? What are some of the issues a researcher should be aware of before undertaking grounded theory?

REFERENCES

Annells, M. 1997a. Grounded theory method, part I: within the five moments of qualitative research. *Nursing Inquiry,* **4** (2), 120–129.

Annells, M. 1997b. Grounded theory method, part II: options for users of the method. *Nursing Inquiry,* **4** (3), 176–180.

Barnes, D. M. (1996). An analysis of the grounded theory method and the concept of culture. *Qualitative Health Research,* 6(3), 429–441.

Blumer, H. 1969. Symbolic Interactionism: Perspective and Method. Englewood Cliffs, New Jersey: Prentice-Hall.

Coghlan, D. & Brannick, T. 2001. Doing Action Research in Your Own Organisation. London: Sage.

Denzin, N. K. & Lincoln, Y. S. (Eds.). 1994. Handbook of Qualitative Research. Thousand Oaks, CA: Sage.

Dunphy, A.P. (2006). *Common Success Factors When Bidding for Sporting Events in New Zealand.* Unpublished master's thesis, Auckland University of Technology, New Zealand.

Eaves, Y. D. 2001. A synthesis technique for grounded theory data analysis. *Journal of Advanced Nursing,* **35** (5), 654–663.

Glaser, B. G. 1978. Theoretical Sensitivity. Mill Valley, CA: Sociology Press.

Glaser, B. G. 1992. Basics of Grounded Theory Analysis. Mill Valley, CA: Sociology Press.

Glaser, B. G. 1998. Doing Grounded Theory: Issues and Discussions. Mill Valley, CA: Sociology Press.

Glaser, B. G. & Strauss, A. S. 1967. The Discovery of Grounded Theory: Strategies for Qualitative Research. NY: Aldine de Gruyter.

Jones, S. A. & Bee, C. C. 2003. Interpreting athletic endorsements from a persuasion knowledge framework. Proceedings of the Sport Marketing Association Conference, Gainesville, FL.

Kendall, J. 1999. Axial coding and the grounded theory controversy. *Western Journal of Nursing Research,* **21** (6), 743–757.

Marshall, C. & Rossman, G. B. 1995. Designing Qualitative Research, 2nd ed. Thousand Oaks, CA: Sage.

Roy, R. J. E. (2004). *A Grounded Theory Approach to the Extension and Revision of Scanlan's Sport Commitment Model.* Unpublished doctoral dissertation, Simon Fraser University, British Columbia, Canada.

Sotiriadou, P., Quick, S., & Shilbury, D. 2003. Identifying the Roles and Interrelationships of Sport Development Stakeholders in Australia, *9th Annual Sport Management Association of Australia & New Zealand Annual Conference Proceedings,* p. 54, University of Otago, New Zealand.

Stern, P. N. 1985. Using grounded theory method in nursing research. In: *Qualitative Research Methods in Nursing* (Ed. by M. Leininger), pp. 149–160. Orlando: Grune and Stratton.

Strauss, A. & Corbin, J. 1990. Basic Qualitative Research: Grounded Theory Procedures and Techniques. Newbury Park, CA: Sage Publications.

Strauss, A. & Corbin, J. 1994. Grounded theory methodology. In: *Handbook of Qualitative Research* (Ed. by N. K. Denzin, Y. S. Lincoln), pp. 273–285. Newbury Park, CA: Sage.

Strauss, A. & Corbin, J. 1998. Basics of Qualitative Research: Techniques and Procedures for Developing Grounded Theory. Thousand Oaks, CA: Sage.

Strauss, A. L. 1978. Negotiations: Varieties. Contexts. Processes and Social Order. London: Jossey-Bass.

Wilson, H. S. 1989. Family caregiving for a relative with Alzheimers dementia: coping with negative choices. *Nursing Research*, **38**, 94–98.

CHAPTER 18

Narrative Inquiry in Sport Management Research

KEY TERMS

Narrative: the consciously formulated, premeditated and coherent account of an experience.

Story: a more informal, provisional and exploratory narrative.

Voice: sometimes "voice" is used synonymously for "story", at other times it means "professional knowledge or orientation". When one calls writing a "voice" one is enlisting the residual power of this tradition to give power to the group or individual concerned. The term "voice" tends to carry with it unconsciously the assumption that the group has a natural authenticity, is identical to itself, uncontaminated by the language and values of other usually more dominant groups.

Metanarrative: an idea that is supposed to be a comprehensive explanation of historical experience or knowledge. The prefix "meta" means "beyond" and is here used to mean "about", and a narrative is a story. Therefore, a metanarrative is a story about a story, encompassing and explaining other "little stories" within totalizing schemes.

KEY QUESTIONS

The key questions raised in this chapter are as follows:

- What is the relationship between narrative and critical reflection?

- What are the implications for utilizing narrative in the field of sport management research?

CHAPTER OVERVIEW

Interest in narrative inquiry as a method of research has been instrumental through the postmodern development in the social sciences. This interest in narrative inquiry is attributed to the postmodern perspective of truth and knowledge. This chapter will explore the qualitative research methods of "story", "narrative" and "voice" and highlight how they can provide rich descriptions of the sport management environment and at the same time provide an alternative research approach. The chapter suggests that this shift in recognition of non-quantitative research paradigms is significant in that it represents a tacit understanding that "narratives" provide a unique insight into the meaning of various social phenomena for any number of social actors. It draws on the work of Bruner (1986, 1991) who argues that narrative is a useful way of approaching the world of sport management research. It suggests that in combination with the process of reflection, narrative inquiry as a qualitative research methodology has the capacity to bring to the field of sport management research an understanding of the unique experiences of sports managers. By sharing narratives, the researcher and sport manager can ultimately aim to understand the complex nature of the practitioner's world, with a resultant improvement in practice and leadership qualities.

WHAT IS NARRATIVE INQUIRY?

The term "narrative inquiry" has been used as an overarching category for a contemporary form of research practice, which includes the collection and analysis of autobiographies and biographies. What counts as narrative inquiry varies widely across researcher practice and those who critique it. Bochner (2001) in arguing for the value of qualitative research that utilizes a narrative inquiry observed:

The narrative turn moves from a singular, monolithic conception of social science toward a pluralism that promotes multiple forms of representation and research: away from facts and toward meanings;

away from master narratives and toward local stories: away from idolizing categorical thought and abstracted theory and toward embracing the values of irony, emotionality, and activism; away from assuming the stance of disinterested spectator and toward assuming the posture of a feeling, embodied, and vulnerable observer; away from writing essays and toward telling stories.
(pp. 134–135)

DEFINING NARRATIVE

There appears to be some disagreement about a precise narrative definition. Riessman (1993) states the term narrative "refers to talk organized around consequential events" which take the listener "into a past time or "world and recapitulates what happens" (p. 3). To give their definition to narrative inquiry, Clandinin and Connelly (2000) outline some of its characteristics:

> *… narrative inquiry is a way of understanding experience. It is collaboration between researcher and participants, over time, in a place or series of places, and in social interaction with milieu. An inquirer enters this matrix in the midst and progresses in this same spirit, concluding the inquiry still in the midst of living and telling, reliving and retelling, the stories of the experiences that make up people's lives, both individual and social. Simply stated … narrative inquiry is stories lived and told. (p. 20)*

Chase (2005) offers a number of definitions for narrative, while acknowledging that the field of narrative analysis often is conceptualized as including any type of textual data. Narrative, Chase states is:

> *a short topical story about a particular event and specific characters such as an encounter with a friend, boss, or doctor; (b) an extended story about a significant aspect of one's life such as schooling, work, marriage, divorce, childbirth, an illness, a trauma, or participation in a war or social movement [or sport]; or (c) a narrative of one's entire life, from birth to the present. (p. 652)*

In her essay on approaches to narrative inquiry Chase (2005) asserted that the term "narrative" has been used to "routinely refer to any prosaic data (as opposed to close-ended or short-answer data)" (p. 651). Chase argues that narrative inquiry included a great number of analytic lenses, stemming from diverse disciplines. Chase considers a number of issues with the "analytic lenses" (p. 656) of narrative inquiry. First, narrative is a unique form of discourse and as such, makes up a meaningful reality for the narrator. Discourse, narrative, and speech acts do not "describe", rather, they "constitute" "social subjects, social relations, and systems of knowledge and belief" (Fairclough, 1992, p. 36). Chase (2005) goes on to advocate a view of narratives as "verbal actions – as doing or accomplishing something–…when someone tells a story he or she shapes, constructs and performs as self" (p. 657). Storytellers or narrators create versions of themselves with the stories they tell. Chase cites a number of works that explore this idea that selves are constructed through narrative: "narrators construct nonunitary subjectivities" (Bloom & Munro, 1995), "revised identities" (Josselson, 1996), "permanently unsettled identities" (Stein, 1997) and "troubled identities" (Gubrium & Holstein, 2001).

Chase (2005) offers a reminder that narratives are "both enabled and constrained by a range of social resources and circumstances… they include the possibilities for self and reality construction that are intelligible within the narrator's community…and cultural and historical location" (p. 657). Finally, in the treatment, construction, and analysis of narrative, Chase acknowledges that qualitative researchers often viewed *themselves* as narrators as well as their research participants. As such, researchers "narrate "results" in ways that are both enabled and constrained by the social resources and circumstances embedded in their disciplines, cultures and historical moments" (p. 657).

The result of narrative research is not a definitive statement or generalization about an aspect of that which is being researched. Brown (2001) uses an analogy of the research resulting in a "traveler's guide" rather than a map or encyclopedia entry. McCormack (2002) also refers to this research not providing a "map" but allowing: "the reader to witness the process of the story's construction and its meaning for the storyteller" (p. 337).

THE NARRATIVE METHOD

By its nature, the sport management researcher undertaking "narrative inquiry" is required to take seriously accounts of the way others see their world and make sense of their roles within it. This method of inquiry as defined by Moustakas (1990) begins with a question or problem "that has a personal challenge and puzzlement in the search to understand one's self and the world in which one lives" (p. 15).

The narrative researcher is also the storyteller because they construct the participant's story and its meaning. Mishler (1995) reminds us that narrative researchers are also the storytellers because they construct the participant's story and its meaning. He continues:

> It is clear that we do not find stories; we make stories. We retell our respondents' accounts through our analytic re-descriptions. We too are storytellers and through our concepts and methods – our research strategies, data samples, transcription procedures, specifications of narrative units and structures, and interpretative perspectives – we construct the story and its meaning. In this sense the story is always co-authored, either directly in the process of an interviewer eliciting an account or indirectly through our representing and thus transforming others' texts and discourses. And a related point: The teller of the tale is also engaged in a retelling. The version we hear or read is shaped both by the context of its telling and the history of earlier retellings. (pp. 117–118)

Through *dialog* and self-inquiry, this process strives to find meaning in the human experiences. This meaning is derived from the sport management researcher's perceptions, beliefs and values, judgments and their own senses. An individual's defining moments can be expressed as a narrative portrait of their lived experiences and the meanings they attach to them. The narrative sport management researcher will often aim to capture and represent the authentic voices of participants, trying to go for a deep insight on a small number of participants.

METHODOLOGY

Chase (2005) does not offer specific recommendations for method. Instead, she referred to narrative inquiry as "a field in the making" (p. 669). The value of this process is that it is used to understand or explain how human experience is made meaningful and how it relies on the social interactions within environments, to provide accounts of people's thoughts, beliefs, interpretations and experiences.

Defining reflective practice in narrative

The term narrative – though it refers to spoken and informal discourse – reflects the professional and conceptual processes through which the original material (the story or stories) has been put. The real point of this distinction is that narratives should contain a *reflective* component. It may not be overt, but the shaping and organization of a narrative would usually reflect and transmit the consequences of a meditative or generalizing process of thought. Narratives do not exist as Bruner (1991) writes:

> in some real world, waiting there patiently and eternally to be veridically mirrored in a text. The act of constructing a narrative moreover, is considerably more than selecting events either from real life, from memory, or from fantasy and then placing them in an appropriate order. The events themselves need to be constituted in the light of the overall narrative. (p. 8)

Reflection is therefore an integral part of narrative inquiry and is linked to the gaining of new understandings. At the root of most concepts of reflective practice is Dewey's (1933) philosophical statement that reflective thought is "the active, persistent, and careful consideration of any belief or supposed form of knowledge, in the light of the grounds that support it and the further conclusions to which it tends" (p. 6). In the past 70 years, the term "reflective practice" has increasingly appeared in the descriptions of education, nursing and management but is only just starting to appear in sport management. Edwards' (1999) article on "Reflective Sport Managers" in Sport Management Review was the first attempt to introduce this concept to sport management.

APPLYING NARRATIVE RESEARCH

Riessman (1993) notes that the analysis of narrative data depends largely on the researcher's personal interests and biography, epistemological and theoretical groundings, and their evolving research question. With that in mind, Riessman recommends that narrative researchers not formulate very specific research hypotheses or questions.

Typically, in qualitative research methodology, the researchers try to listen first to the practitioners' stories. However, some researchers may try telling and responding to one another's stories concurrently so that they could reflect a sincere effort to listen to all the participants. In this way, the story may become richer and more meaningful. Hollway and Jefferson (2000) have developed a method for narrative interviewing. Within the method they call "free-association narrative interview", Hollway and Jefferson work with the premise that all research participants are "defended subjects". They define "defended subjects" as individuals who:

> may not hear the question through the same meaning-frame as that of the interviewer or other interviewees; are invested in particular positions in discourses to protect vulnerable aspects of the self; may

not know why they experience or feel things in the way that they do;
[and] are motivated, largely unconsciously to disguise the meaning of
at least some of their feelings and actions. (p. 26)

The free-association narrative interview allows for potentially threatening topics to be explored in so much as the position, as interviewer, is not that of a questioner.

The agenda of a free-association narrative interview is largely open (Hollway & Jefferson, 2000). This differs greatly from structured interview schedules and even semi-structured interviews in which the interviewer has a fairly established set of questions to ask each interviewee. While establishing a few key topic areas is important to a free-association narrative interview, the order and even manner in which they are broached is not established beforehand.

To facilitate the story gathering techniques for the free-association narrative interview, Hollway and Jefferson (2000) offered a few guidelines. The first is to use open-ended questions rather than closed questions. This allows the storyteller to offer his/her own reflections on the question, rather than respond with short, yes-or-no type answers. Further, Hollway and Jefferson recommended that listeners avoid asking "why questions". In approaching a "why" question, storytellers are compelled to examine and organize motives and often enter into the realm of the abstract or intellectual instead of voicing a somewhat more disjointed but more powerful exploration of feelings. Riessman (1993) suggested an interview guide with as few as five broad questions about the topics of relevance, supplemented by a few probes, such as "Can you tell me more about that?" or "What was that like for you?" (p. 55).

Data management

Hollway and Jefferson (2000) warn against fragmenting narratives. The tendency to handle large amounts of unstructured data by coding passages thematically and retrieving them to form a new text breaks narratives to pieces. This is undesirable within Hollway and Jefferson's narrative approach in so much as it "often leads researchers to overlook the form of their data" (p. 68). Instead, they offer two suggestions for data management. Hollway and Jefferson begin approaching their data by taking detailed notes and identifying a few key passages. From those notes they created a *"pro forma"* summary of those notes to convey some sense of the whole narrative. Additionally, they created *"pen portraits"* of each participant which were intended to make the narrator "come alive for a reader" (p. 70). This approach allows readers and researchers to grasp some sense of the whole narrator, complete with incoherence, inconsistency, and unpredictability. This self-consciousness in writing or "researcher reflexivity" speaks directly to the notion of multiple truths' or "realities".

Role of researcher

In their article, *"Working in the Interpretive Zone"*, Wasser and Bresler (1996) commented on the importance of the researcher's presence and how the interactions of the researcher with the participants serve to shape study outcomes. This shift, they say, is occurring in tandem with the increasing recognition of the collective nature of knowing and our greater attention to social theories of development. By working in *"the interpretive zone"* (Wasser & Bresler, 1996), multiple voices and viewpoints were encouraged, and participants had an opportunity to bring together their different kinds of knowledge, experiences, and beliefs, hopefully forging new meanings through the process of joint inquiry.

Chase (2005) took up the issue of researcher voice in narrative inquiry. She identified three types of voices that narrative researchers may use: an *"authoritative voice"*, *"a supportive voice"*, and an *"interactive voice"*. Authoritative voices separate researcher voice from the voices of the researched and usually follow the pattern of a textual presentation of "data" or narrative followed by a set of interpretations. Supportive researcher voices foreground the researcher's voice over the voices of the researched. Chase suggested that "because the goal of this narrative strategy is to bring the narrator's story to the public, researchers do not usually dwell on how they engaged in [the] interpretive process" (p. 665). Finally, interactive researcher voices seek to disrupt the notion of the all-knowing observer and author. It is with the interactive voice that all aspects of the research process, from the intriguing insights to the downright embarrassing moments are fully exposed. Chase wrote that the interactive voice "displays the complex interaction – the intersubjectivity – between researchers' and narrators' voices" (p. 666).

On a reflective note, Clandinin and Connelly (2000) remind the researcher that in doing narrative inquiry research we continually meet ourselves in past remembrances, present experiences and future dreams and, perhaps, even daydreams. In essence, they are saying:

> … as narrative inquirers we work within the space not only with our participants but also with ourselves. Working in this space means that we become visible with our own lived and told stories. Sometimes, this means that our own unnamed, perhaps secret, stories come to light as much as so those of our participants. This confronting of ourselves in our

narratives past makes us vulnerable as inquirers because it makes secret stories public. In narrative inquiry, it is impossible (or if not impossible, then deliberately self-deceptive) as researcher to stay silent or to present a kind of perfect, idealised, inquiring, moralising self. (p. 62)

Validating narratives

Riessman (1993) acknowledges that there is no single way of evaluating narrative research. She wrote, "There is no canonical approach in interpretive work, no recipes and formulas, and different validation procedures may be better suited to some research problems than others" (p. 69). Even so, she offered a few criteria for evaluation. First, she suggested that validation be conceived of as trustworthiness of the text. If the reader finds the text to be honest, it is a starting point for a positive evaluation. Riessman further noted the persuasiveness, coherence, and the pragmatic usefulness of the text as standards for evaluating the research. Noting the difficulty of establishing criteria for evaluating qualitative work, Sparkes (2002) recommends *verisimilitude*, rather than validity, as a starting point. The extent to which a story evokes a sense of truth within its readers is the foundation for the story's worth. Sparkes reviewed other scholars' views on evaluation, as well, and included in his list of possible evaluative criteria items such as *coherence, insightfulness, parsimony* (Lieblich et al., 1998); *fairness and authenticity* (Lincoln & Guba, 2000); *substantive contribution, esthetic merit, reflexivity, impact, and expression of a reality* (Richardson, 2000).

Narrative ethics

Narrative ethics as an ethical approach has begun to garner attention in a small but vibrant body of literature that has begun to emerge over the past few decades (Nelson, 2001). While there is no agreed upon definition of narrative ethics, nor any one academic discipline that can lay claim to it, many scholars concur that a central tenant of narrative ethics is the idea that narratives "figure importantly into the moral life" (Nelson 2001, p. 36). Moreover as Nelson elaborates, narrative ethics, "accords a central role to stories" (p. 36). But what does it mean to say that narratives figure into the moral life? Nelson (1997, 2001) claims that, from a philosophical perspective, it often means assigning moral significance to stories, not simply as examples or illustrations (although these are legitimate uses of stories for moral purposes as well as for narrative ethics), but rather as a "necessary means to some moral end" (p. 36).

Research Brief

Title: Playing with Stories: Sporting Narratives and the Deliberation of Moral Questions.
Who: Masucci, M.A. University of Tennessee

The purpose of this study was to examine the relationship between sporting narratives and morality. More specifically, Masucci investigated how people can draw upon sporting experiences, as expressed in narrative form, to help shape and inform their moral choices. He argued that sporting narratives play a crucial moral role due, in large part, to their pervasiveness and accessibility. Drawing from, and expanding on, the practical tradition of narrative ethics, and expanding upon Nelson's (2001) conception of the narrative counter-story, Masucci introduces two types of morally valuable sporting stories; *sport as autobiography* and *sport as reflexive narrative*. He also demonstrated how each type of sporting story can lead one to make morally estimable choices.

SPORT AS STORY AND NARRATIVE

There is a rich tradition of telling sporting *stories* in our culture, from local sporting myths to the valorization of certain athletes and the demonizing of others, in various newspaper, book, magazine, radio, television, and virtual accounts. Indeed, as Oriard (1993) claims in his book, *Reading Football*, "it seems obvious that every sporting season tells a story to its various fans: tale of hopes fulfilled or disappointed, of adversity overcome or unsurmounted, of aging heroics or youthful folly or sheer luck triumphant…the numerous plots are familiar" (p. 23). It is clear that sport figures importantly in and as narratives. Moreover, paying close attention to sporting narratives can often reveal insights into larger social and cultural meanings. As Gusfield (2000) suggests: "considering sports as a form of art, as telling and acting out stories within its own specific form, enables us to consider the elements that operate in creating meaning" (p. 70).

Butryn and Masucci (2003), in their investigation of Tour de France champion Lance Armstrong, have articulated the value of this "reorientation toward narrative inquiry" (p. 126), as it relates to examining the experiences of athletes and go on to claim that:

> By investigating the stories that athletes tell about themselves, researchers have been better able to understand the actions, motives, and conflicting identifications that impact and form an athlete's experience. Critical narrative approaches have helped sport studies researchers begin to make sense of the implications of "managing" multiple identifications against more traditional social expectations. Furthermore, narrative research that foregrounds the athlete's perspective, interpretation and evaluation of their own experiences,

has helped to facilitate a reconsideration of seemingly common-sense ideas about technology, masculinity, race, class, ability and sexual orientation. (pp. 126–127)

Within sport management research context *stories* are almost always less finished, less formal and less deliberated than the narrative. Stories and tales are casual, informal and contingent. Narratives are premeditated, organized, formal and have a structure that is their own.

Narrative inquiry is thus a reflective practice whereas *story* is not. And because it is a reflective practice narrative is connected, as story is not, with *authority*. The "narrator" is automatically endowed with power, with control over the material he or she presents, a power that flows to him or her through the position as organizer of the material. In moving from *"story"* to *"narrative"* it has become part of a reflective, self-conscious and interventionary process. In other words, to construct a narrative requires abstract thought. To write a narrative requires intellectual commitment and energy. Moreover, the construction of a narrative involves mediation upon social and ethical issues.

Sport management research *narratives* would mean not merely anecdotal, casual accounts, but involve a blending of theoretical with empirical or experiential materials. It is this capacity to connect theory with experience, to foreground the relationship between daily practice and knowledge, that makes narrative a vital tool for the future of sport management research inquiry. For example, a narrative approach to understanding the lived experiences of sport managers would allow the researcher to connect theory with experience and to establish a relationship between daily practice and knowledge. Moreover, by prompting sport managers to tell their stories, a deeper understanding of how professionals continue to grow and advance their sport management knowledge may be promoted. These narratives can also allow the sport management researcher to extend their understanding of how sport managers construct meaning. In this way, new insights may be derived about the practice of sport management which can be important to adding new knowledge for the discipline.

NARRATIVE AND VOICE

The concept of, *"voice"* is a central controlling metaphor in much of the recent writing in narrative inquiry. Syrjala and Estola (1999) for example use the term "telling and retelling", while Clandinin and Connelly (2000), prominent in contemporary works in this field, argue narrative to be the process by which researchers insert themselves into the story of another, for the purpose of giving that other a "voice". Viewed in this light, narratives are seen as mutual constructions, in which the researcher and participant work together, to produce a story, which is authentic.

Past research (Alvesson, 1993; Goodson, 1991; Schratz, 1993) has attempted to throw light upon the issue of the voices of marginalized groups within the society. In recent years, "many researchers have become disenchanted with the academic process of noise reduction" (Schratz, 1993, p. 1) by suppressing the more disturbing aspects of representing the individuality of human interaction. Recently, researchers have attempted to break down some of the established conventions of objectivity and highlight issues such as gender, race, homophobia, and socio-economic class by representing the marginalized voices within culture (Ball, 1989).

It can be argued that narrative inquiry has been valued by many, not only as a process for eliciting meaning from experience, but also as a legitimate methodological approach for addressing significant research questions. This is especially true for sport management researchers. If narratives do indeed encapsulate a wealth of experience embodied by sport managers and the complexity of understanding of what this type of management entails, then it is clear that narrative inquiry can provide an important platform for giving *voice* to sport managers, by encouraging them to tell their stories.

NARRATIVE AND REMINISCING

When engaged in narrative inquiry researchers have often been accused of using prior knowledge by reminiscing about their own life experiences. Sparkes (1995) refers to this process as *"narrative of self"* (p. 175). Porter and Washington (1993) remark: "the individual is not admitting to the self that he/she is denying the existence of things prior" (p.149). However, the self should be prepared to accept a situation of neutrality before the research begins. For example, the sport managers' life could be interpreted in the context of a narrative report and the act of reminiscing also becomes an important tool for representing the narrative of their life. In other words, the act of reminiscing can have a major effect on the final production of the narrative. Furthermore, and perhaps more importantly, reminiscing is the precursor to reflection which requires a deeper form of thought.

Another form of interference in the narrative comes from the acceptance of *nostalgia*. This can also function as an important perspective in the act of reminiscing. Thus, the nostalgic or positive thoughts of the past may lead some respondents to reminisce and over-emphasize the nature of certain points in the narrative. If the researcher has experienced similar occurrences the passage of narrative might take on a stronger significance than warranted within the text. Porter and Washington (1993) go further and argue that: … the very implicitness of nostalgia' leads one to assume that, previous knowledge and experience must affect the context and overall development of the narrative account of an individual's life or voice (p. 151). In short therefore, researchers should be aware that *nostalgia* may have some influence over the "truth" of the narrative.

Research Brief

Title: Endless punchers: Body, Narrative, and Performance in the World of Japanese Boxing
Who: Goodman, L.S., State University of New York at Buffalo
This study presented the personal "narratives" of professional boxers in Japan in documentary form through interview, participant observation, and research involving translation from Japanese texts. Through presenting in context and analyzing the stories of Japanese boxers, the study aimed to discover why they box, how they construct their identities as boxers and give meaning to their lives, their insights into and conceptions of boxing, and the roles they play in their performance of the sport.

NARRATIVE AND TRUTH

Hollway & Jefferson (2000) suggests the rules of narrative – the conventions of the game – make it difficult for a listener to question the narrative's content. Witten (1993) supports this comment by stating that:

> The presumption, encased in narrative, is shielded from testing or debate; it is a claim to validity that denies the need for justification or proof. In short, the narrative is a powerfully persuasive, presumed claim to truth and correctness that is not ordinarily subject to challenge. (p. 107)

So how can we be sure that the narrative has been written correctly and does not falsify the truth? It appears as though all the normal conventions of interpretative research are followed when writing the narrative, cross checking by the use of triangulation and rereading by the subject can counteract any contradictions of the truth. However, if working in isolation the narrative discourse utilized often relies on its "truth" by the reputation of the writer.

Narrative Case Study

Who: Dr. Allan Edwards (Griffith University), Dr. James Skinner (Griffith University), Dr. Keith Gilbert (University of East London)

What: Sport Management: Varying Directions towards the Narrative

Theoretical framework

Edwards, Skinner and Gilbert utilized narrative inquiry of sport managers to explore what sport managers believe are the core issues that can contribute to successful sport management practice. This narrative approach to understanding the lived experiences of sport managers allowed the researchers to connect theory with experience and to establish a relationship between daily practice and knowledge. It was suggested that understanding the lived experiences of sport managers in this way can allow sport managers to establish new insights into how they interact with their sport organizations and the individuals and communities they serve in their daily operations. This study also highlighted how narrative can be used to enhance a sport manager's understanding of their work environment through critical reflection.

Data collection methods

Edwards, Skinner and Gilbert conducted focus group meetings with sport managers over a period of 10 months. These series of narrative events addressed the overriding issues that the participating sport managers believed provided a unique insight into their everyday lives and the results highlighted some of the major difficulties in their reasoning and provided areas of concern which could be utilized in further research studies.

Typically, in qualitative research methodology, the researchers try to listen first to the practitioners' stories. However, Edwards, Skinner and Gilbert acknowledge that in this research they tried telling and responding to participants' stories concurrently. In this way they believed that they were able to expand on and extend the subjects' stories by adding their own experiences and reflections. By sharing stories, and remaining open to the variety and eloquence of others' stories, Edwards, Skinner and Gilbert pursued a narrative reflection on practice that Schon (1983) discussed as critical to professional development. Audio taping allowed the researchers to preserve the rapport they had developed and concentrate fully on the responses and use these as a basis for further questioning.

Data analysis techniques/presentation

Edwards, Skinner and Gilbert utilized specific critical incidents and experiences to examine the core issues that contribute to successful sport management practice. The research drew on the narrative experiences of sport managers to provide a unique insight into their everyday lives and experiences. The conclusions drawn from this research were therefore based upon the day to day practical experiences of the participants in their work environment.

Major findings

In summary, this research found that the overriding issues that the participating sport managers believed provided a unique insight into their everyday lives centered on: (1) experience and power, (2) accountability; (3) demands of the job; (4) professional development; (5) ways of knowing; (6) collegiality; and (7) critical reflection.

The research concluded by suggesting that through an increased interest in narrative the stories disclosed may move other sport managers to share their own stories and experiences to assist in framing their own identity. Moreover, by prompting other sport managers to tell their stories, a deeper understanding of how professionals continue to grow and advance their sport management knowledge may be promoted. These narratives also taught the researchers about deepening and extending their personal understanding of how sport managers construct meaning.

Suggestions for future research

By examining how sport managers deal with their experiences and how their involvement in their sport organization has created a dominant set of meanings about what constitutes sport management practice, this research showed how critical reflection through the sharing of lived experiences can be beneficial to the development of sport management knowledge. Edwards, Skinner and Gilbert argue that the use of critical reflection and narrative are strong paradigms which could be utilized together to produce research previously not encountered in sport management research. Moreover, they suggested that the sharing of narratives helps shape and frame the unique experiences of sport managers and assist them ultimately in understanding the complex nature of the practitioner's world. They propose that this process of writing, sharing, reflection and analysis should lead to improved sport management practice and improved leadership qualities and should therefore be utilized to further investigate the daily lives of sport management practitioners.

Case study research probes

1. Edwards, Skinner and Gilbert use "Narrative" to gain an understanding of the lived experiences of sport managers. How can they be sure that the data they have collected is an accurate representation of these experiences?

2. Do you feel that by engaging with the "narrative dialog" of the sport managers the researchers were able to expand on and extend the subjects' stories by adding their own experiences and reflections, or alternatively, may have guided the discussion away from the experiences the sport managers wanted to share? Discuss.

CONCLUSION

Unlike more traditional research methods, narrative inquiry captures aspects of personal and human lives that cannot be "quantified into facts and numerical data" (Clandinin & Connelly, 2000, p. 19). Narrative inquiry is a tool that arranges lived experiences to make them comprehensible, memorable and shareable. Because narratives rely strongly on communication and relationships, they can facilitate connections between people and create a sense of "shared history".

Narrative inquiry as a research methodology can engage the researcher in reflective practice of lived experiences and can provide a means for sport management researchers to understand the complex nature of the sport practitioner's world. This narrative process of writing, sharing, reflection and analysis may improve sport management knowledge and practice.

IN PROFILE - Associate Professor Bob Stewart

Bob Stewart is an Associate Professor of sport management at Victoria University, Melbourne, Australia. He has undertaken an array of qualitative research projects that use methodologies framed around document analysis and in-depth interviews. One of his most extensive studies involved an examination of the commercial and administrative evolution of first class cricket in Australia from 1945 to 1980. The minute books of the Australian Board of Control for Australian Cricket were used as a platform for the analysis of the board's decision making systems, and interviews were used to illuminate the political processes that shaped the game's development. Archival documents and interviews also provided extensive data on the relationships that developed between the game's key stakeholders, which included the players, administrators, ground managers, the Australian Broadcasting Commission, commercial television station operators, and corporate sponsors. Bob also used document analysis and interviews to generate data for his

Continued

ongoing examination of the national progress of Australian Rules football in general, and the Australian Football League in particular. Again, he was able to secure extensive archival material that explained not only the ways in which administrative structures and systems developed, but also the impact these structures and systems had on the strategic direction of the game, and how the game adjusted to the expansion of rugby and soccer. As a way of understanding the game's shifting national fortunes from the 1930s to the1960s Bob trawled the minute books of the games national governing body, the Australian National Football Council. These documents provide a rich foundation of contextual forces and strategic initiatives that gave sharp and revealing insights into the factors that shaped the game's development during this time. Bob's most recent research project involves the analysis of the ways in which drugs are used and managed in Australian sport. Working with Professor Aaron Smith, his research colleague from Latrobe University in Melbourne, Bob has developed a methodology built upon narrative analysis, which involves the use of detailed in-depth interviews to construct life histories for the informants, which in the first stage of this study is confined to elite athletes and players. Bob chose a narrative analysis method in order to ensure a strong chronological progression where athletes and players were encouraged to identify pivotal and critical incidents that (1) impacted on their values and attitudes about contemporary sport, and (2) shaped their own individual athletic development. It also allowed them to speak candidly about the role that drugs played in their sport, and the extent to which it posed a problem for the credibility and reputation of their sport. Bob is a great believer in the value of qualitative research in sport management, and how it can provide a rich vein of data by (1) providing a strong context within which to examine the roles played by key stakeholders in shaping the strategic direction of a sport, and (2) drawing out the deeper values and beliefs of the various stakeholders, and the ways they can shape its subsequent structures, systems, culture, and conduct.

REVIEW AND RESEARCH QUESTIONS

Narrative inquiry is a qualitative research methodology that aims to highlight how they can provide rich descriptions of the sport management environment. With an understanding of the key elements of narrative inquiry attempt to answer the following questions:

1. Distinguish between "story" "narrative" and "voice", and in doing so, identify their relevance to narrative research.

2. Discuss the importance of critical reflection to the process of narrative inquiry.

3. Identify three ways in which narrative inquiry can be used in sport management research?

REFERENCES

Alvesson, M. 1993. Cultural Perspectives on Organizations. Cambridge: Cambridge University Press.

Ball, S. 1989. The Micro-Politics of Teaching. UK: Falmer Press.

Bloom, L. R. & Munro, P. 1995. Conflicts of selves: nonunitary subjectivity in women administrators' life history narratives. In: *Life History and Narrative* (Ed. by J. A. Hatch, R. Wisniewski), pp. 99–112. London: Falmer Press.

Bochner, A. 2001. Narratives' virtues. *Qualitative Inquiry*, **7** (2), 131–157.

Brown, N. 2001. The imputation of authenticity in the assessment of student performances in art. *Educational Philosophy and Theory*, **33** (3–4), 293–305.

Bruner, J. 1986. Actual Minds, Possible Worlds. Cambridge, MA: Harvard University Press.

Bruner, J. 1991. Acts of Meaning. Cambridge, MA: Harvard University Press.

Butryn, T. & Masucci, M. 2003. It's not about the book: a cyborg counternarrative of Lance Armstrong. *Journal of Sport & Social Issues*, **27** (2), 124–144.

Chase, S. E. 2005. Narrative inquiry: multiple lenses, approaches, voices. In: *Handbook of Qualitative Research* (Ed. by N. K. Denzin, Y. S. Lincoln), pp. 651–680, 3rd ed. Thousand Oaks, CA: Sage.

Clandinin, D. J. & Connelly, F. M. 2000. Narrative Inquiry: Experience and Story in Qualitative Research. San Francisco: Jossey-Bass.

Dewey, J. 1933. How We Think. Chicago: Regnery.

Edwards, A. 1999. Reflective practices in sport management. *Sport Management Review*, **2** (1), 67–81.

Fairclough, N. 1992. Discourse and Social Change. Malden, MA: Blackwell.

Goodson, I. F. 1991. Studying Teachers Lives. London: Routledge.

Gubrium, J. F. & Holstein, J. A. 2001. From an individual interview to the interview society. In: *Handbook of Interview Research: Context and Method* (Ed. by J. F. Gubrium, J. A. Holstein), pp. 3–32. Thousand Oaks, CA: Sage.

Gusfield, J. 2000. Sport as story: form and content in athletics. *Society*, **37** (4), 63–70.

Hollway, W. & Jefferson, T. 2000. Doing Qualitative Research Differently. London: Sage.

Josselson, R. 1996. On writing other people's lives: self-analytic reflections of a narrative researcher. In: *Ethics and Process in the Narrative Study of Lives* (Ed. by R. Josselson), pp. 60–71. Thousand Oaks, CA: Sage.

Lieblich, A., Tuval-Mashiach, R. & Zilber, R. 1998. Narrative Research. Thousand Oaks, CA: Sage.

Lincoln, Y. S. & Guba, E. G. 2000. Paradigmatic controversies, contradictions, and emerging confluences. In: *Handbook of Qualitative Research* (Ed. by N. K. Denzin, Y. S. Lincoln), pp. 163–188, 2nd ed. Thousand Oaks, CA: Sage.

McCormack, B. 2002. "Removing the chaos from the narrative": preparing clinical leaders for practice development. *Educational Action Research*, **10** (3), 335–351.

Mishler, E. G. 1995. Models of narrative analysis: a typology. *Journal of Narrative and Life History*, **5** (2), 87–123.

Moustakas, C. 1990. Heuristic Research: Design, Methodology and Applications. London: Sage.

Nelson, H. L. 2001. Damaged Identities: Narrative Repair. Ithaca: Cornell University Press.

Nelson, H. L. (Ed.). 1997. Stories and Their Limits: Narrative Approaches to Bioethics. New York: Routledge.

Oriard, M. 1993. Reading Football: How the Popular Press Created an American Spectacle. Chapel Hill: University of North Carolina Press.

Porter, J. R. & Washington, R. E. 1993. Minority identity and self-esteem. *Annual Review of Sociology*, **19**, 139–161.

Richardson, L. 2000. Writing: a method of inquiry. In: *The Handbook of Qualitative Research* (Ed. by N. K. Denzin, Y. S. Lincoln), pp. 923–948, 2nd ed. Thousand Oaks, CA: Sage.

Riessman, C. K. 1993. Narrative Analysis. Newbury Park, CA: Sage.

Schon, D. 1983. The Reflective Practitioner: How professionals think in action. London: Temple Smith.

Schratz, M. 1993. Conversation and narrative in collaborative research: an ethnography of the written literacy. *Mind, Culture, and Activity*, **1**, 209–229.

Sparkes, A. 1995. Writing people: reflections on the dual crises of representation and legitimation in qualitative inquiry. *Quest*, **47** (2), 158–195.

Sparkes, A. C. 2002. Telling Tales in Sport and Physical Activity: A Qualitative Journey. Champaign: Human Kinetics.

Stein, H. F. 1997. Death imagery and the experience of organizational downsizing. *Administration & Society*, **29**, 222–247.

Syrjala, L. & Estola, E. 1999. Telling and retelling stories as a way to construct teachers' identities and to understand teaching. Paper presented at the European Conference on Educational Research, Lahti, Finland. Retrieved February 27, 2008 from http://www.leeds.ac.uk/educol/documents/00001311.htm

Wasser, J. D. & Bresler, L. 1996. Working in the interpretative zone: conceptualizing collaboration in qualitative research teams. *Educational Researcher*, **25** (5), 5–15.

Witten, M. 1993. Narrative and the culture of the workplace. In: *Narrative and Social Control: Critical Perspectives* (Ed. by D. M. Mumby), pp. 97–118. Newbury Park, CA: Sage.

CHAPTER 19

Phenomenology and Sport Management Research

OBJECTIVES

By the end of this chapter, you should be able to

- understand the basic concepts of phenomenology.

- identify the implications of the use of phenomenological methodology in sport management.

KEY TERMS

Descriptive phenomenology: a direct description of phenomena aimed at maximum intuitive content;

Essential (eidetic) phenomenology: seeks to explain essences and their relationships;

Phenomenology of appearances: attends to the ways in which phenomena appear.

Constitutive phenomenology: studies processes whereby phenomena become established in our consciousness.

Reductive phenomenology: relies on suspending belief in the reality or validity of phenomena.

Hermeneutic phenomenology: a phenomenological interpretation which seeks to unveil hidden meanings in phenomena;

Phenomenological reduction: during which attention is narrowed, the superfluous and accidental are ignored, whilst previous prejudice about the world is set aside (also referred to as epoche or bracketing).

KEY QUESTIONS

The key questions raised in this chapter are as follows:

- What is "Phenomenology"?

- What is the difference between Husserl and Heidegger's interpretations of phenomenon?

- Can phenomenology be used as a research methodology in sport management research?

CHAPTER OVERVIEW

This chapter explores the methodology of phenomenology and looks at some possible applications in the field of sport management research. Phenomenology seeks to explore and understand the lived experience of its participants. In sport management literature, phenomenology offers researchers a different perspective and opportunity to explore previously unchartered waters. This chapter will provide an introduction and overview to the major concepts of phenomenology as well as provide some suggestions as to possible frameworks from which to apply the phenomenological methodology to sport management research.

DEFINITION OF PHENOMENOLOGY

Phenomenology is difficult to define simply. The term "phenomenology" is derived from two Greek words: *phainomenon* and *logos*. *Phainomenon* is defined as "appearance" (Spinelli, 1989; Steware & Mickunas, 1990), anything which shows itself (Heidegger, 1962; Spinelli, 1989), without involving "any sense of the strange or spectacular" (Hammond et al., 1991, p. 1). *Logos*, meaning "reason" or "word", leads to one definition of phenomenology as "a reasoned inquiry which discovers the inherent essences of appearances" (Steware & Mickunas, 1990, p. 3).

PHENOMENOLOGY AS A METHODOLOGY

Phenomenology is a qualitative research methodology which has become increasingly employed in social science research, and has the potential to be used with great effectiveness in the field of sport management research.

Edmund Husserl is the acknowledged founder of modern phenomenology and the principal figure in the development of the phenomenological method (Steware & Mickunas, 1990). Husserl held the view that, in striving to build up an objective view of reality, scientific practice has progressively cut off subjective experience from the life-world to such an extent that Western man is in a permanent state of crisis, that is, he feels that science is the only source of facts, and loses consequently his lived relation to the historical and social reality of life (Husserl, 1970). Husserl therefore introduced the concept of the "Life-world" or "Lived experience" which constitutes what is taken for granted or those things which are common sense (Koch, 1995).

Husserl's phenomenology, in describing phenomena, has to cope with the essences of our subjective experience. To reach this essence, one has to go through a multiplicity of possible profiles which convey meaning, the essence (*eidos*) being the sum of all possible profiles (Thines, 1987). For Husserl, all experience could be transformed into its essence through a process of *eidetic intuition* which is the activity of seeing into the essence of a thing (Taylor, 1991).

One of the more contentious aspects of Husserl's work is the notion of bracketing or *epoche* which holds that the point of view of natural science is to be left out of consideration or set aside. This is his act of phenomenological **reduction,** during which attention is narrowed, the superfluous and accidental are ignored, whilst previous prejudice about the world is set aside.

Martin Heidegger was Husserl's student, who then reinterpreted phenomenology and its methods. Heidegger argues that the observer cannot be separated from the world, and that an understanding of the person cannot occur in isolation from the person's world (van Manen, 1990; Walters, 1995). Heidegger's emphasis is on *being-in-the-world* **(dasein)** and how phenomena present themselves in lived experience, in human existence (van Manen, 1990). He argued that Husserl's attempt to describe everything as correlates of consciousness overlooked basic dimensions of human existence such as dread, anxiety, forlornness and death. Heidegger also argued with bracketing as the method of investigating these aspects of existence and instead, wanted to find "the basic modalities of being-in-the-world" (Steware & Mickunas, 1990, p. 69). So, for Heidegger, phenomenology was ontology, a study of the modes of being-in-the-world of human beings. Heidegger's aim was to let the things of the world speak for themselves and asked, "What is the nature of this being?" (van Manen, 1990, p. 184). Heidegger's phenomenology, therefore, is an explication of the meaning of being.

The method that Heidegger used for this explication of being was *hermeneutics* (from the Greek word for "interpretation") which he considered as one of the processes which people use in making sense of their everyday lives (Walters, 1994). He argued that hermeneutics presupposes prior understanding on the part of the interpreter and that it is only possible to interpret something according to one's own lived experience (Walters, 1995). Heidegger coined the term the hermeneutic circle. In simple terms, the hermeneutic circle represents a text, contained within a larger circle which represents all aspects of a particular culture. Both circles are then included with another, larger circle, which is human existence itself. The hermeneutic circle opens up interpretations of the human condition which can lead to an understanding of the possibilities of being.

Additionally, Heidegger's phenomenology differs from Husserlian phenomenology in relation to bracketing. Instead of bracketing or removing presuppositions, Heidegger's phenomenology attempts to discover and explain historical situations and concepts – those aspects of culture that affect the way we view and understand the world. As culture is already in the world prior to a person's existence, a pre-understanding already exists prior to any story being brought to a particular situation. People therefore encounter the world with reference to their own background understanding, and therefore their interpretation of their lived experience will reflect this background.

The value of phenomenology for a sport management researcher is that it serves as a theoretical framework that privileges participants lived experience (Levesque-Lopman, 1988). As such, phenomenological sport management researchers seek to learn what is central to the phenomena being studied (Donalek, 2004). Sport management research done from a phenomenological perspective can allow participants to communicate their experience without the meaning being significantly altered by the sport management researcher and can aid in the empowerment of participants by encouraging them to speak about their own experiences (Levesque-Lopman, 1988).

The differences between the philosophies of Husserlian and Heideggerian phenomenology impact their use as research methodologies. While Husserlian phenomenology is a descriptive methodology (Rogers, 1983), Heideggerian phenomenology rests on an interpretive process (Cohen & Ornery, 1994). These contrasting perspectives on phenomenology are outlined in Table 19.1.

From its beginnings, the catch-cry of phenomenology has been "To the things themselves" indicating that its intent is to uncover, explore and

Table 19.1   Comparing and Contrasting two Theories of Phenomenology Interpretation

Husserlian Phenomenology	Heideggerian Phenomenology
Transcendental phenomenology	Philosophical hermeneutics Hermeneutic phenomenology
Epistemological	Existential–ontological
Epistemological questions of knowing	Questions of experiencing and understanding
How do we know what we know?	What does it mean to be a person?
Cartesian duality: mind–body split	Emphasis is on being-in-the-world (Dasein)
A mechanistic view of the person	Person as self-interpreting being
Mind–body person lives in a world objects	Person exists as a "being" in and of the world
A historical	Historicality
Unit of analysis is the meaning giving subject	Unit of analysis is the transaction between the situation and the person
What is shared is the essence of the conscious mind	What is shared is culture, history, practice, language

Table 19.1 Comparing and Contrasting two Theories of Phenomenology Interpretation *continued*

Husserlian Phenomenology	Heideggerian Phenomenology
Starts with a reflection of mental states	We are already in the world in our pre-reflexive selves
Meaning is unsullied by the interpreter's own normative goals or view of the world	Interpreters participate in making data
Participants' meanings can be reconstituted in interpretive work by insisting that the data speak for themselves	Within the fore-structure of understanding interpretation can only make explicit what is already understood
Claim that adequate techniques and procedures guarantee validity of interpretation	Establish own criteria for trustworthiness of research
Bracketing defends the validity or objectivity of the interpretation against self-interest	The hermeneutic circle (background, co-constitution, pre-understanding)

Source: Koch (1995, p. 832)

describe the "uncensored phenomena" of the things themselves, as they are immediately given (Spiegelberg, 1970). Husserl's (1970) primary objective was to develop "apodietic" foundations (i.e., those evident beyond contradiction, Webster Dictionary, 1977, p. 39) for all human science and, indeed, for human knowledge of any kind. As such, he proposed a method for achieving such a return "to the things themselves" which Kearney (1994) describes as "complex and indeed manifold" (p. 18) and which Husserl presented in a different way in each of his major works. As summarized by Kearney (1994), this method involves five principle phases.

1. Bracketing – suspension of the presuppositions imposed by culture and tradition.

2. Reduction is achieved when the researcher is able to review the real-life interactions before they are overlaid by objectifying constructs.

3. Free variation occurs when meaning is no longer confined but unfolds without the above constraints.

4. Intuition of the essential nature of the phenomenon.

5. A description of the essential structure of the phenomenon.

Through this process, Kearney suggests the basic nature of the phenomena can be revealed.

Heidegger's hermeneutical approach to phenomenology had a considerable influence on the development of existential phenomenology. In his hermeneutical work, Heidegger employed two notions, the hermeneutic circle and historicality of understanding. These notions have influenced contemporary hermeneutics and need to be understood in view of Heidegger's (1977) often cited claim that humans cannot have a world and a life at a sociocultural level except through acts of interpretation. Although not directly included in contemporary discussions of phenomenological methodology, these two notions do much to clarify the underlying assumptions of this hermeneutic phenomenological study in the existential mode.

Reference is often made to European and American Continental Phenomenology, which will only be briefly referred to here. Husserl is considered to be of the European Phenomenology School, whilst Heidegger's views accord more with those of the Continental American phenomenologists. Basically, two major differences exist between the American continental and traditional European approaches to phenomenology. The first of these is that the American continental phenomenological question does not seek for "pre-reflective" experience but includes thoughts and interpretations of experience of the phenomenon in the data collection and analysis. Secondly, American continental analysis focuses on describing participants' lived experience within the context of culture rather than searching for the universal or unchanging meaning of it outside the cultural context as a means of understanding the phenomenon. These differences are further highlighted in Table 19.2.

Table 19.2 Summary of the Differences Between European and American Continental Phenomenology

	European Phenomenology	American Continental Phenomenology
The value of lived experience	"Lived experience" is used as a tool to access phenomena.	Allows investigation of lived-experience itself - experience is explored in its own right.
The way experience is viewed	Seeks pre-reflective experience of phenomena.	Seeks descriptions of experience per se.
	Interpretations and thoughts not included.	Interpretations and thoughts included
The way culture is viewed	Regarded with suspicion	Unchallenged
Assumptions	Phenomena may have universal meanings.	Although not stated, it appears that phenomenal meanings may be constructed culturally.
Epistemology	Constructivist	Constructivist but with somewhat more subjective orientation. There is more focus on individual knowledge based on personal experience.
	Knowledge is regarded as a blend of experience and reason.	

Despite the dynamic and diverse ways in which the phenomenological approach to philosophy has been applied, Steware and Mickunas (1990) suggest that phenomenological philosophy can be characterized as centering on the following basic themes:

- a return to the traditional tasks of philosophy – to articulate the questions arising out of the depths of the human spirit itself, and to develop knowledge and understanding of men and women and their relationship to the world;

- the search for a philosophy without presuppositions – phenomenology aims to suspend assumptions about the nature of reality while turning to the content of consciousness itself, the phenomena;

- the intentionality of consciousness – which holds that consciousness is always directed toward an object, and is often expressed as consciousness is consciousness of, and is tied to the world of experience;

- the refusal of the subject–object dichotomy – by shifting attention from the question of the reality of the world to its meaning as phenomena, the distance between consciousness and its content is overcome.

Van Manen (1990) uses an eclectic approach which he calls *hermeneutic phenomenology*. He outlined the essentials of phenomenological research as

- The study of lived experience.

- The explication of phenomena as they present themselves to consciousness, rather than as conceptualized, categorized or theorized.

- The study of essences of experience which asks, not "how", but rather, what is the "nature" of the experience.

- The description of experiential meanings we live as we live them, examples of which are designed to enable us to see the structure or the deeper significance of the experience being described.

- The human scientific study of phenomena in that it is systematic, explicit, intersubjective, self-critical and examines structures of the lived, human world (rather than the natural world).

- The attentive practice of thoughtfulness whose language awakens a person to the meaning of the experience.

- A search for what it means to be human, which may be achieved by more deeply understanding human experience.

- A poetizing activity insofar as its language reverberates the world rather than speaking "of" it, and so the poem itself is the result rather than a conclusion or summary of the phenomenological study.

Van Manen (1990) spoke of there being no "method" as such if this is understood as a set of procedures, but rather of "ways" or "paths" leading to "clearings". These paths cannot be determined by fixed signposts – they need to be discovered or invented as a response to the question in hand. He spoke, however, of a "tradition" – a set of guides and recommendations which forms the basis of a principled form of enquiry. This tradition is presented as "methodological structure" in which hermeneutic phenomenological research is seen as a dynamic interplay among six research activities. These are as follows:

1. turning to a phenomenon which seriously interests us and converts us to the world;

2. investigating experience as we live it rather than as we conceptualize it;

3. reflecting on the essential themes which characterize the phenomenon;

4. describing the phenomenon through the art of writing and rewriting;

5. maintaining a strong and oriented pedagogical relation to the phenomenon;

6. balancing the research context by considering parts and whole. (pp. 30–31).

PREPOSITIONS AND GENERAL STEPS OF THE PHENOMENOLOGICAL RESEARCH PROCESS

Spiegelberg (1976) and Parse et al. (1985) articulated the general steps of the phenomenological research process to be as follows:

1. *Investigating the particular phenomena.* There are three operations, which constitute the major processes of phenomenological analysis, including: intuiting, analyzing, and describing. They are closely related and though discrete, they occur simultaneously. The researcher lives these processes all-at-once while dwelling with the participants' descriptions of the phenomenon. Intuiting is coming to know the phenomenon as described by the participant; analyzing is the intentional tracing of the phenomenon's elements and structure in order to come to know the nature of the lived experience; and describing is the process of affirming the connection between the phenomenon

and what is written about it, thus culminating in an elaboration of the meaning of the elements and the structure of the lived experience.

2. *Investigating the general essences.* This occurs through eidetic intuiting, where the researcher examines the particulars reflecting on the remembered experiences as written by the participant leading to apprehension of general essences.

3. *Apprehending the essential relationships among essences.* This process involves the examination of the internal relationships between the particulars in a single general essence and relationships among several general essences.

4. *Watching modes of appearing.* This process includes exploration of the way in which something appears, which is significant to understanding the phenomenon as a whole, as it unfolds through dwelling with the participants' descriptions.

5. *Watching the constitution of phenomena in consciousness.* This is an activity of exploring the phenomenon through the process of integrating the familiar with the unfamiliar.

6. *Suspending belief in the existence of the phenomena.* This process is also known as bracketing where the researcher suspends beliefs about a specific phenomenon. The researcher holds in abeyance any preconceived notions about the phenomenon of interest. (As described earlier, this particular step is the foundation of conflicting opinions between phenomenological researchers.)

7. *Interpreting the meaning of the phenomena.* Hermeneutical interpretation is the final activity in the phenomenological analysis process. It is an attempt to interpret the sense of the phenomenon. There is a shift in the level of discourse from the concrete to the abstract.

PHENOMENOLOGY AND SPORT MANAGEMENT

Both the traditional European and the American continental approaches to phenomenology, and indeed the different approaches of Husserl and Heidgger, have value to the field of sport management research. Husserl's approach has value in that it critically analyzes phenomena as they present in sport and sport management, and in doing so, provides for deeper understanding of the universal meanings of the phenomena that occur in these fields. The American continental approach has merit for two reasons: Firstly, it is in keeping with the trend toward more human research in the postmodern world in which people live and in which research is conducted. Secondly, the reorientation of phenomenology toward human science rather than the more "critical" approach of traditional phenomenology (Crotty, 1995) clearly addresses some of the more under-explored areas in sport management research such as the lived experiences of athletes attempting to excel in a non-traditional gender specific sport, or the daily experiences of a sport manager operating at an elite level in a worldwide sporting event, where the researcher seeks to understand the human condition as much as the lived experience of the phenomena itself. For this reason, such research can lead one in the direction of uncovering the meaning of lived experience from the subjective perspectives of the persons who participate. This approach therefore has the ability to foster understanding of many of the complex and perplexing conditions in which sport managers find themselves.

Sports management researchers have already effectively utilized the phenomenological hermeneutic research method when studying human experiences.

Taking the cases of the moves of the Toronto Maple Leafs and the Montreal Canadiens from Maple Leaf Gardens and the Montreal Forum, respectively, Gunderson (2004) utilized a "radical interpretive" approach, involving a critical blend of interpretive theories and methodologies – including semiology, phenomenology, hermeneutics, and dialectical analysis. McAllister (2006) utilized phenomenology to explore how women administrators perceive the benefits of competitive sport experiences.

Several recent research projects addressing the experiences of athletes have also been conducted. These include Czech et al.'s (2004) investigation of athletes' experience of Christian prayer in sport, Dale's (1994) research on elite decathletes' experiences during their most memorable competition, Johnson's (1998) investigation of athletes' experiences of being coached, and Holt's (2003) examination of the coping experience of a professional athlete.

Existential phenomenology appears to be particularly relevant for sport management researchers because one of the four existential grounds of a person's life experience is the body or, to be more precise, the lived body (Pollio et al., 1997). Ironically, relatively little is known about the nature of athletes' lived experiences and its implications for the sport manager. In much the same way as Thompson et al. (1989) contended that consumer research needs to look at consumer's experiences, it might be argued that sport management research needs to examine athletes' experiences to better understand certain athletic phenomena and how the sport manager might develop strategies to cater to these phenomena.

In sport management research, the phenomenological method can attempt to identify and describe the "what" of particular experiences, or what it is actually like to experience something. An in-depth understanding of athletes' experiences could be especially helpful for anyone involved or interested in athletes' lives; be it the coach, sport administrators, friends and family, sports psychology consultants, the media, or the general public. Additionally, rich descriptions of athletes' experiences derived by means of a phenomenological research approach could add to, deepen, or even correct findings obtained in quantitative studies. As Polkinghorne (1989) points out, such revised or expanded understandings could eventually even result in public policy or social changes.

Beyond the athlete, an in-depth understanding of the experience of sport managers across the breadth of responsibility – from local clubs to an International event such as the Olympic games – can provide understanding into the cross-cultural, gender, economic, organizational, interpersonal, and political minefields that the modern sport manager has to traverse on a daily basis.

Research Brief

Title: A Phenomenological Exploration of the Sport-Career Transition Experiences that affect Subjective Well-Being of Former National Football League Players.

Who: Coakley, S.C., The University of North Carolina

Theoretical framework

The purpose of this study was to understand and provide insights into the dynamics of the sport-career transition experiences of former National Football League athletes and examine how subjective well-being is influenced by this developmental stage. Coakley utilized the interpretive tradition of phenomenology and the Conceptual Model of Adaptation to Career Transition as the theoretical framework. Using interview data and the Satisfaction with Life Scale, this study examined the experiences of former National Football League players who reside in North Carolina and began retirement at some point between the 1999 professional football season and June 2005. These findings reveal that former National Football League players experience a time of mild to severe adjustment during the sport-career transition.

METHOD AND SPORT MANAGEMENT EXAMPLE

Below is an example of a phenomenological research approach to a sport management topic using a phenomenological method. The topic is The experiences of a team Manager at the Beijing Olympic Games.

Step 1 – choosing a topic – The topic is chosen. *The experiences of team Managers at the Beijing Olympic Games*

Step 2 – *The bracketing interview*

Once a topic has been chosen and the phenomenological method has been determined to be the most appropriate approach for addressing it, the focus shifts to the participant. To sharpen this focus, a bracketing interview is conducted. During this interview, the primary investigator is interviewed by another researcher familiar with the phenomenological research process. The purpose of the bracketing interview is to explore possible personal biases of the sport management researcher. Bracketing should be considered as an ongoing process during the research project where the sport management researcher continually reflects upon, brackets, and intuits his/her biases. Hector (2003) points out that a bracketing interview is only a first step in an attempt to achieve a suspension of the natural attitude. Besides being aware of his or her own presuppositions and biases regarding the topic, the researcher brackets those biases by using the participant's words, rather than his/her own, when interviewing participants and summarizing their experience. In summary, then, the goal of the bracketing interview is for the sport management researcher to identify his or her presuppositions from the very outset of the research project (Dale, 1996). By making biases visible, the sport management researcher is positioned to be a good listener during the interview process and is less likely to mix his or her own beliefs with the experience of the participant (Thomas & Pollio, 2002).

Step 3 – *Interviewing participants*

The third step in the phenomenological research process is the actual phenomenological interviews (Thomas & Pollio, 2002). Here, the focus is on the participants and their first-person description of the specific lived experience of being a Sport Manager at the Beijing Olympic Games.

Following an initial open-ended question regarding the participant's recollection of the experience, the interview follows the direction given by the participant. The dialog between the interviewer and participant is more circular than linear in nature (Dale, 1996). Thus, it resembles a conversation more than a question and answer session (Thompson et al., 1989). To achieve this conversational dialog, the sport management researcher asks probing follow-up questions to clarify statements or to obtain a more detailed description of certain experiences. Whenever possible, the interviewer uses the participant's own vocabulary when asking these questions. As noted earlier, this is another way the sport management researcher can assure the bracketing of his/her biases (Hector, 2003).

The sport management researcher might also summarize what the participant has said as a way of obtaining clarification (Thomas & Pollio, 2002). The interview concludes once the participant agrees that he or she has described his or her experience in as much detail as possible and that there is nothing else that "stood out" to him or her about the experience. The researcher then summarizes once more what he/she has heard the participant say regarding his or her experience in order to obtain final confirmation.

Step 4 – *data analysis*

After conducting and audiotaping the interview, the sport management researcher uses analysis procedures, such as those described by Dale (1996), Thomas and Pollio (2002), and Polkinghorne (1989) to thematize the data. As Polkinghorne points out, "the aim of phenomenological inquiry is to reveal and unravel the structures, logic, and interrelationships that obtain in the phenomenon under inspection" (p. 50). Dale (1996) suggests that the researcher maintain a methodological log throughout the duration of the study, making notes on his/her thought processes, reasoning, and specific actions undertaken throughout the research project. The steps of data analysis include transcribing and the hermeneutic circle.

Step 4.1 – *transcribing*

The audiotaped interviews are transcribed verbatim, paying close attention to pauses, laughter or other noticeable phenomena during the interview (Thomas & Pollio, 2002). Whenever possible, the sport management researcher should transcribe the audiotaped interviews himself or herself. This allows the sport management researcher to engage the data, containing participants' descriptions of their experiences. Transcribing the interviews himself or herself also enables the sport management researcher to begin the process of data analysis by trying to interpret parts of the text in relation to other parts.

Step 4.2 – *the hermeneutic circle*

In general, the concept of the hermeneutic circle helps to overcome "the seemingly linear character of reading by having an interpreter understand earlier portions of the text in relation to latter portions and, conversely, understand latter portions in the context of preceding ones" (Pollio et al., 1997, p. 49). Smith (1998) notes continuous bracketing by the researcher facilitates the hermeneutic process. Valle et al. (1989) point out that "the ability to deepen one's understanding of the text has to do with one's willingness and ability to reflect one's own *pre-understanding* of the text" (p. 15).

Valle et al. suggest that such reflection should lead researchers/readers to ask themselves questions like: "What have I already assumed which may account for my failure to make sense of this section" (p. 16)? By continuously asking and answering such questions, the sport management researcher maintains a more heightened self-awareness when interviewing participants and also when interpreting the interviews.

Step 5 – *reporting findings to participants*

During the last step of the phenomenological research process the focus shifts back to the participant (Thomas & Pollio, 2002). Here the sport management researcher gives participants an opportunity to review the thematic structure describing their experience and provide feedback as to how accurately and completely the structure does so. This step is important in securing the study's validity (Dale, 1996). Put another way, the sport management researcher is asking each participant "How do my descriptive results compare with your experiences" (Polkinghorne, 1989, p. 53)? Any requests from the participants to add or delete something from the thematic structure are honored and the changes are incorporated into the thematic structure.

Issues of reliability of data need to be addressed. There are some methods phenomenological researchers can use to ensure the reliability of their data. Giorgi (1975) argues that findings from a phenomenological research project are reliable "if a reader, adopting the same viewpoint as articulated by the researcher, can also see what the researcher saw, whether or not he/she agrees with it" (p. 93). Thus, it is the researcher's responsibility to provide the reader with as much information as possible to allow the reader to understand the researcher's perspective.

This information should consist of a thorough bracketing statement outlining the sport management researcher's biases and presuppositions. It should also include a detailed description of the thematic structure, along with many examples and excerpts from participants' interviews that support the themes. Although identical word-for-word replication is not possible in dialogic studies, Thomas and Pollio (2002) point out that thematic consistency is as much a goal of phenomenological research projects as it is of quantitative studies. A phenomenological sport management researcher expects that an overall thematic structure and understanding of participants' experiences that might emerge from another study examining the respective experience would be commensurate with the structure found in the original study. Yet, given the facts that ultimate and complete bracketing is impossible and that interpretations are context-dependent, Thomas and Pollio acknowledge "there may always be more than one legitimate interpretation for any particular set of data" (p. 40). Summing up their notions about the reliability of phenomenological studies, Thomas and Pollio point out that in a sense, the aim of replication is to *extend*, not *repeat*, the themes and relations obtained in the original study.

Phenomenological Case Study

Who: Sebastian Brueckner, The University of Tennessee, Knoxville

What: German Olympians' Experiences of Competing at the 2004 Athens Games

Theoretical framework

The purpose of the study was to provide a detailed description of German Olympians' experience of competing at the 2004 Summer Olympics in Athens. Brueckner utilized in-depth, open-ended phenomenological interviews conducted with 12 German athletes who competed in Athens. The athletes represented various sports. Four grounds emerged from the analysis of the athletes' experience: (1) Time, (2) The Preparation, (3) The Olympics, and (4) The Overall Result.

Data collection methods

The three aspects of the process of data collection were (1) bracketing, (2) selecting participants, and (3) interviewing. In-depth, open-ended phenomenological interviews were conducted. The interviews, originally in German, were transcribed and served as the primary source for data analysis Participants were free to choose the location for their interviews. The existential phenomenological approach with its open-ended interview format allowed these athletes to expand on their experiences in detail.

Data analysis techniques/presentation

Step-by-step procedures suggested by Thomas and Pollio (2002) and Pollio et al. (1997) were used to analyze the phenomenological interview data in this study. These include: (1) transcribing, (2) the hermeneutic circle, and (3) verifying thematic structures with participants.

Major findings

Overall, the findings suggested that while there were considerable individual differences in participants' experiences most of these athletes lacked systematic mental preparation for the 2004 Athens Olympics and also experienced various forms of organizational stress. Based on the results obtained in the study, the following four main conclusions are offered: First, the experiences of these German athletes seemed to be primarily characterized by an absence of systematic mental preparation for the specific challenges they faced during the 2004 Olympic Games. Second, all of these athletes experienced one or more forms of organizational stress described by Woodman and Hardy (2001). Third, the Olympic journeys of all participants were grounded in the context of real life, as they were aware of certain cultural, socioeconomic, and other non-sport related factors influencing their athletic pursuits. Finally, while falling within each of the primary themes, athletes' stories were characterized by considerable individual differences. This approach also allowed the distinct individual aspects of each athlete's experiences to be expressed.

Suggestions for future research

Brueckner suggested that future research investigating the differences in the experiences of German athletes who succeed in major international competitions, including the Olympics, and those who do not could be beneficial for German sport administrators attempting to improve services available to athletes preparing for international and Olympic competition. He further suggests a more detailed analysis of the sources of organizational stress that affect German athletes' preparation for and performance at the Olympics would appear to be another potentially fruitful project.

Case study research probes

1. Explain how the data collection technique of "bracketing" could have been used in this phenomenological study?

2. How would the findings from this study benefit sport managers?

CONCLUSION

This chapter has explored and examined the concepts and methods of Phenomenology. With the aim of studying and understanding the "lived experience", phenomenology offers sports management researchers the opportunity to delve into previously under-researched phenomena. A phenomenological research approach has value in that it critically analyzes phenomena as they present in sport and sport management, and in doing so, provides a deeper understanding of the universal meanings of the phenomena that occur in these fields. Phenomenology can be used to address some of the more under-explored areas in sport management research such as the lived experiences of athletes attempting to excel in a non-traditional gender-specific sport, or the daily experiences of a sport manager operating at an elite level in a worldwide sporting event, where the sport management researcher seeks to understand the human condition as much as the lived experience of the phenomena itself. For this reason, such research can lead one in the direction of uncovering the meaning of lived experience from the subjective perspectives of the persons who participate. This approach therefore has the ability to foster understanding of many of the complex and perplexing conditions in which sport managers find themselves.

IN PROFILE - Dr Lucie Thibault

Lucie Thibault is currently Associate Professor at Brock University in Canada and Editor of the *Journal of Sport Management*. In May 2008, she was awarded the North American Society for Sport Management's Earle F. Zeigler Award. Her research interests lie in Canadian sport policy (CSP) and, in particular, in the involvement of the federal and provincial governments in sport excellence and sport participation. More recently, Lucie's research has centered on policy formation and implementation related to the CSP's focus on sport participation. In the development of the CSP, all provinces and territories agreed to be fully involved in the implementation of the policy in regards to sport participation. As a result, this context provides an excellent and interesting setting for research into sport policy. Using a qualitative approach allowed the research team to examine in-depth the extent, nature, and scope of sport participation policy initiatives at the Canadian federal level. This examination is based on extensive interviews with key policy-makers and leaders responsible for policy implementation as well as on analyses of relevant organizational documents. These data collection strategies were also used to help the research team uncover how these sport participation policy initiatives are enacted in various Canadian provinces. It is through interviews and analyses of relevant documents that the research team was able to identify values, beliefs, and priorities of sport leaders and the issues that may affect their ability to implement sport participation policy within their jurisdiction. Qualitative research provides researchers with the approach to collect data in the field, in the natural setting of policy-makers and sport leaders. Furthermore, in the use of semi-structured interview guides, researchers are able to address in greater detail emergent issues that are raised by the research participants. As such, researchers are in a better position to holistically understand the social phenomenon under study.

REVIEW AND RESEARCH QUESTIONS

Phenomenology seeks to identify and understand the lived experience of individuals. With a basic understanding of phenomenology as an alternative to the more traditional methodologies associated with sport management research, attempt to answer the following questions:

- Is there any place within sport management research for phenomenology? Explain your reasons.

- Identify those key features of Husserl's and Heidegger's approach to phenomenology that you believe would enable an effective analysis of the lived experience of a sport manager.

REFERENCES

Cohen, M. Z. & Ornery, A. 1994. Schools of : implications for research. In: *Critical Issues in Qualitative Research* (Ed. by J. M. Morse), pp. 136–157. Thousand Oaks, CA: Sage. phenomenology.

Crotty, M. 1995. Phenomenology as radical criticism. In: *Proceedings, Asia-Pacific Human Science Research Conference* (Ed. by F. Kretlow, D. Harvey, J. Grubb, J. Raybould, G. Sandhu, H. Dosser), pp. 87–97. Gippsland, Australia: Monash University.

Czech, D. R., Wrisberg, C. A., Fisher, L. A., Thompson, C. L. & Hayes, G. 2004. The experience of Christian prayer in sport – an existential phenomenological investigation. *Journal of Psychology and Christianity*, **2**, 1–19.

Dale, G.A. 1994. *The Experience of Elite Decathlon Participants During Their Most Memorable Performance: Overcoming the Distractions*. Unpublished doctoral dissertation, The University of Tennessee, Knoxville.

Dale, G. A. 1996. Existential phenomenology: emphasizing the experience of the athlete in sport psychology research. *The Sport Psychologist*, **10** (4), 307–321.

Donalek, J. G. 2004. Phenomenology as a qualitative research method. *Urologic Nursing*, **24** (6), 516–517.

Giorgi, A. 1975. An application of the phenomenological method to psychology. In: *Duquesne Studies in Phenomenology* Vol. 2 (Ed. by A. Giorgi, C. Fisher, E. Murray), pp. 82–103. Pittsburgh: Duquesne University Press.

Gunderson, L. (2004). *Memory, Modernity, and the City: An Interpretive Analysis of Montreal and Toronto's Respective Moves From Their Historic Professional Hockey Arenas*. Unpublished master's thesis. University of Waterloo, Canada.

Hammond, M., Howarth, J. & Keat, R. 1991. Understanding Phenomenology. Oxford: Basil Blackwell.

Hector, M. A. 2003. Phenomenology, research, and counseling psychology. *Tennessee Education*, **32/33** (1/2), 25–31.

Heidegger, M. 1962. Being and Time. New York: Harper and Row.

Heidegger, M. 1977. The Question Concerning Technology, and Other Essays. New York: Harper & Row.

Holt, N. 2003. Representation, legitimation, and autoethnography: an autoethnographic writing story. *International Journal of Qualitative Methods*, **2** (1) Article 2.

Husserl, E. 1970. The Idea of Phenomenology. The Hague: Martinus Nijhoff.

Johnson, M.S. 1998. *The Athlete's Experience of Being Coached: An Existential Phenomenological Investigation*. Unpublished doctoral dissertation, University of Tennessee, Knoxville.

Kearney, R. 1994. Modern Movements in European Philosophy: Phenomenology, Critical Theory, Structuralism. Manchester & New York: Manchester University Press.

Koch, T. 1995. Interpretive approaches in nursing research: the influence of Husserl and Heidegger. *Journal of Advanced Nursing*, **21**, 827–836.

Levesque-Lopman, L. 1988. Claiming Reality: Phenomenology and Women's Experience. Totowa, NJ: Rowman and Littlefield.

McAllister, S.L. 2006. *Women Administrators' Perceptions of the Contribution of Competitive Sport Experiences to Their Career Paths and Leadership Practices*. Unpublished doctoral dissertation, Illinois State University, Bloomington.

Parse, R. R., Coyne, B. A. & Smith, M. J. 1985. Nursing Research: Qualitative Methods. Bowie, MD: Brady.

Polkinghorne, D. E. 1989. Phenomenological research methods. In: *Existential Phenomenological Perspectives in Psychology* (Ed. by R. S. Valle, S. Halling), pp. 41–60. New York: Plenum Press.

Pollio, H. R., Henley, T. B. & Thompson, C. B. 1997. The Phenomenology of Everyday Life. Cambridge: Cambridge University Press.

Rogers, M. F. 1983. Sociology, Ethnomethodology, and Experience: A Phenomenological Critique. New York: Cambridge University Press.

Smith, C. P. 1998. The Hermeneutics of Original Argument: Demonstration, Dialectic, and Rhetoric. Evanston: Northwestern University Press.

Spiegelberg, H. 1970. On some human uses of phenomenology. In: *Phenomenology in Perspective* (Ed. by F. J. Smith). The Hague: Martinus Nijhoff.

Spiegelberg, H. 1976. The Phenomenological Movement, 2nd ed. The Hage: Martinus Nijhoff.

Spinelli, E. 1989. The Interpreted World: An Introduction to Phenomenological Psychology. London: Sage.

Steware, D. & Mickunas, A. 1990. Exploring Phenomenology: A Guide to the Field and its Literature. Athens: Ohio University Press.

Taylor, C. 1991. The Ethics of Authenticity. : Cambridge, MA.

Thines, G. 1987. Franz Brentano. In: *The Oxford Companion to the Mind* (Ed. by R. Gregory), pp. 117–118. New York: Oxford University Press.

Thomas, S. P. & Pollio, H. R. 2002. Listening to Patients: A Phenomenological Approach to Nursing Research and Practice. New York: Springer.

Thompson, C. B., Locander, W. B. & Pollio, H. R. 1989. Putting consumer experience back into consumer research: the philosophy and method of existential-phenomenology. *Journal of Consumer Research*, **16** (2), 133–146.

Valle, R., King, M. & Halling, S. 1989. An introduction to existential–phenomenological thought in psychology. In: *Existential-Phenomenological Perspective in Psychology* (Ed. by R. Valle, S. Halling), pp. 3–16. New York: Plenum Press.

van Manen, M. 1990. Researching Lived Experience – Human Science for an Action Sensitive Pedagogy. Ontario: The University of Western Ontario.

Walters, A. 1994. Phenomenology as a way of understanding in nursing. *Contemporary Nurse*, **3** (3), 134–141.

Walters, A. J. 1995. The phenomenological movement: implications for nursing research. *Journal of Advanced Nursing*, **22**, 791–799.

Webster's Dictionary of the English Language. Unabridged, 1977. New York: International Press.

Woodman, T. & Hardy, L. 2001. A case study of organisational stress in elite sport. *Journal of Applied Sport Psychology*, **13**, 207–238.

CHAPTER 20

Emerging Approaches for Sport Management Research

CHAPTER OVERVIEW

This chapter presents two emerging approaches that have significance for sport management research. The first section discusses the process of globalization and how it has impacted the study of sport. Its various definitions are presented and its implications for sport management research are outlined. The next section introduces the research approach of postcolonialism. It defines what this term means and provides a context for how it may be applied in sport management settings. Through this new theoretical lens, it is suggested that postcolonial sport management research has the potential to add new insights into the body of knowledge that informs sport management practice.

GLOBALIZATION AND SPORT MANAGEMENT RESEARCH

Introduction

Constituting an up-and-coming subfield within sport management studies, globalization research brings together different types of theorists, with varied commitments and stakes. Globalization is the subject of a rapidly proliferating theoretical literature and has emerged as a means to explain the intricacy and variability of the ways in which the world is restructuring and, by extension, to assess reflexively the categories used by social scientists to analyze these phenomena.

Researchers in sport management, to varying degrees, have been slow to embrace globalization as a knowledge set because some of its core propositions challenge predominant ontological, methodological, and epistemological commitments. Nevertheless, globalization research has the potential to become a dominant paradigm within sport management discourse.

What is globalization?

Globalization research can be categorized in different ways. For example, it can be characterized based on its focus on specific phenomenon of globalization, that is, economic, political, and social. However, in each of these categories, there are different perspectives, such as neoliberalist, Marxist, neo-Marxist, etc. According to Sklair (2002), research on globalization can be categorized into four broad approaches: These include the *global polity and society, the world systems,* the *global capitalism,* and the *global cultural* approaches.

The *global polity and society* approach maintains that global polity and society can be achieved only in the modern age with the advancement of science, technology, and industry. This body of literature is filled with discussions of the decreasing power and significance of the nation-state and the increasing significance or actually power of super-national and global institutions and systems of belief and value (Sklair, 2002). For those theorists, the most desirable future is the organization of global governance through some global civil society, while globalization is the most potent and necessary drive for that future. British social thinker Anthony Giddens (1990) is one of the leading voices of such arguments. He defines globalization in terms of four dimensions: the nation-state system, the world military order, the international division of labor, and the world capitalist economy. According to Giddens, globalization is a consequence of modernity itself because "modernity is inherently globalizing" (p. 63). The philosophical assumption of this approach is essentially neoliberalism.

The second approach to globalization study is the *world system perspective* (Sklair, 2002). The world systems approach is based on the distinction between core, semi-peripheral and peripheral countries in terms of their positions in the international division of labor demanded by the capitalist world system. Based on the work of Immanuel Wallerstein (1974), social scientific research on world systems has been developed since the 1970s. Unlike other approaches in which writers are grouped based on the tenets of their work, the world systems school is a highly institutionalized academic enterprise. This school of thought has been the most systematic available for the analysis of the global system for more than 20 years. The world system theory closely resembles dependency theory.

An approach that is more sophisticated than *the world system approach* is the global capitalism approach (Sklair, 2002). For these theorists, the main driving force of globalization is the structure of the ever-more globalizing capitalism (e.g., Ross & Trachte, 1990; Robinson, 1996; Sklair, 2002). Unlike the world system approach that focuses on nation-state centered economics, the global capitalism approach strives toward "a concept of the global that involves more than the relations between nation-states and explanation of national economics competing against each other" (Sklair, 2002, p. 46).

The last approach to globalization research is the *global culture* approach (Sklair, 2002). Placing culture at the center is inspired by Marshall McLuhan's (1964) notion of "the global village," the very rapid growth of the mass media in scale and scope that has taken place over the last few decades. As Sociologist Tomlinson (1999) puts it, "Globalization lies at the heart of modern culture; cultural practices lie at the heart of globalization" (p. 1). Huntington (1993, 1996) predicts that the source of future international conflicts lies in the cultural, rather than the political and ideological. Appadurai (1996) developed a fivefold conceptual framework of empirical research on global cultural flows. His categories include ethnoscapes (flows of people), mediascapes (flows of images and information), technoscapes (development and flows of technology), finanscapes (flows of global capital), and ideoscapes (flows of ideologies and movements).

The global culture approach is the most widespread form of research within sport and cultural studies as well as sociology. Edwards and Skinner (2006) have suggested that this is a self-limiting form of research inquiry and have explored the conceptions of a new world order and implications for sport management in their book entitled *Sport Empire*.

Research Brief

What: Globalization: The Structural Changes of the Hungarian Sport Life after the Communist Regime
Who: Molnar, G., Miami University
Molnar utilized globalization theory to present an understanding of the process of globalization and the possible consequences of globalization in Hungary and how Hungarian society is reacting to these changes. He also interpreted the influence of globalization on post-communist Hungary concerning the changes in its sport life. Through his application of globalization we are presented with an understanding of the recent political, economic, historical and cultural situation of Hungary.

Globalization: decentered?

Hardt and Negri (2000), in their influential work, *Empire*, argue that we experience the irresistible and irreversible globalization of economic and cultural exchanges. They suggest that with the development of a global market and global circuits of production, we also see the materialization of a global order or a new form of sovereignty. Together with the processes of globalization, sovereignty of nation-states has weakened. Now, the money, technology, people, and goods move easily across national borders and the nation-state has less power to regulate these flows.

"Empire" and "Multitude" are the governing terms of Hardt and Negri's (2000) discussion. They suggest that along with the global market and global circuits of production a new global order has emerged, a new form of sovereignty based on a new logic and structure of rule. Empire is the political subject that effectively regulates these global exchanges, the sovereign power that governs the world.

Empire does not refer to imperialism. Empire has no territorial center of power and does not depend on fixed boundaries. The divisions among three Worlds (First, Second, and Third) have been blurred. It is a decentered and deterritorializing apparatus of rule that progressively incorporates the entire global realm with its open, expanding frontiers. Empire manages hybrid identities, flexible hierarchies, and plural exchanges through modulating networks of command (Hardt & Negri, 2000, p. xii).

Multitude is opposed to Empire. Multitude is as all those who labor and produce under capital, it is the "class of productive singularities, the class of the operators of immaterial labor" (Hardt & Negri, 2000). The Multitude however has power which is driven by its desire for liberation from Empire's global structures and networks. Edwards and Skinner (2006) have drawn upon this theoretical framework provided by Hardt and Negri (2000) to critique the implications of a new world order on global sport management.

Globalization research approach

In brief, qualitative globalization research may be characterized by three commitments: First researchers employing globalization approaches seek to understand the world through interacting with, empathizing with and interpreting the actions and perceptions of its actors. Globalization research methods are thus used to explore the meanings of people's worlds – the myriad personal impacts of impersonal social structures, and the nature and causes of individual behavior. Second, globalization qualitative research tends to involve the collection of data in natural settings, rather than in artificial contexts. Third, it tends to explore and generate theory rather than test it. Qualitative globalization methods work inductively, that is, building up theory from observations; rather than deductively, that is, testing theories by trying to refute their propositions.

Depending on theoretical or explanatory frames and the quality of interpretation, the data generated by qualitative globalization research can provide powerful and critical insights into particular questions. They can be used effectively with people or places we think are familiar to us, as well as in situations somewhat removed, geographically and otherwise, from our own. Given the interpenetrating contexts generated by globalizing phenomena, together with associated mobile, trans-local and diasporic communities, much research conducted using qualitative approaches include the ways in which communities are both tied into and construct trans-local/transnational networks and discourses, such that while people might be organizing and acting at local spatial scales they are consistently framing their identities with reference to larger scale and global contexts.

Research Brief

Switching Fields: The World Soccer Economy in an Era of Globalisation

Who: Brewer, B, Johns Hopkins University

Brewer seeks to embed an account of the commercial and political transformation of the world soccer economy within the larger world-historical context from which it emerged, with particular emphasis on how this process impacted the shifting (mis)fortunes of Northern (or "First World") and Southern ("Third World") participants within the world soccer system. The analysis demonstrates that significant Third World governance in the early stages of the commercial transformation of the sport yielded structural transformations within the nascent world soccer economy that functionally mimicked what commodity chain analysts have labeled the "buyer-driven" commodity chain model.

Moreover, the research indicates that at present, with the leading edge of the world soccer economy centered on Europe and England, the evidence points to the emergence of a model in line with prototypical "buyer-driven" commodity chain model. Within this emergent buyer-soccer commodity chain, national football associations play only a secondary role to private, commercial football clubs. While Third World participation within the world soccer economy remains significant, the nature of the Third World's role has shifted from that of a significant power to a major source of low-cost labor within the world soccer economy. Overall, Brewer concluded that this is a shift that has greatly diminished the developmental benefits derived from the Third World's participation within the world soccer economy.

Globalization and sport management

Drawing on globalization theorists, six propositions are highlighted as they relate to sport management research.

1. Many contemporary issues in sport management cannot be explained as local interactions and must be construed as global issues. Although this claim is not unique to globalization studies, at issue is a series of sport problems – e.g., doping in sport, the rise of organized crime in sport, global warming threats to sport, and the spread of infectious diseases – which are beyond the regulatory framework of the national sporting organization.

2. Globalization constitutes a structural transformation in world order. As such, sport does not exist in a vacuum separate from the social, economic and environmental context. Questions arise as to how national and international sport organizations respond to this new world order.

3. As a transformation, globalization involves a series of continuities and discontinuities with the past. In other words, there is no escaping historiography. Modern conceptions of sport organization have their foundation in the past.

4. The advent of globalization is fluid. This implies that global sport is an actor in its own right. Transnational sport organizations, national sporting bodies and local sport organizations all influence and are influenced by local and global issues.

5. Given shifting parameters, sport needs to adjust to evolving global structures. International sport organizations, however, are in varied positions vis-a-vis globalizing structures, and need to reinvent themselves differently according to changing global circumstances.

6. Underpinning such differences is a set of new, or deeper, tensions in world sport. For example the global trend to postmodern individualistic leisure pursuits poses a challenge for traditional sport organizations such as the IAAF and the IOC. The next generation of sport consumers are likely to challenge the hegemony of some Olympic sports with little consumer appeal. The challenge is how to respond to these global changes.

Research Brief

Place, Identity and Futbol club Barcelona: A Critical Geography of Sport.

Who: Shobe, H.W., University of Oregon

Shobe looks at Futbol Club Barcelona (FC Barcelona) and its changing relationship to Catalonia/Barcelona as a part of a larger investigation of the nexus among place, identity and sport. The study shows how sport is implicated in how place is socially constructed, from the top down and from the bottom up. To flesh out the ways in which sport clubs and teams are dialectically involved in the production and maintenance of place identities, the dissertation examines the ways in which FC Barcelona is implicated in the construction of urban identity in Barcelona and national identity in Catalonia. The thesis recognized that in recent years, the increasing globalization of sport is straining the bonds between the team and the place where it is located in ways that are likely to alter the place-team dynamic in the years to come. The dissertation also examines the implication of marketing the team as a global brand for the club/place/identity triad.

Globalization and qualitative research method

Research methods have not changed under contemporary globalization processes. Rather, Sullivan and Brockington (2004) note that orientations to research and to the interpretation of "findings" – particularly in relation to certainty, to the implications of notions of difference and "the other", and to aspirations of objectivity – have been much affected by the intertwined theoretical fields of poststructuralism, postcolonialism and feminism (p. 3).

They add that by highlighting the infusion of power in research praxis the Globalization researcher acknowledges the always politically constitutive role(s) of academic engagement.

As a developing sport management research paradigm, globalization is more of a potential than a refined framework, kit of tools and methods, and mode of resolving questions. The efforts to theorize sport globalization have produced an intellectual move rather than a methodological movement to investigate global sport. Globalization research does not have a clearly defined methodology. There is no one correct approach. Qualitative Globalization research utilizes many of the approaches mentioned previously in this book.

Research Brief

Title: Sport Empire
Who: Edwards, A. and Skinner, J.
Sport Empire provides a new theoretical framework to analyze sport in a global context. Drawing on Hardt and Negri's (2000) concept of Empire insight into a new form of globalization is presented and this forms the basis for the conceptualization of Sport Empire. Particular attention is paid to the role of Nation-States and the United Nations. The various forms of bio-political control that exist in Sport Empire are illustrated through a focus on the IOC and FIFA. Issues such as corruption in sport, transnational media conglomerates, genetic engineering and biotechnology, multiculturalism and diversity management, humanitarian projects, environment and health challenges, terrorism and the role of the multitude in producing a new global Post-hegemonic sport order are raised. Through this examination Edwards and Skinner suggest that sport management governance can no longer be isolated from the ever-present cultural, economic and political manifestations of a "society of control" within Empire. Moreover, this will lead inevitably to viewing the practices and principles of sport management from a new global perspective.

POSTCOLONIALISM AND SPORT MANAGEMENT RESEARCH

Introduction

Sport management research to some extent is still perceived as neutral and apolitical, which explains why sensitive issues related to race, gender, and class need to evolve. Postcolonial theory, with its interpretations of race, racialization, and culture, offers sport management scholarship a set of powerful analytic tools unlike those offered by other sport management and social theories. Building on the foundation established by those who first pointed to the importance of incorporating socio-cultural aspects into sport,

sport management scholarship is in a position to move forward. Critical perspectives such as postcolonialism equip us to meet the epistemological imperative of giving voice to subjugated knowledges and the social mandates of uncovering existing inequities and addressing the social aspects of sport. This section makes a case for the integration of postcolonial perspectives into theorizing and sketches out a research methodology based on the post-colonial tradition. Postcolonial discourse offers a theoretical perspective – another lens, so to speak – for insights into the contours of social life. Most importantly, it has given voice to those who were silenced.

Postcolonial ideological discourse

The term *postcolonial* is a problematic one. Just like *poststructuralism* and *postmodernism*, it has multiple meanings and implications when used, not to mention that it is highly criticized (Viruru & Cannella, 2001). As Cannella and Bailey (1999) have argued, postcolonial scrutiny and insights could have potential for influencing research, perhaps even challenging Western constructions of research. "Postcolonial" continues to generate dissatisfac-tion among practitioners and detractors alike and which some (most notably those who equate Postcolonial Studies with postmodernism) now suggest may have outlived its usefulness (see San Juan, 1998, *Beyond Postcolonial Theory*; Hardt & Negri, 2000, *Empire*).

Postcolonial studies is a relatively recent ideological discourse and represents a critical response by the former colonized to the various forms and processes of Western domination and subjugation resulting from the colonial encounter. The colonial enterprise has left former colonies suffering from wounds which appear to deepen rather than heal. In virtually every aspect of their lives, former colonized people contend with the repercussions of their encounter with European colonizers. In response, postcolonial theorists engage in discussions about a host of experiences relating to slavery and colonialism such as suppression, resistance, representation, difference, race, gender, and social class. Within these broader themes, specific issues such as the primacy of the colonizer's language, religion, cultural histories, knowledge and other element of identity over that of the local peoples is topical in the postcolonial conversation.

Postcolonial studies, therefore, is an academic space in which to contest hegemonic ideologies and impositions, which continue to oppress and confuse formerly colonized peoples who now inhabit what is called the "developing world" (here after, Third World or postcolonial societies). McConaghy (2000) suggests that while postcolonialism draws on post-structuralism and postmodernism, it does not overlap neatly with them.

Defining postcolonialism

Postcolonialism challenges Western science as the unique source of knowledge production and uncovers inequities related to gender, race, and class resulting from the process of colonization and postcolonization. What makes this discourse especially pertinent to sport management is that it brings to the forefront these issues and makes explicit how these socially constructed categories have been used in the colonizing process, and the effect that this has had on peoples' lives and life opportunities.

Said (2000) defines colonization as: the expansive force of a people; it is its power of reproduction; it is its enlargement and its multiplication through space; it is the subjugation of the universe or the vast part of it to that people's language, customs, ideas, and laws. Postcolonialism is the process of post-colonializing. Quayson (2000) suggests that to understand this process [postcolonializing], it is necessary to disentangle the term, postcolonial, from its implicit dimension of chronological supersession, that aspect of its prefix, which suggests that the colonial stage has been surpassed and left behind. It is important to highlight instead a notion of the term as a process of coming-into-being and of struggle against colonialism and its after-effects.

More succinctly, the postcolonial approach is directed at uncovering the exclusionary effects of dominant ideologies in "Othering" other forms of knowledge – the subjugated knowledge. Foucault (1980) defines subjugated knowledges as a whole set of knowledges that have been disqualified as inadequate to their task or insufficiently elaborated: naïve knowledges, located low down on the hierarchy, beneath the required level of cognition or scientificity.

Quayson (2000) asserts that postcolonialism focuses on dominant discourses and ideologies that shape the social world to look at the material effects of subjugation. Subjugation is the process by which imperialism and colonialism impose a condition of positional superiority over the colonized (Said, 2000). The process is to ground contemporary world phenomena like immigration, unemployment, health problems, into the real world to unmask the interrelations between these phenomena and new colonial ideologies. Consequently, the researcher's aim is to "relate modern-day phenomena to their explicit, implicit, or even potential relations, to the heritage of colonialism" (Quayson, 2000, p. 11) while decolonizing methodologies and methods (Tuhiwai Smith, 1999), to critique the marginalizing effect of Western science on subjugated knowledge.

Applying postcolonialism to sport management research unveils the reductionist Western discourse of essentializing the "Other" in a unique, crystallized, neutral, rational, and objectivist cultural entity. As well, "decolonializing" methodologies and methods is directed at disrupting the power relations to voice subjugated knowledge. According to Hall (1997), subjectivities emerge from: "the different constellation of social, cultural and economic forces... since we are, in part, constructed as subjects through the particular layering of historical discourses, which we inhabit, then new kinds of sensibilities begin to be clearly discernible" (p. 247). Postcolonial scholarship in sport management research is limited; however, important work has been produced in which issues and concerns of postcolonialism and sport are discussed. One of the beat examples of this form of research in sport is represented in the research of James (refer to research brief).

Research Brief

Title: Postcolonial Cricket: Beyond a Boundary
Who: CLR James (1963)
Many view *Beyond a Boundary* as James' postcolonial cultural manifesto; James primarily focuses on the sport of cricket, but he also interweaves this exploration with analyses of (1) the cultural implications of the region's "uneven" relationship with Britain, (2) the historical progress toward self-government in the West Indies, and (3) the development of a regional West Indian identity. James begins *Beyond a Boundary* with his upbringing in Tunapuna, Trinidad. He examines the imperial cultural hegemony of cricket which seems to have resisted political independence. Cricket is firmly ingrained as *the* national sport of the former British colonies. *Beyond a Boundary* is arguably the earliest cultural studies analysis which focuses on the Caribbean or on cricket – much less the two in one. The text has always received critical praise. Many scholars regard *Beyond a Boundary* as one of the most outstanding works of cultural studies ever produced. As much as the text is indeed about intercultural relations, it is also decidedly about cricket.

How can postcolonialism be articulated in sport management research?

The development of postcolonial scholarship in sport management depends on our abilities to define new theories and methods to explore and understand cultural differences, and to challenge dominant culture stereotypes. Also, sport issues related to racial, gendered, and class discrimination need to be part of the sport management social mandate. The harmful effects of racial, gendered, and social discrimination on sport management must be recognized. Postcolonial research is a theoretical perspective that moves us away from the shortcomings of cultural essentialism, since culture cannot be isolated from the broader social context within which it comes into play together with a constellation of other structural factors. This theoretical approach provides the analytic lens to examine the extent to which sport management research and practice perpetuate dominance through our everyday practice. However, it should be remembered that research cannot be neutral, apolitical, or ahistorical since sport management is governed by normalizing discourses and practices.

Furthermore, there is the complex question of political commitment and its relation to scholarly inquiry. Undoubtedly, it is a core issue to be addressed in sport management, and postcolonial research provides the analytical framework to perform such reflection. Nevertheless, postcolonial research warns us to distance ourselves from the expert role in acknowledging the anthropological construction of sport. Democratization of sport management research can be realized by recognizing "subjugated knowledge" as a legitimate source of theorization, adapting sport management interventions to meet the needs of people located at the margins of pluralist societies. If social justice is ever to be achieved in the sport system, voices of the subaltern have to be heard. In this sense, implementing postcolonialism questions the appropriateness of culturalist theories to correct such issues as managerial imbalances stemming from social discrepancies and neocolonial ideologies.

Finally, postcolonialism is not specifically directed at developing knowledge for the sake of knowledge. Giroux (2002) describes this strategy as the "most retrograde academic use" (p. 98) of knowledge since it evacuates the possibilities of challenging the status quo. Anderson (2000) emphasizes that deconstructing and rewriting taken-for-granted knowledge, and redefining relations of power and privilege is a step toward achieving social justice. Some research has existed which does not recognize that it is in fact postcolonial in nature.

FROM THEORY TO PRACTICE IN SPORT MANAGEMENT

Perhaps the greatest challenge in our call for a postcolonial sport management scholarship lies in the translation of its theoretical tenets into a method of research.

The following describes a postcolonial research method that has evolved from an exploration of the dialectic between theory and research.

Framing the research

The **first** distinction of a postcolonial sport management research method lies in the way in which the entire research project is viewed through a political lens – a lens that attends to the micropolitics and macrodynamics of power. While attending to power relations is certainly a methodological theme of other brands of research (e.g., feminist research may be the most overt example), a postcolonial framing rests on an overarching mindfulness of how domination and resistance mark intercultural encounters at individual, institutional, and societal levels. Thus, postcolonial sport management scholarship pursues matters of how contemporary constructions of race, ethnicity, and culture continue to rely on colonialist images and patterns of inclusion and exclusion within sport management settings. Careful attention to the social and historical positioning of the sport management researcher vis-a-vis research participants also is paramount to the postcolonial project.

Linking self and society

Inherent in contemporary postcolonial efforts is the tension between self and society, the local and the global, the particularities of the hybrid moment and the universality of the colonial experience. It is our ability to understand and explain the nature of the relationship between self and society, the contextualization of subjectivity, that is critical to the progress of sport management. We suggest, therefore, that a feature of postcolonial sport management scholarship is situating human experience (e.g., everyday reality) in the larger contexts of mediating social, economic, political, and historical forces.

Giving voice

The third feature of a postcolonial research method suggested is the deliberate decentering of dominant culture so that the worldviews of the marginalized become the starting point in knowledge construction. A postcolonial commitment results in the weaving of the perspectives and experiences of those marginalized in our society into the very fabric of sport management. Core to the postcolonial movement is the question raised by Spivak (1988) "Can the Subaltern speak"?

A further opportunity for giving voice to previously subjugated voices is the liberal use of polyvocality in research through strategies such as purposive sampling from diverse groups of participants with a range of experiences, listening carefully to the accounts of these participants, and liberally using their verbatim stories in written reports.

A basic question in Postcolonial research has been posed as to whether or not White researchers can truly understand the experiences of issues such as racialization and racism. Some have argued that postcolonial studies in the field are best undertaken by minority scholars; others have argued that such matching of researchers with the researched results in marginalizing certain types of research, making, for example, racism only a concern for racialized groups. We take the position that rather than pursuing the legitimacy of our roles as sport management researchers based on one aspect of one's social identity (i.e., Whiteness), one's legitimacy as a sport management researcher is based on one's ability to explicate the ways in which marginalization and racialization operate.

Emancipatory intent

The final feature of a postcolonial research method is its open commitment to critiquing the status quo and building a more just society. We make the case for emancipatory intent. Praxis-oriented research is research committed to social change. Thus, sport management inquiry within the larger genre of an emancipatory research paradigm is committed to moving beyond the description of what "is" to providing prescription for what "ought" to be, and raises our level of investigation from matters of the individual to consideration of larger sociopolitical forces impacting on the common good. The goal of emancipatory sport management researcher is to foster self-reflection and deeper understanding on the part of the researched at least as much as it is to generate empirically grounded theoretical knowledge.

Research Brief

Title: "Soft Ball" Marketing the Myth and Managing the Reality on Major League Baseball
Who: Lewis (II), R. University of New Mexico
The study traced 'Major League Baseball's' (MLB) uneven progress from an insensitive domestic monopoly to a globally competitive business. Using the thesis of "soft power", it supplemented analysis of cultural, business, economic, and popular research with primary source interviews. The work followed a generally chronological progression that synthesizes four interrelated aspects of MLB: as a sport, a domestic business, a neo-colonialist, and an international business. In so doing, it assessed MLB's management of its ongoing mythical attraction as the "national pastime" in the face of labor and market challenges within the burgeoning entertainment industry.

METHOD

What is important about a postcolonial perspective is that there are no prescribed techniques for data collection or data analysis. Different techniques can be drawn on depending on the focus of the inquiry, as long as they meet the criteria for scientific adequacy and rigor.

The postcolonial methodology sketched out here promises us new and important tools for forms of transformative knowledge that have been largely overlooked within sport management scholarship and practice. With such a commitment, postcolonial sport management scholarship will permit more thoughtful attention to the issues of equity and social justice.

CONCLUSION

In this chapter, it has been argued that contemporary globalizing contexts provide opportunities for sport management globalization research. The key question which will be answered within the next few years is: Does globalization constitute a research paradigm to enhance our understanding of sport management practice in changing times?" In articulating the postcolonial notion to sport management it has been demonstrated that the negotiation of cultural differences and meanings is the basis upon which culturally safe sport management practice can be designed. The issue is to adapt sport management practice to the needs of marginalized people by integrating marginalized knowledge in sport management scholarship. Postcolonial research provides the analytic lens to critically assess the effects of power, race, gender, and social class on sport management practice; to democratize sport management research and practice and to bridge theory and practice by generating transformative sport management knowledge.

IN PROFILE - Dr Thor Indridson

Thor Indridson (B.A., M.Sc., Ph.D.) is a Senior Lecturer in Human Resource Management at the Bristol Business School, University of West of England and lectures in the Sport Management Program. His teaching and research areas in sport include research methods, human resource management and employment relations. He has published several books and articles on Scandinavian employment relations, labor market history and industrial and social policy. He worked for a number of years as a researcher for trade unions in his native country, Iceland. This provided him with the opportunity to observe and follow closely labor market developments, wage negotiations, organizational behavior, and employment relations in the workplace and apply this knowledge to sport organizations. He has served for several years in leadership positions in sport organizations and federations in Iceland. His work in this area includes: membership of the Olympic Committee; representation of the board of the National Sport Federation, the Icelandic

Judo Federation, the Icelandic Weightlifting Federation (where he a previous chair), the Scandinavian and European Weightlifting Federations and numerous sub-committees and task groups. Besides his academic career he has also worked as a management consultant to private companies as well as public sector organizations. Dr Indridson is currently using qualitative research methods in his examination of human resource practices in sport organizations. Through the data collection techniques of observation, focus groups and semi-structured interviews Dr Indridson has been able to provide a 'thick description' of the implications of these practices for the sport organization and how these practices have impacted on individuals in specific ways. Dr Indridson believes it is essential that the data collected is validated through triangulation. This requires verification that the data collected via observation is consistent with what is said in focus groups and individual interviews and is therefore a valid representation of the views presented.

REVIEW AND RESEARCH QUESTIONS

Globalization and postcolonialism are new and emerging methodologies that have the potential to provide new ways of producing sport management knowledge and its implications for practice. With a basic understanding of these concepts attempt to answer the following questions:

- Do the strengths of globalization and postcolonial approaches to sport management research outweigh the possible weaknesses?

- Identify how globalization and postcolonial research approaches would enable an effective analysis of the lived experience of a sport manager.

REFERENCES

Anderson, J. M. 2000. Gender, 'race', poverty, health and discourses of health reform in the context of globalization: a postcolonial feminist perspective in policy research. *Nursing Inquiry*, **7**, 220–229.

Appadurai, A. 1996. Modernity at Large: Cultural Dimensions of Globalization. Minneapolis ME: University of Minnesota Press.

Cannella, G. S. & Bailey, C. 1999. Postmodern research in early childhood education. In: *Advances in Early Education and Day Care vol. 10* (Ed. by S. Reifel), pp. 3–39. Jai Press: Greenwich, CN.

Edwards, A. & Skinner, J. 2006. Sport Empire. Oxford: Meyer & Meyer Sports.

Foucault, M. 1980. Power/knowledge selected interviews and other writings, 1972–77 (C. Gordon, Trans.). New York: Harvester Wheatsheaf.

Giddens, A. 1990. The Consequences of Modernity. Cambridge, UK: Polity Press.

Giroux, H. A. 2002. Breaking into the Movies: Film and the Culture of Politics. Maiden MA: Blackwell.

Hall, S. 1997. The local and global: globalization and ethnicity. In: *Dangerous Liaisons: Gender, Nation, and Postcolonial Perspectives* (Ed. by A. McClintock, A. Mufti, E. Shohat), pp. 173–187. Minneapolis: University of Minnesota Press.

Hardt, M. & Negri, A. 2000. Empire. Cambridge, MA: Harvard University Press.

Huntington, S. P. 1993. The clash of civilizations. *Foreign Affairs*, **72** (3), 22–49.

Huntington, S. P. 1996. The Clash of Civilizations and the Remaking of World Order. New York: Simon & Schuster.

McConaghy, C. 2000. Rethinking Indigenous Education: Cultur-alism, Colonialism and the Politics of Knowing. Flaxton: Post Pressed.

McLuhan, M. 1964. Understanding Media: The Extension of Man. London: Routledge.

Quayson, A. 2000. Postcolonialism: Theory, Practice or Process? Cambridge: Polity Press.

Robinson, W. 1996. Promoting Polyarchy. Cambridge, UK: Cambridge University Press.

Ross, R. J. S. & Trachte, K. C. 1990. Global Capitalism: The New Leviathan. Albany: SUNY Press.

Said, E. W. 2000. The Edward Said Reader, M. Bayoumi, & A. Rubin (Eds.). New York: Vintage Books

San Juan Jr., E. 1998. Beyond Postcolonial Theory. New York, NY: St. Martin's Press.

Sklair, L. 2002. Globalization: Capitalism and its Alternatives. Oxford, UK: Oxford University Press.

Spivak, G. C. 1988. Can the subaltern speak? In: *Marxism and the Interpretation of Culture* (Ed. by C. Nelson, L. Grossberg), pp. 271–313. Urbana & Chicago: University of Illinois Press.

Sullivan, S., & Brockington, D. (2004). Qualitative methods in globalisation studies: or, saying something about the world without counting or inventing it. CSGR Working Paper, 139/04.

Tomlinson, J. 1999. Globalization and Culture. Chicago, IL: University of Chicago Press.

Tuhiwai Smith, L. 1999. Decolonizing Methodologies: Research and Indigenous Peoples. London: Zed Books.

Viruru, R. & Cannella, G. S. 2001. Postcolonial ethnography, young children and voice. In: *Embracing Identities and Early Childhood Education* (Ed. by S. Grieshaber, G. S. Cannella). New York: Teachers College Press.

Wallerstein, I. 1974. The modern world-system. In: *Capitalist Agriculture and the Origins of the European World-Economy in the Sixteenth Century.* New York/London: Academic Press.

CHAPTER 21

Future Directions in Sport Management Research

411

CHAPTER OVERVIEW

This chapter will discuss some emerging issues for future sport management research and demonstrate how they can be situated in the sport management research field. Social Network Theory, Race and Critical Race Studies, Whiteness Studies, Disability Studies, Participant Authored Audiovisual Stories and Visual Sociology are research methods that need to be considered for future research projects. Each in its own way presents opportunities for sport management knowledge to be extended through their application. This chapter briefly outlines the basic principles that underpin these approaches and suggests how they might be applied in the field of sport management.

SOCIAL NETWORK THEORY AND SPORT MANAGEMENT RESEARCH

What is social network theory?

A *social network* is a social structure made of nodes (which are generally individuals or organizations) that are tied by one or more specific types of interdependency, such as values, visions, ideas, financial exchange, friendship, kinship, dislike, conflict or trade. The resulting structures are often very complex. Social network analysis views social relationships in terms of *nodes* and *ties*. Nodes are the individual actors within the networks, and ties are the relationships between the actors. There can be many kinds of ties between the nodes. Research in a number of academic fields has shown that social networks operate on many levels, and play a critical role in determining the way problems are solved, organizations are run, and the degree to which individuals succeed in achieving their goals. In its simplest form, a social network is a map of all of the relevant ties between the nodes being studied. The network can also be used to determine the social capital of individual actors. These concepts are often displayed in a social network diagram, where nodes are the points and ties are the lines.

Social network analysis (related to network theory) has emerged as a key technique in a range of disciplines, that is, modern sociology, anthropology, sociolinguistics, geography, social psychology, communication studies, information science, organizational studies, economics, and biology as well as a popular topic of speculation and study.

People have used the social network metaphor for over a century to connote complex sets of relationships between members of social systems at all scales, from interpersonal to international. In 1954, J.A. Barnes started using the term systematically to denote patterns of ties that cut across the concepts traditionally used by the public and social scientists: bounded groups (e.g., tribes, families) and social categories (e.g., gender, ethnicity). Over time, other scholars expanded the use of social networks.

The benefits of social network analysis

Social network analysis has now moved from being a suggestive metaphor to an analytic approach to a paradigm, with its own theoretical statements, methods, social network analysis software, and researchers. Analysts reason from whole to part; from structure to relation to individual; from behavior to attitude. They either study whole networks (also known as complete networks), all of the ties containing specified relations in a defined population, or personal networks, (also known as egocentric networks) the ties that specified people have, such as their "personal communities".

Several analytic tendencies distinguish social network analysis:

■ There is no assumption that groups are the building blocks of society: the approach is open to studying less-bounded social systems, from non-local communities to links among Web sites.

■ Rather than treating individuals (persons, organizations, states) as discrete units of analysis, it focuses on how the structure of ties affects individuals and their relationships.

■ In contrast to analyses that assume that socialization into norms determines behavior, network analysis looks to see the extent to which the structure and composition of ties affect norms.

The shape of a social network helps determine a network's usefulness to its individuals. Smaller, tighter networks can be less useful to their members than networks with lots of loose connections (weak ties) to individuals outside the main network. More open networks, with many weak ties and social connections, are more likely to introduce new ideas and opportunities to their members than closed networks with many redundant ties. In other words, a group of friends who only do things with each other already share the same knowledge and opportunities. A group of individuals with connections to other social worlds is likely to have access to a wider range of information. It is better for individual success to have connections to a variety of networks rather than many connections within a single network. Similarly, individuals can exercise influence or act as brokers within their social networks by bridging two networks that are not directly linked (called filling structural holes).

The power of social network analysis stems from its difference from traditional social scientific studies, which assume that it is the attributes of individual actors, whether they are friendly or unfriendly, etc. that matter. Social network analysis produces an alternate view, where the attributes of individuals are less important than their relationships and ties with other actors within the network. This approach has turned out to be useful for explaining many real-world phenomena, but leaves less room for individual agency, the ability for individuals to influence their success, because so much of it rests within the structure of their network.

Social networks have also been used to examine how organizations interact with each other, characterizing the many informal connections that link executives together, as well as associations and connections between individual employees at different organizations. For example, power within sport organizations often comes more from the degree to which an individual within a network is at the center of many relationships than actual job title. Social networks also play a key role in recruiting in sport organizations, in business success, and in job performance. Networks also provide ways for organizations to gather information, deter competition, and collude in setting prices or policies.

Applying social network theory to sport management research

Quatman (2006) suggests studies using social network analysis have yet to be explored in any realm of the discipline of sport management. For example, she argues that while the idea of social influence is often implied or referred to in sport management literature on consumer behavior, conceptual and empirical studies specifically integrating the role others play in influencing others' behaviors and attitudes are limited. Although consumer behavior is used as the primary example here, the same critique can be applied to many of the topics of interest in the field.

Quatman (2006) suggests traditionally sport management research has focused on identifying and measuring the personal attributes, attitudes and perceptions of individuals. Similarly, individuals conforming to social norms (i.e. gender, race or ethnic variables) are often used as explanatory elements for many sport management studies. Paradoxically then Quatman suggests that individuals are often assumed to be acting in complete isolation of one another, while at the same time, individuals are construed as strong conformers to social norms. Individuals' behaviors are therefore automatically believed to be a relative function of deliberate choice based on reason, serendipitous contact, or "socially constraining factors" (p. 11). However, Quatman highlights that individuals do not function in vacuums, whether social or environmental, and are driven to action by "both conscious and subconscious motives" (p. 11), yet "decision-making, attitudinal formation, and other processes of interest in sport management research often embrace one of these two extreme approaches taking on either an over-socialized or an under-socialized view of the world" (p. 11).

Quatman (2006) argues that the capabilities of traditional methods of research have not allowed for sufficient integration of social influence into measurement and interpretation techniques. Although sport management studies often explain philosophical and paradigmatic approaches that incorporate social interaction and processes as necessary components, conventional analytical instruments have been insufficient for testing a social reality of such complexity. She suggests "that by providing analytical tools for overturning some of the under-socialized and over-socialized limitations of the more conventional research methods, social network techniques may indeed prove to be a valuable methodological approach for investigating even more diverse topics and domains in the field of sport management" (p. 11).

Research Brief

Title: The Social Construction of Knowledge in the Field of Sport Management: A Social Network Perspective
Who: Quatman, C., Ohio State University
Quatman's study aimed to introduce social network analysis as an alternative methodological approach to researchers in sport management. A network model of co-authorship patterns was generated using several rounds of sampling and archival data collection. The observed network structure was explored both quantitatively and qualitatively for meaningful patterns. The results of the study were intended to essentially tell a story of the evolution and current state of the field of sport management's co-authorship structure and identify potential socio-structural barriers present in the network. Among the themes that emerged was the structural dominance of one particular institution and the presence of a structural gap between researchers in the United States and Canada. The findings of the study were tied to theoretical, methodological, and practical implications for the diffusion of ideas and practices throughout the network structure. Through the incorporation of some techniques associated with social network analysis into the process of a critical investigation of the social construction of knowledge in sport management, Quatman provides a new research direction for the application of network analytic techniques to explore challenging research questions in the future.

RACE THEORY, CRITICAL RACE THEORY AND SPORT MANAGEMENT RESEARCH

What is race theory and critical race theory

Race theory and Critical Race theory are fields of inquiry that investigate the social construction of race and discrimination that are present in society.

Both fields emphasize the socially constructed nature of race, consider the workings of power, and oppose the constitution of all forms of subordination.

Most recent attention in the field of race studies has occurred in the field of Critical Race Studies (CRT). Delgado and Stefancic (1993) note the following major themes in CRT writings:

- A critic of liberalism

- Storytelling/counter-storytelling and "naming one's own reality"

- Revisionist interpretations of American Civil rights law and progress

- Applying insights from social science writing on race and racism to legal problems

- Structural determinism, how the structures of legal thought or culture influence content

- The intersections of race, sex and class

- Essentialism and anti-essentialism

- Cultural nationalism/separatism as well as empowering black nationalism, power or insurrection

- Legal institutions, critical pedagogy and minorities on the bar

- Criticism and self-criticism

Race theory and CRT share an overlapping literature with critical theory, feminist studies and postcolonial theory.

Applications to sport management

Race studies has emerged as an academic area of inquiry since the 1960s; however, it is only recently that race studies have attracted the attention of sport scholars. Although there have been a number of studies investigating under-representation of racial groups and racial stacking in sport, particularly in the USA context, very little ideological analysis has occurred. We would encourage sport management researchers to imbue such studies with an investigation on race studies.

CRT thought has been applied in a variety of contexts where socialized and institutionalized oppression of racial minorities has been litigated in the courts. In world football (soccer) players from many countries have been the subject of racist chants and comments. Whilst FIFA have attempted to develop policies to rid this racism from the game particular problems remain.

In a non-sporting context, Delgado and Stefancic (1993) draw on CRT in calling for tort action for racial insults, looking to the historical action of speech and the serious psychological harm inflicted on its victims as just measure for evaluation hate speech. The application of this type of research would be useful to sport administrators.

Research Brief

Who: de Wet, E. Rand Afrikaans University

What: The Phenomenological Experience of Ethnic Integration by Individuals in High School Rugby Teams

The historical context of sport in South Africa and the role of rugby as mediator in the process of racial integration on the high school rugby field were explored, as well as social concepts influenced by transformation and integration such as prejudice, discrimination, racism and territoriality. De Wet utilized a non-empirical and subjective phenomenological research methodology in this research. The purpose of the study was to examine high school rugby players' perspectives in order to identify points of sameness and difference between players' perspectives. The goal was to gain insight into the phenomenon of integration in rugby at a high school level. Data were obtained from interviewing players so as to potentially shed insights on key facets related to the research issue. Colored and white players between the ages of 16 and 18 years participated in the study. Research took the form of an individual interview with the researcher. The study found that preparing high school rugby administrators, coaches and counselors to be multi-racially competent is a complex process. It requires that a person receives training in multicultural perspectives, both academic and experiential in order to possess the required knowledge, attitudes and skills to work effectively with young people.

WHITENESS STUDIES AND SPORT MANAGEMENT RESEARCH

What is whiteness studies

Whiteness studies is an interdisciplinary arena of academic inquiry focused on the cultural, historical and sociological aspects of people identified as white. Since the mid-1990s, a number of publications across many disciplines have analyzed the social construction of *whiteness* as an ideology tied to social status.

A central tenet of whiteness is that race is said to have been constructed by a white power structure in order to justify discrimination against non-whites. Major areas of research include the nature of white identity and white privilege, the historical process by which a white racial identity was created and the relation of culture to white identity. A reflexive understanding of such assumptions underpins work within the field of whiteness studies.

No longer content with accepting whiteness as the norm, critical scholars have turned their attention to whiteness itself. In the field of *Critical White Studies*, numerous thinkers investigate such questions as:

■ How was whiteness invented and why?

■ How has the category of whiteness changed over time?

■ Can some individual people be both white and non-white at different times and what does it mean to "pass for white"?

■ At what point does pride for being white cross the line into white power and white supremacy?

■ What can whites concerned over racial inequity or white privilege do about it?

OTHER RELATED FORMS OF SPORT MANAGEMENT INQUIRY

Ethnic studies and sport management research

Ethnic studies is the study of ethnicity. It developed toward the end of the twentieth century partly in response to charges that traditional disciplines had a dominant eurocentric perspective. Ethnic studies attempts to investigate minority cultures on their own terms, in their own language, and according to their own value system.

From this perspective, sport managers may investigate the influence of specific ethnic groups and their position in sport within defined cultural contexts, for example, the influence of Latino players in US baseball, African football players, sport in ethnic groups and the problems of integration.

Diaspora studies and sport management research

Diaspora studies is an academic field that was established in the late twentieth century to study dispersed ethnic populations. These groups are referred to as Diaspora peoples. The term Diaspora implies forced resettlement, due to expulsion, slavery, racism, or war, especially national conflict. Areas of interest in Diaspora studies for sport management researchers could include sport in conflict zones such as Iraq and sport and refugees.

Research Brief

What: Sport and Conflict: Is Football an Appropriate Tool to Utilise in Conflict Resolution, Reconciliation or Reconstruction?

Who: Lea-Howarth, J., University of Sussex

This study utilized case studies based on and qualitative interviews with the organizers of football-based grassroots peace-building projects in Sierra Leone and Israel, as well as case studies in Liberia and Bosnia–Herzegovina. Lea-Howarth utilized a theoretical framework based on Lederach's ideas about peace-building through building social networks and Galtung's theories of peace, violence and the "3Rs" of Resolution, Reconciliation and Reconstruction to survey the contribution of team-sports to peace-building, (conceived here as conflict resolution, reconciliation and reconstruction). He advocated team-sports as a tool to address cultural violence, engender reconciliation and aid rehabilitation primarily by building social networks and educating participants.

DISABILITY STUDIES AND SPORT MANAGEMENT RESEARCH

What is disability studies?

Disability studies is an interdisciplinary field of study which is focused on the contributions, experiences, history and culture of people with disabilities. The field of teaching and research in the area of disability is growing worldwide. It is based on the premise that disadvantage typically experienced by those who are disabled reflects primarily on the way society defines and responds to certain types of difference. The definition of disability studies is contested by those coming from different epistemologies. The *Society for Disability Studies* offers the following working guidelines for any program that describes itself as "Disability Studies":

- It should be interdisciplinary/multidisciplinary.

- It should challenge the view of disability as an individual deficit or defect that can be remedied solely through medical intervention or rehabilitation by "experts" and other service providers.

- It should study national and international perspectives, policies literature, culture and history with the aim to placing current ideas of disability within their broadest possible context.

- It should actively encourage participation in disabled students and faculty, and should ensure physical and intellectual access.

- It should make a priority to have leadership positions held by disabled people, at the same time it is important to create an environment where contributions from anyone who shares the above goals are welcome.

Disability studies is not without its critics. It has been suggested that the dominant social model, which developed in the 1970s and has served its purpose well since then, has now been outgrown, and needs major developments. Disability studies has also been criticized for its failure to engage with multiple forms of oppression, such as racism, sexism or homophobia. As a relatively new discipline, it is true that as yet disability studies has seen little progress in this area. More recently the concept of *critical disability studies* has started to emerge in the social sciences. Publications are now beginning to emerge through and in time it is hoped that this issue will be fully engaged in by researchers, including sport management researchers.

Within sport management a few studies have examined disability. However, to date studies have not studied specific sport management issues from a disabilities studies perspective. Research in this area is urgently needed. The Special Olympics and Paralympics provide an important fertile ground for research as opposed to ploughing back over the same farrowed fields of professional sport. Gilbert and Schantz (2008) have recently added tremendously to this area of sport management research on disability through their publication of an edited book on the Paralympics.

Research Brief

Title: Hearing the Voices of Experienced Equestrians with Disabilities

Who: McBride-Conner, A., Texas Woman's University

McBride-Conner utilized constructivist grounded theory to examine the personal meaning of equestrian sport participants with disabilities. Participants in the study were eight (seven female, one male) equestrians aged 38–56. Data were collected through participant observation and semi-structured interviews. Mc Bride-Conner reported four themes: (1) constructing equestrian identity, (2) engaging in equestrian sport, (3) becoming one with the horse, and (4) deriving meaning.

PARTICIPANT AUTHORED AUDIOVISUAL STORIES AND SPORT MANAGEMENT RESEARCH

What is participant authored audiovisual stories?

Participant Authored Audiovisual Stories (PAAS) is a controversial new approach which we believe has possibilities in sport management research particularly in the area of consumer behavior and "insider knowledge". PAAS deals with qualitative research methodology based on sound and image data, in particular with audiovisual stories authored by the research participants.

As a research method, PAAS promises a sound platform from which to explore social phenomena, especially when what is at stake is an understanding of the relationship between the agency of subjects and their socio-cultural contexts.

According to Harrison (2002), visual research is still viewed as a marginal practice. Despite its marginality Ramella and Olmos (2005) argue that:

> …research methodologies based on sound and image data open up a vast field of opportunities, one that is rapidly capitalising on many of the twists and turns of societal change: from the fast development of audiovisual technologies, and the improvements in digital communications, to the growing case made in the social sciences against the hegemony of the written text and the incorporation of audiovisual languages into our everyday lives. (p. 3)

They go on to describe the process in the following way:

> Described in a nutshell, research participants create their own stories around a more or less determined problem. For this purpose they utilize audiovisual media, that is, video cameras or photo-cameras or a radio, just to cite some. Further, they draw on a variety of genre to organize their stories, for example, an autobiography, a documentary or a drama. According to the genre selected, stories may include personal testimonies, or fictional enactment of life episodes; they may also include stories by other people (e.g., street interviews by research participants to lay people). Here the list can be limitless. Also, being in possession of the audiovisual media provide participants ample latitude to situate themselves, and importantly, their stories. Situating a story should not be restricted to a physical location; it also means situating it socially (who else is it?), and culturally (what is in it?). (p. 3)

PAAS has been successfully utilized in many projects and offers in particular the potential for research participants to *own* the story, to express it and articulate it in close relation to their everyday life in a social and cultural context (Ramella & Olmos, 2005).

VISUAL SOCIOLOGY AND SPORT MANAGEMENT RESEARCH

What is visual sociology?

Visual Sociology is an emerging field in the social sciences; yet its theoretical and methodological contributions are just becoming known. Visual sociology is a research approach concerned with the visual dimensions of social life.

It includes the study of all kinds of visual material and the visual social world, and uses all kinds of visual material in its methodologies such as photographs, film, tape and video to study society as well as the study of the visual artifacts of a society. Visual sociology is viewed as suited to data gathering technologies for, small group interactions, ethnography, oral history, etc.

Theory and method

There are at least three approaches to visual sociology:

1. *Data collection using cameras and other recording technology*

In this first sense visual sociology means including and incorporating visual methods of data gathering and analysis in the work of research. Visual recording technology allows manipulation of data because they make it possible to speed up, slow down, repeat, stop, and zoom in on things of interest.

In a sport management context this methodological approach is routinely utilized by venue managers as they collect visual data through security cameras, to monitor the behavior of spectators and to observe behavior patterns which may lead to security or safety issues. These "observations" could be the basis for more formalized research inquiry. In this way new knowledge and understanding of facility management may evolve which assists the facility manager to better understand the behavior of fans in their venues.

2. *Studying visual data produced by cultures*

The second approach of visual sociology is to study the visual products of society – their production, consumption and meaning. Visual images are constructed and may be deconstructed and may be read as texts in a variety of ways.

In a sport management context Gilbert and Schantz (2008) utilized visual sociology methods for understanding the visual culture of the Olympic Games host city of Beijing. They examined a range of visual sub-cultures including architecture, space and place, landscape, art, ceremonies, cultural displays as well as peoples lives and fashion. Gilbert and Schantz suggest that the possibility of conceiving the visual culture of Olympic host cities as a holistic entity raises the problematic of devising broader more encompassing visual-centric methodologies for London 2012.

3. *Communication with images and media other than words*

A third approach of visual sociology is both the use of visual media to communicate sociological understandings to professional and public audiences, and also the use of visual media within sociological research itself.

The research brief below is a sport example of this form of visual sociology research.

In a sport management context, researchers could, for example, use a combination of narrative and photographs to seek a more effective way of understanding just how facility managers see and experience their environment on game day. The importance of subjecting routine understandings and practices to detailed analysis in this way allows the lives of these 'social actors' to be analyzed in a unique way and provide new understanding of their "lived experiences".

Research Brief

Title: Seeing the Way: Visual Sociology and the Distance Runner's Perspective
Who: Hockey, J. and Collinson, J.A (2006). Visual Studies, 21(1), pp. 70–81
Employing visual and auto-ethnographic data from a two-year research project on distance runners, this research examined the activity of seeing in relation to the activity of distance running. One of its methodological aims is to develop the linkage between visual and auto-ethnographic data in combining an observation based narrative and sociological analysis with photographs. This combination aimed to convey to the reader not only some of the specific sub-cultural knowledge and particular ways of seeing, but also something of the runner's embodied feelings and experience of momentum en route. Via the combination of narrative and photographs the authors sort a more effective way of communicating just how distance runners see and experience their training terrain.

CONCLUSION

The emerging research issues discussed in this chapter need to be considered by sport management researchers if we are to broaden our approaches to research and seek knowledge through new and innovative research approaches. Each method presented in this chapter presents its own set of unique challenges while at the same time presenting opportunities to understand social reality through different theoretical lenses.

IN PROFILE - Professor Keith Gilbert

Keith Gilbert is a Professor and Director of the Centre for Disabilities, Sport and Health in the School of Health and Bioscience at the University of East London, United Kingdom. Professor Gilbert has a Ph.D. in Sport Sociology from the University of Queensland and has a strong interest in qualitative and interpretive research methodology. His research interests are firmly grounded in visual sociology and sport and disability. He has used visual sociology methods for understanding the visual culture of the Olympic Games host city of Beijing. He examined

Continued

a range of visual sub-cultures including architecture, space and place, landscape, art, ceremonies, cultural displays as well as people's lives and fashion. In the area of sport and disability he is questioning what the relationship between disability and sport is, and how the lives of disabled people are changed by their involvement in sport.

Through a critical theoretical lens he suggests the Paralympics has initiated change within our current sport system demanding a paradigm shift in thought processes, practices and strategies of sport managers. He argues that by analyzing how and why embedded assumptions guide theory development, research and practice, elite disabled athletes can begin to describe and explain oppressive effects. He suggests that critical approaches promise us the possibility of examining our sporting worlds in terms of moral and political as well as simply technical concerns. In accepting the political, interested nature of our activities Professor Gilbert suggests we are provided with the conceptual tools to theorize our sporting practice, and to reconstruct it. As a consequence of acknowledging this it becomes clear that we should consistently subject to critical scrutiny our understandings and actions of sport and the ways in which we shape and are shaped by our sporting worlds.

REVIEW AND RESEARCH QUESTIONS

Each of the emerging issues discussed in this chapter embrace a unique methodological approach that has significant relevance to sport management research. With a general understanding of these emerging issues, attempt to answer the following questions:

- Is there any place within sport management research for these approaches to sport management research? Justify your answer.

- Discuss the positive and negative features of each approach.

- Provide examples of how two of these approaches could be applied to sport management research.

REFERENCES

Delgado, R. & Stefancic, J. 1993. Critical race theory: an annotated bibliography. *Virginia Law Review*, **79** (2), 461–516.

Gilbert, K. & Schantz, O.J. (Eds.). 2008. The Paralympic Games: Empowerment or Side Show? Maidenhead: Meyer & Meyer.

Harrison, B. 2002. Seeing health and illness worlds using visual methods in a sociology of health and illness: a methodological review. *Sociology of Health and Illness*, **24** (6), 856–872.

Quatman, C. 2006. *The Social Construction of Knowledge in the Field of Sport Management: A Social Network Perspective*. Unpublished doctoral dissertation, The Ohio State University, Columbus.

Ramella, M., & Olmos, G. 2005. Participant authored audiovisual Stories (PAAS). Giving the camera away or giving the camera a way? *Papers in social Research Methods: Qualitative Series no. 10*, June (London School of Economics and Political Science Methodology Institute).

PART 6

Writing the Sport Management Research Report

CHAPTER 22

Preparation of the Sport Management Research Report

CHAPTER OVERVIEW

The Sport Management Research Study is only complete once the findings have been written up and possibly published. There is no definitive format for a qualitative research report; however, this chapter seeks to guide the new researcher in writing up a report in a systematic way. The following sections are included: introduction, aims of the study, literature review, sample, questions guiding the investigation, data collection methods, data analysis methods, findings, discussion, conclusion, references, appendices and abstract.

WRITING UP QUALITATIVE RESEARCH

Just as there are many different qualitative methods and approaches to qualitative data analysis, there are many different writing styles and approaches. For a brief overview of some of these styles as they relate to ethnography, see Harvey and Myers (1995) and Myers (1999).

In writing up qualitative research, we recommend Wolcott's (1990) book. This book has many practical suggestions. For example, Wolcott points out that many qualitative researchers make the mistake of leaving the writing up until the end, that is, until they have got "the story" figured out. However, Wolcott makes the point that "writing is thinking". Writing actually helps a researcher to think straight and to figure out what the story should be. The motto of every qualitative researcher should be to start writing as soon as possible.

A common problem for qualitative researchers is that sport management researchers are expected to publish their work in journals. However, most types of qualitative research leads to the gathering of a significant mass of data. It can be difficult for qualitative researchers to write up their results within the space constraints of a journal article. Another problem is the expectation that singular findings will be presented in each paper, that is, each journal article should have just one main point.

One solution is for qualitative researchers to treat each paper as a part of the whole. That is, a qualitative researcher has to devise a way to carve up the work in such a way that parts of it can be published separately. Then the issue becomes which part of the story is going to be told in one particular paper. A qualitative researcher has to come to terms with the fact that it is impossible to tell the "whole story" in any one paper, so he or she has to accept the fact that only one part of it can be told at any one time. One advantage of such a strategy is that there is potential to publish many papers from just one period of the fieldwork.

For those completing a thesis, the Quality indicators (Table 22.1) modified from Walden University Version 1.2 (8/1/05) may provide a valuable checklist for developing the research plan.

GENERAL PRINCIPLES RELATED TO WRITING THE RESEARCH REPORT

Qualitative research aids researchers in addressing key issues in sport and sport management. The research report should address all aspects of the work carried out and offer an appropriate selection from the findings. A systematic approach to constructing the research report will aid the sport management researcher to produce a cohesive and well-defined report.

Table 22.1 Quality Indicators for Completing a Thesis

Chapter 1: Quality Indicators

1	Abstract	contains a concise description of the study, a brief statement of the problem, exposition of methods and procedures, summary of findings, and implications for social change
2	Introduction	has a clear statement demonstrating that the focus of the study is on a significant problem that is worthy of study. There is a brief, well-articulated summary of research literature that substantiates the study, with references to more detailed discussions in Chapter 2
3	Problem statement	concisely states what will be studied by describing at least two factors and a conjectured relationship among them that leads to an identified problem
4	The nature of the study, specific research questions, or research objectives	(as appropriate for the study) are briefly and clearly described.
5	The purpose of the study	described in a logical, explicit manner.
6	In qualitative studies	The conceptual framework shows which ideas from the literature ground the research being conducted
7	Operational definitions	Of technical terms, jargon, or special word uses are provided.
8	Assumptions, limitations, scope and delimitations	provide descriptions of a. facts assumed to be true but not actually verified b. potential limitations of the study, and c. the scope (bounds) of the study
9	The significance of the study	is described in terms of a. knowledge generation b. professional application, and c. social change
10	Chapter 1 ends with a Transition Statement	that contains a summary of key points of the study and an overview of the content of the remaining chapters in the study.

Chapter 2: Quality Indicators

1	Introduction	that describes a. the content of the review b. the organization of the review, and c. the strategy used for searching the literature.

Table 22.1	Quality Indicators for Completing a Thesis *continued*
2 The review of related research and literature	is clearly related to the problem statement as expressed in: a. research questions and/or b. study questions and study objectives.
3 The review of related research and literature includes the relationship of the study to previous research	
4 The review contains concise summaries	of literature that helps substantiate the rationale or conceptual framework for the study (for qualitative studies)
5 There is literature-based description	of potential themes and perceptions to be explored (qualitative studies).
6 The content of the review	is drawn from acceptable peer-reviewed journals or sound academic journals or there is a justification for using other sources
7 The review is integrated,	critical essay on the most relevant and current published knowledge on the topic. The review is organized around major ideas or themes.
Chapter 3: Quality Indicators	
1 Introduction describes how the research design	derives logically from the problem or issue statement.
2 The Role of the Researcher	in the data collection procedure is described.
3 Measures for ethical protection of participants are adequate.	
4 Criteria for selecting participants are specified and are appropriate to the study	There is a justification for the number of participants, which is balanced with depth of inquiry – the fewer the participants the deeper the inquiry per individual.
5 Choices about which data to collect are justified	Data collected are appropriate to answer the questions posed in relation to the qualitative paradigm chosen. How and when the data are to be or were collected and recorded is described.
6 How and when the data will be or were analyzed is articulated	Procedures for dealing with discrepant cases are described. If a software program is used in the analysis, it is clearly described. The coding procedure for reducing information into categories and themes is described.

Table 22.1	Quality Indicators for Completing a Thesis *continued*

Chapter 4: Quality Indicators

1   Chapter 4 is structured around the research questions   and/or objectives addressed in the study, reporting findings related to each.

2   An integrative summary of the literature   (the main findings of the literature review in Chapter 2 is presented.

3   Overall, data analysis (presentation, interpretation, explanation) is consistent with the research questions   or research questions and underlying theoretical/ conceptual framework of the study

Chapter 5: Quality Indicators

1   In the concluding Chapter 5, outcomes are logically and systematically summarized and interpreted   in relation to their importance to the research questions and hypotheses. There is a 'take-home' message for the reader.

Overall Quality Indicators

The thesis

- follows a standard form and has a professional, scholarly appearance
- is written with correct grammar, punctuation, and spelling
- includes citations for the following: direct quotations, paraphrasing, facts, and references to research studies
- does not have over-reliance on limited sources, and
- in-text citations are found in the reference list.

Source: modified from Walden University Version 1.2 (8/1/05)

The following sections of a research report will be addressed. Not all may be necessary, and the researcher will choose those sections necessary to adequately present their findings:

- Introduction

- Aims of the study

- Literature Review

- Sample

- Questions Guiding the Investigation

- Data Collection Methods

- Data Analysis Methods

- Findings
- Discussion
- Conclusion
- References
- Appendices
- Abstract

Introduction

The introduction sets the scene of the study and puts the research in context. It should aim to start with a sentence that describes exactly what the paper is about. If the research is about the experiences of sport managers at a large international sporting event, then the reader will want to know why the study was done, and how it relates to other research in the area. Include information about recent progress in the field of the research, and the relationship of this proposal to work in the field generally. Where possible use refereed papers that are widely available to national and international research communities

Aims of the study

In this section, researchers describe the research question or the aim of the study. They describe how the research is significant and whether the research addresses an important problem. They describe how the project is relevant to the broader context of sport management research. It is important that, at the end of the paper, researchers are able to reflect back on the degree to which the aim was or was not achieved.

Literature review

This section covers not only an account of the research carried out previously in the same area, but also how the researcher conducted the literature search. This could involve a discussion of the various computer search engines used and the keywords used in the search. Reviews of the research and general literature should be thorough and systematic. The researcher should also specify whether "gray" literature was reviewed. This is literature produced by governments, academics, business and industry, but not that controlled by commercial publishers.

When reading the literature review section, the reader needs to know who did the research and when. Depending on the research topic, fairly current material should be included, although some old-but-good (and still relevant) material can be included.

It is valuable if the researcher can offer a short, critical commentary on the studies reported in the literature. At the end of this section, the researcher will restate the research problem, whereby because of the review of the literature it is apparent that this is a topic worthy of further investigation.

Sample

If sampling has been used in the data collection stage, then the reader needs to know the size and type of sample used in the reported study. If an unusual variant of sampling is used, it is useful to acknowledge its nature, and the researcher could include other comments about the sampling process which the reader would find helpful.

Specific questions guiding the investigation

How were the specific research purposes and aims operationalized into specific research questions? What were the specific research questions?

Good quality research questions are as follows:

■ Clear concise and focused.

■ Informed by the literature.

■ Are motivating or personally meaningful.

■ Are manageable and do-able, are significant in that the values of the answer obtained is likely to justify the effort that you put into it.

■ Do not already have readily accessible answers (Knobel & Lankshear, 1999).

Data collection method

At this stage, there are different views about what might next be reported. Generally, sport management researchers will have approached their qualitative research through one of the theoretical frameworks covered earlier in this book. In this case, the researcher will discuss the data collection methodology as it is located within the chosen theoretical framework.

Each of the data collection methods should be discussed in this section. If interviews were used, then how the interviews were carried out should be discussed; however this does not require a detailed critique of the interview process itself. The same would apply for other data collection methods. The researcher will report what they did and how they did it, but not compile a detailed review or critique of the methods employed.

Data analysis methods

In this section, the researcher will describe the data analysis methods used. There is no requirement that this be extremely detailed, though it should be clear to the reader as to which methods were employed. The sport management researcher may choose to describe the coding process briefly as well as the themes identified as integral to the study.

Findings

In this section, the sport management researcher may choose to either present the findings on their own, without supporting discussion, or else link the findings with the work of other researchers. It should be noted that what one discovers in a qualitative study are "findings" and not "results".

As far as possible, this section should be exhaustive in reporting the data. Depending on the eventual destination of the research report, the researcher will need to decide which information to include and what to leave out. If the report is for a journal, then there will be restricted space, and the researcher may need to limit the number of verbatim quotes, for example, particularly if they are longer quotes.

In this section as well, if links are to be made to existing research, then those links should be clear and obvious. There should be no sense of "bending" the data to make what will be a spurious link with what has gone before. Enough evidence should be presented to establish that such links really are there.

Discussion

The content of this section will be determined, to a considerable extent, on how the researcher has presented findings in the previous section. If links are made to previous research and some sort of critical debate is offered, it might be decided that a separate discussion section is not required.

The discussion should stick to the findings. The researcher should avoid the temptation to speculate about the meaning of his or her findings or to try to "get inside the head" of respondents and somehow "interpret" what that respondent meant.

The best approach would seem to be to both present the findings in a factual way and offer a discussion that never strays further than the limit of the data. However, it is also important that the findings are discussed and that the researcher does not produce merely a bald account of some of his or her findings.

Conclusions

It is in this section that the researcher can both summarize their findings and suggest applications of those findings. Such applications should be realistic and not speculative and no attempt should be made to extrapolate beyond the data. Some may argue that it is impossible to generalize from qualitative data (because of the sampling methods, the ways of collecting data and the methods of analysis) – and most would say that it is not the point of doing qualitative research to generalize in this way. However, it is sometimes a temptation for researchers to project their findings into the future and to attempt to predict its implications through generalizations out to a larger population.

Researchers also need to decide whether or not to be critical of what they have done, or to allow this function to rest with the reader. Researchers also need to be aware of their limitations. Clearly, there are many questions that researchers cannot answer and they need to be open to the possibility that this research project does not answer all that many questions – and never answers any conclusively.

References

Include a list of all references that have been used – that is, those that are actually referred to in the text of the report.

Appendices

Information that is not essential to explain your findings, but that supports your analysis (especially repetitive or lengthy information), validates your conclusions or justifies a related point should be placed in an appendix (plural appendices).

Abstract

Whilst the final part of the writing process is writing an abstract for the paper, the abstract will actually appear at the front of the paper. This is the piece of the work that will represent the researcher on bibliographic search engines and it may be all that many readers know of the work. A good abstract should contain details of the background to the study, the aim, the sample, the data collection and analysis methods and a summary of the findings.

Other topics to include in the research report

Individual researchers will need to decide how much information to include in those sections covered before. Depending on the research study and the destination of the final report, other sections may also need to be covered. These could include the following:

- Ethical approval and how it was obtained.

- Funding sources.

- An account of the division of labor (where more than one researcher was involved).

CONCLUSION

This chapter has offered an overview of the stages involved in writing a qualitative research report. It is not intended to be definitive, but merely provides a guideline to the sport management researcher. Whichever way researchers choose to structure their report – and this will generally depend on the final destination or audience of the paper – the sport management researcher should endeavor to take a systematic and structured approach to the process to ensure that their research findings are presented in the most effective way.

IN PROFILE - Dr Geoff Dickson

Geoff Dickson, located at Auckland University of Technology, is a senior lecturer in sport management and Associate Dean (Research) for the Faculty of Health and Environmental Sciences. He is also an editorial board member for a number of sport management journals. In these roles, he reviews and critiques a lot of research. At one end of the spectrum, there is 'heavy duty' quantitative research and at the other there is 'hard core' qualitative research. A large amount of his sport management research involves single or comparative case studies of organizations. In these studies, he is drawn to qualitative research for a number of reasons. Qualitative does not just scratch the surface; it goes deeper than that and provides an opportunity for the complexities and intricacies to be explored in considerable detail. Geoff also enjoys qualitative research because it provides a greater opportunity for the voices of those being researched to be heard. It is important to recognize the strengths and weakness of both quantitative and qualitative methods. The sport management researcher should beware of anybody professing that qualitative is better than quantitative or vice versa. Both approaches have equal value. It all depends on the research question and what the researcher is trying to achieve. It is important not to confuse qualitative research with a licence to do your own thing. It is very important that qualitative research is scientific and adheres to the best practice. Qualitative is never an excuse to abandon rigor and is more than just the routine application of common sense. Underpinned by a fear of statistics, many novice and future researchers pursue qualitative research believing that it is easier than quantitative research. This is simply not correct. Qualitative research is not just the routine application of common sense. Bad qualitative research is very easy to do. Good qualitative research is very difficult to do, but at the same time, very rewarding for all involved.

REVIEW AND RESEARCH QUESTIONS

When writing a qualitative research report, the sport management researcher needs to take a systematic approach. Now having an overview of this process, attempt to answer the following questions:

- What are the key sections of a researcher report?
- What are some important quality indicators to consider when writing a thesis?

REFERENCES

Harvey, L. & Myers, M. D. 1995. Scholarship and practice: the contribution of ethnographic research methods to bridging the gap. *Information Technology & People*, **8** (3), 13–27.

Knobel, M. & Lankshear, C. 1999. Ways of knowing: Researching Literacy. Newtown, NSW: P.E.T.A.

Myers, M. D. 1999. Investigating information systems with ethnographic research. *Communications for the Association for Information Systems*, **2** (23).

Wolcott, H. F. 1990. Writing up Qualitative Research. Newbury Park, CA: Sage.

Index

Note: Key terms are in **bold** type.